Wine

for
dummies®
A Wiley Brand

Wine

8th Edition

by Michelle Grant, PhD, Mary Ewing-Mulligan, and Ed McCarthy

for dummies®
A Wiley Brand

Wine For Dummies®, 8th Edition

Published by: **John Wiley & Sons, Inc.,** 111 River Street, Hoboken, NJ 07030-5774, www.wiley.com

For general information on our other products and services, please contact our Customer Care Department within the U.S. at 877-762-2974, outside the U.S. at 317-572-3993, or fax 317-572-4002. For technical support, please visit https://hub.wiley.com/community/support/dummies.

Wiley publishes in a variety of print and electronic formats and by print-on-demand. Some material included with standard print versions of this book may not be included in e-books or in print-on-demand. If this book refers to media that is not included in the version you purchased, you may download this material at http://booksupport.wiley.com. For more information about Wiley products, visit www.wiley.com.

Library of Congress Control Number: 2025938156

ISBN 978-1-394-32007-3 (pbk); ISBN 978-1-394-32011-0 (ebk); ISBN 978-1-394-32009-7 (ebk)

SKY10106122_052825

Contents at a Glance

Table of Contents

Introduction

Wine is the intersection between science, art, and culture. In each glass, there are centuries of history and hours of blood, sweat, and tears. We love wine not only for its seemingly infinite spectrum of tastes, but most importantly for the experiences it helps us to create. We want you and everyone else to enjoy wine too — regardless of your experience or budget.

We will be the first to admit that wine's commercial trappings — the ceremony, the fancy language, the paraphernalia — don't make it easy for regular people to enjoy wine. You have to know strange names of grape varieties and foreign wine regions. You have to figure out whether to buy a $20 wine or an $8 wine that seem to be pretty much the same thing. You usually even need a special tool to open the bottle when you get it home. All of this may be the most investment you've ever made in a mere beverage!

While the process of buying, storing, and pouring wine may never get easier, you don't have to let the complications stand in your way. With an open mind and willing palate, you can discover as much as you want and engage as much as you want with wine. Like many people who will open this book, we started out knowing little to nothing about wine. We benefited from years of tasting wines, asking questions, gaining important mentors, and learning from our mistakes over and over again. We want to help you feel more comfortable around wine, and want this book to be your guide. Ironically, what will *really* make you feel comfortable about wine is accepting the fact that you'll never know it all — and neither will we! There's just too much information, and it's always changing. So, sit back, grab a glass, and rest assured that you're in good company as the wine world (and the wine in your glass) evolves.

About This Book

The first edition of *Wine For Dummies* was published in 1995, with several editions that followed. There was no time better than now to release an eighth edition of *Wine For Dummies*, which includes new (to the book) countries and regions, updated price points, and the latest vintage information. It also offers a deeper look behind the scenes, including modern considerations about wine in restaurants, bars, and sommeliers (find out what they are in Chapter 20). Some of our favorite highlights of this edition include:

>> New information on the history and evolution of wine, including the migration patterns of *Vitis vinifera* and their impact on modern winemaking (Chapter 2).

>> Inclusion of sparkling, dessert, and fortified wines in their relevant country chapters to ease your frame of reference and help commit each specialty's homeland to memory.

>> Separate chapters for Spain (Chapter 7), Germany (Chapter 8), Portugal (Chapter 9), central, eastern, and southeastern Europe (Chapter 10), Africa (Chapter 15), the Middle East (Chapter 16), and Asia (Chapter 17), offering more detail on the grapes, the laws and labels, and the most important wines to know.

>> More focused (and color) maps to serve as helpful reference points.

>> A chapter on the science of food and wine pairing (Chapter 18), as well as some of our favorite pairings to try at home or on your travels.

We wrote this book primarily as a reference. You don't have to read it from cover to cover for it to make sense and be useful to you. Simply turn to the section that interests you and dig in. Note that sidebars, which are shaded boxes of text, consist of information that's interesting but not necessarily critical to your understanding of the topic. We italicize many non–English or special words at least the first time they appear, drawing your attention to terms that may be specific to a particular country, region, or established theme in the wine industry. We offer pronunciation guides for some of the most commonly used words in Appendix A.

Finally, wine is a truly global subject and different countries use different methods of measurement. We reflect this variety within the text. Remember that 1 liter equals approximately 2 pints, 1 milliliter (ml) equals approximately 0.03 ounces, and 1 gram (g) equals approximately 0.04 ounces. Temperatures are given in both Fahrenheit (°F) and Celsius (°C) throughout.

Foolish Assumptions

We assume that you picked up this book for one of several reasons:

>> You know little about wine but want to learn more.

>> You do know something about wine, but you want to understand it better, or with more complexity.

>> You're already very knowledgeable but realize that you can always discover more.

You are not a dummy, otherwise you wouldn't be reading this book to learn more about wine. We hope that selecting this book means you don't take yourself too seriously and can move past the wine mumbo jumbo to get to the real stuff that matters. A casual, yet professional approach drives our tone throughout the book, which is after all, about a beverage that's meant to be enjoyed!

Icons Used in This Book

The pictures in the margins of this book are called *icons*, each drawing your attention to different types of information.

REAL DEAL

A bargain's not a bargain unless you really like the outfit. The wines we mark with this icon are bargains because we like them, we believe them to be of good quality, and their price is low compared to other wines of similar type, style, or quality. You can also interpret this logo as a badge of genuineness, as in "This chablis is the real deal."

REMEMBER

Some issues in wine are so fundamental that they are worth commiting to memory. This symbol draws your attention to these critical points of information.

TECHNICAL STUFF

This icon is a bit like the 4-year-old who insists on knowing "Why?" Where you see it, feel free to skip over the technical information that follows unless you're interested. Wine will still taste just as delicious.

TIP

Advice that will make you a wiser wine drinker or buyer is marked by this bull's-eye so that you won't miss it.

WARNING

There's very little you can do in the course of moderate wine consumption that can land you in jail — but you could spoil an expensive bottle and sink into a deep depression over your loss. This symbol warns you about common pitfalls.

WORTH THE SEARCH

Unfortunately, some of the finest, most intriguing, most delicious wines are made in very small quantities. Usually, those wines cost more than wines made in large quantities — but that's not the only problem. The real frustration is that those wines have very limited distribution, and you can't always get your hands on a bottle even if you're willing to pay the price. We mark such wines with this icon, and hope that your search proves fruitful.

Beyond the Book

As if all the great information in this book weren't enough, you can go beyond the book for even more information! Check out this book's online Cheat Sheet by going to www.dummies.com and searching for this book's title. You can also download a PDF of the maps featured in this book at www.dummies.com/go/winefd8e.

Where to Go from Here

We recommend that you go to Chapter 1 and start reading there. But if you don't have time because you're about to head out to a fancy restaurant, then begin at Chapter 21. If you already have bottle in hand or wine in glass, and want to know more about what you're about to sip, turn to the relevant country chapter. Of course if you're considering making your own wine or the story behind what may be in your glass, Chapter 3 may be what you need.

In other words, start wherever you wish, closer to the beginning if you're a novice and closer to the middle if you know something about wine already. On the journey of wine appreciation, *you* get to decide how far to go and how quickly — and you get to choose the route to get there. Pleasure is your final destination!

1

Getting Started with Wine

Chapter **1**

What Is Wine?

What is wine? Wine is an alcoholic beverage made from the fermented juice of grapes. While wine can be made from many other types of fruit, this book focuses on wine made specifically from the *Vitis vinifera* species of grapes.

Most wine marketing highlights the pleasurable, fun aspects of wine: the suspense of the first sip, the bonds strengthened with friends and loved ones over a good bottle, and the memories that connect us as people.

If you work in wine or know anyone who has ever made it, then you know that there are countless hours of blood, sweat, and (often) tears in every bottle. Behind the label, wine is in its most basic form an agricultural product. It is fermented grape juice, processed and packaged as a breathing link between the earth and its people.

In this chapter, we dive into the world of grapes, tracing a vine's life cycle and highlighting key aspects of vineyard management that can impact a winemaker's ability to harvest grapes and make different types of wine. We conclude the chapter with important facts about the most popular grapes to know and the wines they make.

Understanding the Importance of Varieties

Grapes are the starting point of every wine. The grapes that make a particular wine dictate the genetic structure of that wine and how it will respond to everything the winemaker does to it. Think back to the last wine you drank. What color was it? If it was white or amber, the odds are that it came from white grapes. If it was pink or red, the wine likely came from red grapes. Did it smell herbal or earthy or fruity? Whichever, those aromas came mainly from the grapes. Was it firm and tannic or soft and voluptuous? Most of what you will remember is due in large part to the grapes, with a nod to both mother nature and the winemaker.

REMEMBER

The specific grapes that make any given wine are largely responsible for the sensory characteristics the wine offers — from its appearance to its aromas, flavors, alcohol, tannin (a substance that exists naturally in skins, seeds, and stems; refer to Chapter 4 for more details), and acid profile. How the grapes grow — the amount of sunshine and moisture they get, for example, and how ripe they are when they're harvested — is also a factor and can emphasize certain grape characteristics over others. So can winemaking processes, such as oak aging. Each type or *variety* of grape reacts in its own way to the farming and winemaking techniques that it faces. By *variety*, we mean the fruit of a specific type of grapevine: the fruit of the cabernet sauvignon vine, for example, or of the chardonnay vine. Discover more about winemaking in Chapter 3, and about the different varieties later in this chapter. Parts 2 through 5 of this book reveal how different varieties thrive in different wine regions, and how some regions have become known as the best places for wines from those varieties.

TECHNICAL STUFF

The term *variety* has scientific meaning. A variety is a subdivision of a species. Most of the world's wines are made from grape varieties that belong to the species *vinifera* — itself a subdivision of the genus *Vitis*. This species originated in Europe and western Asia. Other distinct species of *Vitis* are native to North America. You can find out more about *Vitis vinifera* and the spread of winemaking in Chapters 2 and 3.

Grapes of other species can also make wine. For example, the concord grape, which belongs to the native American species *Vitis labrusca*, makes concord wine and grape juice and jelly. Non-*vinifera* wines often receive less appreciation compared to wines made from *Vitis vinifera* grapes because they are typically perceived as having less complexity, more inconsistent quality, and a sweeter, fruitier flavor profile, which many wine connoisseurs associate with lower-tier wines, particularly due to the historical dominance of European *Vitis vinifera* grapes in the wine industry. However, there is a growing interest in exploring diverse grape varieties and high-quality non-*vinifera* wines produced by skilled winemakers.

A VARIETY OF VARIETIES

Snowflakes and fingerprints aren't the only examples of nature's infinite variety. Within the genus *Vitis* and the species *vinifera,* as many as 10,000 varieties of wine grapes exist. If wine from every one of these varieties were commercially available and you drank the wine of a different variety every single day, it would take you more than 27 years to experience them all!

Not that you would want to. Within those 10,000 varieties are grapes that can make extraordinary wine, grapes that tend to make very ordinary wine, and grapes that probably shouldn't be turned into wine at all. Most varieties are obscure grapes whose wines rarely enter into international commerce.

An adventuresome grape nut who has plenty of free time to explore the back roads of Spain, Portugal, Italy, and Greece might be able to encounter only 2,000-plus different grape varieties (over five years' worth of drinking) in their lifetime. The grape varieties you might encounter during your normal wine enjoyment probably number fewer than 50.

Living Life as a Vine

Most wine education focuses on winemaking in the cellar: fermentation vessels, different types of fermentations, yeasts, and so forth that can influence the final flavor profile, texture, and more in a wine (find out more about these in Chapter 3). Less attention is paid to what happens to grapes before they enter the cellar. Like any other plant, the grapevine has a life (and often mind) of its own.

The life cycle of a vine

The typical life cycle of a vine happens in phases according to the seasons of the year and location on the globe. See the color section of this book to discover the life cycle of a vine, which is described in more detail here:

1. **Winter pruning:** Up to 90 percent of a vine's previous growth can be removed to prepare it for the coming season. The goal of this step, carried out while the vines are in a dormant state, is to guide the vine's future production, limiting the number of clusters (also known as *thinning,* which packs nutrients and energy into fewer grapes, thereby concentrating sugars and aromatic and phenolic compounds), maximizing sun exposure, and ensuring high-quality fruit.

2. **Spring bud break:** After a winter of dormancy, small buds begin to swell and unfold, revealing the first signs of green growth. This critical step tells winemakers that fruit is on the way, but is in a fragile, not fully formed state. Frost and hailstorms can be serious threats during this phase, permanently damaging new shoots if temperatures are too extreme.

3. **Spring flowering:** Surviving buds develop numerous small flowers, each with the potential to turn into an individual berry (since grapevines are also magical enough to self-pollinate).

4. **Summer fruit set:** As the temperature increases, the tiny, pollinated flowers shed their petals and small, green berries (all grapes start out green, even if they may later become red, blue, or purple) form with seeds at the end of each stem. The fruit set stage gives the winemaker an early sign of potential crop yield. Mid-season, encouraged by the sun's heat, the clusters of green berries begin to show pigmentation and develop more sugar and ripeness. Referred to as *veraison,* some clusters begin to turn red, purple, or bluish in color.

5. **Fall harvest:** Sugar continues to increase (and acidity decreases, marking the importance of this inverse relationship in finished wines as well) as the grapes remain on the vine and exposed to sunlight. This is where the fun begins for winemakers as they taste and test the grapes for sugar content (referred to as *brix*), determining the exact day or moments when to pick grapes and transport them to the winery. Check out Chapter 3 for details of what happens when the grapes reach the winery.

REMEMBER

Each *vintage* (growing season) has a different story to tell based on the conditions of the vine, the soil, the climate, and more. Leading up to the many decisions the winemaker will face at the time of harvest, the approach to vineyard management can play just as important of a role as the winemaking itself.

Pests and other vineyard concerns

WARNING

If you think that humans are the only species that love grapes and the wines that come from them, then think again! Vineyards (and wineries) can be havens for a range of pests and diseases that can permanently damage if not eradicate entire plots if not identified and/or treated immediately. Some of the most common pests include:

>> **Grapevine moths:** These can eat different parts of the plant, with larvae feeding on everything from flower buds, blossoms, and grapes.

>> **Leafhoppers:** As the name implies, these hop from leaf to leaf, nibbling away as they go and leaving white and yellow patches that render the leaves incapable of achieving *photosynthesis* (the process by which plants, algae, and bacteria turn light energy into chemical energy in sugar form).

- >> **Mealybugs:** These typically make their homes inside vine trunks, then venture onto grapes where they infect berries with their egg sacs.

- >> **Phylloxera:** The most infamous pest of them all is by far the historic villain of the wine industry. *Phylloxera* is a sap-sucking insect that feeds on the roots of grapevines. See Chapter 2 for more information on phylloxera and its devastating impact on *Vitis vinifera* in the late 1800s.

- >> **Roundworms:** These pests infiltrate and feed on the area around and inside the vine root.

In most cases (outside of phylloxera and roundworm, that require resistant root-stock to truly combat threats; see Chapter 2), vineyard-generated remedies and insecticides can help winemakers prepare for the worst of pests. But in addition to pests, winemakers must stay vigilant about other potential diseases affecting vines and grapes. The most common include Powdery Mildew (a fungus attacking both the vine and the grapes), Downy Mildew (another fungal disease resulting in oil spots and patches that prevent full photosynthesis), Pierce's Disease (spread by glassy-winged insects called sharpshooters and European sap-feeding insects that inhibit water flow), and various forms of rot. *Botrytis cinerea*, when manipulated with precision by winemakers, is the one exception to unwanted diseases that results in delicious, dessert-style wines. See Chapter 6 for more detail on *Botrytis cinerea* and the process for making wine with "botrytized" grapes.

Exploring Grape Character and Performance

Grapes grow on vines and are made into wine. But what makes some grapes better for winemaking than others? We like to think of the grape universe, if you will, as being defined by two main attributes, which we informally call character traits and performance factors. *Character traits* are the characteristics of the fruit itself — its unaltered flavors that are driven by genetics alone. *Performance factors* refer to how the grapevine grows, how its fruit ripens, and so forth.

Appreciating a grape's true character

REMEMBER

Skin color is the most fundamental distinction among wine grapes. Every grape is considered either a white variety or a red (or black) one, according to the skin color of the ripe grapes. A few red-skinned varieties are further distinguished by having red pulp rather than white pulp, but almost all red varieties have white pulp. Within the white and black categories, each grape variety has its own hue.

THE ROUTE TO RIPENESS

When grapes are not yet ripe, they contain high amounts of acid and very little sugar — which is true for any fruit — and their flavor is tart. As ripening progresses, they become sweeter and less acidic (although they always retain some acid), and their flavors become richer and more complex. Their skins get thinner, and even their seeds and stems ripen. In red varieties, the tannin in the skins, stems, and seeds becomes richer and less astringent. The stage of ripeness that the grapes attain before being harvested is a big factor in the style of a wine that is totally driven by the winemaker's discretion. For more on flavors and pairing with food, see Chapter 18.

Individual grape varieties also differ in other ways:

- » **Aromatic compounds:** Some grapes (such as muscat; see Table 1-1 later in this chapter) contribute floral aromas and flavors to their wines, for example, while others contribute herbaceous (think sauvignon blanc; read more on this superstar later in this chapter) or fruity notes. Some grapes have neutral aromas and flavors and, therefore, make fairly neutral wines.

- » **Acidity levels:** Some grapes are naturally disposed to higher acid levels than others, which makes for crisper, leaner wines.

- » **Thickness of skin and size of the individual grapes (called *berries*):** Black grapes with thick skins naturally have more tannin than those with thin skins. The same holds for small-berried varieties compared to large-berried varieties, because their skin-to-juice ratio is higher. More tannin in the grapes translates into a firmer, more tannic red wine.

The composite character traits of any grape variety are fairly evident in wines made from that grape. For example, cabernet sauvignon grapes tend to have thicker skins and smaller berries compared to merlot grapes, contributing to higher tannins and higher sugar. Due to the higher sugar content in cabernet sauvignon grapes, the resulting wines often have higher alcohol levels.

Understanding a grape's performance factors

How a particular grape variety performs in the vineyard is vitally important to the grape grower because the vine's growth patterns determine how easy or challenging that variety will be to cultivate in a particular site. Considerations include:

- » How much time a variety typically needs to ripen its fruit. In regions with short growing seasons, early ripening varieties do best.

>> How dense and compact the grape bunches are. In warm, humid conditions, dense bunches can have mold and mildew problems.

>> How much vegetation a particular variety tends to have. In fertile soils, a vine that's disposed to growing a lot of leaves and shoots can have so much vegetation that the grapes don't get enough sun to ripen.

TECHNICAL STUFF

The reasons some varieties perform brilliantly in certain places (and make excellent wine as a result) are complex. The amount of heat and cold, the amount of wind and rain (or lack of it), the slant of the sun's rays on a hillside of vines, and the presence of water bodies are just a few of the factors affecting a vine's performance. In any case, no two vineyards in the world have precisely the same combination of these factors or *terroir*. We describe the history and concept of *terroir* with more detail in Chapter 2.

Grape royalty

Bees have their queens, elephants have their matriarchs, and humans have their royal families. The grape kingdom has nobles, too — at least as interpreted by the people who drink the wine made from those grapes. *Noble* grape varieties (as wine people call them, possibly inheriting this term from King Louis the XIV of France who once created a list of grapes to claim his country's economic and artistic superiority) have the potential to make great — not just good — wine. Every noble grape variety can claim at least one wine region where it's the undisputed champion. The wines made from noble grapes on their home turf can be so great that they inspire winemakers in far-flung regions to grow the same grape in their own vineyards. The noble grape might prove itself noble there in its own way, too.

Classic examples of noble grape varieties at their best are:

>> Cabernet sauvignon in Bordeaux, France (Chapter 6)

>> Chardonnay and pinot noir in Burgundy, France (Chapter 6)

>> Chenin blanc in France's Loire Valley (Chapter 6)

>> Nebbiolo in Piedmont, Italy (Chapter 5)

>> Sangiovese in Tuscany, Italy (Chapter 5)

>> Riesling in the Mosel and Rheingau regions of Germany (Chapter 8)

>> Syrah in France's northern Rhône Valley (Chapter 6)

Who's Who in White Grapes

This section includes descriptions of the white *vinifera* varieties whose wines are most popular in today's global industry. These wines can be varietal wines or place-name wines that don't mention the grape variety anywhere on the label (a common practice for European wines). These grapes can also be blending partners for other grapes, in wines made from multiple varieties. We discuss these wines broadly in order of their importance.

Chardonnay

Chardonnay is considered an elite grape variety thanks to its role in producing some of the greatest dry white wines in the world and the greatest sparkling wines — white Burgundies, in the first case, and champagnes (where it's usually part of a blend), in the second case. Today, it also ends up in a lot of everyday wine. The chardonnay grape grows in practically every wine-producing country of the world for two reasons: it's adaptable to a wide range of climates, and the name *Chardonnay* on a wine label is a surefire sales tool.

Traditional chardonnay winemaking involves using oak barrels to ferment the juice or age the wine, and the oak influences the wine's taste. The process can bring smoky, toasty flavors to the wine and diminish the wine's fruitiness. But many chardonnays these days are either unoaked or made in such a way that the oak influence is minor. See Chapter 3 for more on oak.

Chardonnay itself has fruity aromas and flavors that range from tart green apple — in cooler wine regions — to tropical fruits, especially melon or pineapple, in warmer regions. Chardonnay also can display subtle earthy aromas, such as mushrooms or minerals. Chardonnay has medium to high acidity and is generally medium to full-bodied. Classically, chardonnay wines are dry, but many inexpensive chardonnays are sweeter.

REAL DEAL

The top chardonnay-based wines (except for most champagnes and similar bubblies) are 100 percent chardonnay. But less expensive wines that are labeled *Chardonnay* — those selling for less than $12 a bottle in the United States, for example — are likely to have some other, far less distinguished grape blended in, to help reduce the cost of making the wine.

Riesling

The great riesling wines of Germany and the Alsace region of France have put this grape on the map as one of the world's greatest varieties. Riesling shows its real class in a few other places, but certainly not everywhere. Austria, Australia's Clare Valley and Eden Valley regions, and New York's Finger Lakes region are among the few.

In some ways, riesling is the antithesis of chardonnay. While chardonnay is often full and rich, riesling is usually lighter and fresh. Riesling's precision and vivid personality can make many chardonnays taste clumsy in comparison.

REMEMBER

Trademarks of riesling are high acidity, low to medium alcohol levels, and aromas and flavors that range from ebulliently fruity to rocky and mineral driven.

WORTH THE SEARCH

The common perception of riesling wines is that they're sweet, and many of them are — but plenty of them aren't. Riesling grapes can be *vinified* — made into wine — either way, according to the style of wine a producer wants to make. Some riesling wines don't taste as sweet as they might technically be, because their high acidity undercuts the impression of sweetness. Look for the word *trocken* (meaning dry) or *halb-trocken* on German riesling labels and the word *dry* on U.S. labels if you prefer a dryer style of riesling. In general, though, we suggest that you don't get hung up on the sweetness issue and just focus on how delicious riesling can be.

Sauvignon blanc

Sauvignon blanc is a white variety with very distinctive character. It can be very high in acidity and has pronounced aromas and flavors. Besides herbaceous notes (sometimes referred to as grassy or vegetal), sauvignon blanc wines can have tart to ripe stone fruit, tropical fruit, and citrus flavors (particularly grapefruit, lemongrass, and passionfruit), as well as mineral notes. The wines are light- to medium-bodied and dry or dryish. Most of them are unoaked (fermented in stainless steel or other container besides oak).

France has two classic wine regions for the sauvignon blanc grape: the Loire Valley, where the two best-known sauvignon wines are called Sancerre and Pouilly-Fumé (described in Chapter 6), and Bordeaux. In Bordeaux, sauvignon blanc is sometimes blended with Sémillon. Some of the Bordeaux wines that are blends of the two grapes and fermented in oak are among the greatest (and most expensive) white wines of the world.

New Zealand's sauvignon blanc wines are particularly renowned for their intensely flavorful style. Sauvignon blanc is also important in northeastern Italy, South Africa, Chile, and parts of California (sometimes labeled as *Fumé Blanc*).

Pinot gris/pinot grigio

Pinot gris (pronounced *gree*) is one of several grape varieties that begin with the word *pinot*. Others include pinot blanc (white pinot, called *weissburgunder* in Austria), pinot noir (black pinot, called *blauburgunder* in Austria), and pinot meunier (we don't know how that one translates). Pinot gris (gray pinot), called *pinot grigio* in Italian, is considered a white grape, although its skin color is coppery pink, and especially dark for a white variety.

Pinot gris wines are usually not oaky. Those labeled pinot grigio typically are light to medium-bodied and have fairly fresh green apple and pear aromas and flavors, while those called pinot gris can be aged in oak and tend to have more body with notes of dried or baked peaches, apricots, orange peels, and baking spice.

Pinot gris is an important grape throughout northeastern Italy, but the only region in France where pinot gris figures prominently is Alsace, where it really struts its stuff. Oregon makes different styles of pinot gris that can range from light and crisp to fuller and fruit packed. California versions are mainly mass-market wines labeled pinot grigio and modeled after the Italian style with varying levels of quality.

Other white grapes

Table 1-1 describes some other grapes whose names you see on wine labels or whose wine you could drink in place-name wines without realizing it.

TABLE 1-1 ## Other White Grapes and Their Characteristics

Grape Type	Characteristics
Albariño	An aromatic grape from the northwestern Spanish region of Rías Baixas and Portugal's northerly Vinho Verde region, where it's called alvarinho. It makes medium-bodied, crisp, stone fruit, citrus, and tropical fruit-forward wines that are usually unoaked.
Arneis (ahr-*nase)*	A local variety from the Piedmont region of northwestern Italy, where white varieties are uncommon. It makes soft, flavorful wines with notes of melons, almonds, and flowers.
Chenin blanc	A noble grape in the Loire Valley of France, for Vouvray and other wines. The best wines have high acidity and a fascinating oily texture (they feel viscous in your mouth). Other excellent regions for chenin blanc include South Africa's Western Cape and California's Mendocino County.
Garganega	An Italian white grape grown mostly in the Veneto region of Northeast Italy. This grape makes the increasingly popular wine named after the region called Soave. The wines are light to medium-bodied, with lemon zest, orange blossom, and almond characteristics.
Gewürztraminer (geh-*vurz*-trah-mee-ner)	An aromatic grape that makes deep-colored, medium to full-bodied, white wines with aromas of lychee, rose petals, and jasmine. Gewürztraminer is one of Germany's most important grapes. France's Alsace region is also classic domain of this variety. The wines have pronounced floral and fruity characteristics but are dry. Italy's Alto Adige region makes dry, mineral-driven gewürztraminer, as do some wineries in California and New York.
Grüner veltliner	A native Austrian variety most known for its white pepper characteristics. The grape makes clean, precision-focused white wines that can be rich in texture with tart fruit and other vegetal and mineral-driven notes.
Muscat/moscato	An aromatic grape with baked peach and floral aromas that makes Italy's sparkling Asti (which, incidentally, tastes exactly like ripe muscat grapes). Alsace and Austria make a dry muscat wine, and in lots of places (southern France, southern Italy, and Australia, for example) it makes a delicious, sweet dessert wine. Moscato (the Italian name) from California and Australia is a popular mass-market wine in the U.S.
Pinot blanc	This grape can range from light and neutral to more aromatic and richer in texture. High acidity and low sugar levels translate into dry, crisp, medium-bodied wines. Alsace, Austria, northern Italy, and Germany are the main production zones.
Sémillon (seh-mee-yohn)	Sauvignon blanc's classic blending partner but can be made as a varietal wine in its own right. This wine is low in acid relative to sauvignon blanc and has attractive but subtle aromas although it can be slightly herbaceous when young. A major grape in Australia, and southwestern France, including Bordeaux (where it's the key player in the dessert wine, Sauternes).
Verdicchio	A grape from Italy's Adriatic coast that makes varietally-labeled wine with medium body, crisp acidity, and aromas of lemon and sea air.
Viognier (vee-ohn-yay)	A grape from France's Rhône Valley that's grown in California, the south of France, South America, and elsewhere. This wine is known for its richness and body. It can show floral aromas, delicately apricot-like flavors, and be medium- to full-bodied with lower acidity.

The grapes described in this chapter make the most popular wines on the market today. You will (and should) encounter many more varieties and styles to try on your wine journey!

Who's Who in Red Grapes

If you love red wine, lucky you! You have a wide range from which to choose, because so many red varieties make good quality, interesting wines. Some of these varieties grow just about everywhere, while others are specialties of certain countries or regions. You'll encounter these grapes in varietal wines, place-name wines, and sometimes in blends. In Parts 2 through 5, we discuss the common place-name wines within each wine major wine-producing country of the world.

International superstars

Four red grape varieties are so renowned that winemakers all over the world have tried their hands at growing them and making wine from them. Read on to meet these four superstars.

Cabernet sauvignon

Cabernet sauvignon is a noble grape variety that grows well in many climates, except very cool areas. It became famous through the age-worthy red wines of the Médoc district of Bordeaux (which also contain merlot and cabernet franc, in varying proportions — see Chapter 6). But today, California is an equally important region for cabernet sauvignon — not to mention Washington, Australia, South Africa, Chile, Argentina, and so on.

The cabernet sauvignon grape makes medium- to full-bodied wines that are higher in tannin. The textbook descriptors for cabernet sauvignon depend on their age, and can include aromas of dark fruits (blackberries, black currants, plums), earth (leather, tobacco), vegetal or herbal notes (green bell pepper, mint, eucalyptus, cacao), and baking spices (vanilla, cinnamon, cloves, mostly due to oak aging).

Cabernet sauvignon wines come in all price and quality levels. The least-expensive versions are usually fairly soft and very fruity. The best wines are rich, firm, and complex with great depth and classic, concentrated cabernet flavor. Serious cabernet sauvignons can age for 15 years or more (see Chapter 3 for more details on aging as a winemaker decision).

Because cabernet sauvignon is fairly tannic (and because of the blending precedent in the home region of Bordeaux), winemakers often blend it with other grapes such as merlot or cabernet franc. Australian winemakers have a unique practice of blending cabernet sauvignon with syrah (more on that in Chapter 13.)

Merlot

Deep garnet to ruby in color, full body, relatively high alcohol, and softer tannins than cabernet sauvignon are the characteristics of wines made from the merlot grape. The aromas and flavors can include red and black fruits, violets, roses, and chocolate, with a velvety texture in the best examples.

TIP

Some wine drinkers find merlot easier to enjoy than cabernet sauvignon because it's less tannic. But some winemakers believe that merlot isn't satisfactory in its own right, and thus often blend it with cabernet sauvignon, cabernet franc, or both. Merlot makes both inexpensive, simple wines and, when grown in the right conditions, very serious wines.

Merlot is the most-planted grape variety in France's Bordeaux region (read more about its reign in Chapter 6). Merlot is also important in Washington, California, New York's Long Island district, northeastern Italy, and Chile, among others.

Pinot noir

Every winemaker we've spoken to that makes pinot noir detests the process. Cabernet sauvignon is an easier, sensible wine to make — a predictable, steady, reliable wine that doesn't give the winemaker much trouble and can achieve excellent quality. On the other hand, pinot noir is finicky, enigmatic, and challenging. Achieving a high-quality pinot noir is like winning a gold medal at the Olympics after a brutal training season.

The benchmark region for pinot noir wine is red Burgundy from France, where tiny vineyard plots yield rare treasures of wine made entirely from pinot noir. Oregon, California, New Zealand, and parts of Australia, Chile, and Slovenia also produce excellent pinot noir. But pinot noir's production is relatively limited, because this variety is very particular about climate and soil. These are very thin-skinned grapes that are some of the most sensitive to infections and disease in the vineyard. They produce low yields and are sensitive to extreme temperatures. But wait, there's more: pinot noir must be delicately handled in the winery too, as aggressive methods and over-extraction can quickly zap the grape of its inherently delicate and sophisticated flavor profile.

Pinot noir's wine is generally lighter in color than cabernet sauvignon or merlot. It has fairly high alcohol, medium to high acidity, and medium to low tannin (although oak barrels can contribute additional tannin to the wine). Its flavors and aromas can be very fruity — often a mix of red and blackberries — or earthy and woodsy, depending on how it's grown and/or vinified. You can find pinot noir wines in a wide variety of styles. Pinot noir is rarely blended with other grapes in making red wine, but most champagnes combine pinot noir with chardonnay. Chapter 6 explains how a red grape can make a white sparkling wine.

Syrah/shiraz

The northern part of France's Rhône Valley is the classic home for great wines from the syrah grape, but Australia can be considered the grape's second home. Syrah also grows in Washington, California, Italy, Spain, Chile, Argentina, Israel, and Greece.

Syrah produces deeply colored wines with full body, firm tannin, and aromas of black and blueberries, black pepper, cured meat, herbs, and sometimes leather or tobacco. In Australia, syrah (often referred to as shiraz) comes in several styles. Some are charming, vibrantly fruity wines that are quite the opposite of the northern Rhône's powerful, pepper-driven syrah wines, such as Hermitage and Côte-Rôtie, while others are even more powerful than those classic French wines. Turn to Chapter 13 for more on shiraz.

Syrah doesn't require any other grape to complement its flavors, although in Australia, it's often blended with cabernet sauvignon, and in the southern Rhône Valley, it's typically part of a blended wine with grenache and other varieties.

BURIED IN THE BLEND

Knowing the grape variety or varieties of a wine — either because it's the name of the wine, or because you remember which grape varieties are approved for use in the wine's specific region — can really boost your understanding of that wine. But a big trend today is *blended wines,* which contain the juice of several varieties. Only the wine-maker knows which varieties are in the blend (and they're not always willing to tell). The best approach with these wines is to just taste them and decide whether you like them or not — whatever they might be.

Local heroes

Some red grape varieties don't translate well outside their home regions, usually because growing conditions elsewhere aren't ideal. But they can make exciting wines on their home turf — wines that offer a terrific change of pace from the more standard "international" red varieties. Here are five of these varieties, in order of U.S. market presence.

Malbec

This grape originated in Bordeaux and is prominent in the southwestern French region of Cahors. But today, wine drinkers know it far better as Argentina's signature red grape variety. Malbec is a dark grape that makes deeply colored red wines with very firm tannin and spicy, dark-berry aromas and flavors. In the sunny, high elevations of Argentina's Mendoza region, the wines tend to have softer tannin and richer fruit flavors than in France.

Sangiovese

Sangiovese is an Italian grape that excels in the Tuscany region of Italy, especially in the Chianti Classico and Brunello di Montalcino areas. Sangiovese makes wines that are medium to high in acidity and firm in tannin. Sangiovese wines can be light to full-bodied, depending on exactly where the grapes grow and how the wine is made. Tasting notes can include dried to ripe red cherries or cranberries, herbal notes like tomato leaf, oregano, or bay leaves, and floral characteristics such as violets or other purple flowers.

Tempranillo

Tempranillo is Spain's undisputed claim to fame. It gives wines deep color, fairly low acidity, and only moderate alcohol. Modern renditions of tempranillo from the Ribera del Duero region and elsewhere in Spain prove what depth of color and fruit intensity this grape has. In the most traditional wines, such as some in the Rioja region, much of the grape's color and flavor is subdued by long wood aging and by blending with varieties that lack as much color, such as grenache. Tasting notes can still include ripe red and black cherries, dill, cedar, and baking spices. Aged versions will show more coffee, cocoa, leather, and tobacco aromas.

Zinfandel

Although most wine drinkers associate zinfandel with California, research has shown that zinfandel is a Croatian grape called crljenak kastelanski (soorl-*yen*-ak kash-tel-*ahn*-ski.) This is the same grape as Italy's primitivo.

Zin — as California lovers of red zinfandel call it — makes rich, dark wines that are high in alcohol and medium to high in tannin. They can have red, black, and blue fruit aromas, a spicy or tarry character, and a jam-like flavor. Some zinfandels are lighter than others and meant to be enjoyed young, and some are serious wines with a tannin structure that's built for aging. You can usually tell which is which by the price. Zinfandel also makes the popular, inexpensive pink wine called white zinfandel.

Nebbiolo

Outside of scattered sites in northwestern Italy — mainly the Piedmont region — nebbiolo just doesn't make remarkable wine. But the extraordinary quality of Barolo and Barbaresco, two Piedmont wines, proves what greatness nebbiolo can achieve under the right conditions.

Nebbiolo is high in both tannin and acid, which can make a wine tough. Fortunately, the grape also gives enough alcohol to soften the wine. Its wines can be deep in red color when young but can develop orange tinges within a few years. Its complex aroma is fruity (dried to ripe strawberry, cherry), earthy and woodsy (tar, truffles), herbal (mint, eucalyptus, anise), and floral (roses). Aged nebbiolos can take on more dried fruit characteristics (figs, prunes), and softer tannins over time.

TIP

Lighter versions of nebbiolo are meant to be consumed young — wines labeled *Nebbiolo d'Alba* or *Roero,* and some wines labeled *Nebbiolo Langhe,* for example — while some of the finer Barolos and Barbarescos are wines that really deserve a minimum of 5 years' age before drinking.

Other red grapes

Table 1-2 describes additional red grape varieties and their wines, which you can encounter either as varietal wines or as wines named for their place of production.

TABLE 1-2   ## Other Red Grapes and Their Characteristics

Grape Type	Characteristics
Aglianico	From southern Italy, where it makes Taurasi and other age-worthy, powerful red wines, high in tannin.
Barbera	Italian variety that, oddly for a red grape, has little tannin but very high acidity. When fully ripe, it can give big, fruity wines with refreshing crispness. Many producers age this wine in new oak.
Cabernet franc	A parent of cabernet sauvignon and often blended with it to make Bordeaux-style wines. Ripens earlier, and has more expressive, fruitier flavor (especially red berries), as well as less tannin. A specialty of the Loire Valley in France, where it makes wines with place-names such as Chinon and Bourgeuil.
Carménère	Originated in Bordeaux but today is a key player only in Chile. Makes nearly black, flavorful wines with dark berry and spice notes and soft tannins. Some wines can have herbal flavors if the grapes weren't ripe enough.
Gamay	Excels in the Beaujolais district of France. It makes grapey, banana-peel tasting wines that can be low in tannin — although the grape itself is generally tannic.
Grenache	A Spanish grape by origin, called garnacha there, although most wine drinkers associate grenache with France's southern Rhône Valley more than with Spain. Sometimes grenache makes pale, high-alcohol wines that are weak in flavor. In the right circumstances, it can make deeply colored wines with velvety texture and fruity aromas and flavors suggestive of raspberries.

Chapter **2**

How Wine Got Here

You probably didn't think that you would be learning about history and biology in a book about wine. But both are the "secret sauce" to understanding why wine is made from certain grapes, and what differentiates one *terroir* from another (we discuss this term in more detail later in this chapter). This chapter helps you to become more familiar with wine's evolution around the world.

There are an estimated 81 species of *Vitis* — a Latin term defining the *genus* (a taxonomic rank that groups together closely related species) of grapevines that belong to the *viticeae* family of flowering plants around the world. While archaeological evidence places the potential origin of several species in what is now North America, Asia, and Europe, only one of these species dominates the world of winemaking: *Vitis vinifera.* Read on for more about *Vitis vinifera*'s world tour.

Charting the Rise of *Vitis Vinifera*

In short, *Vitis vinifera* is the plant that gifted us wine! *Vitis vinifera*, also known as the common grapevine, is the species of flowering plant from which most of the world's wine is made. Read more about how grapes from vines transform into wine in Chapter 3.

Wine's most simplistic definition is "fermented grape juice." Before the rise of wine as we know it came the discovery of fermentation. Archeological evidence suggests that foods such as cereal, rice, honey, and fruit (likely berries or grapes) were fermented in China as early as 7000 BCE.

Fermentation describes the metabolic process of microorganisms (bacteria or yeast, for example) breaking down carbohydrates through chemical reactions into different substances. The chemical reactions vary, which explains why sourdough bread tastes different from kimchi, yogurt, cheese, or beer. The absence of oxygen is a crucial ingredient to fermentation, which early humans learned they could manipulate, along with other factors, to produce intentionally fermented food and drink. And while the earliest humans probably consumed fermented fruits of some kind (likely not intentionally), the oldest evidence we have of winemaking dates back to 8000 BCE. Here's our estimate of how the story goes:

>> 20,000 BCE: The oldest archeological evidence of humans using pottery to store food.

>> 12,000 to 10,000 BCE: Early humans begin domesticating animals and plants for survival, likely in both in the Caucasus region (now countries of Armenia, Azerbaijan, and Georgia) and parts of the Near East region (now including the countries of Iran, Iraq, Israel, Jordan, Lebanon, Syria, and Turkey).

>> 11,000 BCE: Recent research led by Yang Dong (a lead researcher specializing in plant biology at the Chinese Academy of Science's Institute of Botany) in 2023 revealed that *Vitis vinifera* was likely concurrently domesticated in both Near East and Caucasus regions during this time.

>> 8000 to 7000 BCE: 2017 chemical testing led by Dr. Patrick McGovern (considered the world's leader on the study of wine's origins) shows evidence of *Vitis vinifera* winemaking (including fermentation, storage, and aging) in large clay jars at Shulaveris Gora and Gadachrili Gora, south of Tblisi, Georgia's capital.

>> 6000 BCE: From this time, wine spread east to Greece and western Europe and the Americas primarily from the Near East region, and northwest into Europe from Caucasus.

>> 2470 BCE: The Egyptians have been established as the oldest civilization to extensively document the process of winemaking. Complex tomb paintings and hieroglyphs show regions, harvest, and production.

See Figure 2-1 for the adventures of *Vitis vinifera* across the globe, showing how this species initially spread from its area of origin in the Near East and Caucasus regions.

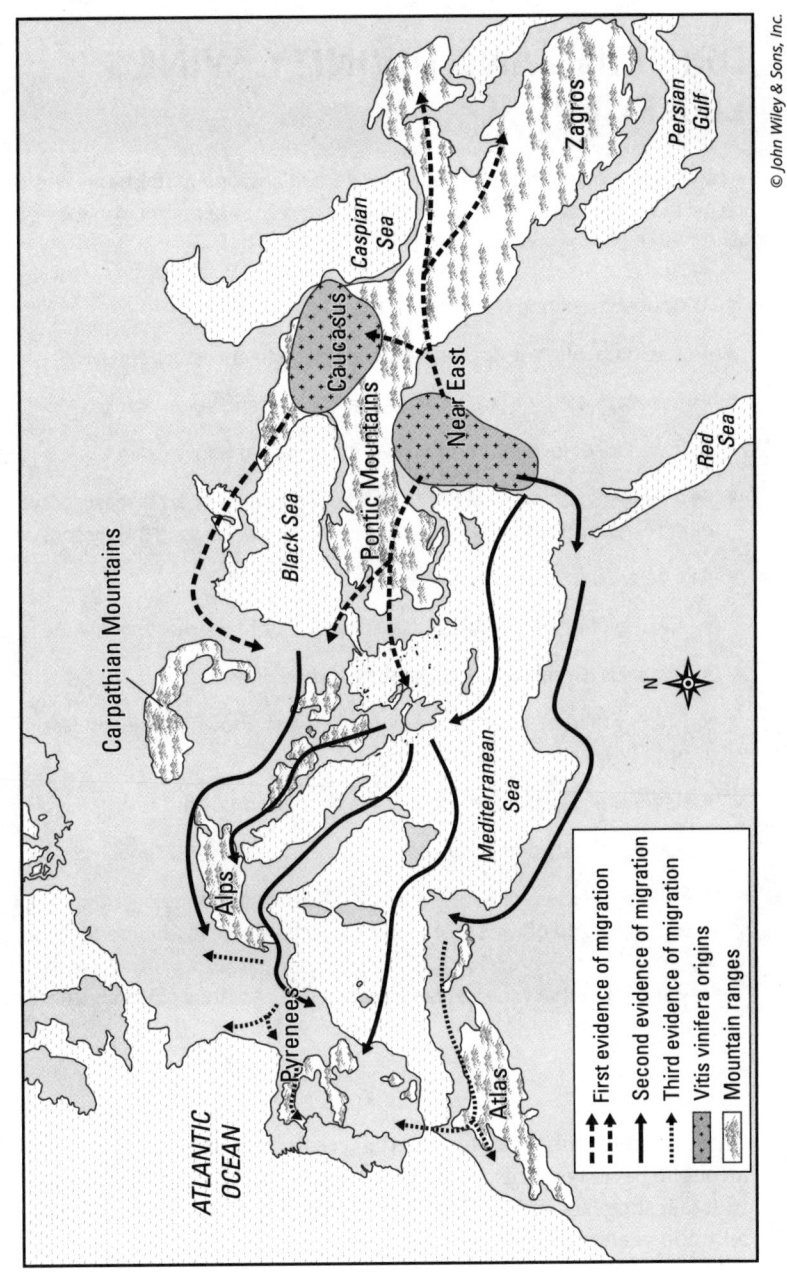

FIGURE 2-1: The early migration of *Vitis vinifera*.

© John Wiley & Sons, Inc.

DRINKING AND DIVINITY: WINE'S LIFE PURPOSE

A combinaton of ancient texts, fables, oral traditions, and modern-day Western science reveal that wine has served many purposes (and gods apparently) in the history of the world. Here are some of our favorites:

- As nourishment and cleansing for the soul.

- As a spiritual offering and/or right of passage to ancestors and gods.

- As a therapy, helping you to release inhibitions and speak freely.

- As a symbol of love, sex, and sensuality, as well as a love potion.

- As a heart-health booster, reducing risk of coronary heart disease, preventing blood clots, and promoting healthy cholesterol when moderately consumed

- As a deity reincarnated; for example:

  - Ash, Egyptian god of the oasis and vineyards of the western Nile Delta

  - Dionysus (Greek) or Bacchus (Roman), god of wine

  - Isis, Egyptian mistress of wine and beer, also known as the goddess of magic, fertility, and protection of women

  - Renenutet, Egyptian goddess of the harvest, important to grape growers

  - Varuni, Hindu goddess of wine

  - Yidi, the goddess of wine and alcohol in Chinese mythology, and Liu Ling, dubbed a Chinese god of wine for his love of the beverage in Chinese folklore

There is no doubt that wine has been considered a spiritual gift if not a necessity on earth for centuries!

TIP

Unfortunately wine can't take the credit for the earliest intentionally made alcoholic beverage. This award goes to beer, as cave evidence from Mount Carmel in Israel suggests that barley or wheat were used to purposely make beer as long as 3,000 years before wine.

Tombs, traders, and monks

So, how did we get from making cloudy, stinky stuff in clay pots to the silky, nectar of the gods now packaged in elegantly blown-glass bottles with fancy corks?

Wine was considered crucial enough to be packed into the ancient tombs of Egyptian pharaohs, ensuring their successful journey to the afterlife (even then, vintage-dated stuff appears to have been the most popular for the elite, as wine packed into luxurious tombs may have shown not only the year the wine was made but also the name of the winemaker). But history also tells us that early civilizatons recognized the commercial potential for wine as an export to other parts of the world. Since at least the sixth century BCE, wine was traded as a commodity, likely beginning with Greek imports to Gaul (modern-day France).

Parts 2 to 5 of this book show how commerce drove the spread of wine and wine culture to various parts of the world, including the Middle East, Europe, and the Americas. The most important periods to know include:

>> The 9th to 13th centuries, when the first of the oldest commercial wineries were established (Schloss Johannisburg of Germany in 817, Château de Goulaine of France around 1000, and Barone Ricasoli of Italy in 1141, to name three), with documented, high-volume sales to churches and monasteries.

>> The 12th century, throughout which Catholic monks of various orders vigorously planted vines and meticulously documented observations about different varieties and the impact of climate and technique on a finished wine across Europe. Catholic monks are largely credited for developing the concept of *terroir* as we know it today (and as described later in this chapter).

>> The 17th to 19th centuries, during which English, French, Spanish, and Portugese colonial empires expanded to the Americas, bringing *Vitis vinifera* vines with them and igniting local and internatonal production and commerce.

>> The 20th century, a period of tremendous growth in the wine industry globally, especially in North America and the Southern Hemisphere.

This chapter only scratches the surface when it comes to the history of wine and its uses. If you'd like to know more, check out *9,000 Years of Wine: A World History* (Whitecap Books, 2017) and *Wine: A Social and Cultural History of the Drink that Changed Our Lives* (Infinite Ideas Limited, 2018), both by Rod Phillips.

The phylloxera threat and vine evolution

With the exception of Australia, Chile, Germany, Greece, and Portugal, virtually every other major winegrowing region of the world has encountered some form of phylloxera. This menacing louse feeds on the roots of grapevines, and is the most important pest to know among many that can damage and kill grapevines.

Phylloxera crawls into soil and attaches itself to a grapevine's roots, where it feeds and lays eggs, essentially infecting the vine from its insides. Consequently, the vine weakens and dies. During the process of deterioration, other opportunistic infections from bacteria and fungi can further exacerbate the vine's condition. It can take anywhere from three to ten years to kill a vine, but this can be much quicker in drier climates, where the struggle for water already stresses the vine.

The world's most devastating phylloxera outbreak took place throughout the late 19th century, decimating entire vineyards and destroying industries in Europe, especially in France. Resilience and determination saved the day (and made important history in the evolution of the commercial wine industry) when French botanist Jules-Emile Planchon (the man credited with discovering phylloxera as the culprit for the death of so many French vines) partnered with Charles Valentine Riley, an American entomologist. The two discovered that grafting European grapevines onto American rootstock could make the vines grow phylloxera-free. Today, an estimated 95 percent of the world's grapevines are planted on tolerant American rootstock!

Understanding the Spirit of *Terroir*

Knowing wine's place and importance in world history, as well as the evolution of the vine as we know it, are important building blocks to understanding what makes this liquid so beloved. While the winemaker puts the magic touches that give us the "ooh's and aah's" on wine in the cellar, something bigger is always at play: the concept of *terroir*, a French term coined by Baron Pierre Le Roy de Boiseaumarié in 1920, associated with the word *terre*, meaning land or earth. The term was coined in 1920 but its application was in use for thousands of years before, likely dating back to the first winemakers who tried to make wine in different years, recognizing that the same grapes made in the same fashion but in different years (now referred to as *vintages*) can taste totally different.

In essence, *terroir* describes the special characteristics of a place and the impact of those characteristics on resulting wines. Every wine has an associated *terroir* based on where the grape (or blend of grapes) was grown. While most factors are naturally occurring, some are human-influenced. Common factors influencing *terroir* include:

>> Soil and its many horizons, including organic matter, topsoil, eluviation, subsoil, parent material, and bedrock.

- >> Climate and microclimate, including dry, continental, Mediterranean, humid subtropical, and maritime as some of the most common for *Vitis vinifera*.

- >> Proximity to water, including oceans, lakes, and rivers that can warm and/or cool a region to varying degrees.

- >> Elevation, including mountain ranges, volcanos, and the impact of varying slope sizes and orientations

- >> Viticultural techniques, including vine training, canopy management, fertilization, irrigation, and use of herbicides, all influencing grape composition and stress response.

What's so fascinating about the concept of *terroir* is its versatility and dynamism between regions and even within plots of the same vineyard. We use the term *terroir* throughout this book to refer to the combination of factors described above and their collective influence on wines made in different styles and regions around the world. We discuss more about these factors and the role of the winemaker in Chapter 3.

Discovering Wine Around the World

Wine is produced in nearly 62 percent of the world's countries, or 120 countries out of the world's total 195 (at the time of writing). Most high-quality vineyards, where the majority of the world's wine is made and consumed, are located in the two *vine belts*, between 40° and 50° North and 30° and 40° South, where *Vitis vinifera* has the best chances of achieving full ripeness, and vineyards are less susceptible to temperature extremes.

On average, the world drinks slightly less wine each year than is produced, which continues to drive down prices on the global market. In 2023, an estimated 6.9 billion gallons of wine were produced worldwide, but only about 6.2 billon were consumed. That's still a lot of wine!

TIP

The highest wine-consuming U.S. states are California, Texas, Florida, and New York — this ranking also corresponds to the highest-populated states in the country. If you live in or around larger populated areas, you may be more likely to encounter larger retailers that can offer more discounted prices on wines that are imported from other countries in the world.

"Yes, they make wine there, too!"

Italy, France, Spain, and the United States dominate world wine production. But there are many other countries to experience great wine from! See Figure 2-2, which shows world wine production by country in 2023.

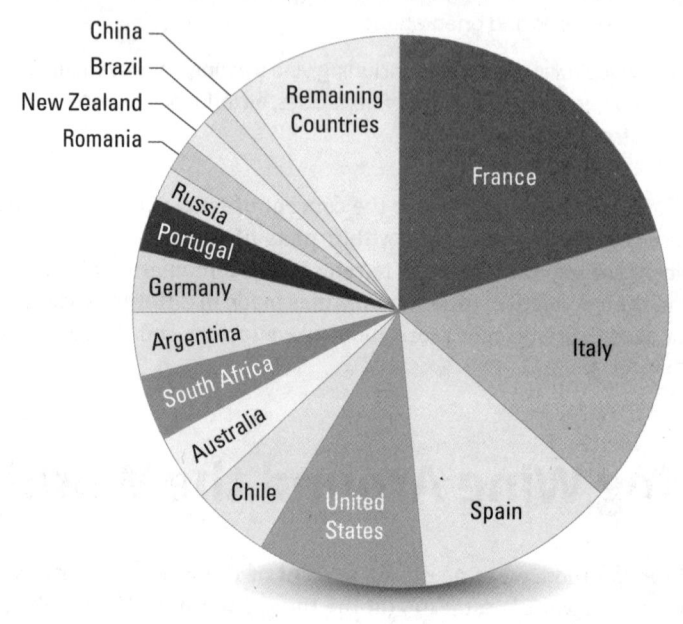

FIGURE 2-2: World wine production by country in 2023.

Many of the "remaining countries" shown in Figure 2-2 are briefly described in Parts 2 through 5 of this book, including their histories, main varieties cultivated, and important producers to know.

Wine laws and classification systems

As wine spread throughout the world, laws were created to regulate, monitor, and enforce standards for winemaking, designate regions for specific grapes and styles, and develop or enhance marketability, particularly on the international scene. While most major winemaking countries have their own laws and classification systems, some also adhere to regional or continental guidelines specific to the geographical and winemaking cultures in those places. The most common frameworks for the world's major wine-producing regions include:

>> European Union: European Union (EU) Protected Geographical Indication (IGP) and Protected Designation of Origin (PDO) systems

- » France: *Appellation d'Origine Contrôlée* (AOC) system

- » Italy: *Denominazione di Origine Controllata* (DOC) and *Denominazione di Origine Controllata e Garantita* (DOCG) system

- » Spain: *Denominación de Origen* (DO) system

- » United States: American Viticultural Areas (AVAs)

REMEMBER

Wine laws and classification systems are important to understanding how to interpret wine labels. Knowing the difference between a DOC and DOCG wine label may help you distinguish between price, quality, and producer on a shelf of countless Italian wines! We cover wine laws and classification systems in Parts 2 through 5.

Chapter **3**

Winemaking 101

Although an estimated 22 billion bottles of wine were consumed in 2023, it's safe to say that most wine drinkers don't actually know much about what wine really is, or even how it's made. The good news is that knowing a lot about wine isn't a prerequisite for buying or drinking it! But familiarity with certain aspects of wine can make choosing wines a lot easier, enhance your enjoyment, and increase your comfort level in different spaces. You can master as much or as little as you like. The journey begins here!

Wine comes in many colors as illustrated in the color section of this book. This chapter describes how different types of wine are produced, as well as the special touches that winemakers add to differentiate their wines from others.

Understanding How Wine Happens

As outlined in Chapter 1, wine is essentially fermented fruit juice. We focus on grapes, although a small portion of the world's wine is also made from other types of fruit (raspberries, blueberries, pineapples, and so forth). The raw recipe for turning grapes into wine goes something like this:

1. **Pick a large quantity of ripe grapes from grapevines.**

2. **Put the grapes into a clean container that doesn't leak.**

3. **Crush the grapes somehow to release their juice (feet have historically performed this step, but not so much these days).**

4. **Wait.**

In its most basic form, winemaking is that simple! After the grapes are crushed, *yeasts* (tiny, one-celled organisms that exist naturally in the vineyard and cellar, and therefore, on the grapes) come into contact with the sugar in the grapes' juice and gradually convert that sugar into alcohol. When the yeasts are done working, your grape juice is wine, and the sugar from the grapes is gone (it's now alcohol). The riper and sweeter the grapes, the more alcohol the wine will have. This process is called fermentation. *Fermentation* is a totally natural process that doesn't require human participation at all, except to put the grapes into a container and release the juice from the grapes. Fermentation occurs in fresh apple cider left too long in your refrigerator, without any help from you. Even milk, which contains a different sort of sugar than grapes, develops a small amount of alcohol if left on the kitchen table all day long.

Alas, if every winemaker actually made wine in as crude a manner as we just described, we'd be drinking some pretty rough stuff that would hardly inspire us to write this book. In the sections that follow, we'll provide more detail on the winemaking process for different styles of wine.

SULFITES: PROBABLY NOT THE CAUSE OF YOUR HEADACHE

TECHNICAL STUFF

Sulfur dioxide, a compound formed from sulfur and oxygen, occurs naturally during fermentation in very small quantities. Sulfur dioxide is found in many foods and beverages, including beer, lemon juice, apple cider, shellfish, dried fruits, and more. Winemakers add it, too. Sulfur dioxide is to wine what aspirin and Vitamin E are to humans — a powerful chemical compound that cures all sorts of afflictions and prevents others. Sulfur dioxide is an antibacterial agent, stopping the wine from turning to vinegar. It inhibits yeasts, preventing sugar that has remained in a wine (if any) from fermenting in the bottle. It's an antioxidant, keeping the wine fresh and untainted by unwanted oxygen. Despite these magical properties, winemakers try to use as little sulfur dioxide as possible because many of them share a belief that the less you add to wine, the better (just as many people prefer to ingest as little medication as possible).

Most wine labels in the United States carry the phrase *Contains Sulfites* (meaning sulfur dioxide) because of a law enacted to protect tiny percentage of the population who are very sensitive to sulfites. That law requires that any wine containing more than 10 parts per million of sulfites carry the *Contains Sulfites* phrase on its label. Considering that about 10 to 20 parts per million of sulfites occur naturally in wine, that covers just about every wine. Ironically, winemakers today need to rely on sulfur dioxide less than ever before because winery hygiene is so advanced, and sulfur dioxide use is probably at an all-time low. Sulfite levels in wine range from about 30 to 150 parts per million (dried apricots have roughly 2,885 parts per million). The legal max for wine in the United States is 350 parts per million.

If you're wondering, it is highly unlikely that the headache you may have after a night of drinking wine is caused by sulfites, simply because there are so few of them in wine, and a very small percentage of the world's population have strong reactions to even the slightest hints of sulfites. If you can eat a dried apricot or other high sulfite food with no side effects, then it's likely that you just need to grab another glass of water with your wine next time! Histamines and other compounds may explain other allergic-like reactions to wine that should be reviewed carefully with your healthcare provider.

Making (Not Quite) White Wine

Whoever coined the term "white wine" must have been colorblind. All you have to do is look at it to see that it's not white: it's yellow (sometimes straw yellow or even golden).

REMEMBER

White wine is wine mainly made from white (technically green, yellow, or even pinkish) grapes. White wine can also be made from red grapes, so long as the skins are separated from the juice early enough. Yellow wines, golden wines, and wines that are as pale as water are all referred to as white wines.

Here's the process for making white wine, with variations according to a winemaker's preferences:

1. **"White" grapes are harvested at the winemaker's discretion of ripeness and acidity and delivered to the winery.**

2. **Grape bunches are pressed and skins and stems are removed before fermentation begins.** The skins are removed from the grapes either by pressing large quantities of grapes so that the skins break and the pulpy juice flows out, or by crushing the grapes in a machine that has rollers to break the skins so that the juice can drain away.

3. **Alcoholic fermentation begins in (generally) stainless steel tanks and at cooler temperatures than red wines to preserve the grapes' freshness and flavors (typically between 45°F and 65°F, or 7°C and 18°C).** Oak-barrel fermentation is an exception here for grapes such as chardonnay or some

torrontés (find out more in Chapter 12). Ambient and/or cultured yeasts activate the fermentation process in both cases.

4. **Most white wines go through a process called *cold stabilization,* which is essentially flash-freezing the wine for a few days to gather and disperse tartaric acid.** This is purely for vanity: the process can give the wine a clean, crisp, and clear look, without which you may find some harmless crystals on your cork or in your glass.

5. **Depending on the winemaker's preferences, the wine may undergo additional stainless steel or oak aging (to introduce more wood-like or baking spice notes verses pure fruit).** This process may be another 6–12 months on average.

6. **Finally, the wine is bottled, labeled, and sold!**

TIP

We like to think of white wines in three broad categories. Michelle often uses these categories on menus to help guests at her wine bar differentiate between styles, especially if they're new to grape names alone:

>> **Fresh and lively:** Includes higher acid, ready-to-drink, and generally lighter white wines such as stainless steel fermented grüner veltliner, pinot grigio, sauvignon blanc, soave, or dry riesling.

>> **Full and rich:** Includes white wines that have undergone some oak or *sur lie* (on the lees, or spent yeast cells) aging. Some chardonnay, sauvingon blanc and sémillon blends, torrontés, viognier, and chenin blanc are some common examples.

>> **Dessert styles:** These can range from medium-bodied with high acid to fuller bodied with thick and syrup-like textures. They are generally dessert wines made from white grapes that are naturally high in sugar or harvested later in a growing season to obtain more concentrated sugar levels. Some examples include late harvest pinot gris, riesling, muscat, Pedro Ximénez, and furmint.

Aromatic wines such as gewürztraminer and muscat (see Chapter 1) may fall into any category depending on their winemaker's style. You can drink white wine anytime and with anything you like. It can be served as a chilled refresher on a hot day, an exciting partner to an appetizer or entrée, or a decadent dessert if it has the right amount of sweetness!

TECHNICAL STUFF

Over time, the world's best winemakers learned that there really wasn't a suitable alternative to oak for barrel-aging wine. Today, American, French, and Hungarian oak are the three most commonly used types for the world's largest wine producers. But a winemaker's decisions don't stop there: the size of the barrel (the most commonly used in the United States is the 225 liter "Bordeaux" or "Barrique" style barrel), the age of the barrel, the level of toast or char that the cooper made on the barrel, and deciding whether to ferment and age versus age alone in oak can all have lasting effects on the wine's ultimate flavor profile and texture.

Making Amber Wine

Everything about amber winemaking is the same as white winemaking, with a few exceptions. Amber, or orange wines are white wines that are fermented with their skins (hence the phrase, *skin contact)* and (sometimes) seeds like red wines (see later in this chapter). The resulting wines from this process can range from deep yellow or gold to caramel and burnt orange. The grape skins and seeds are what create the magical, autumn leave colors, also giving the wine *tannin* (a chemical substance mainly found in the skins and seed of grapes; find out more in Chapter 4) and body similar to that found in red wines. With origins in eastern Europe, particularly in Georgia, amber wines are also a tradition in Italy and Slovenia, with newer examples popping up around the world (see Chapters 5 and 10).

Making Rosé Wine

Rosé is the name that wine people give to pinkish hues of wine. These wines are made from red grapes, but they don't end up red because the grape juice stays in contact with the red skins for just a short time. This is called the *maceration* technique: only a few hours, compared to days or weeks for red wines. Because this skin contact is brief, rosé also absorbs very little tannin from the skins. Therefore, you can chill these wines and drink them as you'd drink white wines. Although the maceration technique is the most common, a less frequently used method is called *saignée*, loosely translated as "bleeding," during which some of the pressed juice is removed from the fermentation vessel and fermented separately to create a rosé wine.

Rosé is not only lighter in color than red wines, but typically also lighter in body (it feel less heavy in your mouth. Chapter 4 explains body and other taste characteristics of wine). They have a fascinating range of color, from pale orange to deep pink or fuscia, depending on the variety.

The popularity of rosé varied over the years, but in the last two decades has taken off, particularly among younger wine drinkers (canned rosé is apparently a thing). All wine lovers are deepening their knowledge of and appreciation for rosé, not just as as a refreshing drink on a hot day, but as a trusted companion to a broad range of snacks, entrées, and desserts.

Making Red Wine

Red wines really are red. They can be purplish red, ruby red, or garnet, but they're red. Red wines are made from grapes that are red or bluish in color. But of course, our world is too complicated so we end up calling the grapes themselves black!

REMEMBER

The most obvious difference between red wine and white wine is color. The red color occurs when the colorless juice of red grapes stays in contact with the dark grape skins during fermentation and absorbs the skins' color. Along with color, the grape skins give the wine tannin (find out more in Chapter 4). The presence of tannin in red wines is one of the biggest differentiators between red, white, and rosé.

On the surface, the process for red winemaking is similar to that for white winemaking (but the slightest changes in the winery can tip the scales from a high-quality wine to something barely quaffable):

1. **Grapes are harvested according to the winemaker's discretion for ripeness and acidity and and delivered to the winery.** This step is crucial for red winemakers: underripe black grapes can lead to tart, harsher tasting wines, while overripe grapes can lead to jammy, flabby wines too high in alcohol.

2. **Grapes are crushed and destemmed.** There are some exceptions like Beaujolais, in which whole clusters of gamay grapes are added to the fermentation vessel. *Cold soaking* (letting the juice sit with its skins at a controlled, colder temperature) to extract more flavor and color from the skins may also take place at this stage.

3. **Alcoholic fermentation begins, with ambient yeasts and/or cultured yeasts introduced by the winemaker.** This is where things may start to change for red wines. The winemaker typically wants to ferment these wines at a higher temperature (usually between 70°F and 85°F, or 24°C and 29°C) in order to extract more tannin and color. If the temperature is too cold, yeasts can become dormant and stop doing their job of eating up the sugars in the grapes. If the temperature is too hot, the wine essentially starts cooking and produces a boiled, undesirable flavor.

   Most red wines are fermented in closed-top vessels, but there are some exceptions in which open-top fermentations intentionally allow more oxygen into the wine. Cap management techniques (described in more detail later in this chapter) may take place in the earlier stages of this step.

4. **After fermentation is complete, the winemaker may elect to put the wine through extended maceration, cold stabilization, fining, or filtering (described later in this chapter) before additional aging.** The period of additional aging can be from months to years depending on the producer.

5. **Wines are bottled, labeled, and sold!**

Red wines vary widely in style — mostly because winemakers have so many ways of adjusting their methods to achieve the kind of wine they want. In each case, what may feel like time and punishment for the winemaker should lead to a high-quality red wine ready for us to drink and enjoy!

We like to put our red wines into three broad categories. Many wines may straddle all categories depending on where they come from and how they're made:

>> **Light and easy-drinking:** These are red wines that are lighter in style, lower in alcohol, and less tannic. Some examples include pinot noir, gamay, grachetto, dolcetto.

>> **Medium-bodied and elegant:** These are red wines that have some tannin but are still moderate in alcohol (less than 13.5%). This category tends to maintain bright acidity, making the wines excellent food pairings. Some examples include cinsault, carignan, mencía, and barbera.

>> **Full-bodied and powerful:** These are the fullest bodied, typically most alcoholic and tannic red wines. Some examples may include cabernet sauvignon, zinfandel, merlot, malbec, syrah, nebbiolo, Douro blends, and Nero d'Avola.

Thanks to the wide range of red wine styles, you can find red wines to go with just about every type of food and every occasion when you want to drink wine. Check out Chapter 18 for more guidance on food and wine pairing.

Making Champagne and Sparkling Wine

Sparkling wines are wines made from either white or red grapes that contain carbon dioxide bubbles. Carbon dioxide gas (CO_2) is a natural byproduct of fermentation, and winemakers sometimes decide to trap it in the wine. Sparkling wine's colors can range from pale yellow to deep, dark red (hello, lambrusco). Just about every country that makes wine also makes sparkling wine. In the eyes of most governments, these bubbles must be a natural byproduct of fermentation in order for a wine to be officially considered sparkling.

In the universe of wine, sparkling wines are a solar system unto themselves. They're produced in just about every country that makes wine, and they come in a wide range of tastes, quality levels, and prices. Champagne, the sparkling wine from the Champagne region of France, is the brightest star in the sky, but by no means the only one. We describe how champagne is made in detail in Chapter 6.

Adding the sparkle

For all wines, when yeasts convert sugar into alcohol, CO_2 is a natural byproduct. If fermentation takes place in a closed container, the CO_2 can't escape. With nowhere else to go, the CO_2 becomes trapped in the form of bubbles.

Most sparkling wines actually go through two fermentations: one to turn the grape juice into still wine without bubbles (called a *base wine*) and a subsequent one (conveniently called the *secondary fermentation*) to turn the base wine into bubbly wine. The winemaker generally has to instigate the secondary fermentation by adding yeasts and sugar to the base wine. The added yeasts convert the added sugar into alcohol and CO_2 bubbles.

WORTH THE SEARCH

Beginning with the secondary fermentation, the longer and slower the winemaking process, the more complex and expensive the sparkling wine will be. Some sparkling wines take years to make, while others are produced in only a few months. The slower route wines can often cost well over $100 a bottle (for example, Billecart-Salmon or Ruinart from France, or Gusbourne Estate from England which is gaining a reputation for traditional method sparkling), while bubblies at the opposite end of the spectrum can sell for as little as $10 (La Marca Prosecco or Freixenet Cava).

The three fermentations

Although many variations exist, most sparkling wines are produced in one of three ways: through *secondary fermentation in the bottle* (the "traditional" or "Champagne" method), *secondary fermentation in a tank* (the tank or "Charmat" method (pronounced *shar-mah*), named for the Frenchman who successfully patented the process in 1907 after others had attempted the same), and via the *ancestral method* or "pétillant naturel" method.

Secondary fermentation in the bottle

The traditional method is to conduct the second fermentation in the individual bottles in which the wine is later sold. Champagne has been made this way for more than 300 years and, according to French regulations, can be made in no other way. Many other French sparkling wines produced outside of the Champagne region use the same process, but are not allowed to call themselves champagne because they do not come from that region. They use the term *Crémant* to indicate their production method (for example, Crémant de Bourgogne, Crémant d'Alsace). The best sparkling wines from other regions around the world also use the traditional method.

Secondary fermentation in the bottle is an elaborate process in which every single bottle is an individual fermentation vessel. Including the aging time at the winery before the wine is sold, this process requires a minimum of 15 months (in the case of champagne) and usually takes 3 years or more. Bottle-fermented sparkling wines are always more expensive than tank-fermented bubblies. Check out Chapter 6 to discover more about the process of making champagne as well as the many different styles of champagne in France.

The traditional method as practiced in Champagne involves several processes that occur way before the secondary fermentation. For example, pressing to extract juice from the grapes must be gentle and meticulous to prevent the grape skins' bitter flavors — and their color, in the case of black grapes — from passing into the juice. Another crucial step in traditional method winemaking is blending various wines after the first fermentation to create the best composite base wine for the secondary fermentation.

This technique of conducting the secondary fermentation in the bottle is called the *classic* or *traditional method* throughout Europe. In the United States, it's called the *Champagne method* or *méthode champenoise*. In South Africa, it's uniquely dubbed *Méthode Cap Classique* or MCC.

Charmat or tank method

This is a fairly new way of producing sparkling wines, dating back about 100 years. The Charmat method of making a sparkling wine involves conducting the secondary fermentation in large, closed, pressurized tanks. Sparkling wines produced in the Charmat method are typically the least expensive to make, and to buy. That's because they're usually made in large quantities and ready for sale soon after harvest. Also, the grapes used in making sparkling wine by the Charmat method (glera, for example) are usually far less expensive than the pinot noir and chardonnay typically used in the traditional or Champagne method (further detailed in Chapter 6), which involves blending several (sometimes hundreds) of base wines, adding sugar and yeasts to ignite the secondary fermentation, then allowing the wine to age for several months to years before adding a dose of sugar and wine, and finally bottling.

Here's how the Charmat method works:

1. **A base wine (already fermented) is seeded with sugar and yeast, and it ferments a second time.** The CO_2 created by the fermentation becomes trapped in the wine, thanks to the closed tank as well as pressure within the tank and cold temperature.

2. **The wine — now a sparkling wine with higher alcohol than the base wine had — is filtered (under pressure) to remove the solid yeast deposits (the *lees*) from the second fermentation.**

3. **Before bottling, some sugar is often added to adjust the wine's flavor, according to the style desired.**

The whole process can take just a few weeks. In some exceptional cases, it can be extended to a few months, allowing the wine to rest between the second fermentation and the filtration.

Popular sparkling wines made in the Charmat method include prosecco and lambrusco from Italy (see Chapter 5), and sekt from Germany (see Chapter 8) and Austria (see Chapter 10).

Ancestral method

This approach predates the Champagne method with its roots traced to early sixteenth-century monks of southwest France. Gaining increasing popularity with new generations and natural wine enthusiasts, this method describes a spontaneous secondary fermentation that happens in the bottle without adding any yeast or sugars! Essentially, grape juice is fermented to a desired level of sweetness, but is bottled before all of the juice's sugars become alcohol. The remaining sugars are then fermented by the naturally present yeasts in the bottle, and CO_2 is produced. Bubbles are a consequence of this spontaneous fermentation. For today's winemaker, the ancestral method is a low-cost, low-intervention technique that can produce wines with a range of effervescence, natural fruit flavors, and other unique characteristics.

Making Dessert and Fortified Wines

Some wines have more than 14% alcohol because the winemaker added alcohol during or after the fermentation. This may sound like an unusual way of making wine, but certain parts of the world, such the sherry region of Spain, and the port and madeira regions of Portugal, have made legends from it. We discuss those wines in Chapters 7 and 9 respectively.

Dessert wine is the legal United States terminology for such wines, even if they're not necessarily sweet and not necessarily consumed after dinner or with dessert. In Europe, this category of wines is called *liqueur wines,* which carries that same unfortunate connotation of sweetness. We prefer the term *fortified wine,* which suggests that the wine has been "strengthened" with additional alcohol. Separate from fortified wines, there is a subset of wines that we call dessert wines for the purposes of this book. These are wines that are intentionally made in a sweeter style, to be consumed after a meal, with a dessert, or as a dessert on their own.

The most common dessert wine styles (not fortified with additional alcohol) involve picking grapes at distinct times and under very specific conditions:

>> **Late harvest:** Picking grapes later in the harvest season to ensure fuller ripeness levels and sugar concentration (a widely used approach that can be applied to any varietal, with some popular examples including German riesling and Italian vin santo made mostly from trebbiano and malvasia).

>> **Drying grapes:** Concentrating sugars in harvested grapes by drying them on mats and/or hanging them from the ceiling of a temperature-controlled (or moderated) room (a traditional technique used for *passito* styles in Italy).

>> **Botrytizing grapes:** Harvesting grapes affected by *Botrytis cinerea* or "noble rot", described in Chapter 6 (the key ingredients for famous wines such as French Sauternes or Hungarian Tokaji).

>> **Freezing grapes:** Leaving grapes on their vines to freeze in extreme temperatures (referred to as *icewine* in parts of Canada and Germany, for example).

We describe these winemaking techniques in more detail in Parts 2 through 5 of this book according to country of production.

REMEMBER

If you thought the process for red winemaking was painstaking, dessert wines take the cake. These wines are made in very small quantities because of the strict requirements that must be met from the time the grapes are harvested (often by hand, sometimes one grape at a time) to the time the (very small quantities of) concentrated juice is delicately pressed off the skins. Making even just a few bottles of excellent dessert wine is a tremendous feat. This also explains why the bottles of dessert wine you see on shelves are typically smaller, sold in a 500-ml bottle instead of the standard 750ml for dry wines. Some dessert wines are also more expensive, with the priciest examples in the thousands of dollars per bottle. But reasonable examples exist under $50 a bottle that are worth the investment!

Appreciating Winemakers as Magicians

The preceding sections detail the winemaking process for different types of wine. But there's even more sophistication and meticulousness involved. A finished wine is the result of hundreds of decisions the winemaker has made. Many of these decisions are also a consequence of the tools and resources that each winemaker has at their disposal. Winemakers are indeed magicians!

Many of today's winemakers have the advantages of new knowledge, technology, equipment, and a range of tools that are used to craft wines according to their individual vision and preferences. This explains why no two wines ever taste exactly the same. Here are some examples of the tricks in a modern winemaker's bag, as well as their impact on the winemaking process:

>> **Container types for fermentation:** These include stainless steel tanks, oak barrels, concrete casks, and giant clay pots or amphorae (called *qvevri* in Georgia and used in other countries of eastern Europe as well). The type of container used can influence freshness, flavor profile, texture, and complexity by moderating oxygen flow and transfer of different chemical compounds to the wine. The size of the container and the temperature of the juice during fermentation (which winemakers can intentionally decrease or increase) are also important factors that can impact a finished wine.

>> **Type and quantity of yeasts:** Some winemakers choose to add cultured, commercially made yeasts in addition to the ambient or native yeasts that naturally occur in the vineyard or cellar. This helps winemakers control the fermentation process and ensure the development of certain flavors. For example, a sauvignon blanc winemaker may add certain strains of cultured yeasts to enhance the flavors of grapefruit or green grass.

>> **Cold soaking:** Immediately after grapes are crushed and before the alcoholic fermentation begins, some winemakers may choose to soak the *must* (the grape skins, seeds, pulp, and/or stems) in a temperature-controlled vessel at a low temperature (usually somewhere between 50° and 60°F, or 10°C and 16°C). This process can help extract even more flavor and color, for red wines in particular.

>> **Cap management:** This describes a set of (less violent than they sound) activities referred to as "punching down" or "pumping over" the cap of grape skin, seeds, and pulp that rise to the surface of fermenting must as CO_2 separates the grape solids from their liquids. A *cap* is formed in this fashion for any wine that a winemaker chooses to ferment with its skins (some whites and ambers, but mostly reds). *Punching down* (referred to in French as *pigéage)* involves using specialized tools to break up the cap and push it back down into the wine to enrich colors, flavors, and aromas. *Pumping over* requires a heavy-duty pump strong enough to collect the must from the bottom of the fermenting vessel and refunnel it back over the floating cap, resulting in a gentler, less concentrated and tannic extraction (due to more limited interaction with grape skins). The shape and size of tools used varies widely depending on the winemaker and size of winery.

>> **Fining and filtering:** These are ancient practices used by winemakers to add the finishing touches (think lip gloss or a dash of perfume before a night out if you're into that) although the tools and methods have evolved:

- *Fining* involves adding a substance, or agent, to help eliminate unwanted particles in a finished wine. These can include excessive tannin, proteins, or other compounds that can cloudy a wine's final appearance. Today's most common agents include bentonite (a clay made from volcanic ash), casein (milk protein), gelatin, and isinglass (a type of gelatin that comes from fish bladder proteins).

- *Filtering* describes the process of passing a wine through porous material, again to remove unwanted particles and/or sediment from the finished wine.

After fermentation, winemakers can choose how long to let the wine *mature* (a stage when the wine polishes itself into the winemaker's ultimate vision) and in what kind of container. Fermentation can last for days or months, and the wine can then mature for a couple of weeks, years, or anything in between.

TECHNICAL STUFF

While there isn't a formal definition of *natural wine* (at least not in the United States at the time of this writing), the term is usually applied to wines that are made using more traditional techniques, incorporating native or ambient yeasts, applying minimal intervention in the cellar, and utilizing few to no additives, filtering, or fining agents.

REMEMBER

One of the biggest factors in making one wine different from the next is the nature of the raw material, the grape juice. Besides the fact that riper, sweeter grapes make a more alcoholic wine, different varieties of grapes (chardonnay, cabernet sauvignon, or merlot, for example) make different wines. Grapes are the main ingredient in wine, and everything the winemaker does, they do to the particular grape juice they have. Of course, grapes don't grow in a void. Where they grow — the soil and climate of each wine region, as well as the traditions and goals of the people who grow the grapes and make the wine — affects the nature of the ripe grapes and the taste of resulting wine. This is why so much information about wine revolves around the countries and regions where wine is made. In Parts 2 to 5, we cover all the world's major wine regions and their wines.

Chapter **4**

Honing Your Particular Taste (Buds)

U nless you are in the estimated less than 3 percent of people in the entire world who suffer from *anosmia* (partial or total loss of smell), then you can smell and taste wine. It is true, however, that some people are genetically wired to be more sensitive to a wider range of flavors than others. Tasting wine is an excellent test of your hypersensitivity to flavor. It's also something that, with time and practice, you can improve no matter how sensitive your taste buds may be.

In this chapter, we talk about the science of perception and encourage you to think about wine as an intersection between science and winemaker-crafted art! We share our simple process for wine tasting: See, Smell, Sip (or Swallow), and Speculate. We then discuss the building blocks of wine tasting, offering tips and tricks along the way to decode wine speak and detect quality in all its splendor!

Exploring the Science of Perception

Wine professionals tend to throw around words like "aromas" and "flavors." As pretentious as it sounds when it comes to wine, there is a method to our madness. The term *flavor* describes the perceptual experience (that is engineered by our brains) when we eat or drink. For all substances, our senses of smell and taste work together at distinct points to make sense of whatever we put in our mouths. The process of flavor perception has three basic steps:

1. **An odor or olfactory assessment happens,** during which your brain associates the smell of a substance with as many as a trillion different memories of other smells you've experienced before.

2. **A taste assessment occurs,** during which the gustatory cells in your taste buds (located on your tongue, roof, and back of your mouth) bind to the chemicals in food and drink and travel through your nerves and into your brain.

3. **A conclusion is mentally made,** during which a powerhouse part of your brain called the gustatory cortex helps you consciously differentiate between different tastes.

Here's what's so special about wine: until you cut your nose in on the action, all you can taste in the wine are sensations, including sweet, sour, bitter or salty. Flavors are actually *aromas* that you taste, not through tongue contact, but by inhaling them up an interior nasal passage in the back of your mouth called the *retronasal passage* (see Figure 4-1). When you draw in air across the wine in your mouth, you're vaporizing the aromas just as you did when you swirled the wine in your glass.

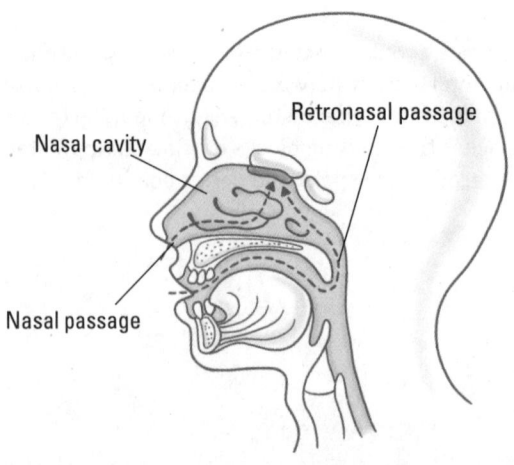

FIGURE 4-1:
The trail of wine flavors.

Illustration by Lisa S. Reed.

Using the Four "S" Method

Let's get back to the basics. You drink beverages every day, tasting them as they pass through your mouth. But when it comes to wine, drinking and tasting are not synonymous. Wine is much more complex than other beverages: there's more going on in a mouthful of wine. For example, most wines have a lot of different (and subtle) flavors, all at the same time, and they give you multiple, simultaneous sensations, such as softness and sharpness together.

TECHNICAL STUFF

Are there really red cherries or black plums in your wine? Not exactly. The fermentation process is the key to unlocking different chemical compounds in grapes that are shared by other fruits, vegetables, and organic matter. When you hear about a wine that tastes like ripe strawberries and forest floor, it's because there are chemical compounds in the wine that are also found in these materials.

If you just drink wine by gulping it down the way you do water or lemonade, you miss a lot of what you paid for. But if you *taste* wine, you can discover its nuances. In fact, the more slowly and attentively you taste wine, the more interesting it gets.

The process of tasting a wine — systematically experiencing all the wine's attributes — has four steps, which we discuss in the following sections. The first two steps don't involve your mouth at all: First, you see the wine (and we mean, *really* see the wine, using a technique), and then you smell it. Finally, you get to savor the taste and speculate about it (if you're into that kind of thing or studying to become a *sommelier* (a trained wine professional specializing in wine service, storage, and food and wine pairing). Otherwise, you can simply enjoy it with food or friends — the best ingredients for a great time!

See

Call us wine weirdos if you want, but we do enjoy looking at wine in our glass, noticing how brilliant it is and the way it reflects the light, and trying to decide precisely which shade of white, pink, or red it is!

TIP

To observe a wine's appearance, tilt a (no more than half-full!) glass away from you and look at the color of the wine under white light and against a white background, such as a tablecloth, napkin, or a piece of paper (a colored background distorts the color of the wine). Notice how dark or how pale the wine is and what color it is. Also notice whether the wine is cloudy, clear, or brilliant (most wines are clear. Some *unfiltered* wines — Chapter 3 explains filtering — can be less than brilliant.

One of the important clues a wine's color can give has to do with something called *rim variation*. This is the difference in color from the inner core of your glass to the outer rim (again, while the glass is tilted at an angle away from you). In many cases, older wines will have greater variation. For example, an aged Bordeaux (see Chapter 6) may have a deep red core that transitions to lighter shades of brown towards the edge of your glass.

At this point, you can also swirl the wine around (see the next section) and observe the way the wine runs back down the inside of the glass. Some wines form *legs* or *tears* that flow down around the inner circumference of the glass. Once upon a time, these legs were interpreted as the sure sign of a rich, high-quality wine. Today, we know that a wine's legs are a complicated phenomenon related to the surface tension of the wine and the evaporation rate of the wine's alcohol. They may or may not tell us about the details of a wine, so it's important for us to collect more information.

Smell

After you observe a wine's appearance, you get to the really fun part of tasting: swirling and smelling. This is the stage when you can let your imagination run wild, and no one will ever dare to contradict you! If you say that a wine smells like wild strawberries to you, how can anyone prove that it doesn't?

Before we explain the smelling ritual, and the tasting technique that goes along with it (described in the next section), we want to assure you that (a) you don't have to apply this procedure to every single wine you drink; (b) you won't look foolish doing it, at least in the eyes of other wine lovers (we can't speak for the rest of the human population); and (c) you will not be tested on these techniques unless you are studying for a certification from an organization like the Court of Master Sommeliers (CMS) or the Wine and Spirits Education Trust (WSET). So, don't put too much pressure on yourself and just have fun with it!

To get the most out of your smelling, swirl the wine in the glass first. But don't even *think* about swirling your wine if your glass is more than half full.

Keep your glass on the table and rotate it three or four times using the pads of your fingertips from the base of the stem so that the wine swirls around inside the glass and lets oxygen in. Then, quickly bring the glass to your nose. Stick your nose into the airspace of the glass and smell the wine. Is the aroma fruity, woodsy, fresh, cooked, intense, mild? Your nose tires quickly, but it recovers quickly, too. Pretend you're in a department store fragrance aisle and wait just a moment before you try again. If you're tasting in a group, listen to your friends' comments and see if you find similar or different smells. As you swirl, the aromas in the wine vaporize so that you can smell them. Wine has so many aromatic compounds that whatever you smell is probably not merely a figment of your imagination.

The point behind this whole ritual of swirling and sniffing is that what you smell should be pleasurable to you, maybe even fascinating, and that you should have fun in the process. But what if you notice a smell that you don't like? Hang around wine geeks for a while, and you'll start to hear words such as *petrol, wet rocks, burnt match*, and *asparagus* used to describe the aromas of some wines. "Yuck!" you say? Of course you do! Fortunately, the wines that exhibit such smells are not the wines you'll be drinking for the most part — at least not unless you really catch the wine bug. And when you do catch the wine bug, you might discover that those aromas, in the right wine, can really be a kick. Even if you don't come to enjoy those smells (honestly, some of us really do), you'll appreciate them as typical characteristics of certain regions or grapes.

WARNING

Wine can also have bad smells that nobody will try to defend. These are called *wine faults.* It doesn't happen often, but it does happen, because wine is a natural, agricultural product with a will of its own. Often, when a wine is seriously flawed, it shows immediately in the nose of the wine. Sometimes a bad cork is to blame, and sometimes the problem lies with some issue in the winemaking or even the storage of the wine. Just rack it up to experience and open a different bottle. We review the most common wine faults later in this chapter (see "The blame game: Wine faults").

TIP

TIPS FOR SMELLING WINE

When it comes to smelling wine, many people are concerned that they aren't able to detect as many aromas as they think they should. Smelling wine is just a matter of practice and attention. If you start to pay more attention to smells in your daily activities, you'll get better at smelling wine.

Try these techniques to get more out of sniffing:

- **Be bold.** Stick your nose right into the airspace of the glass where the aromas are captured. Give your nose enough space to take it all in without snorting the wine!

- **Don't wear a strong scent or sit in a smoky room.** These odors will compete with the smell of the wine.

(continued)

(continued)

- **Don't smell a wine when strong food aromas are present.** The meat you smell in the wine could really be a stew cooking on the stove!

- **Become a smeller.** Smell every ingredient when you cook, everything you eat, the fresh fruits and vegetables you buy at the grocery store, even the smells of your environment — such as leather, wet earth, fresh road tar, grass, flowers, your wet dog, shoe polish, and your medicine cabinet. Pack your mental database with smells so you'll have aroma memories at your disposal when you need to draw on them. We find that people who cook a lot (and well) tend to have great wine-tasting skills because they're constantly engaged with new smells and flavors.

- **Try different smelling techniques.** Some people like to take short, quick "rabbit sniffs," while others like to inhale a deep whiff of the wine's smell. Keeping your mouth open a bit while you inhale can help you perceive aromas. Some people even hold one nostril closed and smell with the other. Whatever floats your boat.

Sip (or Swallow)

After you've looked at the wine and smelled it, you're finally allowed to taste it. Here are the steps to follow:

1. **Take a medium-sized sip of wine.** This means more than a few drops but less than a gulp.

2. **Hold the wine in your mouth, purse your lips, and draw in some air across your tongue, over the wine.** Be careful not to choke or dribble.

3. **Swish the wine around in your mouth as if you're chewing it.** Some people describe this as gargling (like mouthwash) with your mouth closed or rolling the wine around your mouth with your tongue as if you're kneading bread dough. The point is, don't get so violent that the wine isn't getting a chance to engage with your taste buds. You have the option to either spit your first taste of wine into a bucket or other vessel so that you can make some initial conclusions (writing them down if you're serious), before you taste again. A professional wine taster may do this several times for just one wine, uncovering different fruit, earth, or other characteristics with each taste.

4. **Swallow the wine.** Again, this is if you're not studying to become a sommelier or tasting for the sake of guessing before you move onto another wine. Some professional tasters will swallow a bit of the wine so that it has a chance to reach their retronasal passage in full.

The whole process should take several seconds, depending on how much you are concentrating on the wine.

Taste buds on the tongue can register various sensations, which are known as the *basic tastes* — sweetness, sourness, saltiness, bitterness, and *umami* (a savory characteristic). Of these tastes, sweetness, sourness, and bitterness are those most commonly found in wine. By moving the wine around in your mouth, you give it a chance to hit all your taste buds so that you don't miss anything in the wine (even if sourness and bitterness sound like things you wouldn't mind missing).

As you swish the wine around in your mouth, you're also buying time. Your brain needs a few seconds to figure out what the tongue is tasting and make some sense of it. Any sweetness in the wine often registers in your brain first. Acidity (which, by the way, is known outside the wine world as *sourness*) and bitterness register subsequently. While your brain is working out the relative impressions of sweetness, acidity, and bitterness, you can be thinking about how the wine feels in your mouth — whether it's heavy, light, smooth, rough, and so on.

Speculate

After all this rigmarole, it's time to reach a conclusion: Do you like what you tasted? The possible answers are yes, no, an indifferent shrug of the shoulders, or "I'm not sure, let me take another taste," which means that you have serious wine-nerd potential!

WINES HAVE NOSES — AND PALATES, TOO

With poetic license typical of wine tasters, someone once dubbed the smell of a wine its *nose* — and the expression took hold. If someone says that a wine has a nice nose, they mean that the wine has a very strong, attractive aroma. If they say that they detect lemon *on the nose,* they mean that the wine smells something like lemons (including lemon zest, lemon peel, baked lemons, and so forth).

In fact, most wine tasters rarely use the word *smell* to describe how a wine smells because the word *smell* (like the word *odor*) seems pejorative. Wine tasters talk about the wine's nose or aroma. Sometimes they use the word *bouquet,* although this one seems to be slowly dying.

Just as a wine taster might use the term *nose* for the smell of a wine, they might use the word *palate* for the taste of a wine. A wine's palate is the overall impression the wine gives in your mouth, or any isolated aspect of the wine's taste — as in, "This wine has a harmonious palate," or "This wine is smooth on the palate." When a wine taster says that they detect raspberries *on the palate,* they mean that the wine has the flavor of raspberries.

SECRETS OF THE SOMMELIER: DEDUCTIVE TASTING AND COMMON AROMAS

Have you ever watched the TV series *Drops of God* (2023) or the *Somm* documentary movie (2012)? In many scenes from these productions, you're observing an all-star sommelier (or actor) taste a wine, say a few words about fruit and mushrooms or volcanos, then viola! They guess the exact wine, region, producer, and even vintage. Is it true that some wine professionals are this good at tasting? Sure. But this is not the case for most of us mere mortals. We use established methodologies and tools to deduce what a wine is and where it may be from. Check out this list of common wine-tasting elements and descriptor categories.

Tasting Element	Common Categories and Descriptors
Sight	Clarity, color intensity, primary or secondary colors, rim variation, staining, tearing.
Nose	Aromatic intensity, fruit (for example, cherries, strawberries, green apples), fruit condition (for example, tart, dried, baked, stewed), non-fruit (from the grapes or from the winemaking): herbs (bell pepper, asparagus, petrol, butter, cream, vanilla, cheese), organic and/or inorganic earth (forest floor, mushrooms, potting soil, wet stone, volcanic minerals).
Palate and Palate Structure	Sweetness, acidity, alcohol, tannin, texture.

TECHNICAL STUFF

If you've *blind tasted* the wine, meaning you didn't know what the wine was to begin with, this is the point at which you get to guess what region it may be from, what the grape may be, and even how old the wine is. Herein lies the difference between your everyday taster and a professional. Professionals are trained to look for clues and distinguish between different wines made in different parts of the world in different styles. A trained professional may know the difference between a New Zealand sauvignon blanc and a Sancerre from the Loire Valley (same grape, different *terroir* — see Chapter 2 for more on *terroir*) because of patterns that have been established over time between the fruit characteristics, fruit condition, and more in the most common examples of these wines. If you are beginning your wine journey, focus for now on just perfecting your own tasting technique and learning about which wines you enjoy the most!

The tastes of a wine reveal themselves sequentially as the tongue detects them and your brain registers them. But there is one step between knowing how to taste wine and always drinking wine that you like. That step is putting taste into words. You wouldn't have to bother with this detail if only you could always choose your wines the way that people choose cheese in a gourmet shop ("Can I try that one? No, I don't like it, let me taste the one next to it. Good. I'll take half a pound.").

"Like" and "don't like" is a no-brainer when you have the wine in your mouth. But most of the time, you buy the stuff without tasting it first. So, unless you want to drink the same wine for the rest of your life, you're going to have to decide what you like or don't like in a wine and communicate that to another person who can steer you toward another wine you'll like. There are two hurdles here: Finding the words to describe what you like or don't like, and then getting your audience to understand what you mean. Naturally, it helps if everyone speaks the same language.

WARNING

Unfortunately, wine speak is a dialect with an undisciplined and sometimes poetic vocabulary whose definitions change all the time, depending on who's speaking and how they were trained. In the following sections, we address a few of the elephants in the room when it comes to wine-tasting vocabulary.

Sweetness

As soon as you put the wine into your mouth, you can usually notice sweetness or the lack of it. In wine speak, *dry* is the opposite of sweet. Sweetness in a wine is a deliberate decision of the winemaker. Chemically speaking, it concerns the amount of actual sugar that is left in the wine after fermentation (referred to as *residual sugar*). A winemaker can decide whether to make a dry, off-dry, or sweet style of wine by determining when they want to stop the fermentation process (see Chapter 3). Sweetness can also come from the grapes themselves. Botrytized grapes, frozen grapes, and dried grapes are all harvested with highly concentrated sugars that in turn, make naturally sweet wines.

TIP

Classify the wine you're tasting as either *dry, off-dry* (in other words, slightly sweet), or *sweet.*

Acidity

All wine contains acid (mainly *tartaric acid,* which exists in grapes), but some wines are more acidic than others. Acidity is a key taste factor for both white and red wines, although you will hear it more often in relation to whites. For white wines, acidity is the backbone of the wine's taste (it gives the wine firmness in your mouth). White wines high in acidity feel *crisp,* and those without enough acidity feel *flabby.*

Beginning wine tasters sometimes describe dry wines as sweet because they confuse fruitiness with sweetness. Here's the difference:

- **A wine is fruity when it has distinct aromas and fruit flavors. You smell the fruitiness with your nose. In your mouth, you "smell" it through your retronasal passage.** The condition of said fruit on your nose or palate can be *ripe, baked, stewed, candied,* or some other characteristic that implies sweetness, giving the impression that you're having a sweet wine. But for dry wines (meaning those fermented to dryness, with little to no residual sugar in the finished wine), this is just the fruit flavors at work.

- **Sweetness, on the other hand, is a tactile impression on your tongue.** When in doubt, try holding your nose when you taste the wine. If the wine really is sweet, you'll be able to taste the sweetness, despite the fact that you can't smell the fruitiness.

You generally perceive acidity in the middle of your mouth — what wine tasters call the *mid-palate*. How much you salivate after tasting a wine can be a clue to its acidity level, because high acidity triggers saliva production (think about how your mouth and face changes when you drink ice-cold lemonade). You can also sense the consequences of acidity (or lack thereof) in the overall style of the wine — whether it's tart or soft and generous, for example.

TIP

Classify the wine you're tasting as *crisp, soft,* or *round* (think "Pillsbury Doughboy"). Wine professionals will use words like *low, medium* or *medium-plus* to sometimes describe acidity levels in wine. Learn more about how acidity in wine (and other common characteristics) interact with different foods to create ideal pairings in Chapter 18.

Tannin

Tannins are polyphenols, or plant-based chemical compounds, that exist naturally in the skins, seeds (or *pips*), and stems of grapes. Because red wines are fermented with their grape skins and pips, and because red grape varieties are generally higher in tannin than white varieties, tannin levels are far higher in red wines than in white wines. Aging wine in new oak barrels can also contribute tannin to wines (both reds and whites).

Have you ever taken a sip of a red wine and rapidly experienced a dried-out-mouth feel, as if something had blotted up all your saliva or you just swallowed a black tea bag? That's tannin.

To generalize a bit, tannin is to a red wine what acidity is to a white: a backbone. Tannins alone can taste bitter, but some wine tannins are less bitter than others. Also, other elements of the wine, such as sweetness, can mask the perception of bitterness. You sense tannin — as bitterness or as firmness or richness of texture — mainly in the rear of your mouth, on the inside of your cheeks, and on your gums.

TIP

Depending on the amount and nature of its tannin, you can describe a red wine as *astringent, firm, soft, smooth, or elegant.*

Texture

Softness and firmness are actually *textural impressions* a wine gives you as you taste it. Just as your mouth feels temperature in a liquid, it also feels texture. Some wines literally *feel* soft and smooth as they move through your mouth, while others feel hard, rough, edgy, or coarse. In white wines, acid is usually responsible for impressions of hardness or firmness (or crispness). In red wines, tannin is usually responsible. Low levels of either substance can make a wine feel pleasantly soft — or *too* soft, depending on the wine and your taste preferences. Unfermented sugar and alcohol also contribute to an impression of softness. But very high alcohol — which is increasingly common as we experience global warming and more ripeness in harvested grapes — can give a wine an edge of hardness. Initially, it's enough to notice a wine's texture, without figuring out what factor is creating that sensation.

Alcohol and body

A wine's *body* is an impression you get from the whole of the wine — not a basic taste that registers on your tongue. It's the impression of the weight and size of the wine in your mouth, which is usually attributable mainly to a wine's alcohol. We say *impression* because, obviously, one ounce of any wine will occupy the same space in your mouth and weigh the same as one ounce of any other wine. But some wines *seem* fuller, bigger, or heavier in the mouth than others. Think about the wine's fullness and weight as you taste it. Imagine that your tongue is a tiny scale and judge how much the wine is weighing it down.

TIP

Classify the wine as *light-bodied, medium-bodied,* or *full-bodied.*

The flavor dimension

Wines have flavors (uh, we mean *mouth aromas*), but wines don't come in a specific flavor. Although you may enjoy the suggestion of chocolate in a red wine that you're tasting, you wouldn't want to go to a wine shop and ask for a chocolaty wine! We can guarantee you that even the most experienced staff will have a difficult time helping you because this is a common characteristic of several (especially red) wines.

TIP

Instead, refer to *families of flavors* in wine. You have *fruity wines* (the ones that make you think of all sorts of fruit when you smell them or taste them), *earthy wines* (these flavors make you think of minerals and rocks, walks in the forest, turning the earth in your garden, dry leaves, and so on), *spicy wines* (cinnamon, cloves, black pepper, or other Asian spices, for example), *herbal wines* (mint, grass, hay, rosemary, and so on), and so on, and so on. So many flavors exist in wines that we could go on and on (and we often do!), but you get the picture. Sometimes describing these families of flavors to a shop attendant will help them steer you in the right direction of regions, varieties, or even producers where you're more likely to find the flavor families you like. For example, if you're into the green bell pepper or eucalyptus thing, a sales associate may escort you to red wines from Australia (we're thinking shiraz or cabernet sauvignon; see Chapter 13) where you may be more likely to encounter those flavor families.

Another aspect of flavor that's very important to consider is a wine's *flavor intensity* — how much flavor the wine has, regardless of what those flavors are. Some wines are as flavorful as Madras curry, while others have flavors as subtle as unseasoned fillet of sole. Flavor intensity is a major factor in pairing wine with food (as you can read in Chapter 18) and it's also an important factor to consider in determining what type of wine is best for you and the occasion.

Detecting Quality

Did you notice, by any chance, that nowhere among the terms we use to describe wines in the previous section are the words *great, very good,* or *good?* Instead of worrying about crisp wines, earthy wines, and medium-bodied wines, wouldn't it just be easier to walk into a wine shop and say, "Give me a very good wine for dinner tonight"? Isn't *quality* the ultimate issue — or at least, quality within your price range, also known as *value?*

REMEMBER

A lot of wine marketing revolves around the notion of quality, except in the case of the least expensive wines. Wine producers constantly brag about the quality ratings that their wines receive from critics, because a high rating — implying high quality — translates into increased sales. However, quality wines come in all colors, all degrees of sweetness and dryness, and all flavor profiles. Just because a wine is high quality doesn't mean that you'll enjoy it any more than a Michelin star means that you'll love a particular restaurant. Personal taste is simply more relevant than quality in choosing a wine. Degrees of quality do exist among wines. But a wine's quality is not absolute: How great a wine is or isn't depends on who's doing the judging.

The instruments that measure the quality of a wine are a human being's nose, mouth, and brain. Because everyone is different, everyone has a different opinion on how good a wine is. The combined opinion of a group of trained, experienced tasters (also known as wine experts) is usually considered a reliable judgment of a wine's quality.

Critiquing the critics

TECHNICAL STUFF

The process of rating wines and ascribing value to them based on their rank is centuries old. As early as the 19th century, wines were being reviewed and sold based on their ratings by traders and merchants of different kinds (hello, 1855 Bordeaux Classification — read more on this in Chapter 6). The world of modern-day wine critics is much broader than ever before. It includes journalists, sommeliers, major buyers, and more. The most famous of the 21st-century critics is Robert Parker — creator of the 100-point system that was published in *The Wine Advocate* magazine in the late 1970s. Since Parker, several other influential critics have risen to fame and written extensive reviews and tasting notes on oceans of wine labels, including James Suckling, Jancis Robinson, and Antonio Galloni among others. In truth, many critics have shaped American wine culture in particular, and even helped some brands rise to success. Just because a wine has a certain critic rating, it does not necessarily mean you will like it. We find reviews and scores to be most helpful in some retail settings, especially when staff knowledge may be limited, or the selection of wines is vast. The problem here is that wines that aren't rated above 80 or 90 points don't necessarily have a sticker that says so. But to not have a sticker does not mean that the wine isn't good (maybe it just wasn't rated). We understand why producers would don these accolades on their wine (for marketing purposes because ultimately, selling the wine that one makes is the goal). In the end, we still prefer to taste and see for ourselves.

TIP

There are countless online resources and apps that tell you what other (regular) people think about different wines, including their aroma and flavor profiles, and even what you can expect to pay retail based on where you're located. Two of our favorite wine rating apps that focus more on the wisdom of regular crowds versus paid wine professionals or tasters include Vivino (www.vivino.com) and Cellar-Tracker (www.cellartracker.com).

What is a good wine?

A good wine is, above all, a wine that you like enough to drink, because the whole purpose of a wine is to give pleasure to those who drink it. After that, how good a wine is depends on how it measures up to a set of (more or less) agreed-upon standards of performance established by experienced, trained experts. These standards involve mysterious concepts such as balance, length, complexity, depth, finish, and trueness to type (*typicity* in wine speak), which we explain in the following sections. None of these concepts is objectively measurable, by the way.

Balance

Balance is the relationship among sweetness, acidity, tannin, and alcohol in a wine. A wine is balanced when nothing sticks out, such as harsh tannin or too much sweetness. Each sip is a harmony of multiple instruments playing at the same time from start to finish on your palate. Most well-made wines are balanced to most people. But if you have any pet peeves about food — if you really hate anything tart, for example, or if you never eat sweets — you might perceive some wines to be unbalanced. If you perceive them to be unbalanced, then they are unbalanced for you. Professional tasters know their own idiosyncrasies and adjust for them when they judge wine.

REMEMBER

Tannin and acidity are *hardening elements* in a wine (they make a wine taste firmer and less giving in the mouth), while alcohol and sugar (if any) are *softening elements*. The balance of a wine is the interrelationship of the hard and soft aspects— and a key indicator of quality.

Length

When we call wines *long* or *short,* we're not referring to the size of the bottle or how quickly we empty it. *Length* describes a wine that gives an impression of going all the way on the palate — you can taste it across the full length of your tongue — rather than stopping short halfway through your tasting of it. Many wines today are very upfront on the palate — they make a big impression as soon as you taste them, but they don't go the distance in your mouth. In other words, they're *short.* Length is increasingly used also to describe a wine with a long after-taste (see the section "Finish," just ahead.) Length in the mouth can more precisely be called *palate length,* to avoid confusion. Length on the palate, or how long the wine's pleasant flavors endure in your mouth, is a sure sign of high quality.

Complexity

Nothing is wrong with a simple, straightforward wine, especially if you enjoy it. But a wine that keeps revealing different things about itself, always showing you a new flavor or impression — a wine that has *complexity* — is usually considered better quality. Generally, experts use the term *complexity* specifically to indicate that a wine has a multiplicity or combination of aromas and flavors, some that hit you at different parts of your tasting experience (mid-palate and on the finish, for example).

Depth

Depth is another subjective, unmeasurable attribute of a high-quality wine. We say a wine has *depth* when it has a concentration of flavors — that is, it doesn't taste flat and one-dimensional in your mouth. If you can really taste the fruitiness of tart cherries and ripe blueberries, then juxtapose that with aromas of potting soil and mushrooms that still make the wine taste pleasurable in one sip, and you're drinking a wine that has both depth and complexity!

Finish

The impression a wine leaves in the back of your mouth and in your throat after you swallow is its *finish* or *aftertaste.* In a good wine, you can still perceive the wine's flavors, such as fruitiness or spiciness, at that point. The more enduring the positive flavor perception is, the *longer* the finish is. Some wines may finish *hot,* because of high alcohol, or *bitter,* because of tannin — both shortcomings. Or a wine may have nothing much at all to say for itself after you swallow, which tells you that it is probably not the highest-quality wine.

Typicity

To judge whether a wine is true to its type, you have to know how that type of wine is supposed to taste. In other words, you must know the textbook characteristics of wines made from the major grape varieties and wines of the world's classic wine regions. For example, the cabernet sauvignon grape typically has an aroma and flavor of black currants, and the French white wine called Pouilly-Fumé typically has a slight gunflint aroma. Turn to Chapter 1 for more details on common flavors in the world's most famous wine grapes.

The blame game: Wine faults

Strangely enough, the right to declare a wine *good* because you like it doesn't carry with it the right to call a wine *bad* just because you don't. In this game, you get to make your own rules, but you don't get to force other people to live by them!

There are some universal characteristics of bad wines, and these have more to do with chemical faults that unfold during the winemaking process than a winemaker's drive to make a bad wine. In most cases, you can usually return the (almost full) bottle for a refund or exchange.

Watch out for the following:

>> **Volatile acidity:** Referred to as *VA*, this is a measure of gaseous acids in a wine. Many wines can (and are legally permitted to) contain very small amounts of volatile acidity. In large amounts, wine can smell like nail polish remover or even vinegar.

>> **Brettanomyces:** Referred to as *Brett*, this is a yeast that sometimes forms alongside other yeasts in the winery. In high amounts, it can smell like a barnyard, sweaty socks, or old cheese. Some people enjoy these smells (we know a guy whose whole wine bar menu features Bretty-ish wines), but others, not so much.

>> **Oxidization:** This is a fancy term to describe wine that has been in contact with more oxygen than desired before the bottle is opened. The wine often changes color (brownish orange in red wines and brownish in white wines), and can have aromas and flavors of vinegar, unpleasant caramel, straw, or sherry.

>> **Reduction:** In some ways the opposite of oxidization, reduction occurs when wine isn't exposed to enough oxygen during the winemaking process. Reductive wines can have aromas and flavors of rotten eggs, cooked cabbage, or burnt matches.

>> **Cooked or maderized wines:** When a wine has been stored or shipped in heat, it can taste cooked or baked as a result (wine people use the term *maderized* for such wines). Often there's telltale leakage from the cork, or the cork has pushed up a bit inside the bottle. Unfortunately, every other bottle of that wine that experienced the same shipping or storage will also be bad. The same result is also possible when wines are overexposed to sunlight during storage.

>> **Cork taint:** The most common flaw, referred to as *corked* wine, is caused by 2,4,6-Trichloroanisole or TBA (a chemical compound characterized by moldy, musty, or earthy odors). It comes across as a smell of damp cardboard or wet dog that gets worse with air, along with diminished flavor intensity. It's caused by a defective cork, and any wine in a bottle that's sealed with a cork is at risk. Fortunately, only a very small percentage of wines are corked.

REMEMBER

Let's not dwell too long on what can go wrong with a wine. If you find a bad wine or a bad bottle — or even a wine that's considered a good wine, but you don't like it — just move on to something you like better. Drinking a so-called great wine that you don't enjoy is as time-wasting as watching a television show that bores you. Change the channel.

2
The World of Wine: Europe

Discover the rich wine history and main regions of Italy, from Piedmont to Sicily.

Find out why France is wine's "super model." Go deep with wines from regions such as Bordeaux, Burgundy, and Champagne.

Take in Spain's wine culture, from Galicia to Andalucía. Get to know sherry — Spain's best kept dessert secret.

Explore how Germany rose to a league of its own with riesling, pinot noir, and more.

Uncork Portugal's vast world of wine, from still in the Douro to sparkling in Bairrada, and dessert and fortified from Porto and Madeira.

Get a snapshot of more wine regions from central, eastern, and southeastern Europe, from Austria to Greece, Switzerland, and elsewhere.

Chapter **5**

Italy: Wine and Passion

More than 2,000 years after Julius Caesar conquered Gaul, the Italians continue to take the world by storm. With passion, artistic flair, impeccable taste, and flawless workmanship, Italy is at the center of fashion, food, and of course wine. Tiny Italy — merely 60 percent the size of France — is an over-achiever in its wine production. Wine is the lifeblood of its people. Vines grow all over, in every one of Italy's regions. At the heart of Italy is a rich history and culture of people who have made wine for centuries to enjoy with food (or to replace with food, depending on the circumstances). No solid Italian dinner can possibly occur without a bottle of wine on the table.

Italy also has more different grape varieties than any other country in the world — over 1,300, with at least 350 legally authorized for winemaking. The beauty of Italy as a wine region is that most wines are made from native grape varieties that don't exist elsewhere. When transplanted to other parts of the world, they don't perform nearly as well as in Italy. Grapes such as nebbiolo, barbera, sangiovese, and garganega can make outstanding wine in Italy, but are not as common in other major world wine regions.

Italy's sheer volume of wine production is mind boggling. At the time of writing, it is the second largest wine-producing country in the world after France (detailed in the next chapter). It's usually France or Italy that takes the top spot depending on the year, making almost 22 million hectoliters (that's 2.2 billion liters) of wine in 2023 and exporting nearly $8 billion dollars of it worldwide.

REMEMBER

Much has changed about Italian wine in the last three decades. First, the availability and variety of high-quality wines from regions that were once lesser known makes the market much more interesting and delicious overall. Second, newer generations of winemakers who are marrying ancestral knowledge with modern technology are making the Italian wine scene more rigorous than ever before. While regions like Piedmont, Tuscany, and Veneto remain the homes of Italy's most prized (and expensive) wines, other regions of the country not only have their own grapes, but also their own styles which makes each of them unique.

The Laws and the Labels

Italy's wine laws have evolved to arguably confusing levels of nuance since the first denominations of origin were named in 1966. Beyond helping winemakers classify sites and grapes, the laws can be helpful for people like us who want to understand the basics, including what to expect in price and quality of different Italian wines.

REMEMBER

Similar to France's *Appellation d'Origine Contrôlée* (AOC) system (see Chapter 6), Italy started developing its own classification scheme in the early 1960s to designate regional wines and establish quality standards in the global market. With different tiers added over time, Italy's system has four levels, increasing in quality from lowest to highest as follows:

>> *Vino d'Italia,* **formerly** *Vino d'Tavola* **(VdT):** Entry-level table wine with no requirements for site, varieties, or styles.

>> *Indicazione Geografica Tipica* **(IGT) or the European Union's (EU's)** *Indicazione Geografica Protetta* **(IGP):** Historically a step above VdT for wines that do not meet Italy's original DOC/DOCG rules; often includes international varieties and blends, especially many of Italy's award-winning wines.

>> *Denominazione di Origine Controllata* **(DOC) or EU's** *Denominazione di Origine Protetta* **(DOP/PDO):** The majority of today's Italian wine zones (332 at the time of writing); this category includes rules for geographic origin, permitted varieties, aging requirements, and vinification methods.

>> *Denominazione di Origne Controllata e Garantita* **(DOCG) or EU's** *Denominazione di Origine Protetta* **(DOP/PDO):** Rigorous standards for geographic origin, permitted varieties, minimum yields, aging requirements, and quality; these are often (but not always) more expensive than DOC or IGT wines.

The terms DOC and DOCG refer both to the zones and the wines made within them. The DOC Soave, for example, is both a place (a specific production zone defined and regulated by Italian law, named after a town called Soave) and the wine of that place.

IGT wines have a geographic name on the label, but that name represents a broader territory than that of DOC/DOCG wines. For example, although the DOCG wine Brunello di Montalcino must derive from grapes grown in a very specific section of the region of Tuscany, a wine with the IGT name of "Tuscany" may come from anywhere in the entire region. Many IGT wines carry a grape variety name in addition to the name of the geographic area. Today, most Italian wines will have some designation on their label (or wrapped around the bottle's neck) specifying the category to which they belong.

Keep in mind that a DOCG wine isn't always necessarily better than an IGT wine (although it is usually more expensive). But the idea is that more rigorous standards ensure consistently higher-quality wines that represent the specific places they are from.

Regions, Varieties, and Styles

Italy has 20 major wine regions that mirror its political regions. A map of the most important Italian wine regions is included in this book's color section. What we would call a *wine region* in France, such as Burgundy or Alsace, we refer to as a *wine zone* in Italy to avoid confusion with the political regions.

Italy's northern wine zones generally have more continental climates (thanks to the Alps and Apennines that make for cold winters best enjoyed with the northern specialty brandy, grappa), while southern zones bask in the warmth of the Mediterranean. Soil also varies, from limestone and sandstone in northwest zones like Piedmont, to clay and volcanic soils in southern zones like Campania (the home of Mount Vesuvius). Steep hills and winding roads are the name of the game for many Italian wine zones, making some of the world's most picturesque vineyards (and best drivers).

The northwest

This section details the northwest of Italy, including Piedmont, Lombardy, Valle d'Aosta, and Liguria.

Piedmont: The Burgundy of Italy

Bordered by France to the west and Switzerland to the north, Piedmont is one of Italy's most prized wine zones. Surrounded by the Alps on three sides, Piedmont (which actually translates as "foothill") has a climate of cool, wet winters and dry, but hot summers that make the zone a perfect viticultural fit. Clay, limestone, and sand soils dominate.

REMEMBER

Although the zone isn't Italy's largest wine producer by volume, Piedmont is home to the country's most DOCG zones. Similar to France's Burgundy region, Piedmont is best known for its *single varieties* (wines made from one type of grape), and focuses exclusively on producing excellent wines with the same grapes vintage after vintage. Piedmont's primary red grapes include nebbiolo (neb-bee-oh-lo), barbera (bar-bear-uh), and dolcetto (dohl-*chet*-to). Although not as popular as nebbiolo, Piedmont's white wines — particularly its indigenous varieties such as arneis, nascetta, and timorasso — are on the rise. Finally, although often times overshadowed by the proseccos of Veneto, Piedmont's Asti, Moscato d'Asti, and other sparkling wines are available at a range of price points.

TIP

Nowhere else in the world can the phrase "what grows together goes together" be more appropriate than in Piedmont. Home to a delicious fungus commonly known as the white truffle, Piedmont is world-renowned not only for this rich, expensive, umami-flavored goodness (starting at $1,000 per pound), but also for its stellar pairing potential with Piedmontese cuisine and wine. White truffles can elevate almost any dish, and are best known for their (very thin) raw shavings on pasta, meat dishes, risotto, and even eggs. For more on pairing food and wine check out Chapter 18.

BAROLO AND BARBARESCO

Piedmont's most prized possession is nebbiolo. This is a thick-skinned red grape that makes a sometimes deceptively lighter color of wine. If you examine a recent vintage nebbiolo in a glass, you may think you're going to drink something that tastes like Burgundian pinot noir. Although it may have Burgundian pinot noir's elegance and finesse, nebbiolo is totally different. It is a delicious conundrum of high acid, tannin, and alcohol with fruit that can range from dry to ripe depending on the producer and vintage. Typical nebbiolo aromas include cherries, strawberries, violets, roses, mushrooms, and tar. Well-aged nebbiolos are softer in tannin, and more pronounced in dried fruit, leather, and truffle notes.

REAL DEAL

Barolo and Barbaresco are DOCG zones and wines made entirely from the nebbiolo grape in the Langhe (long-hay) hills around the town of Alba. Each is named after a village or commune within its production zone. Communes have become increasingly important for Barolo and Barbaresco, each with their own character and reputation (similar to the *crus* of Burgundy). Barolo is usually more full-bodied than Barbaresco and typically requires a bit more aging. Like most Italian wines, both show their best with food. High-quality Barolo and Barbaresco wines usually start at $50 retail and run to well over $100. Most Barbarescos are slightly less expensive than Barolos.

For years, many of the top Barolo wines have carried the names of specific vine-yards, such as Cannubi or Lazzarito, on their labels. Since 2010, the use of site names has been codified into the DOCG regulation for Barolo: 181 site names are now official *Menzioni Geografichee Aggiuntive* ("additional geographic mentions," or MGAs). The site name appears on the label, but the Italian phrase correspond-ing to MGA usually does not. In the Barbaresco zone, 66 specific sites are now official MGAs — although it is less common to see a site name on Barbaresco labels than on Barolo labels. The presence or absence of a vineyard or site name does not suggest higher or lower quality.

Barbarescos are some of the longest aged wines in Italy. By law, Barolo isn't Barolo until it has aged for at least three years at the winery, or for five years if it's called *Riserva* (meaning it has been aged longer). Barbaresco's minimum aging is two years, or four for *Riserva*. Despite this long production regime, both wines benefit from additional aging.

A few high-quality Barolo producers include Azelia, Ceretto, Elio Altare, Gaja, Parusso, Pio Cesare, and Scavino. Some top Barbaresco producers are Albino Roca, Bruno Giacosa, Gaja, Produttori del Barbaresco, and Roagna.

Some producers — including Giacomo Conterno, Giuseppe Mascarello, Giuseppe Rinaldi, Cappellano, and Bruno Giacosa — make traditionally styled wines; others — such as Gaja and E. Pira e Figli — make modern-style wines. Up until the 1980s, most traditional Barolo and Barbaresco winemaking involved long *macerations* (soaking grape seeds, skins, and stems with pressed juice), large Slovenian oak cask aging (imparting slight oak flavors to the wine), and minimal intervention. The resulting wines were highly acidic and tannic, requiring at least 10-15 years of aging to soften the wines for enjoyment. Considered revolutionary at the time, now-famous winemakers such as Elio Altare and Angelo Gaja led a movement to produce wines with shorter macerations aged in smaller, French oak barrels that were meant to be enjoyed much sooner. Many winemakers followed this modernizing suit: both Barolo and Barbaresco are becoming more approach-able with softer tannins and the ability to be enjoyed within a much shorter period from the vintage. Many Barolos from the 2019 vintage are enjoyable now, for example. Today, most producers make wines that incorporate both traditional and modern styles that can be enjoyed now but also have amazing aging potential.

REAL DEAL

Two good nebbiolo-based wines, the DOCGs Gattinara (gah-tee-*nah*-rah) and Ghemme (*gae*-mae), come from northern Piedmont, where the nebbiolo grape is called *spanna.* Although Gattinara and Ghemme seldom get the praise that the two big Bs (Barolo and Barbaresco) enjoy, they offer the same enticing nebbiolo aromas and flavors — especially Gattinara — in a less full-bodied style. Priced at $29 to $43 a bottle, Gattinara from a good producer may be one of the world's most underrated wines. Look for the Gattinaras by Antoniolo and Travaglini (Antoniolo is a bit more expensive). Antichi Vigneti di Cantalupo (about $35) is the leading Ghemme producer.

PIEDMONT'S EVERYDAY REDS

The Piedmontese serve serious wines such as Barolo and Barbaresco for Sunday dinner or special occasions. What they drink on an everyday basis are the red wines dolcetto, barbera, and nebbiolo. These are made from grapes grown outside of the prestigious DOCGs Barolo and Barbaresco. Of the three wines, dolcetto is generally the least complex, most quaffable, and is often the first red wine served in a Piedmontese meal:

>> **Dolcetto.** If you know enough Italian to translate the phrase *la dolce vita,* you could think that the name dolcetto indicates a sweet wine. Actually, the dolcetto grape tastes sweet off the vine, but the wine produced is distinctly dry and has some noticeable tannin, although the tannin isn't so pronounced when you drink the wine with food (more on tannin in Chapter 4). Dolcetto is a cross between two indigenous varities from the region, dolcetto bianco and moissan. Aromas include blackberries, plums, violets, pepper, licorice, and cocoa. Most dolcetto wines sell for $15 to $30 retail. The best dolcetto wines are from the zones of Dogliani, Diano d'Alba, and Alba. With the exception of Dogliani — a DOCG wine — the labels of these wines carry the grape name, Dolcetto, along with the name of the area. High-quality producers include Giuseppe Rinaldi, Luigi Einaudi, and Quinto Chionetti.

>> **Barbera.** As high profile as it is, nebbiolo (featured earlier in this chapter) is not Piedmont's most planted grape — barbera is. Although this variety is planted in many other Italian zones with varying degrees of quality, it excels in Piedmont — specifically in the Asti, Alba, and Monferrato wine zones. Increasing attention to site and detail has dramatically improved the variety and quality of Barbera since the 1980s, evolving it from a simple table wine to a rich, splendid red wine. The wine's weight varies according to the area where the grapes grow and the producer's style. Today's barberas can be lighter and easygoing, or powerful and juicy with chewy tannins. Barbera happens to be one of our favorite everyday wines, especially with pasta, pizza, or anything tomato-based. Barbera d'Alba is generally a bit fuller, riper, and richer than the leaner Barbera d'Asti and Barbera di Monferrato. But Barbera d'Asti from certain old vineyards rivals Barbera d'Alba in richness and in power (link the *d'*

with the word following it when pronouncing these names: *dal*-ba, *dahs*-tee.) What had been a subzone of Barbera d'Asti is now a DOCG zone called Nizza. Nizza wine is 100 percent barbera, but it does not necessarily state the grape name on the label. A few top-quality barbera producers include Braida, Camparo, Gaicomo Conterno, Luigi Tacchino, Massolino, and Vietti.

» **Nebbiolo.** A third weekday red from Piedmont is Nebbiolo d'Alba or Langhe Nebbiolo. Nebbiolo d'Alba, grown from vineyards outside the Barolo/Barbaresco wine zones, must be 100 percent nebbiolo. Langhe Nebbiolo, which can come from vineyards in the Barolo/Barbaresco territory and beyond, must have a minimum of 85 percent nebbiolo. We see more Langhe Nebbiolo wines these days, perhaps because its larger wine zone gives producers more flexibility in choosing their grapes than Nebbiolo d'Alba. Both wines are lighter in body and easier to drink than either Barolo or Barbaresco, and they sell for about $20 to $30 a bottle. Another nebbiolo-based wine is Roero, made in the Roero DOCG north of the town of Alba. Roero Rosso must be made almost entirely from nebbiolo.

Drinking all of these wines is a no-brainer for us because they have the wonderful aromas and flavors that we love without the several-year wait for the wines to mature.

PIEDMONT'S WHITE WINES

Piedmont's increased production and improved quality over time has resulted in a few delicious white wines too. In addition to the rise of international varieties such as chardonnay, seek out these native varieties:

» **Gavi (*gah-vee*).** Named for a town in southern Piedmont, this is a refreshing, mineral-forward, dry wine with pronounced acidity made from the cortese grape. It has aromas of stone fruit, chamomile, and white flowers with a bright, citrus-forward finish. This wine is light pasta and seafood-friendly. Top-quality producers include Broglia, La Mesma, and La Raia.

» **Arneis (*ahr-nase*).** A white wine produced in the Roero zone near Alba from a once-forgotten grape also called arneis. The grape was rescued from extinction by the late Alfredo Currado of the Vietti winery more than 40 years ago. Arneis is a dry wine with rich texture, intended to be consumed young. Great arneis comes from Broccardo, Giacomo Genocchio, Bruno Giacosa, and Tenuta Carreta among others. Roero DOCG more generally is a hotspot for excellent arneis wines.

» **Timorasso.** Another white Piedmontese varietal garnering more attention, thanks to Walter Massa's push towards site specifics and quality in the last 30 years. Timorasso is dry, straw yellow wine with tropical fruit flavors, flint, and floral notes.

PIEDMONT GETS BUBBLY

Behind the shadow of Veneto's prosseco (see later in this chapter) lies the *spumante* (sparkling) Asti and Moscato d'Asti of Piedmont, the earliest production of which dates back to the 19th century. These two sparkling wines are made from the aromatic moscato grape, which is also known as Muscat Blanc a Petits Grains in France. Asti and Moscato d'Asti are made in the Charmat method (see Chapter 3) whereby secondary fermentation happens in a large tank rather than in the bottle.

Considered a step above Asti, Moscato d'Asti's main differentiator is the amount of fizz: Moscato d'Asti's *frizzante*, or just slightly sparkling character, comes from less sugar being added for the second fermentation. This slight change results in fewer bubbles in your glass. Moscato d'Asti is still refreshingly fruity and can still feel sweet on the palate. It is also always *vintage-dated* (meaning all the grapes used to make the wine were harvested in the same year) to maintain consistent taste unlike Asti that can be blended across several different vintages. Excellent Moscato d'Asti producers include Ceretto, Icardi, Giuseppi Rivetti, and Piazzo.

WARNING

As with other wines from Piedmont and Italy more generally, Asti and Moscato d'Asti got bad reputations two to three decades ago — low prices and lower quality dominated the global market. The opposite is true now, with more high-quality examples available at different price points. Modern, excellent *spumantes* are made in dry to semi-sweet styles. These are light and refreshing with white peach, orange blossom, and honeydew notes.

Lombardy: The brut and the beautiful

Lombardy is the land of both leisurely reds and luxurious sparklers. Near the northern Swiss border, high-quality, lighter styles of nebbiolo are made in Valtellina Superiore DOCG. In the east lies Franciacorta (Fran-chee-ah-court-ah) DOCG — Italy's core for *metodo classico* (or Champagne method, made by secondary fermentation in the bottle) sparkling wine. Produced from blends of mostly chardonnay and pinot noir (and small amounts of pinot bianco and the indigenous variety, erbamat), Franciacorta is mostly made in brut and brut rosé styles (defined as 0-12 grams per liter of residual sugar; see Chapter 6 for more information on Champagne method classifications). It ages anywhere from 18 to 60 months for *Riserva* versions. Renowned Franciacorta producers include Ca'del Bosco, Bellavista, Colline della Stella, Ferrari, and Ferghettina.

You may see the term "satèn" on some Franciacorta — these are slightly less carbonated, sometimes lower alcohol, 100 percent chardonnay sparklers that were topped off with smaller amounts of sugar to jumpstart the secondary fermentation. They are generally softer, creamier, and aged for longer than standard Franciacorta. Given their process and varietal specificity, they are generally more expensive.

Valle d'Aosta: Fresh fruit from high peaks

Wedged between Piedmont to the south and Lombardy to the northwest, Valle d'Aosta is an (unfortunately) lesser-known, highly elevated zone that borders both France and Switzerland. This mountainous area produces still white, rosé, red, and dessert wines, in addition to sparklers made in Charmat and *metodo classico* styles. Both indigenous and international varieties are vinified, including petite arvine, petite rouge, pinot noir, nebbiolo, and moscato for dessert styles.

Liguria: Wines for pesto

Liguria is a narrow coastal zone south of Piedmont. Taste Liguria with whites such as vermentino (known here as pigato), Cinque Terre (a blend of vermentino and the indigenous grapes arbarola and bosco), and the light- to medium-bodied dolceaqua (made from the indigenous grape rossesse). The Genovese of Liguria hold an important claim to fame as the originators of basil pesto. This dish simply cannot be enjoyed without a refreshingly chilled glass of vermentino!

The northeast

This section features the wines of the northeast, including Veneto, Trentino–Alto Adige, Friuli-Venezia Giulia, and Emilia-Romagna.

The Tre Venezie

The three zones in the northeastern corner of Italy are often referred to as the *Tre Venezie* (ven-etsy) — the Venices — because they were once part of the Venetian Empire.

VENETO: BARDOLINO, SOAVE, AND VALPOLICELLA

Two generations ago, consumers were introduced to Italy through a trio of popular wines from the Veneto: Bardolino (*bar-do-lee-noh*), Soave (swah-vay), and Valpolicella (*val-po-lee-chel-lah*). Bardolino and Soave are each named for communes in the picturesque province of Verona — Romeo and Juliet's hometown. Valpolicella is a wine zone east of Lake Garda. Despite facing ups and down in popularity, these three DOC wines continue to be among the most important of northeastern Italy. Each of these zones produces white (Soave) and red (Bardolino and Valpolicella) wines that are among the most popular both in and outside of Italy.

Both Bardolino DOC and Valpolicella DOC wines are made from three or four native, local red grape varieties including corvina, corvinone, rondinella, and others in smaller quantities. Valpolicella wines are generally fuller-bodied and made in more styles than the quaffable, lighter stuff of Bardolino (with the exception of Bardolino Superiore DOC, which makes some fuller-bodied styles). One of our favorite types of Bardolino, chiaretto (*key-ah-ret-toh*) — a rosé wine — epitomizes the vivacity and charm of the Bardolino area.

Entry-level Valpolicella can come from anywhere in the Valpolicella DOC and has no aging requirements. Valpolicella Classico refers to wines that come from the original and most popular area of the zone, and are generally better in quality. Valpolicella Classico Superiore must be oak aged for at least a year and is considered a step above Classico. In the Valpolicella Ripasso DOC, plusher styles are made using a double fermentation, *ripasso* ("re-passed") method: newly made Valpolicella wine is refermented with the *pomace* (pulp, seeds, skins, and sometimes stems) of Amarone wine over the course of several weeks to saturate colors, enhance structure, and make the wine more tannic than basic Valpolicella.

Amarone della Valpolicella DOCG (also simply known as Amarone) is another even richer version. One of Italy's most popular, full-bodied red wines, it's made from the same native Italian varieties as Valpolicella (corvina, corvinone, rondinella, and molinara), but minimum proportions of each type are mandated by law. Amarone grapes are picked later than standard Valpolicella grapes, and are then spread across shelves methodically hung in the air to dry in rooms called *fruttaio* for anywhere from two to four months. The grapes are then crushed and pressed to make a powerful, luscious wine that is then aged in either French oak or Slovenian casks for a minimum of 24 months (48 months for *Riservas*). Amarone is generally higher in alcohol (15–16%), long-lived, and perfect with a plate of mature cheeses. The time-consuming and laborious process of producing Amarone is what drives its higher pricing compared to Valpolicalla Classico or Valpolicella Superiore. Some recommended Amarone producers include Allegrini, Masi, Tomassi, and Speri. Finally, there's Recioto della Valpolicella DOCG — a zone specializing in *passito*-style dessert wines from the same grapes.

The Soave DOC zone encompasses several hillsides of clay, limestone, and volcanic soils and produces some of Veneto's most important white wine. Soave wines are blends made mostly from garganega, trebbiano di Soave and chardonnay in smaller quantities. Soave has ascended the ranks over the years from an inexpensive, standard white wine to one of Italy's finest whites in the hands of the best producers. Similar to other wines of the Veneto, Soave's quality improves in Soave Classico DOC and Soave Classico Superiore DOC. The same is true for dessert styles with Recioto di Soave DOCG at the top of the line. At its best, dry Soave is a smooth (the English translation of *soave*, luckily enough), medium-bodied, *unoaked* (meaning fermented and aged in stainless steel tanks) white with flavors of apricot, citrus, apple, and nuts. Look for Soave wines from Inama, La Cappuccina, Pieropan, and Prà among others.

PROSECCO

This quintessential sparkling wine is all the rage in the United States, which is now the leading export market. Today, prosecco accounts for the largest share of sparkling wine sales in the United States. It is on the rise in the United Kingdom and Germany, often outpacing champagne in sales volume (although not necessarily in revenue).

Prosecco is made from a grape called glera, which is native to central Veneto (from the village of Prosecco near Trieste, if you ask a Venetian). Prosecco is both the name of the wine and its DOC zone. Most affordable prosecco is made in the Charmat method of secondary fermentation in a tank versus a bottle. It is a straightforward, delicious bubbly wine, moderate in alcohol (about 11–12%) and boasting aromas of apple, pear, stone fruit, and fresh citrus. It comes in dry, off-dry, and sweet styles. Besides the fully-sparkling *spumante* version, prosecco also comes in a *frizzante* (lightly sparkling) style, which is less common. Prosecco is the perfect wine to enjoy with Italian antipasto, such as pickled vegetables, calamari, anchovies, or spicy salami. Its fresh, fruity flavors cleanse your palate, open up a great brunch, and serve as a festive cocktail ingredient if you need more than just the bubbles.

REAL DEAL

The highest-quality prosecco comes not from the large DOC zone but from a much smaller DOCG called Conegliano Valdobbiadene Prosecco *(coh-nel-lee-ah-no val-doh-be-AH-deh-nay)*; this name refers to two villages in northern Veneto and applies to the hillside vineyards surrounding them. Another prosecco DOCG is Asolo Prosecco, just south of Conegliano–Valdobbiadene, around the picturesque town of Asolo *(AH-so-lo)*. These wines are sometimes made in *metodo classico* styles and as such, command a higher price point. Prosecco wines labeled simply as DOC can be as budget-friendly as $10 a bottle; prosecco DOCG wines are a few dollars more at $20 and up.

APPASSIMENTO, RIPASSO, AND *PASSITO* TECHNIQUES

Appassimento is a winemaking process whereby grapes are dried or *raisinated*. *Ripasso* refers to the process of re-fermenting a base wine with leftover pomace from a previous fermentation. *Passito* is a general term used to describe any wine (dry or sweet) that is made with dried grapes. All of these techniques are designed to concentrate sugars, enhance flavor and aromatics, and add body or weight to a wine.

TIP

On your next visit to the grocery store or wine shop, you will likely encounter an ocean of prosecco to choose from. If you have time and a few extra dollars, consider some top-quality producers, including Bisol, Canella, Nino Franco, Ruggeri, and Villa Sandi.

Trentino–Alto Adige: Italy's German side

To some people, Italy isn't one unified country but 20 or more politically conjoined entities. Consider Trentino–Alto Adige. This mountainous region is the northernmost in Italy and is dramatically different from the rest of Italy socially and culturally. The mainly German-speaking Alto-Adige (or *Süditrol*) in the north looks and feels completely different from the Italian-speaking Trentino in the south. The wines of the two areas are different, too. Well-drained clay, limestone, gravel, and sand throughout the zone make for amazing white, red, sparkling, and dessert wines from both native and international varieties.

Trentino–Alto Adige is known for crisp, clean, and refreshing wines with bright acidity, tart to dry fruit characteristics, and more mineral-driven profiles. The most important white varieties to know include the frost-resistant (necessary at such high altitudes) kerner, pinot grigio, gewürztraminer, pinot blanc, sauvignon blanc, and chardonnay. Reds include the native, increasingly popular varieties of schiava, lagrein, and the medium- to full-bodied, acidic, and tannic teroldego. Sparkling wines or *Trentodocs* are *metodo classico* wines made in Trentino from chardonnay, pinot noir, pinot blanc, and pinot meunier.

Although Trentino-Alto Adige is best known for its white wines, along with nearby Friuli (see the next section), most producers in the zone make both white and red wines. Producers to look for are Alois Lageder, Elena Walch, Girlan, Hofstätter, Tiefenbrunner, and Terlan.

WORTH THE SEARCH

Vin santo, or "holy wine" is a dessert-style wine made with the *appassimento* technique. While *vin santo* is made in other zones of Italy like Tuscany, the Veneto, Umbria, and Emilia-Romagna, Trentino's *vin santo* is made using indigenous nosiola (nose-ee-oh-la) grapes and aged for a minimum of three years by law. These wines are typically sold in smaller bottles and a little pricer given the painstaking *appassimento* process.

Friuli-Venezia Giulia: The white wine garden

Italy is most known for its red wines, but today, driven by its best-selling inot grigio and prosecco wines, Italy produces more whites than reds. In the arena of elite white wines, the smaller but mighty, mountain-packed zone of Friuli-Venezia Giulia was the first to make the world conscious of the indisputable quality of Italy's white wines. Near the zone's eastern border with Slovenia, the districts of Collio Goriziano — usually referred to as simply "Collio" — and Friuli Colli Orientali produce the best white wines of Friuli (as the zone is generally called). Red wines do exist in Friuli, but the white wines are renowned. Friulano, pinot grigio, pinot bianco, sauvignon blanc, and ribolla gialla are among the leading wines, mainly labeled with the grape name. Great producers include Livio Felluga, Gravner, Miani, Ronco del Gnemiz, and Vigna Petrussa.

TIP

Similar to many other Italian zones, Friuli has evolved its international reputation over the years from basic, water-like pinot grigio to better expressions of this variety, plus many other grapes and styles. While household (sometimes pricier, ironically) names like Santa Margherita are widely available, you can easily find other smaller producers and styles to taste the difference. So much entry-level wine comes from Friuli that this is one of the zones we would suggest looking for a DOC (there are ten) or DOCG label (there are four) on your bottle. The four DOCG zones of Friuli are Friuli Grave, Colli Orientali del Friuli, Collio, and Carso.

WORTH THE SEARCH

Highly coveted dessert wines made from the indigenous picolit and Ramandolo grapes (made in both late harvest and *passito* styles) are also made in smaller quantities between the central Gorizia and Udine provinces. Picolit is rare and more expensive, starting at $100 for a half bottle. Ramandolo is more affordable, with some wines available in the $20 and up range. These wines are meant to be enjoyed with popular desserts from the region, including gubana (a ring-shaped cake made with dried fruit and nuts) and tiramisu!

FRIULI AND THE SKIN CONTACT REVOLUTION

We would be remiss not to mention the rise of Friuli's "amber" or "orange" wines. Popularized by winemakers such as Josko Gravner, these wines are made from any of the zone's white grapes. The harvested grapes spend a few hours to a couple of years in contact with their skins (hence the term *skin contact*), and are then aged in a vessel of the winemaker's choice. More time results in amber to deeper orange and even golden or caramel hues. Dry styles have distinct tasting notes of orange peels, apricots, blossoms, resin, and baking spice. Today, amber or orange wines are made in countries around the world with increasing popularity among adventurous wine drinkers. Top-quality Friuli producers to try include Borgo Savaian, Radikon, Princic, and Livio Felluga.

Emilia-Romagna: Lambruscoland

Emilia-Romagna describes two Italian provinces situated between Veneto to the north and Le Marche to the south. White wines such as trebbiano and red wines like sangiovese and nebbiolo are made here. But this isn't really what the zone is about, at least in Emilia. Here, it's all about juicy, fizzy Lambrusco made from the red grape with the same name. Contrary to popular belief, Lambruscos can range from dry to sweeter styles, with some of the top-quality producers making a range of dry and semi-sweet, or *amabile* versions. Lambrusco has three DOC zones of note: Grasparossa, Salamino, and Sorbara, each with their own characteristics. Lambrusco is also designed to complement the rich Bolognese and Parma (hello, lasagna and prosicutto) cuisine. Some top producers include Cleto Chiarli, Fiorini Lini, and Venturini Baldini.

Central Italy

This section moves farther down Italy's "boot" to Tuscany, Umbria, Lazio, Le Marche, and Abruzzo.

Tuscany: Wine as art

With the cities of Florence and Siena, Michelangelo's David, and the leaning tower of Pisa, Tuscany has more than its share of attractions. Only one Italian wine can possibly compare in fame — and that, too, comes from Tuscany: Chianti (*key-awn-tee*). Read on to discover more about Chianti and other great wines from Tuscany.

CHIANTI: ITALY'S ICONIC RED WINE

Central Tuscany's rolling hills have formed the backdrop for some of the world's most prized works of art. The region is surrounded by natural beauty, with the Appennine Mountains to the northeast and Ligurian and Tyrhenian seas to the west. Winemaking was documented here as far back as the 13th century. The red wines from this area, based on the sangiovese grape variety, are among the best known and most loved of all Italian wines. Quality has come a long way in Chianti, from blending sangiovese with pretty much any grape (white or red) that could be found to focusing on quality that formed the foundation for two distinct zones: Chianti DOCG and Chianti Classico DOCG.

REMEMBER

Chianti DOCG is massive, covering nearly 38,000 acres across Florence, Siena, Arezzo, Pisa, Pistoia and Prato. Its seven subzones are permitted to make wines from at least 70 percent sangiovese. Less strict rules are imposed for the general DOCG designation, but this changes for *Superiore* and *Risvera* labels, with the two terms translated to different aging requirements. Chianti wine must contain at least 70 percent sangiovese grapes and can be entirely sangiovese. Both native and international varieties can be part of the wine, but depending on the subzone, cabernet sauvignon or cabernet franc is limited to 10 or 15 percent. *Riserva* wines must age for two years or more at the winery, and for some subzones six or eight months of aging is mandated. Chianti producers may use the name of the subzone where their grapes grow or the simpler appellation, Chianti, if their production does not qualify for a district name (if grapes from two subzones are blended, for example, or if the grapes come from outlying parts of the zone that have no subzone status). *Superiore* wines are aged for a minimum of 9 months, of which 3 must be in the bottle. A minimum 12% alcohol level must also be met.

REAL DEAL

A benchmark for quality is the tiny Chianti Rufina (*roo*-fee-nah) area (not to be confused with the famous Chianti Classico producer Ruffino). Of the remaining subzones, the Colli Senesi and Colli Fiorentini areas (Siena hills and Florence hills, respectively) enjoy the best reputations for their wines.

Chianti DOCG wines are a mixed lot, stylistically and qualitatively. Some are easy-drinking, fairly light, and inexpensive reds selling for as little as $14, while others are age-worthy and substantial and can cost up to $35. Like Chianti Classico (see the next section), Chianti DOCG wines often have aromas of cherries, violets, and tomato leaf.

WORTH THE SEARCH

Two outstanding producers making Chianti DOCG wines are Frescobaldi and Selvapiana, both in the Rufina subzone.

CHIANTI CLASSICO

Chianti Classico is a DOCG where grapes have grown for more than ten centuries. Soils throughout this 100-square-mile zone vary with mostly clay, limestone, marl, and sandstone. Southern parts of the zone are fairly warm, while northern, more elevated areas are cooler. The impact is a range of flavor profiles and body according to site.

Sangiovese must constitute at least 80 percent of any Chianti Classico wine. In practice, some producers use only sangiovese; of those who use additional grape varieties, many use only native Tuscan varieties, such as canaiolo or mammolo, while others use international varieties, such as cabernet sauvignon or merlot.

REMEMBER

Besides varying according to their vineyard location and grape blend, Chianti Classico wines also vary in style according to their aging. *Riserva* wines must age for two years or more at the winery. Although oak aging is not required for any Chianti Classico wine, some of the aging for *Riserva* often occurs in French oak barrels. *Gran Selezione* wines, an elite category of Chianti Classico that must come only from a winery's own estate-grown grapes, must age at least 30 months. Both *Riserva* and *Gran Selezione* bottlings of Chianti Classico are worthy of aging.

Chianti Classico tasting notes include tart to ripe cherries, raspberries, violets, and more earthy characteristics like tomato leaf, clay, and leather when compared to the standard Chianti DOCG. These are dry, tannic wines that are usually best enjoyed five to eight years after the vintage, although in good vintages they have no problem aging for 20 or more years. Today's Chianti Classico DOCG wines are richer and more concentrated than ever before. This is due in part to warmer climates and winemaking styles that have favored more fleshiness, fruit-bomby flavors, and higher alcohol. The addition of international varieties and the use of French oak barrels for aging have amplified this trend. Given all of this variation, you must choose your Chianti Classico producers with care.

WORTH THE SEARCH

Chianti Classico wines retail generally between $19 and $28 a bottle, while Chianti Classico *Riserva* and *Gran Selezione* wines are a bit more costly, ranging from $35 to $60 and up per bottle. Three exceptional recent vintages to look for in Chianti Classico are 2019, 2018, and 2016. Some excellent Chianti Classico producers include Antinori, Castellare, Castello di Ama, Isole e Olena, Monsanto, and Terreno.

BRUNELLO DI MONTALCINO

Although Chianti has been famous for centuries, Brunello di Montalcino exploded on the international scene over 50 years ago when the Biondi-Santi family, a leading producer, presented some of its oldest wines to writers. The 1888 and 1891 vintages were still drinking well — in fact, they were in excellent shape! The rest is history, as they say.

Brunello di Montalcino takes its name from the town of Montalcino, a walled fortress town south of the Chianti Classico zone, and from its grape variety, which once was referred to as Brunello. The grape in fact is a particular clone, or strain, of sangiovese, often called sangiovese grosso. Brunello di Montalcino is an intensely concentrated, tannic wine that demands aging (up to 20 years) when traditionally made and can benefit from several hours of aeration before serving (see Chapter 20 for more on aeration). More recently, some producers in Montalcino have been making a more approachable, ready-to-drink (at least after fewer years) style of Brunello.

Today, Brunello di Montalcino (*brew-nel-lo dee mon-tahl-chee-no*), a DOCG wine, is one of the greatest, long-lived red wines in existence. It has a price tag to match from $65 to $80 for the better examples of Brunello to $150-plus for Biondi-Santi's, and as much as $500 or more a bottle for wines by Soldera, arguably Brunello di Montalcino's greatest producer.

REAL DEAL

Rosso di Montalcino is a less expensive ($20 to $25), readier-to-drink wine made from the same grape, sometimes from younger vines, and grown in the same production area as Brunello di Montalcino. Rosso di Montalcino from a good Brunello producer is good value, offering you a glimpse of Brunello's majesty without breaking the bank.

Some of our favorite classic Brunello di Montalcino producers include Antinori, Banfi, Biondi-Santi, Castiglion del Bosco, Fattoria del Colle, Il Colle, and Il Poggione. If you're not up for waiting 15-20 years to open a bottle, Brunellos from avowed modern-style producers such as Altesino, Caparzo, Col d'Orcia, Gaja, and Le Potazzine can be enjoyed within 10 years or less from the vintage. Great recent vintages include 2019, 2015, 2012, and 2010.

MONTEPULCIANO'S NOBILITY

Vino Nobile di Montepulciano (*no-be-lay dee mon-tay-pul-chee-ah-no*) is a DOCG wine that is often mentioned in the same breath as Chianti Classico and Brunello di Montalcino, because it is a historic wine from a neighboring area. The wine got its *nobile* tag (meaning "noble") from a local governor in 1787. Prior to his writing, the wine had been described by poets and historians as a wine fit for popes, royals, and the aristocracy of the times.

The Montepulciano wine zone, named after the town of Montepulciano, lies southeast of the Chianti Classico zone and within the larger boundary of the Chianti zone. Vino Nobile's principal grape is Prugnolo Gentile, a local name for Sangiovese. Of central Tuscany's big three red DOCG wines — Chianti Classico, Brunello di Montalcino, and Vino Nobile di Montepulciano — Vino Nobile is generally the most delicate in style, and with shorter aging requirements (two years for standard and three years for *Riserva*). Like Chianti, it is at least 70 percent sangiovese. Most Vino Nobile producers also make a lighter, readier-to-drink wine, Rosso di Montepulciano. Some recommended producers include Avignonesi, Boscarelli, Dei, and Salcheto.

Vino Nobile di Montepulciano is primarily made from sangiovese; another similar-sounding but totally different wine called Montepulciano d'Abbruzo is made from a grape called montepulciano in Italy's Abruzzo zone.

OTHER WINES FROM CENTRAL TUSCANY

Two more noteworthy central Tuscan wine zones include one red, Carmignano DOCG (*car-mee-nyah-no*), and one white, Vernaccia di San Gimignano DOCG (*ver-nah-cha dee san gee-mee-nyah-noh*). The Carmignano zone, directly west of Florence, produces elegant wines from sangiovese and cabernet sauvignon. Although sangiovese is the main grape of carmignano, cabernet sauvignon is also one of this zone's traditional grapes. Two outstanding producers of Carmignano are Ambra and Villa di Capezzana. Vernaccia di San Gimignano takes its name from the white vernaccia grape and the medieval walled town of San Gimignano in the western part of the Chianti territory. Vernaccia is generally stainless steel fermented, crisp, and fresh with citrus, floral, and tropical fruit notes. Look for wines from Casale-Falchini, Cecchi Montenidoli, Mormoraia, and Teruzzi & Puthod.

The coast: Super-Tuscan central

Historically, hilly central Tuscany was the zone's only important wine-producing area. But in recent years, Tuscany's coast — in particular the Maremma — has emerged as a significant wine zone, producing fine wines too numerous to list here. The wines feature native red and white varieties such as sangiovese and vermentino as well as international varieties such as cabernet sauvignon and chardonnay.

Most important in the Maremma is the Bolgheri DOC zone, where both native and international grapes are used to make velvety, opulent red wines worthy of aging and higher price tags (some well over $100 a bottle). The Maremma is the land of several star-powered vineyard sites making Super-Tuscan wines within the larger Bolgheri DOC framework, including Masseto (IGT Toscana, all merlot, made by Tenuta dell'Ornellaia), Ornellaia (DOC Bolgheri, mainly cabernet sauvignon with some merlot or cabernet franc), and Sassicaia (DOC Bolgheri-Sassicaia, 75 percent cabernet sauvingon, 25 percent cabernet franc, made by Tenuta San Guido). Additional outstanding producers associated with Super-Tuscan styles include Tignanello from Guado al Tasso, Le Macchiole, Marchesi Antinori, Michele Sata, and Solaia.

TECHNICAL STUFF

Super-Tuscan wines came into existence almost five decades ago when some producers in the Chianti Classico zone (featured earlier in this chapter) sought to make great wines without following the grape variety constraints that the DOC regulations imposed. As renegade wines, they could not carry the DOC name, and were labeled as merely "Tuscan" wines. Despite having lowly legal status outside the DOC arena, the wines sold for high prices and developed an elite following. Subsequent changes to the regulations have enabled many of these wines to return to the DOC or DOCG fold, but some still carry the Toscana IGT designation by choice. You could say that their quality makes them "super" Tuscan wines. Unfortunately, many unremarkable red wines carrying the Toscana IGT designation have jumped on the Super-Tuscan marketing bandwagon, when in truth there is nothing super about them at all. We foresee that the Super-Tuscan category will either become more meaningless or just obsolete over time.

The Tuscan coast also is home to affordable wines. The first is Morellino di Scansano (*moh-rehl-lee-no dee scahn-sah-no*) from the hilly area around the town of Scansano in southwest Tuscany. Morellino is the local name for the sangiovese grape. Morellino di Scansano DOCG wines offer an easy-drinking, inexpensive ($15 to $22) alternative to Chianti, although a few high-end wines exist, such as Fattoria Le Pupille and Morisfarms. The second is vermentino, a varietal wine from an aromatic white grape also grown in Sardinia and Liguria. Vermentino has become a hot variety in Tuscany, especially along the coast. The wine is a crisp, medium-bodied, flavorful white that's usually unoaked, and sells for $20 to $35. Many leading Tuscan producers, such as Antinori and Cecchi, are making excellent vermentinos.

Umbria: Orvieto and Sagrantino

Home to the towns of Perugia and Assisi, Umbria makes several high-quality whites. Orvieto is widely available for $12 to $15 from Tuscan producers such as Antinori and Ruffino. Two interesting red wines are Torgiano DOCG and Montefalco Sagrantino DOCG (an intense, powerful, and inky red wine made from the local sagrantino grape). Try Montefalco Sagrantino wines from Arnaldo Caprai, Cantina Fratelli Pardi, Tabarrini, and Terre de la Custodia.

Lazio

This region of southern Rome makes the ubiquitous, inexpensive Frascati that has improved in quality over the years. This wine is made with Malvasia Bianca di Candia and Malvasia del Lazio in both *secco* (dry) and *amabile* (off-dry or medium sweetness) styles. Additional grapes are permitted in smaller quantities, including Trebbiano Toscano and Greco Bianco among others. Try the Frascati Superiore DOCG wines of Fontana Candida, Casal Pilozzo, and Vinea Domini.

Le Marche

Le Marche (*Mar-kay)* is situated on Italy's Adriatic coast, with Emilia-Romagna to its north and Abruzzo to its south. The zone's position gives it mostly Mediterranean climate (mild winters and hot summers) with some cooler seasonal variations inland and towards the north. Le Marche is most known as a distinctive white wine zone, featuring native varieties such as verdicchio (*ver-dee-kee-oh)* — a dry, inexpensive white wine that's widely available and seems to improve in quality with every vintage — and pecorino (no relation to the cheese). The zone also produces some excellent *metodo classico* wines from verdicchio that make for a great sparkling alternative. A few top-quality verdicchio producers include Andrea Felici, Colonnara, Tavignano, Umani Ronchi, and Villa Bucci. Le Marche also produces smaller quantities of red wine. The DOCG to note here is Cònero, made mainly from Montepulciano.

Abruzzo: Montepulciano d'Abruzzo

Abruzzo is a sunny, high-altitude region on Italy's eastern Adriatic coast. The star of the show here is the red grape montepulciano, which makes rosés and medium to full-bodied wines with red fruit, savory herbs, violets, lavender, and peppered cocoa notes. Once relegated to a cheap, homely, gulpable wine to be enjoyed with a slice of pizza, montepulciano has come a long way in the last two decades, producing more wines of sophistication and elegance, particularly in the Montepulciano d'Abruzzo DOC. Top-quality producers include Cataldi Madonna, Cirelli, Emidio Pepe, Masciarelli, and Valentini.

WORTH THE SEARCH

The Cerasuolo d'Abruzzo DOC is exclusively dedicated to making rosé from the montepulciano grape, and should be on your next list of interesting rosé zones to try!

Although not as popular as montepulciano, whites are also made in Abruzzo, mostly from the Trebbiano d'Abruzzo grape in the Trebbiano d'Abruzzo DOC.

The south

Rome is generally regarded as the dividing line between northern and southern Italy. Northern Italy is generally more industrial and affluent, with several major cities, such as Milan and Turin, and it is the home of Italy's most renowned wines — Barolo, Chianti Classico, Brunello di Montalcino, Soave, Amarone, and so forth (discussed earlier in this chapter). Southern Italy is mainly agricultural, and besides Rome has only one major city, Naples. But it also boasts the beautiful, heart-stopping Amalfi Coast. Until recently, few world-renowned wines came from southern Italy.

Italy's south used to produce more wine than the north. Two southern zones, Puglia and Sicily, for decades were the most productive in all of Italy until they were eclipsed in recent years by Veneto, thanks to pinot grigio and prosecco. Historically, many southern Italian wines were pedestrian in quality, and much of the huge production was sold in bulk to northern Italy and nearby countries. But a wine renaissance has taken place in southern Italy in the last 30 years. Sicily and Campania in particular are now making some of Italy's best wines. The richness of the south today encompasses both whites and reds. Here we give you a portrait of southern Italy's most important wine zones.

Campania

Campania's stunning natural beauty ranges from the Tyrhennian Sea's Amalfi Coast and Capri to its endless hillsides against the backdrop of Mount Vesuvius. The Avellino province, near Naples, produces some of the finest wines here. A full-bodied, tannic red, Taurasi — a DOCG wine from the indigenous aglianico variety — is one of the legendary, long-lived red wines in Italy. Premium producers are Mastroberardino, Feudi di San Gregorio, and Terredora. The same producers also make two unique whites, Greco di Tufo and Fiano di Avellino. They're rich, complex, viscous wines with great aging capacity that sell in the $20 to $40 range. Coda di volpe and falanghina are additional noteworthy white Campania varieties to enjoy with your next chilled seafood or light pasta dish.

Basilicata

Mountainous (thanks to the nearby southern Apennines), cool Basilicata is Italy's smallest wine zone. It is the humble home of southern Italy's greatest red variety, aglianico, which produces Aglianico del Vulture (named after the once-active Mount Vulture). The wine is similar to Taurasi but not so intense and full-bodied. Elena Fucci, Cantine del Nataio, D'Angelo, and Paternoster are leading producers.

Puglia

This generally hot, southeastern zone is one of the leading producers of red wine in Italy — mainly more affordable, full-bodied red wines such as negroamaro, nero di troia, and primitivo (which has been shown through DNA analysis to be the same grape as zinfandel).As you may guess, primitivo from Puglia is just as luscious and thick as its zinfandel counterpart when planted in warmer areas of California (see Chapter 11). It's jam packed with ripe berry and fruit punch flavors, rich but often velvety (with the right producer) tannins, and a long finish. These are medium- to full-bodied wines that typically range from 13–15% percent alcohol by volume. Some of the best expressions of primitivo are made in the Primitivo di Manduria DOC. *Passito* styles of primitivo are also made in the Primitivo Dolce Naturale DOCG.

The native variety of negroamaro is mostly planted in the zone's best-known wine district, the Salento Peninsula. This is a dark, inky wine with black fruit, dried herbs, licorice, and balsamic notes. While more affordable than some of the top wines of Tuscany or Piedmont, the full-bodied reds from Puglia are to be taken seriously. Recommended producers from the zone include Agricole Vallone, Antinori (whose Puglia estate and wines are named Tormaresca), Cantine San Marzano, Cosimo Taurino, and Leone de Castris.

Calabria

Probably known more on a world scale for its red chillies and bergamot, Calabria is another sun-soaked region where both dry and *passito*-style wines are made. Calabria's most popular red grape is the native gaglioppo (*gah-yo-po*) variety which makes full-bodied, high tannin, high alcohol wines with flavors of crushed cherries, violets, licorice, and spice. The Cirò DOC is known for gaglioppo. Sweet, *passito*-style white wines are also made in Calabria from the indigenous variety Malvasia delle Lipari (also known as Greco di Bianco).

Sicily and Sardegna

Sicily, Italy's prized island possession, is the country's biggest zone by landmass and one of its largest wine producers. Similar to other zones throughout the country, Sicily continues to evolve in its quest for quality over quantity in wine. Sicily's established wineries, such as Duca di Salaparuta (also known as Corvo), Regaleali, and Planeta, now also have the company of exciting, new wineries, such as COS, Morgante, Palari, Salvo Foti, and Benanti.

One of Sicily's most exciting wine zones is Etna, on the slopes of the active northeastern volcano, Mount Etna. This zone produces superb cool-climate red and white wines with distinctive flavors influenced by Mount Etna's black volcanic soils. The reds, called Etna Rosso, are based on nerello mascalese, a genetic cross of sangiovese and the indigenous variety, mantonico bianco. The same grape is the mainstay of other red wines in eastern Sicily, including the great Faro wine produced by Palari near the city of Messina. Nerello mascalese wines resemble pinot noirs in their weight and aromas but generally have more mineral-forward (hello again, Mount Etna) finishes. Many of Sicily's other top reds come from the island's superb variety, ero d'Avola, and some excellent wine comes from the native frappato grape. The DOC Vittoria wines blend both grapes. Back in the Etna zone, the indigenous white variety called carricante makes some of Italy's finest white wines, including Etna Bianco — of which Palmento Costanzo and Pietra Marina are stellar examples.

Other wines of note that are not associated with Mount Etna include the fresh, fruity, saline-mineral-forward grillo (a white grape cross of native varieties catarrato and zibibbo), Muscat of Alexandria that is also used in the production of the cooking wine Marsala (see Chapter 18), and the dessert wines of Moscato Passito di Pantelleria and Malvasia delle Lipari (both made in smaller islands of the coast of Sicily).

Sardinia is a large Mediterranean island off the western coast of Italy. This zone makes crisp whites and medium- to full-bodied reds that are full of ripe fruit flavors and saline mineral characteristics. Both native and international varieties are planted. Whites includes nasco, malvasia, and vermentino. Reds include carignano and cannonau, also known as grenache. Argiolas, Santadi, and Sella & Mosca are three leading producers.

Molise

Molise is a small, lesser-known zone located south of Abruzzo and bordered by Campania to the southwest and Puglia to the southeast. Although the zone is smaller, winemaking here dates back to 500 BCE. Both indigenous and international varieties are planted here. The most important wine production zones are the Biferno DOC (with wines made mostly from montepulciano, tintilia, trebbiano, and aglianico) and Pentro di Isernia (with wines made from montepulciano, sangiovese, and Trebbiano Toscano).

Chapter **6**

France: The Super Model

aute couture, baguettes, romance, the Eiffel Tower — these are just a few things that come to mind when we think of France. For centuries, wine has been at the center of it all, with evidence of early viticulture dating to at least 500 BCE. Today, France is the world's largest wine producer (around 45 million hectoliters in 2023), and still holds the title for some of the most coveted and expensive wines in the world. France is home to more than 360 wine appellations (or AOCs, more on this distinction later in this chapter) and several United Nations Education, Scientific, and Cultural Organization (UNESCO, www. unesco.org) world heritage sites. It sets the standard not only for great winemaking, but also for today's shared understanding and vocabulary of wine culture around the world.

France sets the trend for the majority of the world's wines. Most wine-producing countries now make their own versions of wines from French varieties thanks to the success of these grapes in French vineyards and the international market. Due to this, our chapter on France is a long one — so settle in and enjoy the tour!

HOW DID FRANCE BECOME THE MOST FAMOUS PLACE IN THE WORLD FOR WINE?

Beginning in the first century CE, France emerged as a commercial wine influence within Gaul, which at that time included not only France but also parts of Belgium, west Germany, and northern Italy. France's well-documented, pioneering efforts increased exports to English and Dutch markets, and later to countries in the Americas, Australia, and South Africa. Today, France remains the world's largest exporter of wine, with nearly 16 billion Euros' worth leaving the country in 2024 alone.

In addition to France's contributions over centuries to global cuisine and the art of food and wine pairing, it gave the world a lot of its current day wine speak, including: *vigneron* (veen-yer-awn), vine grower; *terroir,* the combination of factors that give a wine its character; and *château* (shat-oh), which technically refers to castles or fortresses. A château is any structure (including farmhouses or garages) with adjoining vineyards where wine is produced and stored.

Finally, France is the birthplace of almost all the renowned varieties in the world — cabernet sauvignon, chardonnay, merlot, and pinot noir, for example. See Chapter 1 for more information on grape varieties.

The Laws and the Labels

France's early attempts to develop a wine enterprise resulted in many unintended consequences, one of which included an increase in demand that outpaced supply due to phylloxera (a pest native to North America that decimated most of Europe's vines by feeding on their roots; discover more in Chapter 3). By 1895, phylloxera had destroyed nearly half of France's vineyards, resulting in drastic declines in production and sales. Around the same time, as word spread about the industry's potential for profit, wine fraud increased. Tampered wines (some mixed with acid, plaster, sugar, and/or syrup) were made and sold within France and across the Atlantic.

France's first attempt to codify standards for wine were documented in 1889, followed by best practices for making châteauneuf-du-pape by Baron Le Pay in 1923, and finally the system of *Appellation d'Origine Contrôlée* (AOC, translated as "regulated place-name" or "regulated origin name") in 1935. Today, the AOC system not only regulates which products can grow where, but also serves as a stamp of approval for both domestic and international consumers. Some examples of AOCs include Alsace, Bordeaux, Burgundy, and Champagne. The European Union's *Protected Designation of Origin* (PDO) framework of wine laws, within which the AOC system now operates, is also modeled on the French system. French producers operate under both laws, but can choose which designation they prefer for marketing purposes.

REMEMBER

To understand French wine laws, you need to know five things:

>> Most French wines are named after defined and registered places. Regions, sub-regions, *communes* (similar to a township or municipality), or *villages* (the equivalent of of U.S. cities) can all be included in a wine's name.

>> Most of the time, the wine and the region have the same name (as in Sancerre wine, from Sancerre AOC).

>> The French AOC system is hierarchical and highly contentious. Wines from some places are classified or ranked higher than others. Some producers fight to have their wines classified or ranked to improve their standing in the marketplace. Others choose not to be involved at all.

>> Generally, the smaller and more specific the place for which a wine is named, the higher its classification or rank.

>> A wine with a high classification or rank isn't necessarily better than the next wine; it just means that it may be better and/or more expensive. The laws classify or rank the potential of the place where the wine comes from.

Approved and regulated French wine regions fall into two categories:

>> ***Appellation d'Origine Contrôlée* (AOC); known in the EU system as *Appellation d'Origine Protégée* (AOP).** This is the higher designation. On the label, the place-name of the wine usually follows the French phrase (AOC Alsace, for example).

>> ***Vin de Pays* (meaning "country wine"); known in the EU system as *Indication Géographique Protégée* (IGP).** On the label, the phrase is followed by a place-name, such as Vin de Pays (or IGP) de l'Hérault, which indicates the area where the grapes grew. Geographically, the places or regions are generally much larger than the places or regions referred to in the AOC category. The IGP covers 75 distinct regions, including IGP Vin de Pays, IGP Méditerranée, and IGP Val de Loire and others.

These categories generally appear on a French wine's label. AOC wines are often pricier than *Vin de Pays.* If a French wine does not have one of the preceding official terms on its label, then it is simply *Vin de France,* a wine from grapes grown anywhere in France rather than in a specific region. *Vin de France* is a broad category that enables producers to blend grapes or wines from different regions. These wines are usually labelled with the grape name (a rare exception for French wines) and may or may not carry a *vintage* (the year in which the grapes were harvested).

TIP

Figure 6-1 shows an example of a typical French wine label and how to interpret it. Many of the terms shown are also printed on wine labels from other countries (some required by law, others by choice), including producer, vintage, and special regional designations.

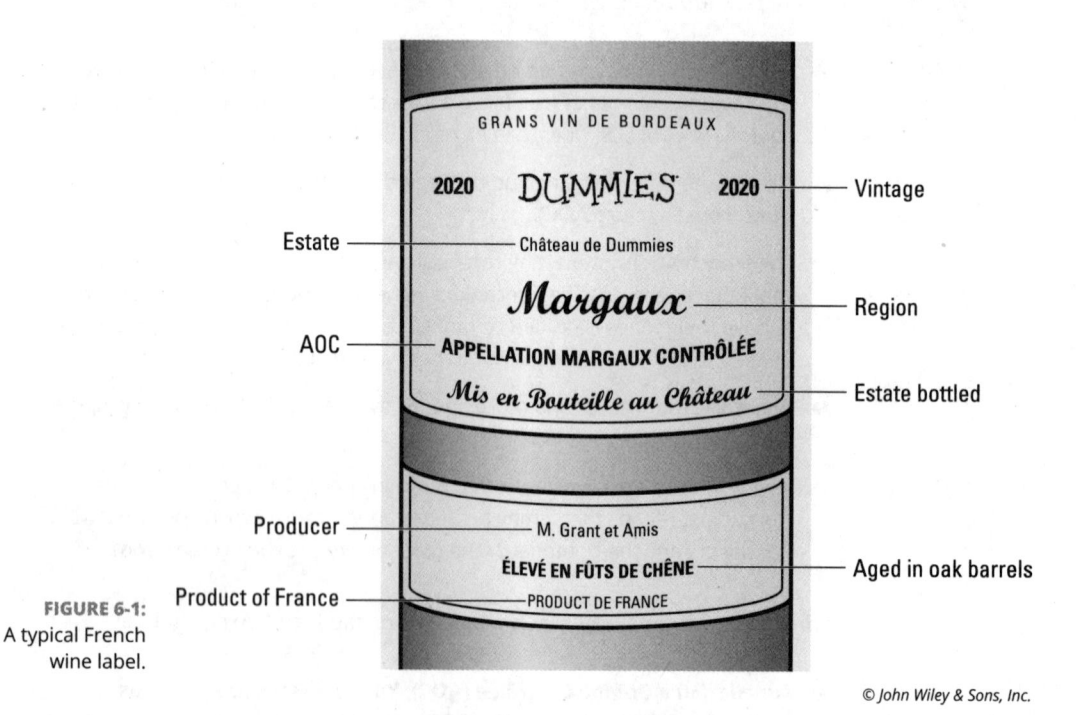

FIGURE 6-1: A typical French wine label.

Regions, Varieties, and Styles

France is home to over 200 indigenous grape varieties across 11 major wine regions, as shown in the color section of this book. Each region specializes in certain varieties and styles based on local traditions, distinctive *terroirs* (discussed in Chapter 2), and competitive advantage. Let's begin our tour!

Bordeaux: Famous reds

Bordeaux, named after the city with the same name, is France's largest AOC, located in the southwest of the country with a climate ideal for vineyards. Bordeaux's reputation as one of the greatest wine regions in the world revolves around the legendary elite red wines of the region — powerful, opulent wines made by historic *châteaux* and capable of improving for many decades. A recent vintage of Château Pétrus, Bordeaux's most expensive, can sell for just over $4,000 today! These legendary wines represent the pinnacle of a red Bordeaux pyramid; quantitatively, they're less than 2 percent of the region's red wine production. Middle-level red Bordeaux starts at about $45 a bottle. The least expensive red Bordeaux can cost as little as $10 to $20 a bottle, and are enjoyable young within 2 to 5 years of the vintage date. The vast majority of red Bordeaux (about 70 percent) fall into the least expensive category.

REMEMBER

Bordeaux produces about 500 million bottles per year from nearly 7,000 producers. The region previously boasted almost twice as many producers, but larger estates annexed many of the smaller ones in the past 30 years. There are 53 named AOCs in Bordeaux. Approximately 90 percent of the region's wines are dry, red styles made with cabernet sauvignon and/or merlot. The remaining 10 percent include dry and sweet whites (including the infamous Sauternes), rosés, and sparkling.

Bordeaux's climate makes for warm, humid summers and mild winters. Water influences drive fluctuations in harvest quality and quantity, resulting in varied character and quality of wines. The main soil types found in Bordeaux include clay, gravel, limestone and sand. While most of Bordeaux's vineyards are not highly elevated, there are some properties situated on hills or areas with well-drained soils that many *vignerons* (winegrowers) can agree are the keys to excellent wines. Some of Bordeaux's most lauded vintages include 2005, 2010, 2015, and 2016 — years in which there was rainfall (but not too much), warm days (but not too hot or humid for too long), and cool evenings (but not cold enough to freeze). A vintage chart for Bordeaux and other major wine-producing regions is included in Appendix C.

TECHNICAL
STUFF

British media and trade professionals sometimes refer to red Bordeaux wines as *clarets*. This is a British term dating back to the 16th century derived from the French *clairet*. The term was historically used to describe a lighter red wine that could be differentiated from other still and/or fortified wines of the time. Today, claret is still used in reference to general red Bordeaux. However, clairet (spelled slightly differently) is a style of Bordeaux characterized by darker pink colors more reminiscent of rosé. This style is still available in smaller quantities today.

Knowing your Left (Bank) from your Right (Bank)

Modern wine writers and media use the terms "Left Bank" to refer to the communes on the left side of the Gironde Estuary, including Médoc, Graves, Sauternes, and Barsac. "Right Bank" refers to the communes on the right side of the Gironde Estuary, including Saint-Émilion and its satellites (Montagne, Lussac, Puisseguin, St. Georges), Pomerol, Fronsac, Canon-Fronsac, Blaye Côtes de Bordeaux, Bourg Côtes de Bordeaux, Francs Côtes de Bordeaux, and Entre Deaux Mers.

TECHNICAL STUFF

The Left Bank and the Right Bank differ primarily in soil composition: Gravel dominates on the Left Bank, and clay rules on the Right Bank. As a result, cabernet sauvignon, which has an affinity for gravel, plays a key role in Left Bank wines. Merlot, which does well in clay, dominates Right Bank wines. Both areas grow cabernet sauvignon and merlot, as well as cabernet franc (adds aromatics, herbal, and spicy notes), petit verdot (boosts tannin and red flower notes), malbec (adds weight and body), and small amounts of carménère (now nearly eliminated from Bordeaux).

REMEMBER

Left Bank and Right Bank Bordeaux wines are, therefore, markedly different from one another although they both have tremendous aging potential (see Chapter 3 for more on aging). The Left Bank generally produces firm, tannic wines with more pronounced black fruit, earthy, and spice notes. Right Bank wines are more approachable because they're mainly merlot: you can enjoy even the best of them long before their Left Bank cousins, often as soon as five to eight years after the vintage. They're less tannic, more supple in texture, and velvety in flavor. Right Bank wines typically include floral, meaty, chocolate, and perfumed notes.

Merlot is the most widely planted variety throughout Bordeaux. Cabernet cauvignon is second, followed by cabernet franc. Even on the Left Bank, a trend exists for a higher amount of merlot in the blend, thus making the wines more accessible at an earlier age.

Bordeaux also comes in white

Although Bordeaux is predominantely a red wine–producing region, there are two areas to note that specialize in both dry and sweet white wines. The dry styles range from inexpensive and intended for drinking young to wines so distinguished and age–worthy that they rank among the great dry white wines of the world.

REMEMBER

Two areas of Bordeaux are important for white wine production:

>> Pessac-Léognan (directly north of Graves, pronounced grahv) and Graves both south of Bordeaux city. These districts are home to some of the best wines of Bordeaux, both dry and sweet. Graves contains five sweet wine–producing communes: Barsac, Bommes, Fargues, Preignac, and Sauternes. These areas constitute the cradle of wines made with *Botrytis cinerea*, otherwise known as "noble rot." Learn more about Sauternes and noble rot later in this chapter.

>> Entre-Deux-Mers (ahn-truh-duh-mair), between the Garonne and Dordogne Rivers and east of Graves and Pessac-Léognan. This district is also known for its dry, semi-dry, and sweet white wines in addition to inexpensive, dry reds. We share more about Entre-Deux-Mers later in this chapter.

Sauvignon blanc and sémillon, in various combinations, are the two main varieties in both dry and sweet white Bordeaux. It's a match made in heaven: sauvignon blanc offers immediate citrus and floral flavors, while the slower-developing sémillon gives the wine richness and depth, enabling it to age well. In general, a higher percentage of sémillon is a good indicator of the wine's age-worthiness. The top dry white Bordeaux are crisp and lively when they're young, but they develop richness, complexity, and a honeyed bouquet with age. In good vintages, the best whites need at least ten years to develop and can live many years more.

A few white wines also come from the predominantly red wine Haut-Médoc district, such as the high-end Pavillon Blanc du Château Margaux. Although special and expensive, these wines qualify only for simple Bordeaux Blanc AOC appellation status because the more specific, commune-level AOCs of the Haut-Médoc apply only to reds.

The Left Bank: Highly classified

Beyond soils and grapes, Bordeaux's Left Bank history of classification is arguably the most ambitious (and longstanding) attempt to assess quality and value of fine red wine. At the order of Napoleon III to the Bordeaux Chamber of Commerce, the 1855 classification began. The Chamber of Commerce delegated the task to wine brokers, the companies who bought and resold the wines of Bordeaux. Bordeaux brokers still exist today. The classification was presented at the *Exposition Universelle de Paris* (a major world fair showcasing achievements in science, various industries, and the arts). It included 60 dry red-producing *châteaux* or *crus* (in Bordeaux, a *cru* refers to a classified wine estate) in the Médoc. One was included from Pessac-Léognan from what was then Graves (Château Haut-Brion), making a total of 61. This ranking assigned each estate to a category from *Premiers Crus* (also referred to as *first growths*) through *Cinquièmes Crus* (also known as *fifth growths*). Nonetheless, to this day, these classified growths enjoy special, powerful (and sometimes disdained by other Bordelais) prestige. These wines fetch prices in the hundreds to thousands of dollars, depending on the vintage, and are mostly enjoyed by the wealthier (or luckier) wine collectors of the world. Read on for more about the Left Bank's main sub-regions.

HAUT-MÉDOC AND ITS COMMUNES

The Haut-Médoc is Bordeaux's most prestigious district. It encompasses the northern and southern Médoc peninsula which is the entire area west of the Gironde Estuary. The term "Médoc" is frequently used as an umbrella for the combined districts of Médoc and Haut-Médoc. The Haut-Médoc district is very important because it encompasses four famous wine communes (from north to south): Saint-Estèphe, Pauillac, Saint-Julien, and Margaux.

Two other communes in the Haut-Médoc, south of Saint-Julien are Listrac (lee-strahk) and Moulis (moo-lees). These communes are lesser known but make excellent wines at great value (some starting at just $20 per bottle retail). Similar to their neighbors, Listrac and Moulis châteaux produce wines that range from light to full in body, soft to firm tannins, and dry to ripe fruit flavors. Vineyards that aren't located in the AOC territories of the six communes described in this section carry the districtwide appellation, *Haut-Médoc*, rather than that of a specific commune.

REAL DEAL

Cru Bourgeois, Cru Bourgeois Supérieur, and Cru Bourgeois Exceptionnel describe an additional three-tiered classification of Bordeaux that includes excellent, wallet-friendly wines. This classification includes nearly 35 percent of the region's wineries in Haut-Médoc, Saint-Estèphe, Pauillac, Saint-Julien, Listrac, Moulis, and Margaux. The *Cru Bourgeois* classification was created in 1932 and, today, 250 Left Bank estates carry this designation. The wines are classified by a committee through a process of blind tasting and review of fruit quality, vineyard management, and other factors. *Cru Bourgeois Exceptionnel* is the highest-ranking category. You can find these wines for great prices in a range of wine shops and even some grocery stores.

SAUTERNES AND NOBLE ROT WINES

If you're seeing red (pun intended) from all the red wines of Bordeaux, take a quick sip of the Left Bank's white wines in this section! Towards the southern tip of the Left Bank are Sauternes and Barsac, two neighboring sub-regions of Graves situated along the Garonne River. Sauternes vineyards technically stretch across several communes, including Barsac, Bommes, Fargues, Preignac, and Sauternes. The maritime climate in these communes is unique given their closeness to the Ciron and Garonne rivers. This climate is also the key ingredient for *Botrytis cinerea*, a fungus known as "noble rot." *Noble rot* is one of few beneficial fungi that infects grapes in warm, humid circumstances, resulting in wines with flavors of honey, orange peels, baked apricots, caramel, nuts, and mushrooms.

TECHNICAL STUFF

Ever wondered why some dessert wines come in such small bottles? The painstaking process of growing and harvesting grapes made with noble rot is not for the faint of heart. These wines are made primarily from sémillon, sauvignon blanc, and smaller quantities of muscadelle. Here's how the grapes in places like Sauternes and Barsac begin to rot (nobly, of course):

1. **Grapes remain on the vines into the Fall (past the period of other dry, white grapes).**

2. **If and when temperatures fall between 59°F and 77°F (15°C and 25°C), and if and when humidity reaches or slightly exceeds 90 percent for at least**

four hours (a true formula for divine intervention), *Botrytis cinerea* can begin to grow and infect the grapes.

3. **The *Botrytis cinerea* fungus starts to break down the grapes' skins, which helps it to spread and search for water to survive.** This process slowly evaporates the grape's water, shriveling and shrinking each berry, and revealing a grey, velvet-like growth (the "rot").

4. **As the grapes dehydrate and shrink in size, the sugar becomes more concentrated and different types and quantities of acidity are retained by the fruit.** Acidity is crucial to giving sweet wines balance. The acidity is also what helps to give sweet wines their food-friendliness (see Chapter 18 for more).

5. **Next comes the challenge of harvest.** Could too much rain and (bad) gray mold completely destroy the perfectly spreading fungus? Could hail or frost throw nobly rotted grapes to the ground, ruining entire clusters in just one night? Between late September/early October and November, the laborious process of picking one grape (or cluster, if grape pickers are lucky) at a time.

6. **Finally, the delicate berries are gently pressed to extract as much juice as possible from a grape that's essentially almost a raisin.**

Finished wines have anywhere from 120 to 220 grams per liter of residual sugar and range from 13.5% to 14.5% alcohol by volume. World-renowned (and pricey, starting around $200 per bottle depending on vintage) Sauternes and Barsac include châteaux such as D'Yquem (Sauternes), Climens (Barsac), Guiraud (Sauternes), Suduiraut (Sauternes), and Caillou (Barsac). Relatively less expensive, great quality options are also available from Château Massereau (Barsac), Domaine De L'Alliance (Sauternes), and Château Doisy-Védrines (Sauternes).

The Right Bank: Small but mighty

On the right side of the Gironde Estuary lie the small but mighty Right Bank sub-regions. Anchored by the cities of Libourne and St. Émilion, a visit to this part of Bordeaux would instantly erase any remnants of grandeur obtained in the Médoc (see the previous section on the Left Bank). The Right Bank has more hillsides or *côtes*, less sprawling *châteaux*, smaller vineyards, and more of a conservative culture (thanks to a history of monastic orders dating back to the Middle Ages). Considering the numbers alone, the Médoc is home to over 6,000 châteaux of all types and sizes. St. Émilion and Pomerol (the Right Bank's most famed sub-regions) combined include around 1,200.

The maritime influence of the Left Bank is less apparent in the Right Bank, which means the Right Bank can get hotter and have less rainfall. The Right Bank is also more susceptible to frost which has unfortunately reduced crop yields substantially in the past (2017 is the most recent example).

The two most dominant sub-regions (and neighbors) of the Right Bank are St.Émilion and Pomerol — both specializing in dry red wines made predominantly from merlot blended with cabernet franc. Some *vignerons* also add malbec, petite verdot, and cabernet sauvignon to their blends.

ST. ÉMILION

St. Émilion wines are known for their plush and juicy character. Typical aromas and flavors include red, black, and blue fruit, as well as pronounced evidence of oak-aging via baking spices, vanilla, or chocolate.

TECHNICAL STUFF

St.Émilion wines are (infamously) reclassified every ten years (2022 was the last classification). The classification includes three quality categories, which are indicated on the labels: *Grands Cru Classés* (64 producers total) and *Premier Grands Crus Classés* (14 producers) further categorized into Group A (2) and Group B(12). As of the latest reclassification in 2022, the two *Premier Grand Cru Classé* properties in Group A are Château Pavie and Château Figeac.

WARNING

Grand Cru Classé, is vastly superior to the more than 600 St. Émilion Grand Cru AOC wines that do not have the word "Classé" attached. If you're thinking that the St.Émilion classification categories should be renamed, you are right: "Grand Cru" is a misnomer for the third category.

POMEROL

Not nearly as large or historically famed as the Haut-Médoc, Sauternes, or St. Émilion, Pomerol's rise to popularity has been most documented through a small handful of outstanding producers. To the west of Libourne lies this unassuming region full of relatively smaller properties specializing in merlot-based blends. Pomerol is known for wines made with finesse: juicy but soft red, black, and blue fruits, velvety tannins, and decadence. Pomerol is also home to some of Bordeaux's most expensive red wines from Château Pétrus and Le Pin. The wines of Pomerol have never been officially classified.

TECHNICAL STUFF

Pomerol's fame is also due in part to a special subsoil that exists at many of its *châteaux*. Dubbed *crasse de fer* (iron slag), the soil includes sand, gravel, clay, and an iron-rich stone on its bottom layer. This soil is believed to give Pomerol wines a distinctive minerality uncommon to other properties of the Right Bank.

CÔTES DE BORDEAUX

The northeast of St. Émilion is surrounded by a small group of four satellite regions. Together, they are called the Côtes de Bordeaux and include Blaye, Bourg, Castillon, and Francs. Vines from these regions are some of the oldest in

Bordeaux, made in both white and red dry styles. The wines are generally made young and intended for immediate, everyday consumption. Merlot dominates the red blends, and sauvignon blanc the whites (similar to the rest of the Right Bank).

ENTRE-DEUX-MERS

Translating to "between two seas" (aptly named given the Gironde Estuary's position in Bordeaux), Entre-Deux-Mers *vignerons* make both white and red wines. However, the AOC name *Entre-Deux-Mers* applies to dry white wines only on a label. Red wines made here must be called either Bordeux or Bordeaux Supérieur.

Entre-Deux-Mers wines are made primarily with sauvignon blanc (adding citrus and floral characteristics), sémillon (adding richness and weight), and muscadelle (adding a floral, perfumed element). These wines are best known for their simplicity, acidity, and food-friendliness. Entre-Deux-Mers wines are also known for their great value — they make a promising white wine companion for dinner and are usually available in specialty wine shops.

FRONSAC AND CANON-FRONSAC

When you leave the Médoc peninsula and cross over the Dordogne River into the Right Bank region, the first wine districts you actually encounter are Fronsac and Canon-Fronsac. Of the lesser Bordeaux appellations, Canon-Fronsac and Fronsac have the highest reputations for quality, and they're priced accordingly, in the $30 to $40 range per bottle. Like St.Émilion and Pomerol, Fronsac and Canon-Fronsac produce only red wines with merlot as the dominant grape variety.

BUYING BORDEAUX WITHOUT BREAKING THE BANK

Younger generations and new propietors of family-owned *châteaux* are eager to refocus while maintaining the integrity of Bordeaux's historic *terroir*. These *vignerons* are using creativity, technology, and new techniques to experiment with biodynamics, canopy management, reverse osmosis, and new oak to name a few. Some names to look out for in the Médoc include Claire Villars Lurton, Guillaume Pouthier, Michel Théron and Stephanie Destruhaut, Sophie Martin, and Pascale and Bruno Rey.

If you're worried you won't be able to taste the *grand vins* (best lots) from Bordeaux as a mere mortal for $3,000 a bottle, cheer up! Many other options exist to enjoy the region

(continued)

(continued)

for less than $200 per bottle, especially through *second wine* releases (wines that may not come from the top tier seletion of grapes or represent a producer's flagship, but still maintain high quality standards). These wines may or may not have the same label as the *grand vin*. Second wines can be just as good (and probably a little pricier than your average red wine) with the same style, age-worthiness, and commitment to quality. On the Left Bank, look for Petite Mouton from Château Mouton-Rothschild, Pavillion Rouge from Château Margaux, and Les Forts de Latour from Château Latour. Right Bank suggestions include Fleur de Clinet by Château Clinet, Le Carillon d'Angélus by Château Angélus, and Mondot by Château Troplong Mondot. Although these wines are seconds, they won't be sloppy at all!

Red Bordeaux without a more specific appellation can carry the general *Bordeaux* or *Bordeaux Supérieur* appellations. Grapes are predominantly merlot and can grow anywhere throughout the region. These are fairly lighter-bodied wines that sell for $12 to $14 per bottle. Sometimes, the labels identify the wines as specifically merlot or cabernet sauvignon. Whether leading brands such as Mouton-Cadet and Michel Lynch or less-known generic Bordeaux brands from good vintages, such as 2015, these wines can be excellent buy. The highest-rated Bordeaux vintages are 2020, 2019, 2015, 2015, 2010, and 2005 — all of which show promise of being great. Wines from 1989, 1986, and 1982 are excellent mature vintages.

Burgundy: Understated elegance

Burgundy (or, as the French call it, *Bourgogne*, pronounced boor–guh–nyuh), is a wine region in eastern France, southeast of Paris. Burgundy stands shoulder to shoulder with Bordeaux as one of France's two greatest regions for dry white and red wines. Of France's 363 wine appellations, 84 are in Burgundy. This region is the coolest and farthest north of all popular red wine regions in the world.

REMEMBER

Unlike Bordeaux, Burgundy's fame is split nearly equally between its white and red wines. Also unlike Bordeaux, good Burgundy is often scarce. The reason is simple: Not counting the Beaujolais area (which is technically Burgundy, but different in soil types, grapes, and more), Burgundy produces only 25 percent as much wine as Bordeaux, at best. Considering the fact that less than half of Burgundy's wine production is red, the scarcity of red Burgundy becomes all the more dramatic.

TECHNICAL STUFF

Burgundy's history of winemaking dates back to the first century CE. The region's most influential period was the stretch between the eighth century and the French Revolution (1789-1799). It was during this period that Burgundy became a Catholic center in France. Over the centuries, several new laws regarding land ownership were implemented, and Benedictine and Cistercian monks started meticuluously defining and documenting Burgundy's grapes and *terroir*. Some argue that the work of these monks strengthened and formalized the concept of *terroir* as a foundation for understanding the factors contributing to great wines.

Burgundy has a continental climate with warm summers and cold winters. Many *domaines* (wine estates) are located on steep slopes or hills reaching as high as 1,300 feet above sea level. Burgundy is always susceptible to fluctuations in sunlight, rain, and hail. In years without enough sunlight, grapes are more underripe when harvested, leading to wines that are less juicy or flavorful. In years with summer hailstorms, grapes can rot and die. Just as in Bordeaux, when the perfect combination of climactic factors is at play, Burgundy's wines can be some of the most complex, elegant, and opulent in the world.

Burgundy's *domaines* are smaller and more fragmented than Bordeaux's. The soils vary from one hillside to the next and even from the middle of each slope to the bottom. You can find two different vineyards growing the same grape but making distinctly different wines only six feet (two meters) apart from each other across a dirt road! The few large vineyards that do exist have multiple owners, with some families owning only two or three rows of vines (thanks to the Napoleonic Code of 1804 that mandated equal land inheritance among family members).

The typical Burgundy winemaker's production varies from 50 cases to 1,000 cases of wine a year, per type — far from enough to satisfy wine lovers all over the world. Compare that to Bordeaux, where the average Left Bank château owner makes 15,000 to 20,000 cases annually.

REMEMBER

Because soils vary so much in Burgundy, a wine's specific vineyard site is extremely relevant to the taste, quality, and price of that wine. A wine from a tiny vineyard with its own particular character is more precious and rare than a wine blended from several vineyards or a wine from a less-favored site. The AOC structure (discussed earlier in this chapter) for Burgundy wines recognizes the importance of site. While there are regionwide AOCs, districtwide AOCs, and commune AOCs, there are also AOC names that refer to individual vineyards. In fact, some of these vineyards are recognized as better than others: some of them are *Premier Cru* (prem-yay crew), meaning "first growth," while the very best are *Grand Cru*, meaning "great growth."

Bordeaux producers use the terms *Premier Cru* and *Grand Cru*, most importantly in St. Émilion. In Burgundy, *Premier Cru* and *Grand Cru* are always official distinctions within the AOC law. Their meaning is extremely precise; Table 6-1 gives examples of AOC names in Burgundy, listed in order of increasing specificity.

TABLE 6-1   **The Structure of Burgundy AOC Names**

Specificity of Site	Examples
Regional	Bourgogne Rouge; Crémant de Bourgogne
District	Beaujolais; Bourgogne Côte d'Or
Village or commune (44 villages)	Chambolle-Musigny; Gevrey-Chambertin; Puligny-Montrachet
Premier Cru (640 plots)	Chambolle-Musigny Les Amoureuses; Gevrey-Chambertin Clos Saint.-Jacques; Puligny-Montrachet Les Pucelles
Grand Cru (33 vineyards)	Le Musigny; Le Chambertin; Le Montrachet

REMEMBER

Just in case site classification isn't specific enough for you, Burgundy has a few terms that define place, ownership, and geography in more detail:

>> **A *climat* refers to a specific winegrowing plot of vineyards.** For example, the Grand Cru Climat Montrachet includes Puligny-Montrachet and Chassagne-Montrachet vineyards in Côte de Beaune. Some winemakers will include the name of of a wine's *climat* on the bottle's label.

>> **A *lieux dit* is often confused with a *climat*, but is a vineyard that can contain multiple plots.** These plots typically share a historic or geographical element in common. The term *lieux dit* is not typically on a Burgundy wine label.

>> **A *monopole* refers to an estate owned by a single person or winery.** The term *monopole* is often added to a Burgundy label as an indication of quality and rarity.

The availability and price of a Burgundy wine varies according to the specificity of its site, with *Premier* and *Grand Crus* at the most expensive end of the spectrum.

The grapes: Pinot noir, chardonnay, and gamay

Burgundy's soil is mainly limestone and clay. The *terroir* is particularly suited to the two main grape varieties of the region, pinot noir (for red Burgundy) and chardonnay (for white Burgundy). Other white grapes are grown in smaller quantities throughout the region, including aligoté and césar.

Pinot noir is known to winemakers around the world for being very fickle (sensitive to soil types and pruning techniques, susceptible to harsh climate conditions, labor-intensive harvesting and winemaking requirements, and so on). Whether through luck or centuries of experience, nowhere in the world does pinot noir perform better than in Burgundy.

In Burgundy's southerly Beaujolais district (described later in this section), the soil becomes primarily granitic but also rich in clay and sand — very suitable for the gamay grape predominantly planted in this area.

White Burgundy combines a richness of flavor — peaches, hazelnuts, and honey in Meursault; florals and butterscotch in Puligny or Chassagne-Montrachet — with lively acidity and a characteristic touch of oak. Many white wines around the world (including chardonnay from places such as Argentina, California, Spain, and South Africa), are aged in oak to add flavors of baking spice, toast, brioche, caramel, or mocha. For more on oak aging, see Chapter 3. With age, even more flavor complexity develops. Chardonnay from other regions and countries can be very good, but white Burgundy is certainly the benchmark.

TIP

The producer and the vintage are considerably more important than the appellation in Burgundy. Good vintages for red Burgundy are 2020, 2019, 2015, 2010, 2009, and 2005. For white Burgundy, 2022, 2015, 2014, 2010, and 2008 — 2008 especially for Chablis.

Red Burgundy is paler than Bordeaux, ranging from light ruby red to deep cardinal or garnet. This is due to the lower pigmentation levels in pinot noir grapes compared to cabernet sauvignon or merlot. Red Burgundy can range from 12.5% to 13% alcohol, and is typically lower in tannin compared to the bigger bodied wines of Bordeaux. The characteristic aroma is of red or black cherries, raspberries, currants, florals, potting soil, forest floor, and sweet spices. As a red Burgundy ages, it can develop more baked than fresh fruit flavors, in addition to more leather, gamey, or mushroom notes. Time also gives Burgundy more of a silky texture and richness that makes it so highly addictive to wine collectors. With some exceptions (for example, a powerful wine from a great vintage such as 2015, 2014, 2010, 2009, or 2005), fine red Burgundy should normally be consumed within ten years of the vintage — and even sooner in a lesser-celebrated vintage (see Appendix C). The 2020, 2019, and 2015 vintages will be especially long-lived for red Burgundies.

Districts, districts everywhere

Burgundy has five districts, all of which make very distinct wines. The districts, from north to south, are Chablis (shah-blee), the Côte d'Or (coat dor), the Côte Chalonnaise (coat shal-oh-naz), the Mâconnais (mack-coh-nay), and Beaujolais (boh-jhoe-lay).

The heart of Burgundy, the Côte d'Or (which literally means "golden slope"), itself has two parts: Côte de Nuits (coat-deh-nwee) in the north and the Côte de Beaune (coat-deh-bone) in the south. The Chablis district makes only white wines, and the Mâconnais makes mainly white wines. The Côte Chalonnaise and Côte d'Or make both white and red wines. Beaujolais makes almost exclusively red wines from the gamay grape.

REMEMBER

The term *red Burgundy* refers primarily to the red wines of the Côte d'Or and also to the lesser known and less expensive red wines of the Côte Chalonnaise. Like-wise, when wine lovers talk about white Burgundy, they are usually referring to just the white wines of the Côte d'Or and the Côte Chalonnaise. They'll use the more precise names, Chablis and Mâcon, to refer to the white wines of those other parts of Burgundy. When in doubt, the general term "Burgundy" can include any wine from the region.

CHABLIS: EXCEPTIONAL WHITE WINES

The village of Chablis, northwest of the Côte d'Or, is the closest Burgundian com-múne to Paris (about a two-hour drive). Although Chablis's wines are 100 percent chardonnay just like those from Côte d'Or, they're quite different in style. For one thing, almost all Côte d'Or white Burgundies ferment and age in oak barrels, but many Chablis producers use stainless steel tanks (at least for some of their wines). Chablis's climate is also cooler, and its soil is different from the rest of Burgundy. These factors result in wines that are intrinsically lighter-bodied, crisper, and more mineral-driven.

In 1938, the *Institut National des Appellations d'Origine* (INAO, France's national institute tasked with overseeing the country's standards for all appellations of origin) created the AOC region for Chablis. Four appellations were created in order of increasing quality and prestige:

>> **Petit Chablis:** A village-level appellation that can include wines produced in any Chablis commune. Portlandian limestone is the dominant soil type. Wines are generally floral, citrus-forward, and mineral-driven.

>> **Chablis:** The region's biggest appellation with wines produced in the communes of Beines, Béru, Chablis, Fyé, Milly, Poinchy, La Chapelle-Vaupelteigne, Chemilly-sur-Serein, Chichée, Collan, Courgis, Fleys, Fontenay-Près-Chablis, Lignorelles, Ligny-le-Châtel, Maligny, Poilly-sur-Serein, Préhy, Villy and Viviers. Kimmeridgian limestone and fossilized oysters dominate the soil. Wines are more complex than Petit Chablis, with a richer mouthfeel and often longer finish.

>> **Chablis Premier Cru:** Includes wines made from 40 *climats* in the communes of Beines, Chablis, La Chapelle-Vaupelteigne, Chichée, Courgis, Fleys, Fontenay-Près-Chablis, Fyé, Maligny, Milly and Poinchy. Soils are mainly Kimmeridgian marl (a mix of clay, fossils, and limestone). Wines are more structured and can range in minerality and florals, with greater aging potential than Petit Chablis and Chablis.

>> **Chablis Grand Cru:** Includes the seven *climats* of Blanchot, Bougros, Les Clos, Grenouilles, Preuses, Valmur, and Vaudésir. Soil is predominantly Kimmeridgian marl. Wines are stronger in their flinty notes, and can include aromas of almonds, florals, honey, mushrooms, and preserved lemons. These wines can be aged 10–15 years or more.

THE CÔTE D'OR: THE HEART OF BURGUNDY

The Côte d'Or, a narrow 40-mile stretch of land with some of the most expensive real estate in the world, is home to all the famous red and white Burgundies. The northern part of the Côte d'Or is named the Côte de Nuits, after its commercially most important city, Nuits-Saint-Georges. This area makes red Burgundies almost exclusively, although one superb white Burgundy, called Musigny Blanc, and a couple other white Burgundies do exist. The names of these communes are also the names of their wines that tend to have certain characteristics depending on vintage:

>> **Marsannay (mahr-sah-nay):** Known for lighter-bodied reds and rosés

>> **Fixin (fee-san):** Medium- to full-bodied, earthy, herbal red wines

>> **Gevrey-Chambertin (jehv-ray-sham-ber-tan):** Full-bodied, rich red wines; nine Grand Crus, including Chambertin and Chambertin Clos de Bèze

>> **Morey-Saint-Denis (maw-ree-san d'nee):** Full-bodied red wines; *Grand Crus* include part of Bonnes Mares, Clos de la Roche, Clos Saint-Denis, and Clos de Tart, Clos des Lambrays

>> **Chambolle-Musigny (shom-bowl-moo-sih-nyee):** Medium- to full-bodied, supple, elegant red wines; *Grand Crus* include Musigny and part of Bonnes Mares

>> **Vougeot (voo-joe):** Medium- to full-bodied red wines; *Grand Cru* is Clos de Vougeot

>> **Vosne-Romanée (vone-roh-mah-nay):** Full-bodied, elegant, rich, velvety red wines; the six *Grand Crus* are Romanée-Conti, La Tâche, Richebourg, Romanée-Saint-Vivant, La Romanée, and La Grand Rue

>> **Flagey-Échézeaux (flah-jhay-eh-sheh-zoe):** Hamlet of Vosne-Romanée; *Grand Crus* are Grands Échézeaux and Échézeaux

>> **Nuits-Saint-Georges (nwee-san-johrj):** Full-bodied, higher tannin red wines; no *Grand Crus*; fine *Premier Crus*

The southern part of the Côte d'Or, the Côte de Beaune, is named after its most important city, Beaune. The Côte de Beaune makes both white and red Burgundies, but the whites are more renowned. The following communes, from north to south, make up the Côte de Beaune:

>> **Ladoix (lah-dwah):** Seldom-seen, full-bodied, inexpensive white and red wines; part of the *Grand Cru* vineyards. Corton (red) and Corton-Charlemagne (white) are in this commune

- » **Pernand-Vergelesses (per-nahn-ver-jeh-less):** Lesser-known, full-bodied white and red wines; excellent value

- » **Aloxe-Corton (ah-luss-cor-tohn):** Full-bodied wines; several red *Grand Crus* that all include the name Corton and one magnificent white *Grand Cru* (Corton-Charlemagne)

- » **Chorey-lès-Beaune (shor-ay-lay-bone):** Mainly good-value, medium- to full-bodied red and a little white wine

- » **Savigny-lès-Beaune (sah-vee-nyee-lay-bone):** Mostly medium- to full-bodied red wines; fine value

- » **Beaune (bone):** Supple, medium- to full-bodied reds; some whites; 42 *Premier Crus*

- » **Pommard (pohm-mahr):** Full-bodied red wines; 28 *Premier Crus* (including Rugiens and Epénots)

- » **Volnay (vohl-nay):** Light- to fuller-bodied, red wines; 29 *Premier Crus*

- » **Auxey-Duresses (awk-see-duh-ress):** Medium- to full-bodied whites and reds; includes 9 *Premier Crus*

- » **Meursault (muhr-so):** The northernmost important white Burgundy commune; full-bodied, nutty wines; 19 *Premier Crus*

- » **Puligny-Montrachet (poo-lee-nyee-mon-rah-shay):** Home of elegant white Burgundies (although some red wine is made here too); 4 *Grand Crus* include part of Montrachet, Chevalier-Montrachet, part of Bâtard-Montrachet, and Bienvenues-Bâtard-Montrachet. This commune is also home to 19 *Premier Crus*

- » **Chassagne-Montrachet (shah-sah-nyuh-mon-rah-shay):** Full-bodied white and red wines; includes three Grand Crus, the rest of Montrachet, Bâtard-Montrachet, and Criots-Bâtard Montrachet

- » **Santenay (sant-nay):** Light-bodied, inexpensive reds and a small amount of whites; 12 *Premier Crus*

- » **Maranges (ma-rahnj):** Lesser-known, mostly red, inexpensive wines; 7 *Premier Crus*

REMEMBER

All the red wines are entirely pinot noir, and the whites are entirely chardonnay. The different characteristics from one wine to the next are mainly due to the wines' individual *terroirs*.

The wines of many Côte de Beaune villages can carry the specific name of their commune, or they can use the AOC of *Côte de Beaune Villages*. Not only does the AOC provide more recognition than that of a lesser-known village, but it also enables blending of wines from multiple villages, which can increase quantity and make the wine more marketable.

CÔTE CHALONNAISE: BARGAIN BURGUNDIES

REAL DEAL

The sad fact about Burgundy is that many of its best wines are costly. But one of Burgundy's best-kept secrets is the Côte Chalonnaise, the district that lies directly south of the Côte d'Or. Five villages here are home to some excellent Burgundies. While Côte Chalonnaise Burgundies are not as velvety or opulent as Côte d'Or Burgundies (they're a bit earthier and less refined in flavor and texture), they can still be quality wines — and we're talking $30 to $40 retail per bottle here.

From north to south, five villages or communes whose names appear on wine labels include: Bouzeron (boo-zuh-ron), which specializes in aligoté (Maison Chanzy, Domaine de Villaine, and Julien Cruchandeau are some of Bouzeron's top producers); Rully (rouh-yee); Mercurey (mer-cure-ay); Givry (gee-vree); and Montagny (mon-tah-nyee).

MÂCONNAIS: AFFORDABLE WHITES

REAL DEAL

The best buys in white Burgundies — and many of the best white wine buys in the world — come from the Mâconnais district. The Mâconnais lies directly south of the Chalonnaise and north of Beaujolais. It has a milder, sunnier climate than the Côte d'Or to the north. Wine production centers around the city of Mâcon, a gateway city to Provence and the Riviera. The hills in the Mâconnais contain the same chalky limestone beloved by chardonnay that can be found in many Burgundy districts to the north. In Mâcon, you can even find a village called Chardonnay!

Mâcon's white wines are 100 percent chardonnay. Most of them are simply called Mâcon or Mâcon-Villages (a slightly better wine than Mâcon, because it comes from specific villages), and they retail starting at around $15 per bottle. Often better are Mâcons that come from just one village. In those wines, the name of the village is appended to the district name, Mâcon (as in Mâcon-Lugny or Mâcon-Viré).

Mâcon whites are medium-bodied, crisp, fresh, and often mineral-driven. They're usually unoaked (meaning fermented or aged in stainless steel). You should enjoy them while they're young, generally within three years of the vintage. A few red wines are made in the Mâcon district (mainly from gamay) and, like the whites, are good value.

REAL DEAL

The best Mâcon whites come from the southernmost part of the district and carry AOC names of their communes Pouilly-Fuissé (pwee-fwee-say) and Saint-Véran (san-veh-rahn):

>> Pouilly-Fuissé is a richer, fuller-bodied wine than a simple Mâcon, is often oaked, and is a bit more expensive (starting at $28 and up). A few top producers include Château-Fuissé, Domaine Ferret-Lorton, and Domaine Leflaive.

>> Saint-Véran can be found in the $18 to $25 range, and is possibly the best-value wine in all of Mâcon. Some reputable producers include Domaine de la Chapelle, Domaine du Château de Vergisson, Domaine Frantz Chagnoleau, and Guy Voluet.

BEAUJOLAIS: DELIGHTFUL AND AFFORDABLE

The Beaujolais district is situated south of the Mâconnais, in the heart of one of the greatest gastronomic centers of the world. Good restaurants abound in the area, as well as in the nearby city of Lyon. As a wine, Beaujolais is so famous that it stands apart from the other wines of Burgundy. It even has its own red grape, gamay. The fact that Beaujolais is part of Burgundy is merely a technicality.

REMEMBER

Each year on the third Thursday in November, the new vintage of Beaujolais — called *Beaujolais Nouveau* — is released all over the world with special, creative labels and great fanfare. This youngster — only about six weeks old — is a very grapey, easy-to-drink, delicious wine with practically no tannin but lots of fruitiness. Typical tasting notes include cranberries, strawberries, bubblegum, and bananas. In the United States, *Beaujolais Nouveau* graces many holiday tables because of the timing of its annual debut. This wine is typically only available in wine shops and wine bars between November and December and sells between $12 and $15 a bottle.

In addition to *Beaujolais Nouveau*, generic Beaujolais and *Beaujolais Supérieur* (1% higher in alcohol) are the easiest Beaujolais wines. Their AOC zones extend across the whole Beaujolais district, but in practice, these wines come from the southern part of Beaujolais where the soil is mainly clay and sand. They're fresh, fruity, uncomplicated, fairly light-bodied wines that sell for $12 to $16 and are best a year or two after the vintage. Their lightness and chilling potential makes them excellent options for warm weather.

REAL DEAL

Beaujolais has its serious side, too. The best Beaujolais are made in the northern part of the Beaujolais district where the soil is granite-based, producing fuller, more substantial wine than basic Beaujolais. Beaujolais-Villages is a wine blended from grapes grown in (some of) 39 specific villages. It can cost more but be well worth the difference.

Beaujolais that's even higher quality comes from ten specific areas in the north. The wines of these areas are known as *Cru Beaujolais*, and only the name of the *Cru* appears in large letters on the label (the wines aren't actually named Beaujolais). *Cru Beaujolais* have more depth and, in fact, need a little time to develop. Some of the *Crus* can age and improve for five or six years or more. They range in price from about $18 to $30.

WORTH THE SEARCH

Most Beaujolais is sold by large *négociants* — firms that buy grapes and wine from growers and then blend, bottle, and sell the wine under their own labels. Two of the largest Beaujolais *négociants* are Georges Duboeuf and Louis Jadot. Jadot also owns *domaines* in Moulin-à-Vent and Morgon. Seek out some of the small Beaujolais producers, including Anne-Sophie Dubois, Domaine Chapel/Smith-Chapel, Pierre Cotton, and Domaine Anita for bargain, high-quality Beaujolais.

Champagne: The couture of wine

Champagne (*sham-pahn-yah*). Does any other word convey such a sense of celebration? Think of it: Whenever people want to celebrate, you can hear them say, "This calls for Champagne!" ("This calls for iced tea!" just isn't quite the same).

Champagne chic

REMEMBER

Champagne is a type of sparkling wine that is made from either white grapes, red grapes, or both. Most champagne is made from three varieties: pinot noir contributes fruitiness, power, and aging potential to the blend. Pinot meunier provides texture and fruitiness, and chardonnay offers delicacy, freshness, elegance, and longevity. At its finest, champagne can range from light, crisp, and refreshing to rich, mouthfilling, and powerful. Champagne can impart flavors of citrus, dried fruits, nuts, toast, brioche, cream, yeast, florals, minerals, and baking spices.

Champagne, the real thing, comes only from the region of Champagne (the northernmost vineyard area) of France. Many of the important champagne houses are located in the city of Reims. Around Reims and Epernay are the main vineyard areas, where three permitted grape varieties for champagne flourish. The names of these areas may or may not appear on the wine labels. These areas, and the grapes they specialize in, are: the Montagne de Reims (south of Reims), where the best pinot noir grows; the Côte des Blancs (south of Epernay), home of the best chardonnay; the Vallée de la Marne (west of Epernay), most favorable to pinot meunier (a black grape, although all three grape varieties grow here); Côte de Sézanne (south of Côte des Blancs), relatively smaller than the others, producing mainly chardonnay; and Côte des Bar, or the Aube (furthest south of all), mostly pinot noir and many emerging, newer generation winemakers.

Besides its appeal to the rich and famous, Champagne's *terroir* also differentiates it from other sparkling wine regions of the world. The cool climate in Champagne is ideal for its grape growing, and the grapes struggle to ripen sufficiently in some years. The chalky, limestone soils are also important factors contributing to champagne's excellence. The other important elements that help distinguish champagne from all other sparkling wines include: its more than 300 *crus* (wine-producing villages in this region); its cold, deep, chalky cellars mostly built during Roman times; and the more than 300 years of experience the *Champenois* (the people of Champagne) have in making it!

Bordeaux has *châteaux*, Burgundy has *domaines*. Champagne has *domaines* and *maisons*. The key difference between a *domaine* and a *maison* is that a *domaine* is a winery that grows its own grapes and bottles its own wine. A *maison* blends grapes from different vineyards and/or sub-regions.

TECHNICAL STUFF

Although champagne was made as early as the second century CE, champagne as we now know it rose to fame as a luxurious beverage within French courts of the 17th century. Increase in demand among the elite of England and Georgia led to the establishment of several *maisons* (or champagne houses) in the 18th century. It wasn't until the 19th century that many *maisons* began marketing champagne within France and around the world. From the beginning, *maisons* used champagne's favor among nobility and the elite as their marketing plea.

Today, France leads the world in champagne consumption, drinking more than 50 percent of all the champagne produced, followed by the United States and United Kingdom. But the United States buys the most *prestige cuvée* champagne (a champagne house's most prized offering), with more than 26.9 million bottles imported in 2024.

TECHNICAL STUFF

Champagne has become popular not just for its association with luxury and celebration, but also for the meticulousness of its method. Here's how champagne is made:

1. **Grapes are harvested and base wines are formed. Some *maisons* may make hundreds of base wines.**

2. **Base wines are blended, most often using wines from different years for non-vintage champagne.** The final blend is called the *assemblage*.

3. **A special mix of yeast, sugar, and wine called the *liqeur de tirage* is added to the final blend.**

4. **The wine is bottled, capped, and left to rest. Inside the bottle, the yeasts consume the sugar, which generates alcohol and carbon dioxide.** This process is often referred to as the *secondary fermentation in the bottle*. This is when *riddling* takes place — the process of rotating bottles to move the spent yeast cells

or *lees* into the neck of the bottle. The carbon dioxide produced throughout this process is released through the bubbles we see when we open the bottle.

5. **After at least 15 months (or several years, depending on the *maison*), the neck of the bottle is submerged in a cold solution to freeze the "plug" of spent yeast cells that's been created.**

6. **The bottle is *disgorged* (opened) and the desired amounts of *liquer de expedition* (wine and sugar, also known as *dosage*) are added which will determine the champagne's sweetness level.**

7. **The bottle is corked, caged with a small wire wrapper, and labeled.**

REMEMBER

Champagne is required by French law to age for at least 15 months. Most producers let their bottles rest for three years or more.

Blanc de blancs and blanc de noirs

Champagne derived only from chardonnay is called *blanc de blancs* — literally "white (wine) from white (grapes)." A *blanc de blancs* can be a vintage champagne or non-vintage (explained later in this section). *Blanc de blancs* come in a range of styles and price points depending on the *maison*. Not every champagne producer makes a *blanc de blancs*. Some of the most coveted *blanc de blancs* — all vintage champagnes (meaning champagnes made from grapes that were all harvested in the same year) — are Taittinger Comtes de Champagne, a *prestige cuvée* (top product); Billecart-Salmon Blanc de Blancs (also made as a non-vintage), Philipponnat Grand Blanc, Pol Roger Blanc de Blancs; and Dom Ruinart Blanc de Blancs. Two of the priciest Blanc de Blancs (both *prestige cuvées*) are Krug Clos du Mesnil and Champagne Salon S, also from Le Mesnil.

WORTH THE SEARCH

Blanc de noirs (made entirely from black grapes, usually just pinot noir) is fairly rare but does exist, especially among smaller producers. Top *blanc de noirs* are Bollinger's PX TX17 and Vielles Vignes (old vines), Gosset's Grand Blanc de Noirs, Billecart-Salmon's Le Clos Saint Hilaire, and Philipponnat's Blanc de Noirs.

Rosé champagne

Rosé (French for "pinkish") champagnes can also be vintage or non-vintage. Pinot noir, pinot meunier, and some chardonnay may be used in various proportions. Rosé champagne can be made using two methods:

>> **Rosé d'assemblage:** This involves adding still red wine (usually pinot noir) to base white wines before bottling (this is the most prevalent approach used in champagne today).

>> **Rosé de saignée:** This involves leaving grapes in contact with pinot noir skins until the desired level of pinkness is achieved.

SWEETNESS CATEGORIES

Champagnes always carry an indication of their sweetness on the label, but the words used to indicate sweetness are cryptic: Extra dry may not be really dry on the palate, for example. Amounts of sugar permitted to carry certain designations is required by law. In ascending order of sweetness (measured in grams per liter of residual sugar), champagnes are labeled:

- Brut nature or brut zero: 0–3 grams per liter

- Extra brut: 0–6 grams per liter

- Brut: 0–12 grams per liter

- Extra dry: 12–17 grams per liter

- Dry: 17–32 grams per liter

- Demi-sec: 32–50 grams per liter

- Doux: 50+ grams per liter

Brut is the most popular and widely available style for champagne, but brut and extra brut can be confusing! A champagne can be called *brut* as long as it has less than 12 grams per liter of residual sugar. This is a broad range which means that some champagnes will feel sweet to you that are technically brut, and others may feel bone dry to you even if they technically have more residual sugar (as long as it's less than 12 grams per liter). We don't make the rules — we just share them!

TIP

Rosés are typically fruitier, fuller, and more intense in flavor than other champagnes. Their pinkish hues have made them popular choices for wedding anniversaries and Valentine's Day, but many champagne lovers, (like us) drink them at any time of the year! Because of the extra steps involved in making rosé champagne, it usually costs a bit more than its lighter counterparts. Not every *maison* makes one, but those that do are usually successful! Some of the top, widely available rosé producers include Armand de Brignac, Bollinger, Dom Ruinart, Laurent-Perrier, Louis Roederer, Piper-Heidsieck, Moët & Chandon, Taittinger, and Veuve Clicquot.

Vintage versus non-vintage

Vintage champagne is made entirely from the grapes harvested in a single year, and is not blended with reserve wines from previous years. Historically, only about four or five years of every decade had weather good enough to make a vintage champagne — that is, the grapes were ripe enough that some wine could be made without the help of reserve wines. Since 1995, Champagne's climate has changed, and producers have been able to make vintage champagne more consistently. Some of the best recent champagne vintages include 2002, 2008, 2012, and 2015.

The minimum aging requirement for vintage champagne is three years. But many houses age their vintage champagnes for four to six years in order to enhance the wines' flavor and complexity. Vintage champagnes can be *regular vintage,* with a price range of $65 to $120 a bottle, carrying a vintage date in addition to the name of the producer. They can also be *premium vintage* (also known as *prestige cuvée* or *tête de cuvée*) with a price range of $125 to $300 or more per bottle. Examples include Pommery's Cuvée Louise, Moët & Chandon's Dom Pérignon, Perrier Jouet's Belle Epoque, or Veuve Clicquot's La Grande Dame.

Non-vintage (NV) champagne is any champagne without a vintage year on the label. This category accounts for about 85 percent of all champagne. The wine has no specific vintage year because wine from multiple harvests might have been used in the blend. Each *maison* blends its non-vintage champagne to suit its own style.

Most non-vintage champagnes retail for $35 to $70 a bottle. Often, larger retailers buy large quantities of a few major brands, obtaining a good discount that they pass on to customers. Seeking out stores that do a large-volume business in champagne is worth your while if you want to taste the more popular *maisons.* Smaller wine shops may carry some of these labels, but also offer deals on lesser-known producers or grower champagnes (see the next section).

Vintage champagne is almost always superior to non-vintage for the following reasons:

>> The best grapes from the choicest vineyards are included (this is especially true for *prestige cuvées*). Vintage champagne usually tastes more complex, flavorful, fuller-bodied, and with a longer finish.

>> Usually, only the two finest grape varieties (pinot noir and chardonnay) are used in vintage champagne. Pinot meunier is present mainly in non-vintage champagne.

>> Most champagne houses age vintage champagnes longer than their non-vintage wines. The extra aging assures more complexity.

>> The grapes all come from a year that's above average in terms of growing conditions. In the Champagne region, this means cooler temperatures but enough sunshine and moderate rainfall without the devastating effects of frost or hail.

Besides containing various grape varieties and wines from multiple vintages, champagnes can also contain base wines from 30 or 40 different villages (or more). The champagne producer is by necessity a master blender! Most *maisons* age their non-vintage champagne for at least three years before selling it, even though the legal minimum for non-vintage is just 15 months. The extra aging prolongs the marrying time for the blend and enhances the wine's flavor and complexity. With great cellar conditions, you can age non-vintage champagne for one to three years after you purchase it and can sometimes detect improvements in its flavor and richness.

Grower champagnes

In the last three decades, the number of grower champagnes has been on the rise. *Grower champagne* is champagne made by the same person who grew the grapes from their own vineyard. Contrastingly, a *maison* typically purchases most of the grapes for its wines.

While a few growers, such as Paul Bara, have been making and selling champagne for many decades, two-thirds of the region's 15,000 growers are content to sell their grapes rather than make wine. Around 5,000 growers who now sell the champagnes that they themselves have made account for about 18 percent of all champagne sales. Most of these sales take place in France, but the number of exports is growing. Grower champagnes are often available by the glass in wine bars and restaurants for a fraction of larger *maisons*' prices.

TIP

You can recognize a grower champagne by the initials *RM* (*Récoltant-Manipulant*, meaning a person who grows their own grape and makes their own wine from said grapes*)* or *RC* (*Récoltant-Coopérateur*, a person who sells champagne made from grapes that were vinified at a co-op*)* in small print on the bottom of the label.

WORTH THE SEARCH

Some of the better-known grower champagnes in the United States include Pierre Gimonnet, Gaston Chiquet, Champagne Aurore Casanova, Paul Launois, Champagne Elise Dechannes, Champagne Gamet, André-Jacquart, Champagne Moussé & Fils, Cédric Moussé, Champagne Bereche & Fils, Pierre Pallard, Pierre Péters, Pierre Bertrand, Guillaume Selosse, and Vilmart. Most of these producers make 7,000 or fewer cases per year, a pittance compared to the production of the larger *maisons*.

The Rhône Valley's rich wines

The Rhône (rone) Valley, which takes its name from the Rhône River, lies in southeastern France, south of Beaujolais, between the city of Lyon in the north and Avignon directly south (just north of Provence). The Rhône Valley is actually two distinct areas, a narrow swath of vineyard land in the north and a larger, more open landscape in the south. White, rosé, red, and fortified wines are made here ranging from 11% to 14.5% alcohol. To varying degrees, the red wines are full, robust, and fairly high in alcohol. Even some of the white wines tend to be full and powerful. But the wines from the southern Rhône are distinctly different from those in the northern Rhône.

Regal wines of the north

The vineyards of the northern Rhône cover hillsides and terraces along the Rhône River and have a climate that is cooler than that of the southern Rhône. The two most prestigious red wines of the entire Rhône Valley — Côte-Rôtie (coat-roe-tee) and Hermitage (er-mee-tahj) — hail from the northern Rhône. Like all northern Rhône reds, both are made from the great syrah grape, the only red grape in the north.

>> Although both Côte-Rôtie and Hermitage are rich, full-bodied wines, Côte-Rôtie is known for more complexity, floral and earthy aromatics, spice, and distinctive bacon fat aromas. A small percentage of white viognier is permitted and sometimes used in Côte-Rôtie, and this can contribute floral notes. In good vintages (see Appendix C), Côte-Rôtie can age for 20 years or more. Many Côte-Rôties are in the $49 to $75 price range, but a few of the best ones retail for more than $100. Reputable Côte-Rôtie producers include M. Chapoutier and Guigal. Guigal's single-vineyard Côte-Rôties — La Mouline, La Landonne, and La Turque — are legendary but rare and expensive (well over $100, and up to $200-plus).

>> Red Hermitage is the most full-bodied, longest-lived Rhône wine. It is a complex, rich, tannic wine that needs several years before it begins to develop. It ages easily for 30 years or more in good vintages. The best red Hermitages sell today for $65 and up, with a few of the top wines over $100. Three of the top Hermitage producers are Jean-Louis Chave, M. Chapoutier, and Paul Jaboulet Aîné (for its top Hermitage, La Chapelle).

Cornas, made entirely from syrah, is another distinguished northern Rhône red wine. Cornas resembles Hermitage in that it is a full-bodied, tannic wine that needs 10 to 20 years of aging. It ranges in price from $50 to $90 for the best examples. Top Cornas producers include Auguste Clape, Jean-Luc Colombo, Alaine Voge, Thierry Allemand, Yves Cauilleron, and Noel Verset.

Two less-expensive red wines from the northern Rhône are Crozes-Hermitage, from an area surrounding the Hermitage zone, and Saint-Joseph. Both can sell for $18 to $40 per bottle.

A small amount of white Hermitage is produced from the marsanne and roussanne grape varieties. White Hermitage is traditionally a full, rich, oak-aged, earthy wine that needs 8 to 10 years to fully develop, and can age for 15 years or more. Chapoutier's fine Hermitage Blanc, Chante Alouette, however, is all marsanne (about $100) and made in a more approachable style. Other notable Hermitage Blanc producers include Domaine Jean-Louis Chave, Domaine Marc Sorrel, and Cave de Tain.

Condrieu (cohn-dree-uh), made entirely from viognier, is the other white northern Rhône wine to try. It's one of the most fragrant, floral dry wines in existence. Its flavors are delicate but rich, with delicious, fresh apricot and peach notes. Similar to white Hermitage, most Condrieu is oak-aged, which gives it some cellaring potential. Depending on the producer, Condrieu can be enjoyed within 2 to 4 years from harvest, but may also age for anywhere from 5 to 20 years. Condrieu starts at $40 for some of the youngest vintages to upwards of $100 per bottle. Look for Condrieu in finer wine shops and French restaurants.

One wine, Château-Grillet, made from viognier, is difficult to find and expensive. You might be fortunate to find a few older vintages of Château-Grillet in the $200 to $280 range, depending on the vintage. Like Condrieu, Château-Grillet is a wine to drink young.

Generous wines of the south

About 95 percent of Rhône wines come from the southern Rhône. In a warm, Mediterranean climate, the grapes develop reliable levels of ripeness and make generous, easy-drinking wines. The wines are mainly reds blended with several grape varieties. The major player is grenache, which makes juicy wines that are higher in alcohol and low to medium in tannin. Some blends contain significant amounts of syrah or other varieties, which makes for somewhat gutsier wines.

The largest AOC designation is Côtes du Rhône, the Rhône Valley's everyday red wine, which comes mainly from the southern part of the region. For a good, reliable dry red wine that costs about $14 to $25, look for Côtes du Rhône. The southern Rhône Valley makes more serious wines — mostly red — but Côtes du Rhône is one of the best inexpensive red wines in the world.

Nearly 90 percent of Côtes du Rhône wines are red, with the balance being white and rosé. Besides Côtes du Rhône itself, other southern Rhône wines to look for are: Côtes du Ventoux (vahn-too), which is similar to but lighter than Côtes du Rhône; Côtes du Rhône-Villages, a fuller and slightly more expensive wine than Côtes du Rhône; and the single-village wines from Gigondas (jhee-gohn-dahs) and Vacqueyras (vah-keh-rahs).

Châteauneuf-du-Pape (shah-toe-nuf-doo-pahp) or "Pope's New Castle" is the king (or pope) in the southern Rhône. Its name recalls the 14th century, when nearby Avignon was the temporary home of the Catholic popes. John Paul XXII relocated from Rome to Avignon and built a castle in this region. During this time (and to this day), the popes were avid wine enthusiasts — so much so that the wines from the region came to be dubbed *Vin de Pape* or "wine of the popes." Almost all Châteauneuf-du-Pape is red wine blended from different grapes. As many as 13 varieties can be used, but grenache, syrah, and mourvèdre predominate. At its best, Châteauneuf-du-Pape is full-bodied, rich, round, and ripe. In good vintages, it will age well for 15 to 20 years. Most red Châteauneuf-du-Pape wines retail in the $45 to $85 price range, but the best ones can cost up to $90 or more. Top Châteauneuf-du-Pape producers include Château Rayas (nearly 100 percent grenache from very old vines), Château de Beaucastel (which can age 20 years or more), and Domaine de Marcoux. A small amount of complex, earthy-style, white Châteauneuf-du-Pape is also made from grenache blanc, clairette, roussanne, and bourboulenc.

Two interesting dry rosé wines of the southern Rhône are Tavel (tah-vel) and Lirac (lee-rahk). Lirac can also be white or red, but all Tavel wines are rosés. Tavel is the first official rosé AOC in France (named in 1936). Both Tavel and Lirac are made from grenache (blanc or noir) and cinsault grapes. They can be delightful on hot, summer days or at barbecues. As with most rosé wines, they are best when they're very young.

Dessert wines

The Rhône Valley is also home to two important sweet wine types (commonly referred to as *Vins Doux Naturels or VDNs*): Muscat Beaumes-de-Venise and Rasteau. The AOC Vin Doux Naturels classification was given to these wines in 1932 (in addition to similar wines from Languedoc-Rousillon and northern Corsica). The wines can range from 16% to 19% alcohol and are typically fortified by adding neutral grape spirit (around 95% alcohol by volume) to still wines. For more on fortified wine production, see Chapter 3.

Muscat Beaumes-de-Venise is a fortified wine made with a grape called Muscat à Petits Grains. It is the specialty of a village called Beaumes-de-Venise in the southern Rhône Valley, but is also made in surrounding areas and the town of Aubignan. These are sweet, aromatic wines with flavors of orange blossoms, lychees, mangos, pears, honeycomb, apricots, and almonds.

Northeast of Châteauneuf-du-Pape, between the Aigues and Ouveze rivers lies the village of Rasteau. Fortified wines from this region are made from grenache vines that are 50-80 years old. Legally, Rasteau wines must be made from 90 percent grenache (gris, blanc, or noir). Resulting wines include flavors of red and black fruits, damp soil (nicer than it sounds!), cigar box, licorice, and spices. Reputable producers of VDN include Rasteau, Domaine de Rancy, Domaine Vaquer, Domaine des Amadieu, and Cave de Rasteau.

The Loire Valley: The garden of France

In contrast to the regions of Bordeaux, Burgundy, and even Champagne, the Loire Valley offers much more diversity in both varieties in styles. Although the Loire Valley is most famous for its white wines, you can find red wines and some dry rosés, too!

The Loire Valley stretches across northwest France, following the path of the Loire River from central France in the east to the Atlantic Ocean in the west. The rather cool climate, especially in the west, produces relatively light-bodied white wines. The Loire Valley has three sections, each of which features different grape varieties.

The Upper Loire

In the eastern end of the Valley (called the Upper Loire), just south of Paris, are the towns of Sancerre and Pouilly-sur-Loire, located on opposite banks of the Loire River. Here, sauvignon blanc makes lively, dry wines that have smoky, green grass, and mineral-driven flavors. The two principal wines in this area are Sancerre (sahn-sair) and Pouilly-Fumé (pwee-foo-may).

>> There are nearly 300 wineries in Sancerre. The Sancerre AOC includes 14 communes and 3 hamlets (rural communities typically too small to be named a village). Sancerre can be made from either sauvignon blanc or pinot noir (typically referred to as Sancerre Rouge). Sancerre is lighter and more vibrant when compared to Pouilly-Fumé. Sancerre has risen to fame in recent years, selling out both in France and the United States. Top Sancerre producers include Domaine Vacheron, François Crochet, Domaine Durand, and Domaine Jean-Paul Ballanc.

>> Pouilly-Fumé is still sauvignon blanc, but slightly fuller than Sancerre with attractive flinty, mineral flavors. Pouilly-Fumé can be quite a fine wine when made by a good producer, such as Didier Dagueneau or Ladoucette.

The Central Loire Valley

The Central Loire Valley is known for both its white and red wines. The white chenin blanc grape reigns supreme here. These wines can be dry or sweet, and they carry the names of the areas where their grapes grow.

- ›› Savennières (sah-vehn-nyair), is one of the world's greatest dry chenin blanc wines, selling at about $23 and up.

- ›› Vouvray wines come in three styles: dry (*sec*), medium-dry (*demi-sec*), or sweet (*moelleux*, pronounced m'wah-leuh). Vouvray sec is a less austere and less full-bodied wine than Savennières, however. Vouvray also can be a sparkling wine. Most Vouvray is 100 percent chenin blanc.

- ›› Coulée de Serrant (cool-eh-duh-say-han), Bonnezeaux (bon-zoo, translating to "good waters") and Quarts-de-Chaume (caa-duh-shum) are dessert wines made from 100 percent chenin blanc.

The sweet wines of Vouvray can be made only in warm vintages of unusual ripeness, which occur infrequently. These wines need several years to develop and can last almost forever, thanks to their remarkable acidity. Three renowned Vouvray producers are Philippe Foreau of Clos Naudin, Gaston Huet-Pinguet, and Didier Champalou.

TIP

The central Loire Valley also boasts some of the region's best red wines. Made mainly from cabernet franc, they carry the place-names of the villages where the grapes grow: Chinon (she-nohn), Bourgueil (boor-guh'y), Saint-Nicolas-de-Bourgueil (san-nee-co-lah-deh-boor-guh'y), and Saumur-Champigny (soh-muhr-shahm-pee-n'yee). Most are oak-aged, but some are not depending on the producer. These wines can range from light to full-bodied with notes of red and dark berries, violets, bell pepper, pencil shavings (if we're being particular), and baking spice. Central Loire Valley reds can range from $18 to $45 a bottle retail.

Pays Nantais

Close to the Atlantic Ocean is the third wine district of the Loire Valley — Pays Nantais (pay-ee nahn-tay), named after the city of Nantes, right where the Loire River empties into the Atlantic Ocean. This area is the home of the muscadet grape (also known as *Melon de Bourgogne*). The wine, which is commonly known as muscadet (moos-cah-day), is light, bracing, and very dry, with apple and mineral flavors. It's perfect with clams, oysters, mussels, and river fish (and ideal for summer drinking).

TECHNICAL STUFF

Most muscadet comes from the Sèvre-et-Maine AOC zone, and those words appear on the label. Frequently, you also see the term *sur lie*, which means that the wine aged on its *lees* (dead fermentation yeasts) and was bottled straight from the tank. This procedure gives the wine liveliness, freshness, and sometimes a slight prickle of carbon dioxide on the tongue.

Alsace: German roots

Alsace is a picturesque wine region in northeastern France, just across the Rhine River from Germany. Alsace wines are unique among French wines in that almost all of them carry a grape variety name as well as a place-name (that is, Alsace). All Alsace wines come in a long-necked bottle called a *flûte*.

TECHNICAL STUFF

Considering Alsace's northerly latitude, you'd expect the region's climate to be cool. But, thanks to the protection of the Vosges Mountains to the west, Alsace's climate is quite sunny and temperate, and one of the driest in France.

Alsace has two sub-regions, or parts: the Bas-Rhin (bah-han) to the North and the Haut-Rhin (oh-han) to the South, along the lower slopes of the Vosges Mountains. As with most French wine regions, Alsace is divided into AOCs, with three major AOCs producing most of its wines: Alsace AOC (making more than 75 percent of the region's wines that are mostly still whites), Crémant d'Alsace AOC (nearly 25 percent of production focusing on sparkling wines from white and red grapes), and Alsace Grand Cru AOC (51 smaller but higher-quality production vineyard plots).

Although Alsace makes some red wine and a little rosé from pinot noir, 90 percent of Alsace's wines are white. Four are particularly important: riesling, pinot blanc, pinot gris, and gewürztraminer. Commonly dubbed the "Noble Grapes of Alsace," each reflects the characteristics of its grape, but they all share a depth of aromatics that can only be described as the flavor of Alsace.

>> Riesling is the king of Alsace wines. Alsatian riesling has a fruity aroma but a firm, dry, almost steely taste. Although it can be consumed young, riesling from a good vintage can easily age and improve for ten years or more. Rieslings are in the $22 to $50 price range. *Grand Cru* Rieslings can be more costly.

REAL DEAL

>> Pinot blanc is the lightest of the four wines. Some producers make their pinot blanc medium-dry, while others make classic, bone-dry pinot blanc. Either way, it's best young. Pinot blanc can sell for $17 to $30 a bottle.

>> Pinot gris is made from the same variety that you find in Italy as pinot grigio (see Chapter 5). Here in Alsace, it's a rich, spicy, full-bodied, wine full of character. Alsace's pinot gris retails for $20 to $40 per bottle and is known to stand up to spicier and/or sweet and sour foods.

TIP

>> Gewürztraminer has such intense, tropical fruit (lychee in particular), and spicy aromas that it's a love-it-or-leave-it wine. In fact, the name *Gewürz* translates to spice in German, while *Traminer* is the older name of this beloved grape. If you haven't tried an Alsace gewürztraminer yet, you haven't tasted one of the most distinctive wines in the world. Alsatian gewürztraminer gives an impression of both fullness and softness. Gewurztraminer sells mainly for $18 to $22, with the best examples over $25. It does not age as well as riesling so drink it when it's young.

TIP

Besides the grape variety name, you'll see many other words on labels of Alsace wines, such as *Reserve* (an unofficial term) and *Grand Cru*, as well as single-vineyard names. Most producers make numerous wines from each grape variety because the vineyards can differ markedly, and they use these label designations to distinguish their various wines.

Two types of dessert wine are made in Alsace: Vendanges Tardives (late harvest) and Sélection de Grains Nobles. Vendages Tardives wines are only produced using riesling, pinot blanc, pinot gris, and gewürztraminer grapes. These wines may be made from grapes that have been infected with *Botrytis cinerea* (discussed earlier in this chapter). Typical tasting notes include dried and baked fruits, white flowers, honey, and spice. Sélection de Grains Nobles must be made from *Botrytis*-affected grapes only and can be designated as either Alsace AOC or Alsace Grand Cru AOC. Tasting notes may include pineapple, passionfruit, candied fruits, and spice.

Bugey, Jura, and Savoie

Three of France's more obscure wine regions have something in common: they're located in the foothills and slopes of the Alps in eastern France, next to Switzerland — where skiers are probably the most avid fans. They are Bugey, the Jura (joo-rah) and Savoie (sah-v'wah) — sometimes anglicized as "Savoy."

Bugey lies south of Jura and west of Savoie, and makes sparkling, white, rosé, and red wines. It is most known for its sparkling wines made from jacquère and mondeuse blance, also known as molette.

Jura makes two interesting wines that are the region's specialties:

>> Vin Jaune (van-joh'n), from the savagnin variety, is comparable to a light Spanish fino sherry (see Chapter 7), but it's not fortified. Some of the highest-quality Vin Jaune producers include Château-Chalon, Rolet Père et Fils, Domaine de Savagny, and Raphael Fumey et Adeline Chatelain.

> **»** Vin de Paille (van deh pah'ee) is known as *Straw Wine* because of the tradi-tional way in which it's made: The grapes (savagnin, chardonnay, and others) are harvested late and arranged to dry on straw mats or in baskets in attics — similar to Tuscany's specialty, *vin santo* (see Chapter 5). The resulting wine is rich, concentrated, nutty, and raisiny.

Savoie's wines, mainly white, are typically dry but fruit-forward and bright in acidity. The main grapes include jacquère, altesse, and chasselas. Seyssel (say-sell), Savoie's best-known AOC, is known for its slightly sparkling wines as well as its still whites made from altesse and molette.

The south and southwest: Fun in the sun

The south of France is its oldest wine-producing area: The Greeks made wine in Provence as early as 500 BCE! The south is also the part of France that makes the most wine. Languedoc-Roussillon produces from 30 to 40 percent of France's wine in most years!

Southwest France

Southwest France, the huge area between Bordeaux and the Spanish border, has experienced a wine renaissance. There are 30 AOCs in Southwest France alone. The region is France's fifth-largest wine producer. Like the south (detailed later in this section), it's mainly red wine country, but you can find some interesting whites, rosés, sparkling wines, and dessert wines as well.

The Southwest is comprised of four sub-regions with their own AOCs that differ in *terroir*, grapes, and wines. They are named for proximity to their rivers and mountain ranges.

> **»** Bergerac and Dordogne River, specializing in sauvignon blanc, sèmillon, chenin blanc, muscadelle, and other indigenous varieties for whites, in addition to cabernet franc, merlot, malbec (called *Côt* here), and indigenous varieties such as mérille.

> **»** Tarn-et-Garonne, growing grapes from Bergerac and Dordogne River areas plus gamay, pinot noir, syrah, and native varieties such as duras. Whites include native varieties like mauzac and saint côme.

> **»** Lot River — held up by the Cahors (cah-or) AOC — is the most famous region for French malbec. Nowhere else in the world, except Argentina (see Chapter 12),

does this variety play such an important role. The best wines of high-quality producers like Château Vigouroux, Château Lagrezette, or Château de Haute-Serre Clare are dark, tannic reds selling for $100 or more and need about ten years of aging before they mature.

>> Pyrénées, specializing in petit and gros manseng, manseng noir, tannat, and indigenous varieties like courbou.

Three other districts to note in this region specialize in white dessert wines: Gaillac (gah-yack), Jurançon (joo-rahn-sohn), and Monbazillac (mon-bah-zee-yak). Gaillac also makes fruity, lightly sparkling wines. Other red wines of note include madiran (a full-bodied, tannic red made from tannat along with cabernet sauvignon and cabernet franc), and irouléguy (ee-roo-leh-gee; a spicy, tannic red wine made from tannat, cabernet franc, and cabernet). Some irouléguy rosé and white wines are also made.

The large IGP designation (see the earlier section on "The Laws and the Labels") of Côtes de Gascogne lies between Bordeaux and the Spanish border. It includes the area of Armagnac, the popular home of a brandy with the same name. Wine laws in this region are generally more relaxed in terms of permitted grapes and styles, which allows for greater flexibility and experimentation. Whites, ambers, rosés, and reds are emerging from Côtes de Gascogne with increasing popularity in export markets.

Not to be confused with cognac, armagnac is made by distilling wine from a blend of grapes, typically some combination of baco, colombard, folle blanche, and ugni blanc. The resulting spirit is aged in French oak barrels for at least one year, and typically consumed as a *digestif* (a beverage typically consumed after dinner to aid with digestion).

Languedoc-Roussillon

The sunny, dry Languedoc-Roussillon (lahn-gweh-doc-roo-see-yohn) region, also known as the *Midi* (mee-dee), is France's largest wine-producing area. The region makes mainly red wines. In fact, more than half of France's red wines come from here. Traditionally, these robust red wines came from typical grape varieties of the south, such as carignan, cinsault, and grenache. But in the last two decades, more prestigious varieties, such as syrah, cabernet sauvignon, and merlot, have become common. Winemakers use these grapes both for varietal wines and in blends.

REAL DEAL

From this region, look for the red wines from the AOC zones of Corbières, Minervois, Saint-Chinian, Fitou, and Costières de Nîmes. In addition, many varietal wines carrying the designation *Vin de Pays d'Oc* are often good value. They're made from grapes that come from anywhere in the Languedoc-Roussillon region, rather than from a specific AOC zone. One amazing white varietal wine is picpoul de pinet, a racy, lively, mineral-driven wine that sells in the $12 to $15 range. Look for it!

Provence

Provence (pro-vahns) — southeast of the Rhône Valley, east of Languedoc-Roussillon, and west of northern Italy — may be France's most beautiful region. Home of the Riviera, Nice, and Cannes, it's certainly the country's most fashionable and touristy region. But it's also an ancient land, with a thriving old capital, Aix-en-Provence (eks-ahn-proh-vahns). The stunning sunlight and climate have always attracted great artists (including Vincent van Gogh) who painted many of their best works here.

Wine has always been part of Provence's culture and economy. Provence is best known for its rosés, which so many tourists enjoy on the Riviera. There are more than 600 rosés made in Provence alone! Rosé wines dominate in the region's largest AOC wine zone, Côtes de Provence; but in three other important AOC zones—Coteaux d'Aix-en-Provence, Les Baux-de-Provence, and Bandol — red wines rule.

Bandol is often considered the only region of Provence where mourvèdre grapes can thrive at their full potential. The region's *terroir* is ideal for mourvèdre, with lots of sun, clay soils, and cooling ocean breezes. In addition to mourvèdre, red wines are made from carignan, cinsault, grenache, and syrah. Whites are made from clairette, bourboulenc, marsanne, ugni blanc, and vermentino. Some of Bandol's top producers include Domaine Tempier, Château Pibarnon, Domaine Marie Berenice, Domaine Le Galantin, Château Vannières, and Domaine La Suffrène.

Cassis (no relation to the blackcurrant liqueur of the same name), a small AOC zone on the Mediterranean coast near Marseilles, makes distinctive, aromatic white wines. The main varieties in white cassis are clairette and Marsanne.

Corsica

Corsica is a large, very mountainous island 100 miles southeast of Provence. North of the Italian island of Sardinia, Corsica traces its winemaking at least as far back as the 13th century when it was under control of the Italian city-state of Genoa. Corsica was ceded to France in 1768, but maintained a rich mixture of French and Italian culture. Corsica has nine AOC wine zones.

Corsica came into international prominence for its wines in the last decade. Its warm, dry climate lends the island to the production of red wines. It is best known for its medium-bodied, well-priced rosés and reds. The Patrimonio wine region on the northern coast of Corsica became the island's first AOC zone in 1968, and it still produces Corsica's best red wines, called patrimonio, made from sangiovese (called nielluccio locally). Patrimonio also produces a white wine, patrimonio blanc (made from vermentino or vermentinu locally), and some rosé wine. Ajaccio is a second important AOC region on the southwestern coast, mainly known for red wines. Grenache is a major red variety on Corsica, along with many other typical Rhône varieties.

WORTH THE SEARCH

Although much of patrimonio and its other wines are consumed on the island, Corsica continues to develop its export market focused on great value wines. They start at $15 and can go up to $40 for some of the more prestigious producers.

Chapter **7**

Spain: Con Vino

La Liga, flamenco, matadors, tapas — so much of the world's experience with Spain revolves around these cultural traditions. None of them are complete without *vino* (wine). Although Spain can sometimes feel tucked away behind wine giants such as Italy and France (see Chapters 5 and 6, respectively), it's actually the country with the most vines planted in the entire world. While production and export typically trails that of France and Italy, Spain's quality and distinct character is in a league of its own.

In this chapter, we discuss the major wine regions of Spain, taking into account the vast differences in *terroir* from region to region (check out Chapter 2 for more on *terroir*). This chapter should be enjoyed as it would in Spain — *con vino* (with wine)!

The Laws and the Labels

Spain's system of classification shares similarities to those of France, Italy, and Portugal, especially in its recognition that certain wines and their styles are tied to distinct regions. The modern-day system also follows the European Union (EU's) Protected Geographical Indication (IGP) approach by identifying unique geographical areas for wine throughout the country (see Chapter 2).

Spain's modern-day system includes four tiers, from least to most prestigious:

>> ***Vino de La Tierra*** **(VT):** The only EU IGP category, allowing the most flexibility for winemaking grapes and styles.

>> ***Denominación de Origen Protegida*** **(DOP):** This includes most of Spain's wine zones (68 at the time of writing) and has requirements for permitted varieties, styles, and aging. It includes still, sparkling, and fortified wine regions.

>> ***Vino de Pago:*** This is for individual wine estates (*pago*) that have earned special status separate from the DOP zone the estate is in. Requirements for this category include single-estate production and bottling. Twenty-five wine estates are classified at the time of writing.

>> ***Denominación de Origen Calificada*** **(DOCa):** The highest designation, including requirements for regional production, bottling, aging, and cost. Only Rioja and Priorat currently hold this status.

Interestingly, producers in Spain are not required to include any of this information on their labels, allowing winemakers the opportunity to emphasize those aspects of their wines that they believe are most important. Instead of focusing on the denomination, many producers prefer to use aging categories to give consumers a sense of what they will discover when they open the bottle.

You may see some of the following terms on a Spanish wine label. Here's what they mean:

>> **Blanco (*blan-ko*):** White.

>> **Tinto (*teen-toe*):** Red. "Tinto Fino" refers to the tempranillo grape specifically in Ribera del Duero, but it can refer to other red grapes more generally in other regions. On labels from places like Toro, you may see the phrase "Tinta de Toro." This too, is tempranillo.

>> **Bodega:** Winery.

>> **Cosecha (*coh-seh-cha*)** or **Vendimia (*ven-dee-me-yah*):** Vintage year.

>> **Crianza (*cree-ahn-tha*):** For red wines, this means that the wine has aged for two years with at least six months in oak. For white and rosé wines, *crianza* means that the wines aged for a minimum of 18 months with at least six months in oak barrels for whites specifically (for more on the role of oak in wine production, see Chapter 3). These rules sometimes vary by region.

>> **Reserva:** Wines produced in the better vintages: red *reservas* must age for a minimum of three years, including one year in oak barrels, while white *reservas* must age for two years, including six months in oak barrels.

>> **Gran reserva:** Wines produced only in exceptional vintages: red wines must age at least five years, including a minimum of two years in oak barrels. White *gran reservas* (made mostly in Rioja) must age at least four years before release, including six months in oak barrels.

Regions, Varieties, and Styles

Spain is an extremely mountainous country, and while most of the country is hot and dry, it's also home to a range of *mesoclimates* (the climate of a distinct area that is larger than a microclimate of one vineyard, for example) that make for wines of distinct styles and character. Mountains are almost everywhere in Spain. These mountains influence winemaking by tempering climates, allowing for more vine exposure to sunlight, and offering better drainage. The resulting wines can have balanced acidity and a range of dry to more ripe fruit flavors.

Spain has 12 major wine regions (see the color section of this book) with a range of soil types that impact wines. These include clay, limestone, slate, granite, schist, and of course the beautiful white, chalky soils of the southwest known as *albariza (al-ba-ree-za)*, which are special for the Jerez (*he-reth*) region in particular. We discuss each of the major regions based on their geographic location within the broader Iberian Peninsula.

TECHNICAL STUFF

Spanish winemaking history dates back to at least 1100 BCE, when Phoenicians (semitic populations that lived in the eastern Mediterranean, covering what is now Israel, Lebanon, and Syria) starting making sweet wines and aging them in large clay amphorae. Evidence suggests that the Phoenicians brought the tempranillo (*tem-pra-nee-yo*) grape with them, which happens to be Spain's most popular grape to this day. Fast-forward to the 20th century, a period of tremendous growth for Spain as a serious wine contender on the global stage, with Rioja as its first named *Denominación de Origen* (DO, now called *Denominación de Origen Protegida*, or DOP) in 1925. The 1932 creation of the DO statute permitted wine regions to also form their own *Consejo Regulador*, tasked with the responsibility of monitoring quality control, inspecting facilities, deciding regional boundaries, and so forth.

While there is still a wave of Spanish wine with questionable quality making its way to the shop shelf for under $8 a bottle, Spain's higher-quality options are on the rise for white, rosé, red, sparkling, and of course, sherry.

The north

The north is the heart of Spain's high-quality wine renaissance. It's home to the powerful trifecta of Rioja, Ribera del Duero, and Priorat. It's also the center for some of Spain's most popular white wines.

La Rioja: Spain's lady in red

The northern DOCa region of La Rioja (or simply Rioja, pronounced *ree-oh-hah*), has historically been the country's preeminent red wine epicenter. Red wines seriously dominate: About 85 percent of the region's wines are red, while 15 percent are *rosado* (rosé) and white. Nearly 600 wineries now exist in Rioja.

The principal grape in Rioja is tempranillo — Spain's greatest red variety. This is a thick-skinned red grape that can vary significantly depending on vinification and aging preferences of the winemaker. Some common tasting notes include ripe red or black cherries, savory herbs, and vanilla. Aging often adds notes of leather, tobacco, and forest floor. Regulations permit another three varieties of grape for reds: garnacha (*gar-nah-cha*), known elsewhere as grenache; graciano (*gra-thee-awn-oh*), known elsewhere as carignan; and mazuelo (*mah-thu-e-lo*). Red Rioja wine is typically a blend of these varieties. Marqués de Riscal is one of a few wineries legally allowed to use cabernet sauvignon in its Rioja blend, because this variety was growing on its property before regulations for Rioja existed.

The Rioja region has three districts: the cooler, Atlantic-influenced Rioja Alta and Rioja Alavesa, and the warmer, more southern Rioja Oriental zone. Most of the best Riojas are made from grapes in the two cooler districts, but some Riojas are blended from grapes of all three.

Rioja winemaking historically involved lengthy French oak-aging processes that resulted in pale, light, and lifeless wines because of overexposure to oxygen. Beginning in the 1990s, winemakers increasingly adopted the economical approach of importing American oak for local cooperage, rather than importing pre-made French oak barrels. The practice has generally stuck since then with some variations according to region. A more recent trend has been to replace some of the oak aging with bottle aging, resulting in wines that taste much fresher and vibrant. Today, more progressive winemakers use a combination of French and American oak. The American oak has traditionally given Rioja its characteristic vanilla aroma.

Red Rioja wines come in several versions, and the amount of time they're aged before release drives their designation and marketing:

>> **Some wines receive no oak aging at all and are released young. These youthful, lighter wines are usually referred to as *joven* (young).** Some producers use the term *Sin Crianza,* meaning "without aging." Sometimes, only the absence of one of the three terms below tells you that the wine is not aged. Most *rosado* and white wines are *joven*.

>> **Some wines age for two years (with at least 12 months in the barrel and 12 months in the bottle) at the winery and are labeled *Crianza*.** These wines are still fresh and fruity in style.

>> **Other wines age for three years (with at least 12 months in barrel) and carry the designation *Reserva*.**

>> **The finest wines age for five years or longer (with at least two years in the barrel), earning the status of *Gran Reserva*.**

The aging terms appear on the labels — if not on the front label, and on a rear label, which carries the seal of authenticity for Rioja wines.

Prices generally start at $14 for the youngest Riojas, including *rosados* and whites, $14 and up for *crianza* reds, and $20 and up for Rioja *Reservas*. *Gran Reservas* can start at $25 and increase substantially from there. The best recent vintages for Rioja are 2021, 2019, and 2015.

TIP

Many of Rioja's top producers are exported and readily available in larger wine shops or grocery stores. The names to know include Bodegas Faustino, Bodegas Muga, CVNE (Compañía Vinícola del Norte de España) commonly referred to as CUNE (*coo*-nay), Marqués de Murrieta, La Rioja Alta, Marqués de Riscal, and Roda.

WORTH THE SEARCH

White Rioja also exists. Most of them are fresh, clean, fairly neutral wines, but Marqués de Murrieta and R. López de Heredia still make traditional white Rioja: golden-colored and oak-aged, from a blend of local white grape varieties, predominantly viura.

Ribera del Duero: Rocky red paradise

Ribera del Duero, two hours north of Madrid in Castilla y León, is one of Spain's most dynamic wine regions. Perhaps nowhere else in the world does tempranillo (called *Tinto Fino* here, technically a set of tempranillo clones different from that in Rioja) reach such heights. This region makes mostly ferocious, gritty, full-bodied red wines. If you visit Ribera del Duero, you will understand why we use such strong words to describe it: this is a dry, extremely rocky region where very old vines (most over 35 years old) continue to struggle and strive. Only red wines are categorized into *Crianza*, *Reserva*, and *Gran Reserva*.

For many years, one producer, the legendary Vega Sicilia, dominated the Ribera del Duero area. In fact, Spain's single most famous great wine is Vega Sicilia's Unico (mainly tempranillo, with 20 percent cabernet sauvignon) — an intense, concentrated, tannic red wine with enormous longevity. This wine ages for ten years in casks and then sometimes ages further in the bottle before it's released. Unico is available mainly in top Spanish restaurants. Its latest vintage in the United States, 2010, sells for nearly $800 in retail stores. Even Unico's younger, less concentrated, more available sibling, Vega Sicilia Tinto Valbueno, retails for about $200.

Many other prestigious wines have come on the Ribera del Duero scene since Vega Sicilia. Alejandro Fernández's Pesquera, entirely tempranillo, has earned high praise over the past few decades, and comes in both *Crianza* and *Reserva* styles. Additional producers to note are Aalto, Bodegas Mauro, Bodegas Téofilo Reyes, Pingus, and Viña Pedrosa.

Priorat: Keeping faith in the mountains

In the 12th century, Carthusian monks founded a monastery (or *priory*) in the isolated Sierra de Montsant Mountains of Catalonia, about 100 miles southwest of Barcelona. They meticulously planted vines on the steep hillsides, and used wine to celebrate Catholic mass and generate income for the monastery. Similar to the Benedictine and Cistercian monks of Burgundy, the Carthusian monks also conducted a lot of research on viticulture to evolve their techniques and enhance each harvest. The 1800s marked a period of dramatic shift for life in the mountains: the Spanish government appropriated most church-owned land, including vineyards, and restributed it to citizens who (it was argued) would use the land more efficiently. Coupled with the phylloxera outbreak of the 1880s (see Chapter 2), winemaking became somewhat of an afterthought for the smaller populations who remained in the region, and many vineyards either remained dormant or closed all together.

Winemaking slowly came back to the fore in the 1950s, but the most notable revival period took place from the late 1970s through the 1990s. Enterprising winemakers, among them Alvaro Palacios and René Barbier among others re-engaged the area and determined that conditions were ideal for making powerful red wines, especially from old vines planted in the 20th century. Wines from previously hidden (quite literally in the mountains) vineyards became serious contenders in the spotlight. The region's dark (dubbed *llicorella*) volcanic soils, composed mainly of slate and schist, turned out to be the bedrock of amazing red wines in particular. The climate is harshly continental: very hot, dry summers and very cold winters. The steep slopes are terraced, requiring that most vineyards be worked by hand. Grape yields are very low, forcing the vines to dig deep and produce wines with pronounced structure and intensity. Today, Priorat is the only other wine region in Spain apart from Rioja to hold a DOCa designation.

Amazingly rich, powerful red wines — made primarily from garnacha and cariñena (Carignan), two of Spain's native varieties — have emerged from this challenging landscape. Additional planted varieties include cabernet sauvignon, merlot, syrah, and tempranillo. Many are as rugged as the land, tannic, and alcoholic. Some wines are so high in alcohol that they have an almost port-like sweetness, with a rich, black molasses look to them (find out more about port in Chapter 9). Because winemaking in Priorat isn't cost-effective, to say the least, and the quantities of each wine are so small, the wines are necessarily quite expensive (prices begin at about $40 per bottle). Clos Erasmus, arguably the finest Priorat, retails in the $300 range.

TIP

Top-quality Priorat producers include Alvaro Palacios, Clos Erasmus, Clos Martinet, Clos Mogador, Marco Abella, Morlanda, Mas d'en Gil, and Pasanau.

A LITTLE FRENCH IN PRIORAT

Priorat winemakers have developed their own culture for winemaking that fits the *terroir* of the region and reflects the expertise of its "newer" generation. The region has its own classification system that is tied very closely to site quality and vineyard age. Similar to France's AOC system described in Chapter 6, the Priorat system includes (from least to most prestigious): *DOQ Priorat* (entry-level); *Vi de Vila* (village-level designated areas); *Vi de Paratge* (more prestigious areas, requiring that 90 percent of vineyards must be at least 15 years old and the remaining 10 percent must be at least five years old); *Vinya Classificada* (similar to France's *Premier Crus*, requiring that 80 percent of vineyards must be at least 20 years old and the remaining 20 percent must be at least five years old); and *Gran Vinya Classificada* (similar to *Grand Crus* of Burgundy, requiring that 80 percent of the vineyards must be at least 35 years old and the remaining 20 percent must be at least 10 years old). Finally, the current system requires that vines be at least 75 years old to be labeled "old vines." This term can be applied all classifications where the 75-year rule is met. The designation process is managed by the *Consejo Regulador* in Priorat.

You may see the term *Clos* (vineyard in French) attached to certain Priorat producers. This practice and the use of more French than American oak (some producers believe French oak imparts more subtle flavors to grapes such as cariñena and garnacha) and you've got more than a little French in your Spanish wine!

Penedés: Pop, fizz, and Torres

The Penedés wine region is in Catalonia, which is technically an autonomous community (considered a nationality with its own language) of Spain's northeast. Besides being home to some of Spain's most famed artists and architects (including Antonio Gaudí, Pablo Picasso, and Salvador Dalí, to name a few), Penedés is best known as the home of cava. Dating back to 1872, *cava* is Spain's traditional method (*método tradicional*) sparkling wine that is required by law to be made in this style. Cava has its own DOP, but it can technically be produced in the eight regions of Aragon, Castilla y León, Extremadura, La Rioja, Basque Country, Navarra, and Valencia.

TECHNICAL STUFF

While legends like Dom Pérignon and Madam Clicquot changed the way champagne would be made forever (see Chapter 6), Spaniards were simulataneously trying to find their own ways to drive efficiency in production. Although the original design is sometimes disputed as having come from French winemakers, the gyropallate as we know it — called a *girasol* in Spanish — was invented and first implemented successfully in Penedès. The *gyropallate* saves thousands of hours traditionally spent *riddling* bottles (rotating them a fraction of a turn to push all sediment into the neck of the bottle, also called *remuage*) by automating this process for hundreds of bottles at at time (504 bottles to be exact for a standard size).

Most cavas use Spanish grape varieties — specifically macabeo, parellada, and xarello (pronounced *cha-rey-yo*) along with chardonnay, the native subirat variety, garnacha, monastrell, pinot noir, and treppat (also native to the region). As a result, these sparklers taste distinctly different from champagne in France or Franciacorta in Italy. Cava wines come in all sweetness levels, from *brut nature* (bone dry) to *dulce* (sweet) and in various aging categories, including *Reserva* and *Gran Reserva*.

REMEMBER

In the last ten years, two major groups have established separate, higher standards of quality for cava production. The first group devised the *Clàssic Penedès* category, which requires organic viticulture and stricter aging requirements (15 months instead of 9 months for entry-level cava; *Reservas* require 18 months and *Gran Reservas*, 30 months). The second group developed an association of producers called Corpinnat. Wines made with this distinction require both organic and sustainable certifications, a minimum of 90 percent indigenous varieties, estate-grown fruit, and at least 18 months of aging on the *lees* (spent yeast cells). While these subgroups and their requirements may seem daunting, we can taste a real difference in the cavas from Corpinnat. Some of our favorite producers include Gramona, Julia Bernet, Llopart, and Mas Candí.

TIP

Two gigantic wineries dominate Cava production — Freixenet (pronounced *fray-shuh-net*) and Codorníu (*koh-dor-new*). Freixenet's frosted black Cordon Negro bottle has to be one of the most recognizable wine bottles in the world. Other cava brands to look for are Jaume Serra Cristalino, Marqués de Monistrol, Mont Marçal, and Paul Cheneau. Juve y Camps, a vintage-dated, upscale Cava, is a worthwhile find.

Any discussion of Penedés's non-sparkling wines must begin with Torres, one of the world's great family-owned wineries. Around 1970, Miguel Torres pioneered the winemaking in Spain from French varieties, such as cabernet sauvignon and chardonnay, along with local grapes, such as tempranillo and garnacha. All the Torres wines are clean, well-made, reasonably priced, and widely available. Prices start around $14 for the red called Sangre de Toro (garnacha-carignan), $12 to $14 for Coronas (tempranillo/cabernet sauvignon), and $15 for the white Viña Sol. The top-of-the-line "Mas La Plana" black label, a powerful yet elegant cabernet sauvignon, starts at $65 to $70.

Rías Baixas: A breath of fresh (salty) air

Galicia — a province in northwest Spain, bordering the Atlantic Ocean and Portugal — historically was not known for its wine, probably because of its cool and rainy climate. But a small area in southern Galicia, called Rías Baixas (*ree-aahs by-shas*), has achieved international fame for an exciting white wine called Albariño (*al-bah-reen-yo*, called alvarinho in northern Portugal), made from the albariño grape. This region now boasts about 200 wineries, compared to only 60 in 1990, with many women winemakers as stars on the scene. Modern winemaking, the cool local climate, and low-yielding vines have combined to make albariño wines a huge success, especially in the United States, its leading market.

If you think that most of the region's albariño would taste the same, think again! This exciting region is divided into five subzones: Condado do Tea, O Rosal, Val do Salnés, Ribeira do Ulla, and Soutomaior. The wines from coastal subzones such as O Rosal and Val do Salnés can often have tart, green mango and pineapple-flavored wines with a special saline minerality suggesting the Atlantic Ocean's influence. Inland subzones such as Condado do Tea, Ribeira do Ulla, and Soutomaior are known for richer, more mouthfilling and even creamy wines packed with riper, juicier citrus and stone fruit flavors. While the majority of Rías Baíxas Albariño is stainless steel fermented to preserve freshness and allow the grape's natural expression to shine, others are given some oak or concrete aging which can add more texture, richness, and baked notes to the finished product. Bright acidity is common in wines throughout the region regardless of style.

Albariños to look for include Bodega Morgadío, Condes de Albarei, Fillaboa, Pazo de Barrantes, Pazos de Lusco, Pazo de Señorans, Pazo San Mauro, Terras Gauda, and Valminor.

Another white varietal wine, godello (go-dey-yo), grows mainly in Galicia (outside of Rías Baixas) and nearby locations in northwest Spain. The Cinderella story is that godello was practically extinct in 1970, but then rediscovered and replanted. Now it is one of the hottest wines in Spain: it is spicy, fruity, and ages well.

Navarra: Bullish reds

Once upon a time, the word *Navarra* conjured up images of inexpensive, easy-drinking dry rosé wines (or, to the more adventurous, memories of running the bulls in Pamplona, Navarra's capital city). Today, the Navarra region, just northeast of Rioja, is known for its red wines, which are similar to but somewhat less expensive than the more famous wines of Rioja.

Many Navarra reds rely on tempranillo, along with garnacha, but you can also find cabernet sauvignon, merlot, and various blends of all four varieties in the innovative Navarra region. Look for the wines of Bodegas Guelbenzu, Bodegas Julián Chivite, and Bodegas Magaña.

País Vasco: Ancient wine and culture

Translating literally to "Basque Country", this northernmost region has its own distinct history and culture in Spain. First and foremost, the Basque people are likely descendents of North African migrants that arrived in the region somewhere between 4,000 and 8,000 years ago. Second, they speak a language called Euskara — a dialect that is not related to any other language on the continent of Europe. Third — and most exciting for us — the Basque people have grown grapes and made their own wine on the cold, Atlantic Ocean-facing limestone hills of the region for centuries. The Basque people even have their own way of pouring local wines into a glass (often times from mid-air)!

The main wine to note here is txakoli (*cha-ko-lee)*, a white wine made primarily from a group of native varieties collectively referred to as hondarribi zuri (*hon-dah-ra-bee zoo-ree*). These include courbu blanc, crouchen, and noah. Additional white grapes planted include folle blanche, petit manseng, and gros manseng. Txakoli wines are light and full of tart, stone fruit and citrus flavors. They have a fresh, light, sometimes slightly effervescent, punch-you-in-the-face acidity that makes them unique. Hondarribi beltza is the most well-known red variety, producing mineral-driven, lighter-style reds and rosés meant for immediate drinking.

Aragón: Garnacha and more

Sandwiched between the cold Pyrenees Mountains in the north and the hot Montenegros desert to the south, this small area is home to Calatayud, Campo de Borja, Cariñena, and Somontano regions. Soils of clay, iron, limestone, and black and red slate result in wines that vary based on location and DOP. The most preeminent wines to note are the grenache-driven reds from Calatayud and Campo de Borja. Top-quality producers include Bodegas Aragonesas (Campo de Borja), Baltasar (Calatayud), Bodegas Osca (Somontano), Bodegas San Valero (Cariñena), Borsao (Calatayud), and Cuevas de Arom (Campo de Borja).

Bierzo: Mencía on the rise

Bierzo is another smaller region in northwest Spain, east of Rías Baixas. Bierzo is a mountainous area with steep vineyard slopes, specializing in godello for white wine and mencia (*men-thee-ah)* for red. Nearly 60 percent of red wine from Bierzo is mencia. Wine production is fairly small, but Bierzo's wines are developing something of a cult following among Spanish wine lovers. The godello wines tend to have white flower, citrus, mineral, and nutty flavors, and a medium to fuller body. Red wines are what we would call "spicy" with lively acidity and red fruit notes. Most Bierzo wines retail in the $15 to $25 range, although a few are quite expensive. High-quality producers include Emilio Moro, Descendientes de J. Palacios, and Raúl Pérez.

El Toro: Tinto de Toro

The Toro region in northwest Spain, northwest of Ribera del Duero, made wines in the Middle Ages that were quite famous in Spain. But it's a hot, arid area with poor soil that rendered winemaking almost impossible for centuries. Toro has been rediscovered among other regions in Spain's recent wine boom. Winemakers have determined that the climate and soil are actually ideal for making powerful, tannic red wines — mainly from the tempranillo variety (called *Tinto de Toro* here) — which rival the wines of Toro's neighbors in Ribera del Duero. Toro wines to find include those of Bodegas Fariña, Bodegas y Vinedos Dos Victorias, Dehesa La Granja, Bodegas Estancia Piedra, Gil Luna, and Vega Saúco. Retail prices start at about $16, but the best examples can be $50 and higher.

Rueda: The best verdejo

REAL DEAL

The Rueda (*roo-eh-dah)* region, west of Ribera del Duero, produces one of Spain's best white wines from the verdejo grape. The wine is clean and fresh, has delicious fruitiness, and sells for an affordable $12 to $18 per bottle. The Rioja producer Marqués de Riscal makes one of the leading and most available examples.

Central Spain

Probably known more for its medieval history (hello, Don Quixote!), garlic, Manchego cheese, and saffron, Castilla-La Mancha is the largest wine-producing region (and DOP) in Spain and one of the largest in the world. There are oceans of wine made here in the region's more than 30,000 square miles, most of which are in higher altitudes. Castilla-La Mancha is mostly on the southern plateau of the Maseta, and surrounded by the Central, Iberian, and Sierra Morena mountain ranges. Most days are hot, dry, and sunny. Most nights are cool, but still dry. Both native and international varieties are planted here, including airén, macabeo (viura), chardonnay, and viognier among others for whites, in addition to the increasingly popular bobal, listán prieto, garnacha, monastrell, tempranillo, and red Bordeaux varieties. High-quality producers from this region include Envínante, Bodega Loranque, and Bodegas Ponce La Casilla.

The south

Moving south of Madrid, things get a little warmer and spicier in Spain's southern wine regions. Read on for more about Jumilla (the Spanish heart of monastrell), Jerez and Montilla (Spain's sherry-producing centers), and the Canary Islands (offering unique varieties such as listán negro and malvasia volcanica).

Jumilla: Monastrell, anyone?

Although vineyards are still at high altitudes in Spain's southern regions (as are most throughout Spain thanks to mountains everywhere), many vineyards are planted in the valleys west of the Mediterranean sea. Jumilla DOP is monastrell land, brought to the region from France as mourvèdre and now known locally as either monastrell or mataró.

Most of the exported monastrell in the 1990s and early 2000s were lighter to medium-bodied wines that were more simple and straightforward in red fruit and spice. However, there are many examples on today's market that are rich, powerful, and full of character. High-quality producers include more storied estates and new generations: Alceño, Bleda, Fuente Álamo, Juan Gil, José Maria Vicente, Silvano Garcia, and Viña Elena.

Jerez: The sherry bomb

We aren't sure why, but somehow sherry got a reputation for being the unwanted stepsister of other *fortified wines* such as port and madeira (detailed in Chapter 9). This is changing, and fast! Sherry is a wine of true quality and diversity, but it remains undiscovered by most of the world, including much of Spain itself (try getting a glass of sherry in a bar in Madrid or Barcelona). But even as wine drinkers find pleasure elsewhere, some connoisseurs are becoming ever more passionate about sherry, and gradually raising awareness about this delicious wine.

THE JEREZ TRIANGLE

Sherry comes from the Andalucía region of sun-baked, southwestern Spain. The wine is named after Jerez (*her-eth*) de la Frontera, an old town of Moorish and Arab origin where many of the sherry *bodegas* are located (*bodega* can refer to the actual building in which sherry is matured or to the sherry firm itself.) Actually, the town of Jerez is just one edge of a triangle that makes up the Jerez-Xérès DOP. Another edge is Puerto de Santa María, a beautiful, old coastal town southwest of Jerez and home to a number of large bodegas. The third edge of the triangle, Sanlúcar de Barrameda (also on the coast but northwest of Jerez), is so blessed with sea breezes that the lightest and driest of sherries, *manzanilla* (*mahn-zah-nee-yah*), can legally be made only there. Aficionados of sherry swear that they can detect the salty tang of the ocean in manzanilla. Traveling from Sanlúcar to Jerez, you pass vineyards with dazzling white, rocky soil. This is *albariza*, the region's famous chalky earth, rich in limestone from fossilized shells. Summers are hot and dry, but balmy sea breezes temper the heat.

The palomino grape — the main variety used in sherry — thrives only in the hot sherry region on albariza soil. Palomino doesn't work so well for table wines because it is so neutral in flavor and low in acid, but it's perfect for sherry production. Two other grape varieties, pedro ximénez (*pay-dro he-men-ez*) and moscatel blanco (Muscat of Alexandria), are used for dessert styles of sherry.

THE SHERRY-MAKING PROCESS

Sherry is made on a complex spectrum that can be divided into seven or more distinct styles. At the lightest end of the spectrum are manzanilla and fino sherries that are light and very dry. At the heaviest end are cream and pedro ximénez. These tend to have higher levels of fortification and sweetness (with sherries like pedro ximénez sweet enough to serve as dessert on their own). Sweeter sherries are made in one of two ways. One approach is to use varieties that are naturally high in sugar, such as moscatel or pedro ximénez, which are often sun-dried to concentrate their sugars. The second approach is to blend a dry style sherry with a naturally sweet sherry like pedro ximénez to achieve a desired sweetness level.

After initial fermentation, the winemaker decides which sherries will evolve into which styles (see the next section) by judging the appearance, aroma, and flavor of the young, unfortified wines. If a wine is to become a manzanilla or fino, the winemaker fortifies it lightly by adding neutral grape spirit until its alcohol level reaches about 15.5%. Olorosos can be strengthened to 17% or more, and cream and pedro ximénez to upwards of to 22%.

At this point, when the wines are in casks, the special sherry magic begins: A yeast called *flor* grows spontaneously on the surface of the wines destined to be manzanillas and finos. The flor eventually covers the whole liquid surface, protecting the wine from oxidation. Unlike other yeasts that feed on sugar in the grapes, flor feeds on oxygen in the air and on (already converted) alcohol and glycerin in the wine. It changes the wine's character, contributing a distinct aroma and flavor and rendering the wine thinner and more delicate in texture. Flor doesn't grow on oloroso, cream, or pedro ximénez sherries because their higher alcohol content prevents it. Without the protection of the flor (and because the casks are never filled to the brim), these wines are exposed to oxygen as they age. This deliberate oxidation is also what protects them against further oxidation (for example, after you open a bottle).

TECHNICAL STUFF

All styles of sherry age in a way that's unique to sherry production. To make sherry, the young wine isn't left to age on its own (as most other wines would) but is added to casks of older wine that are already aging. To make room for the young wine, some of the older wine is emptied or drawn out of the casks and is added to casks of even older wine in a magnificent, symphonic pyramid of 500 liter (usually black) casks called *butts*. Imagining rows of casks in a pyramid, each level is called a *criadera*. The oldest wines sit at the base of the pyramid. To make room in the older casks, some of that wine is transferred to casks of even older wine, and so on. At the end of this chain, four to nine generations away from the young wine, some of the finished sherry is taken from the oldest casks and bottled for sale. This system of blending wines is called *solera*. It takes its name from the word *solera* (floor), the term also used to identify the casks of oldest wine. See this book's color section for an illustration of this process.

As wines are blended — younger into older, into yet older, and eventually into oldest — no more than a third of the wine is emptied from any cask. In theory, then, each *solera* contains small (and ever-decreasing) amounts of very old wine. As each younger wine mingles with older wine, it takes on characteristics of the older wine. Within a few months, the wine of each generation is indistinguishable from what it was before being refreshed with younger wine. Thus, the *solera* system maintains infinite consistency of quality and style in sherry. It is also never vintage-dated for this reason.

REMEMBER

Because sherry ages in casks of dry, airy bodegas above ground (rather than humid, underground cellars like most other wines), some of the wine's water evaporates, and the wine's alcoholic strength increases. Some sherries aged for more than ten years can be as much as 24% alcohol, compared to their starting point of 18%.

THE SHERRY SPECTRUM

So far, so good: a spectrum of sherry styles — delicate manzanilla and fino aged under protective flor on one end, and fuller oloroso, cream, and pedro ximénez aged oxidatively. New styles occur when the natural course of aging changes the character of a sherry so that its taste no longer conforms to the extreme ends of the spectrum. Deliberate sweetening of the wine also creates different styles.

The seven main styles of sherry that you will encounter are:

>> **Fino:** Pale, straw-colored, light in body, dry, and delicate. Fino sherries always mature under flor, either in Jerez or Puerto de Santa María. The aroma of fino sherry is often compared with almonds. After they lose their protective flor (by bottling), finos become very vulnerable to oxidation spoilage, and you must store them in a cool place, drink them young, and refrigerate them after opening. Best when chilled.

>> **Manzanilla:** Pale, straw-colored, delicate, light, tangy, and very dry, made only in Sanlúcar de Barrameda. The temperate sea climate causes the flor to grow thicker in this town, and manzanilla is thus the driest and most pungent of all the sherries (some say it gets its name from chamomile, which is the English translation of manzanilla). Handle it similarly to a fino sherry. A *manzanilla pasada* has been aged in cask about seven years and has lost its flor. It's more amber in color than a *manzanilla fina* and fuller bodied. It's close to a dry amontillado in style, but still crisp and pungent. Serve cool.

>> **Amontillado (*ah-mon-tee-yah-doh*):** An aged sherry that had flor but lost it in the process of cask aging. It's deeper amber in color and richer and nuttier than the previous styles. Amontillados are said to smell like hazelnuts. These are dry, retaining some of their pungent tang from the lost flor. Serve amontillado slightly cool and, for best flavor, finish the bottle within a week.

>> **Palo cortado (*palo-cort-ado*):** The rarest of all sherries. In general, it starts out with flor and develops as an amontillado, losing its flor. But then, for some unknown reason, it begins to resemble the richer, more fragrant oloroso style, all the while retaining the elegance of an amontillado. In color and alcohol content, palo cortado is similar to an oloroso, but its aroma is quite like an amontillado. Like amontillado sherry, beware of cheap imitations. It keeps as well as oloroso. Serve at room temperature.

>> **Oloroso:** Dark gold to deep brown in color (depending on its age), full-bodied with rich, raisiny, walnut-like flavors, but dry. Olorosos lack the delicacy and pungency of flor-based sherries. They're usually between 18% and 20% alcohol and can keep for a few weeks after you open the bottle because they have already been oxidized in their aging. Serve at room temperature.

>> **Medium:** Made by blending amontillado or oloroso with sweeter sherries or wines, including pedro ximénez or muscatel. This is a sweeter style with residual sugar that ranges anywhere from 5 to 115 grams per liter! Medium sherries can be amber or burnt orange in color with aromas of quince jam or apple pastries.

- **» Cream:** Cream and the lighter "milk" sherries are rich *amorosos* (the term for sweetened olorosos). They are popular and vary in quality, depending on the oloroso used. They can also improve in the bottle with age. Pale cream is made by blending fino and light amontillado sherries and lightly sweetening the blend. They have a very pale gold color. Pale cream is a fairly new style.

- **» Pedro ximénez and moscatel:** Extremely sweet, dark brown, syrupy dessert sherries. Often lower in alcohol, these Sherries are made from raisined grapes of these two varieties. As varietally-labeled sherries, they are quite rare.

TIP

See the color section of this book for the differing colours of sherries.

There is another style of sherry on the rise called *en rama*. This is essentially sherry that is bottled straight from the cask (typically when flor is at its thickest around April or May) without any additional filtering to remove sediment or other biproducts.

WARNING

Some wines from elsewhere in the world, especially the United States, also call themselves sherry. Many of these are inexpensive wines not necessarily made from palomino that have artificial color and/or sugar added. Occasionally, you can find a decent one, but usually, they're unpleasantly sweet and not very good (hence their association as a cooking wine). Authentic sherry is made only in the Jerez-Xérès-Sherry DOP of Spain and carries this official name (the Spanish, French, and English names for the town) on the front or back label. Similarly, true sherry vinegar — which is made using a similar *solera* process — is aged to perfection, and actually has its own DOP. This vinegar is rare and relatively expensive compared to store-bought white or red wine vinegar.

REAL DEAL

Sherries are among the great values in the wine world: you can buy decent, genuine sherries for $12 to $15. But if you want to try the best wines, you may have to spend $15 or more. Some of our favorite producers include Emilio Lustau, González, Hidalgo, Pedro Domecq, and Valdespino.

Montilla: The sherry doppelgänger

REAL DEAL

Northeast of Jerez is the Montilla-Moriles region (commonly referred to as Montilla, pronounced *mon-tee-yah*), where wines very similar to sherry are made in a range of styles. The two big differences between Montilla and sherry are first that pedro ximénez is the predominant grape variety in Montilla, and second that Montilla sherries usually reach their high alcohol levels naturally (without fortification). Alvear is the leading brand of Montilla sherry. Reasonably priced ($23 to $25 for a half-bottle), these wines are often vintage-dated and widely available as finos or amontillados.

Canary Islands: Volcanic treasures

Scattered in the Atlantic Ocean 60 miles west of Morocco lie the Canary Islands. Wine has been made here since the 15th century. There are eight main islands, seven producing wines across ten DOPs: Abona, El Hierro, Gran Canaria, La Gomera, La Palma, Lanzarote, Tacoronte-Acentejo, Valle de Guimar, Valle de la Orotava, and Ycoden-Daute-Isora.

Climates range depending on each island's positioning and the mineral composition of their black volcanic soils. Wines here come from mostly native varieties, and are known to have distinctive volcanic mineral and ash characteristics. Most planted whites include listán blanco, malvasía volcanica and albillo criollo. Reds include listán negro, negramoll, and vijariego. Both the whites and reds are generally dry, acid-forward, light, and fruity, with some variations and longer aging for reds.

If you visit the Canary Islands, you will find the region's *Cordon Trenzado* (braided vines) as its signature — a vine-growing technique designed to maximize space on tight island plots. Great producers from the Canary Islands include El Grifo, Envínate, Viñátigo, and Tajinaste.

Chapter **8**

Germany: A League of Their Own

The earliest mention of German wine comes from the Roman poet Decimus Magnus Ausonius around 370 CE. Germany's wine history is similar to France's — involving churches and monks of the Middle Ages followed by Napoleonic conquest and sweeping landownership reform — all of which resulted in fragmented vineyard ownership among individuals and families.

Although Germans consume five times more beer each year on average, the country remains a key protagonist on the world wine stage. There are more than 42,000 wine producers in Germany. The country is known for its clean, elegant, and lively white wines, but is also increasing in popularity for both sparkling and reds. The trend is due in part to winemakers' enterprising efforts over time, and also in part to climate change which has increased temperatures and encouraged diversity in many regions.

Germany is the northernmost major wine-producing country in Europe, with most vineyards located near the borders of Luxembourg and France to the west, and Switzerland to the south (see the color section of this book).

TECHNICAL STUFF

Naturally, Germany's climate is cool with temperatures ranging from 60°F to 66°F (16°C to 19°C), which means winemakers must go to great lengths to expose grapes to as much sun as possible for as long as possible. Germany's climate is also known to vary from year to year, resulting in considerable differences from vintage to vintage, especially for some of Germany's more high-end wines. Many of the most prestigious vineyards are situated along rivers such as the Rhine and the Mosel, and on steep, south-facing, sunny slopes to temper the extremes of weather and help grapes ripen.

The Laws and the Labels

Germany is home to 13 distinct wine regions, each referred to as *anbaugebiet* (ahn-baw-guh-beet, *anbaugebieten* is the plural form, and more than 15,200 producers, all falling under the umbrella of German laws.

REMEMBER

Germany's system of assigning the highest rank to the ripest grapes was established with the Wine Act of 1971. This is completely different from the practice of most other European systems, which is to bestow the highest status on the best vineyards or districts (although ripeness can certainly be associated with the best vineyards or sites in Germany's case). Germany's system underscores the country's traditional grape-growing priority of ripeness while instituting very specific rules about both ripeness and sweetness in a wine's final designation. The three most important Wine Act of 1971 components are detailed below.

>> **A classification system with three tiers of quality from lowest to highest:**

- *Landwein/Deutscher Wein* (table wine). This designation only requires that 85 percent of the grapes come from one of Germany's 26 defined *Landwein* regions. Finished wines must be either dry or off-dry.

- *Qualitätswein*. This categorizes wines based on sweetness level; wines must come from one of Germany's 13 *anbaugebieten* (described later in this chapter); sweetness categories are often printed on labels but this is not required by law.

- *Prädikatswein*. This meets standards of Qualitätswein and includes additional categorization of grape ripeness as well as restrictions on enriching wine with additional sugar (*chaptalization*), adding oak chips, or making other alterations. All Prädikatswein are Qualitätswein, but not all Qualitätswein are Prädikatswein.

» **A set of six ripeness designations, or *Prädikats* (*pray*-di-cat).** These are designations within the Prädikatswein category described previously, measured by the density of *grape must* (meaning grape skins, juice, stems at the time of harvest versus in the weight of a finished wine). Each uses a unit of measure called *Oechsle* (erks-leh) from least to most ripe:

- Kabinett (kab-ee-net)

- Spätlese (*shpate*-lay-zeh)

- Auslese (*owsch*-lay-zeh)

- Beerenauslese (*bear*-en-*owsch*-lay-zeh), abbreviated as *BA*

- Eiswein (*ice*-vine)

- Trockenbeerenauslese (*trauk*-en-*bear*-en-*owsch*-lay-zeh), abbreviated as *TBA*

» A set of four sweetness categories that define the amount of residual sugar in grams per liter of a finished wine:

- **Trocken (trok-en) or dry:** less than or equal to 9 grams per liter

- **Halbtrocken (halb-trok-en) or "half"-dry:** between 9 and 18 grams per liter

- **Mild (meld) or "Lieblich" (leeb-lick):** 18–45 grams per liter

- **Süss (soose):** More than 45 grams per liter

RIPENESS VERSUS SWEETNESS

Auslese, Beerenauselese, and Trockenbeerenauslese wines can be made with some or all botrytized grapes (see Chapter 3). Although deliciously sweet, Eiswein is made from grapes that freeze on their vines prior to fermentation versus warming up enough to welcome the *Botrytis* fungus in.

At the three highest Prädikat levels, the amount of sugar in the grapes (ripeness) is so high that the wines are inevitably sweet. Many people, therefore, mistakenly believe that the Prädikat level of a German wine is an indication of the wine's sweetness. Remember that the Prädikat is an indication of the amount of sugar in the *grapes at harvest* — not the amount of sugar in the finished wine. At lower Prädikat levels, the sugar in the grapes can ferment fully to dryness. For these wines, there's no direct correlation between Prädikat level and sweetness of the wine.

(continued)

(continued)

Many winemakers craft wines at different ripeness and sugar levels given fluctuations in climate and their impact on wine styles. Just imagine multiple trips to a vineyard throughout the harvest season, with different batches of grapes picked at different ripeness levels! While you may not experience the hard work and joy of a German wine harvest, you can certainly taste the difference. If you walk into a wine shop that carries a great selection, you may see "Riesling Kabinett Trocken" and a "Riesling Kabinett Mild" from the same producer.

Several high-quality producers have also adopted standards created by the *Verband Deutscher Prädikatsweingüter* (a private organization with around 200 members, also known as the VDP). The VDP was officially established in 1910 by owners of some of Germany's most prized estates.

The VDP established a common set of quality standards similar to the Crus of Burgundy in 2012 (see Chapter 6 for more details). These standards prioritized vineyard location versus grape ripeness or sweetness levels alone. The VDP system acknowledges the complex set of factors contributing to a site's *terroir* (see Chapter 2) and the wines it can produce as a result. The system classifies vineyard sites based on location, quality, and aging potential. From least to most prestigious, the categories are:

>> *Gutswein* **(goots-vine):** Estate wine; basic, everyday drinking wines from less-coveted sites.

>> *Ortswein* **(oughts-wine):** Mid-tier wines akin to French village wines from average sites.

>> *Erste Lage* **(eh-stuh-lag-uh):** "First Site" wines similar to Premier Cru Burgundy or Alsace.

>> *Grosse Lage* **(grooz-lag-uh):** "Great Site" wines similar to Grand Cru.

In this system, ripeness is still important, but it is linked to the potential of a place. Although the VDP is a private organization run by about 5 percent of Germany's winemakers (mostly families and family-owned estates), many modern-day German wine laws are following a similar trajectory of the VDP standards. Beginning in 2026, a new classification system based on geographic origin will be mandated by German law alongside the Prädikatswein system of grape must concentration described earlier in this section.

Like most European wines, German wines carry place-names. The place named can be an entire wine region, such as Mosel, or it can be a smaller area. For the best wines, the place-name is usually a combination of a village name and a vineyard name, such as Piesporter (pees-port-er, town) Goldtröpfchen (gold-truh-fien, vineyard), for example. Unlike most European wines, however, the grape name is also usually part of the wine name (for example, "Piesporter Goldtröpfchen Riesling"). The finest German wines have yet another element in their name — a Prädikat as described earlier in this section (for example, "Piesporter Goldtröpfchen Riesling Spätlese").

REMEMBER

Wines with a Prädikat hold the highest rank in the German wine system. A helpful German wine label should tell you the producer, grape variety, sweetness (and possibly ripeness) levels, and vintage. Others may include specific classifications (for example, villages or vineyards). Most higher-quality German wines are Qualitätswein and Prädikatswein as described earlier in this section. These follow labeling requirements specific to their classifications (made from just one district in an *anbaugebiet*, meeting a prescribed minimum alcohol content, and so forth).

WARNING

Try to be patient with German wine labels that vary from so simple that quality could be questionable, to so complicated that you just give up and move on to the next aisle!

Besides its classification systems and emphasis on ripeness versus sugar, German nomenclature for winemakers and estates is also in a league of its own. A *doctor* producer refers to a winemaker with an advanced or graduate degree in *viticulture* (the study of grape growing), *enology* (the study of wines and winemaking), or other wine-related field. This distinction highlights a certain level of technical knowledge and/or winemaking know-how (somewhat of a gold badge for the wine estate). *Schloss* is the German word for castle (similar to the French *château*), after which many German wine estates are named. These are actual castles that may have been converted into modern day homes or wineries. Wines made in historic castles are not required to have *Schloss* on their labels, but the word certainly has a nice ring to it.

TIP

DECIPHERING GERMAN WINE NAMES

If you're like most of us who don't speak German or know German geography intimately, deciphering German wine names can be tricky, to say the least. But here's a bit of information that can help. In the German language, "-er" signals origin. When you see names such as Zeller or Hochheimer — names that end in *-er* — on a wine label, the next word is usually a vineyard area that is from the commune or district with the *-er* on its name (for example, Zell's Swartze Katz, Hochheim's Kirchenstück). The name of the region itself always appears on labels of Qualitätswein and Prädikatswein wines.

Regions, Varieties, and Styles

Of Germany's 13 *anbaugebiet*, 11 are in the western and two are in the eastern part of the country. The most prestigious include the Mosel (named for the Mosel River, along which most vineyards lie), the Rheingau (along the Rhine River), and Pfalz. The Rhine River also lends its name to both Pfalz (formerly called the Rheinpfalz) and Rheinhessen, as well as the smaller Mittelrhein region. Baden, Ahr, Nahe, and Franken, and Württemberg are other important regions to know.

To know German wine, you need to know riesling. A staggering 40 percent of the world's riesling (rees-ling) imports come from Germany. It is the dominant grape in most German wine regions.

Unfortunately, the mass production and consumption of riesling — particularly in the United States which is Germany's biggest riesling customer — has everyone in a frenzy. The people who hate it think they hate it because it's too sweet. The people who love it think they love it because they love sugar. But sweeter rieslings, when made to higher quality standards with the perfect balance of sugar and acid (acid is a real thing for German winemakers, probably even more serious than the grapes themselves) are actually quite rare and often times expensive. More importantly, the simplification of "dry" versus "sweet" rieslings undermines the diversity, precision, and attention to detail in every glass we drink from Germany's 13 *anbaugebiet*.

Nearly 50 percent of Germany's vineyards grow just riesling, müller-thurgau (moo-la tua-gow, a genetic cross of riesling and madeleineroyale), and spätburgunder (shpate-burg-under, or pinot noir). Additional white wines are made from weissburgunder (pinot blanc), grauburgunder (pinot gris), kerner (a genetic cross between riesling and a red grape called trollinger), scheurebe (another genetic cross between riesling and a white grape called bukettraube), and silvaner (a genetic cross between gewürtztraminer [gev-ootz-tra-mee-nah] and an Austrian variety called österreichisch Weiß [oosta-rye-hish vise]).

The modern trends in Germany, wine-wise, are clear:

>> Rieslings have ruled for centuries, and continue to do so. The majority are dry with increasing quantities of off-dry styles exported to the United States.

>> Pinot blanc, pinot gris, and other white wines are becoming popular alternatives to riesling but are still not major competition.

>> Red wine, especially pinot noir, has become much more popular since the turn of the century. The wine regions of Baden, Ahr, the Pfalz, and Württemberg lead the way but are still lesser known than riesling when it comes to German wine.

German rosés and sparkling wines are also on the rise internationally.

REMEMBER

Wine connoisseurs all over the world recognize Germany's sweet, dessert-style wines as among the greatest. Most of these legendary wines owe their sweetness to a magical fungus known as *Botrytis cinerea* (pronounced bo-try-tis sin-eh-ray-ah), commonly called "noble rot." See Chapter 6 for more information on how this makes some of France's most expensive dessert wines; the wine from the infected berries is sweet, amazingly rich, and complex beyond description. It can also be expensive, sometimes sold for $100 or more per bottle for German wines.

Wines at the BA and TBA Prädikat levels (described earlier in this chapter) are usually made entirely from botrytized grapes. They are generally richly textured and sweet. Auslese wines often come from partially botrytized grapes, and when they do, they are likely to be sweet, although never to the extent of a BA or TBA.

Lusciously sweet German wines are also made by freezing grapes on the vine in early winter. When the frozen grapes are harvested and pressed, most of the water in the berries separates out as ice. The sweet, concentrated juice that's left to ferment makes a decadent, sweet Prädikat-level wine called *Eiswein* (literally, icewine). Eisweins differ from BAs and TBAs because they lack a certain flavor that derives from Botrytis, sometimes described as honey, nuts, or caramel.

TECHNICAL STUFF

Both botrytized wines and Eisweins are often referred to as *late harvest wines,* not only in Germany but all over the world, because the special character of these wines comes from conditions that normally occur only when the grapes are left on the vine beyond the usual point of harvest.

TIP

You can take a good stab at determining how sweet a German wine is by reading the alcohol level on the label. If the alcohol is low — around 10% or less — the wine probably contains grape sugar that didn't ferment into alcohol and is, therefore, only somewhat sweet. Higher alcohol levels suggest that the grapes fermented completely, and will taste sweeter.

GRAPE CROSSING: GERMAN WINE HOPSCOTCH

Many of Germany's grapes are genetic crosses. Besides what we know about Germany's history of great scientists (Albert Einstein, Johannes Kepler, and Max Planck to name a few), we also know that historically, winemakers had to get creative in Germany's cooler climates. The primary purpose of developing many hybrids throughout the 19th and 20th centuries was to create grapes that could ripen earlier and withstand harsher temperatures while still producing higher-quality, acid-driven wines.

The following sections explain more about each region and its contribution to the German winescape.

The Mosel: Steep slopes and (sometimes) prices

The Mosel, formerly known as Mosel-Saar-Ruwer (*moh*-zel-zar-*roo*-ver) named for the river's two tributaries, is one of the world's most picturesque wine regions. With its vineyards rising steeply (the steepest in Germany, in fact) on the slopes of the twisting and turning Mosel River, these wines are known as some of the most majestic, racy, and charismatic white wines of the world. They are also some of the most respected because of the sheer level of skill and effort required to grow grapes on slopes where sun is scarce. The majority of the region's vineyards are located in the Middle Mosel, or *Mittelmosel*. Mosel is most importantly known for its slate soils that range in color from amber and red (thanks to volcanic material) to deep blue and grey.

Riesling dominates here, planted to more than 62 percent of vineyards. Mosel wines can range from bone dry to lusciously sweet. Distinctive Mosel riesling tasting notes include lime juice, stone fruit, honeydew melon and (surprise!) slate. With age, Mosel rieslings can develop notes of apricots, honeycomb, and petroleum.

TECHNICAL STUFF

If you detect a petroleum aroma in your riesling, not to worry: there isn't unleaded fuel in your glass. This aroma is caused by a chemical compound called Trimethyldihydronaphthalene, or TDN. This compound is a natural byproduct of the grape's *carotenoids* (pigments) that protect the grape from UV radiation (essentially, sunburn for grapes which decreases acidity, increases bitterness, and compromises quality). Riesling is known to have higher concentrations of this pigment, leading to more pronounced TDN aromas as the wine ages.

REAL DEAL

Although the Mosel is home to some of Germany's most prized and expensive wines (Egon Müller and Joh Jos Prüm have sold in the thousands), the Mosel boasts dozens of excellent wines at a range of price points. Some of our favorites include Dr. Loosen, Dr. Thanisch, Karthäuserhof, Karlsmühle, Selbach-Oster, and Zilliken.

Rheingau: Small but mighty

The Rheingau (*ryne*-gow) is among Germany's smaller but mightier wine regions with some of the richest wine history in the country. This is where Cistercian monks began to develop a theory of wine classification based on ripeness in the early 1700s (and used the term *cabinet* which back then, referred to wine of superior quality to be stored away for later drinking or sale). The Rheingau is also home to Germany's first documented wine made with botrytized grapes. Like the Mosel region, it has some dramatically steep vineyards bordering a river, but here the river is Germany's greatest wine river, the Rhine (of which the Mosel River is a tributary).

In addition to slate which is also found in the Mosel, Rheingau sites have loess, limestone, marl, and sandstone soils. Riesling occupies 80 percent of the Rheingau's vineyards (the highest of all 13 *anbaugebiet*), many of which are south-facing slopes that add a luxurious, mouthfilling sensation to the wines. Wines range in style from Trocken (dry) to Süss (sweet).

Wines made from spätburguner (pinot noir) are increasing in popularity and made throughout the Rheingau. Spätburgunder wines are known for their dried to ripe red and black fruit aromas, herbaceousness, and hints of spice. Recommended Rheingau producers include August Kesseler, Weingut Eva Fricke, Franz Künstler, Kloster Eberbach, and Schloss Johannisberg.

Pfalz: Dancing in the sun

Farther south and almost as big as the Rheinhessen (described in the next section) the Pfalz *(fallz)* is Germany's second-largest wine producer. Although climate change continues to rear its head across Europe, the Pfalz remains the sunniest place in Germany with the highest number of sunshine hours annually. The region has a wide array of soils, including basalt, sandstone, limestone, loess, loam, gravel, and even red clay. The Pfalz's *terroir* make the region a perfect place for a variety of wines.

Although riesling still takes the cake, a few other grape varieties are planted in smaller quantities, including both whites and reds:

>> Weissburgunder (vice-boor-gun-duh) or pinot blanc

>> Grauburgunder (grau-boor-gun-duh) or pinot gris (also known as pinot grigio in Italy)

>> Gewürztraminer (gev-ootz-tra-mee-nah)

>> Kerner (a cross of the red grape trollinger and riesling)

>> Scheurebe (schoy-reh-beh)

>> Spätburgunder (pinot noir)

>> Dornfelder (a cross of the red grapes helfensteiner and heroldrebe)

The Pfalz is also well-known for its sekt (zek-t) or sparkling wine. These wines can be made in Champagne or Charmat method styles (see Chapter 3), and are typically blends of riesling, weissburgunder, blauburgunder, grauburgunder, and chardonnay. Similar to champagne, sekt can be made in a range of styles from brut nature to mild . . . which is a bit of a misnomer since this is the highest sweetness category with 50 grams per liter of residual sugar!

A few of Pfalz's top-quality producers include Dr. Bürklin-Wolf, Weingut Reibold, Weingut A. Christmann, Müller-Catoir, and Dr. Basserman-Jordan.

Rheinhessen: Home of the Roter Hang

South of the Rheingau is Rheinhessen (*ryne-hess-ehn*), Germany's largest wine region historically producing large quantities of simple wines for everyday enjoyment. Liebfraumilch (leeb-frow-milsh) — a still white wine blend from Riesling, Silvaner, Müller-Thurgau, and Kerner — originated here, and it's still one of the most important wines of the region, commercially speaking. The Rheinhessen's highest-quality wines come from the Rheinterrasse, a vineyard area along the Rhine River.

The *Roter Hang* (meaning red slope, named after the red hues of sandstone soil found along the hillside) includes the most celebrated sites with wines from Weingut Wittmann, Wagner Stempel, Keller, George Gustav Huff, and Dressigacker. The Rheinhessen's image continues to evolve towards higher quality with increasing numbers of producers joining the VDP.

Mittelrhein: Grapes and cherries

This is one of Germany's smallest wine regions, situated northeast of the Mosel and Ahr. Peppered with several historic castles, this region includes mostly riesling and sekt styles, with celebrated vineyards positioned in the south. Notable producers include Toni Jost, Weingut Weingart, and Weingut Ratzenberger.

Baden: Spätburgunderland

South of Pfalz is the red grape loving region of Baden (bah-den), now Germany's most important region for spätburgunder (pinot noir). The warmer climate of recent years has helped Baden's producers improve both quality and quantity of their red wines. Today, about 44 percent of Baden's wines are red (and primarily spätburgunder). These wines are luscious but elegant, showing ripe red and blue fruits, medium body, and smooth tannins.

TIP

While tasting in Germany, we were delighted by the quality of Baden's spätburgunder and spätburgunder rosés, certainly a far cry from some of the very light, thinner German pinot noir wines of the past, and among the best in Germany. Increasing comparisons can be made between some of Burgundy's pinot noirs and those from places like Baden in Germany. The somewhat cooler, northern part of Baden also produces weissburgunder and grauburgunder, as well as dry rieslings.

Although *cooperatives* or *co-ops* (groups of winegrowers who collaborate by sharing grapes, making wines, and selling wines under one or more labels) make 80 percent of Baden's wines, independent producers to look for in Baden include Franz Keller, Weingut Heitlinger, Weingut Dr. Heger, Salwey, and Zierseisen. Because some of these are more difficult to find in the United States, prices may start at $25 per bottle and up.

Württemberg: More than Mercedes-Benz

Sometimes referred to as an "up and coming" wine region, Württermberg is home to some of Germany's (relatively) newer winemakers blessed with the warm days (increasingly warmer now due to climate change) and cool nights needed for full ripeness of red grapes. When compared to Baden and the Ahr (described below) that both produce red wines, Württemberg actually leads the charge with nearly 80 percent of Germany's red wine production. Württemberg is located northeast of Baden, and moderated by the Neckar River with most vinyards along the valleys and banks of its tributaries. Similar to most other *anbaugebiet*, vineyards are planted on slopes. Like Baden, the majority of wines are produced and sold by co-ops.

In addition to reds and rosés made from grapes like trollinger, lemberger (blaüfrankisch, which is an Austrian cross between gouais blanc and blaue zimmettraube), spätburgunder, and schwarzriseling (schvaats-rees-ling, or pinot meunier), whites such as riesling and kerner are also well-known here. Sekt is also produced and enjoyed from blends of these grapes. High-quality Württemberg producers include Weingut Beurer, Weingut Karl Haidle, Weingut Knauss, and Weingut Schnaitmann.

The locals of Württemberg love their wine. Indeed the highest per capita wine consumption in all of Germany is in this region! This may or may not have anything to do with the fact that Württemberg is considered the cradle of automobiles (where Karl Benz is said to have invented the automobile). Either way, what better way to spend a day than checking out the headquarters of Mercedes-Benz and Porsche in Stuttgart while drinking delicious local wines made just 30 minutes away in Württemberg!

Ahr: Size doesn't matter

Ahr is one of Germany's smallest wine regions, located north of the Mosel. This is the northernmost red wine region of Germany, producing spätburgunder and spätburgunder rosé that differs from Baden in its more lean, mineral-driven, and slate notes. The Ahr region gets its red-grape growing potential from the Mediterranean-style microclimate, Ahr River, and precision-built, south-facing vineyards which create the warmth needed to ripen red grapes such as spätburgunder. This variety accounts for nearly 65 percent of all wine made in Ahr. The Ahr is also the only German region where 85 percent of all wine produced is red!

WORTH THE SEARCH

Although Ahr wines can be difficult to find, they really are worth the search! Notable producers include Jean Stodden, Weingut Sonnenberg, Weingut Meyer-Näkel, and Weingut Bertram-Baltes.

Nahe: Different soils, different wines

Southwest of the Rheingau lies Nahe (*nah*-heh). Nahe is among Germany's smallest wine regions, but is simultaneously the most diverse in soil types, including sandstone, clay, limestone, slate, and volcanic rock. The region is named for the Nahe River and is most well-known for its intense, juicy, and elegant rieslings. Additional planted varieties include müller-thurgau, silvaner, and dornfelder. Higher-quality producers include Diel, Kruger-Rumpf, Prinz zu Salm-Dalberg, and Dönnhoff.

Franken: Beer and wine

If you need a break from thinking about German riesling, Franken is the perfect excuse! Further east of the Mosel, Rheingau, and Rheinhessen you will find this (significantly colder) region, with winter temperatures ranging from from 30°F to 38°F (-1°C to 3°C). Franken is located in the north of the state of Bavaria (which is world famous for both beer and Oktoberfest, a 16-day festival celebrating Bavarian food and culture that attracts more than six million visitors annually).

Limestone is the main soil type here, and like most other German wine regions, vines planted on slopes is the name of the game. Franken is known for very dry wines made from müller-thurgau, silvaner, kerner, scheurebe, and bacchus (a cross between silvaner and riesling). Well-known producers include Weingut Juliusspital, Bürgerspital, Weingut Horst Sauer, Castell, and Weingut Hans Wirsching.

Chapter **9**

Portugal: Força!

ichelle's travels to Portugal taught her two things: first, that there are more native Portugese varieties than she could have ever imagined and second, that Portugal has some of the highest-quality wines at the most affordable prices in the world. Unlike most people that came to know Portugal primarily through port, which is its most famous wine style, Michelle fell in love first with its dry, unfortified styles stretching from north to south of this Atlantic coast gem.

Whether for the wines or national legends such as football player Cristiano Ronaldo, the phrase, "Força!" applies (meaning "strength" in Portuguese).

The Laws and the Labels

In 1756, the Douro was established as the only legal region where port wine could be produced (there's much more on port later in this chapter). It was from this foundation that the concept of wine classification was further developed for port and other wines over time. Portugal's entrance to the European Union in the 1980s was a key to igniting research, creativity, and technological advancements that would stamp the country as a serious wine producer worldwide.

Portugal created its own *Denominação de Origem Controlada* (DOC) in 1986 that, similar to the DOCs of Italy and AOCs of France (see Chapters 5 and 6), established quality standards and differentiated between wines of various styles and geographies. The Portuguese system has three tiers:

>> **Vinho (Vinho):** Entry-level, table wine.

>> **Vinho Regional:** A step above vinho in quality. There are 14 regions.

>> **Denominação de Origem Controlada (DOC):** Wines of exceptional quality with strict standards for varieties, yields, and so forth. The *Comissão Vitivinícola Regional* oversees the process of designation at this level. There are 31 DOCs in Portugal.

Producers are only required to state the DOC designation on their labels if applicable. Otherwise, labels are fairly flexible in Portugal, with many not including much more than the producer, region, and alcohol level. This is just as well: many Portugese wines are blends of several different grapes, which could make for a lengthy label anyway!

REMEMBER

The following terms may appear on Portuguese wine labels:

>> **Adega:** Winery or cellar.

>> **Branco (*brahn-ko*):** White.

>> **Colheita (*col-hay-tah*):** Vintage year.

>> **Garrafeira (*gar-ah-fay-rah*):** A *reserva* that has aged at least two years in a cask and one in a bottle if it's red, or six months in a cask and six months in a bottle if it's white.

>> **Quinta (*keen-ta*):** Estate or vineyard.

>> **Reserva:** A wine of superior quality from one vintage.

>> **Tinto (*teen-toe*):** Red.

Regions, Varieties, and Styles

Although written accounts of winemaking in Portugal exist from first-century Romans, archeological evidence suggests that grapes were harvested for winemaking by the Tartessians (an ancient civilization of what is now southwest Spain) in at least 2000 BCE. This rich history explains why there are now at least 250 native Portuguese grapes.

A QUICK SIP ON COOPERATIVES

Portugal has numerous winemaking cooperatives. Historically, vineyard holdings were smaller and more fragmented, making it more difficult for winemakers to produce and market their wines on their own. Cooperatives help small producers pool the resources and costs associated with commercial wine production and export. This practice has been encouraged by the Portuguese government through regulatory frameworks, marketing platforms, and support for regional and sub-regional winemakers.

Portugal's natural beauty is vast. Steep mountain ranges, terraced vineyards, river valleys, and even hot winds from the Sahara Desert create a mélange of *mesoclimates* (the climate influenced by local geography) resulting in truly fascinating wines. Climate varies significantly by region and soil types are also different, including loam, granite, schist, sand, and even volcanic soils in some areas. Portugal technically has 14 wine regions (see Figure 9-1). This chapter explores ten of the most important ones to know.

Minho: "Green" white wines

The Minho region, also known as Vinho Verde (*veen-ho ver-day*, translating to green wine) is in the northwest corner of Portugal, directly south of Spain's Rías Baixas (see Chapter 7). This lush, fertile region is particularly verdant because of the rain from the Atlantic Ocean (a theory behind the wine's name). The term "Vinho Verde" refers not only to the region and DOC, but the wine as well that can be made from a number of grapes.

WORTH THE SEARCH

While mineral-driven red wines are produced here, this is primarily white wine country. Although most people think that Vinho Verde is just that light, slightly fizzy stuff you can get for $7 a bottle in the grocery store, the term applies to any wine made in the region from any combination of twenty white or three main red varieties. Generally speaking, the $7 bottles are on the lower end of the quality spectrum, offering mass-produced, almost sparkling water-with-lemon-like wines for quick, cheap enjoyment. While the more expensive, varietal-focused wines can be harder to find, they're worth the search and extra few bucks.

The main grapes for Vinho Verde white wines include alvarinho (called albariño in Spain), arinto, avesso, azal, loureiro, and trajadura. The main red varieties include alvarelhão, Espadeiro, and Vinhão. There are both single variety wines and blends. The majority of Vinhos Verdes are stainless steel fermented to preserve freshness and allow the grape's inherent, vibrant characteristics to shine (discover more in Chapter 3). However, some producers are increasingly incorporating oak aging to add depth and texture. Some of our favorite producers are Anselmo Mendes, Quinta da Raza, Quinta do Ameal, and Soalheiro.

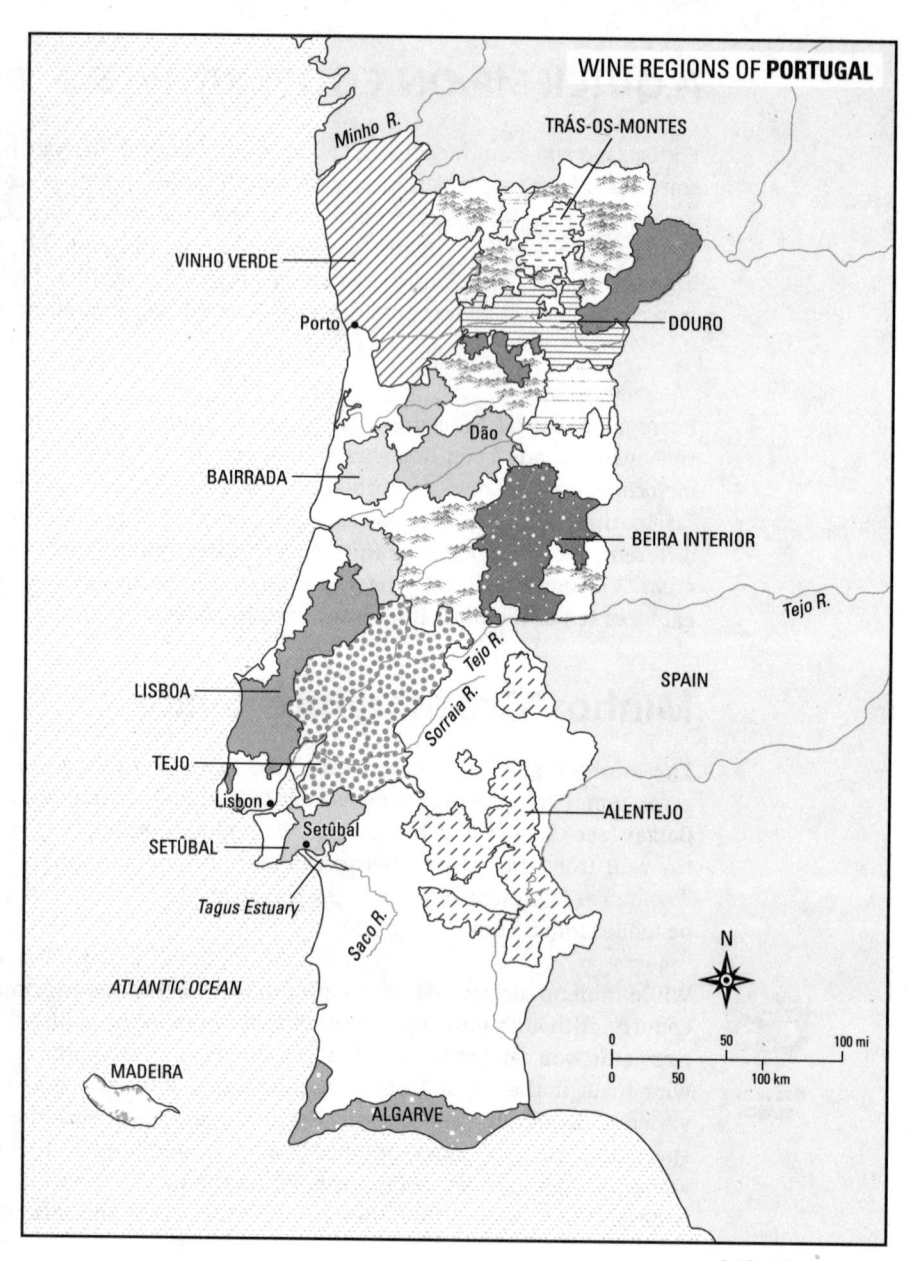

FIGURE 9-1:
The wine regions
of Portugal.

© John Wiley & Sons, Inc.

Douro: The home of port

Still in the north of Portugal, Douro is the home of the Douro and Porto DOCs. In addition to port, the Douro also produces high-quality, age-worthy dry reds. Climate in the Douro can be extreme: blazing hot summers and cold, chilling winters. The Douro River flows into the Atlantic Ocean, creating a hotbed for humidity that can result in summer diseases and winter frosts — both less than ideal for winemaking. On the bright side, the Douro makes rich, powerful, weighty red wines that taste totally different from the Bordeaux blends of France or the tempranillo blends of Spain. Winemakers can choose from up to 80 permitted varieties, although most use some combination of aragonez or tinta roriz (known as tempranillo in Spain), alicante bouschet, castelão, tinta cão, touriga franca, and touriga nacional. These wines are excellent value for money and food-friendly because of their balance and approachability.

Whites from the Douro are few and rare, but they do exist. Some top-quality Douro producers include Adega de Borba, Casa Ferrerinha, Duorum, Niepoort, Quinta do Crasto, Quinta do Vale, and Sogrape (Sogrape is also one of Portugal's biggest rosé exporters, popular for its juicy, gulpable rosé called Mateus).

Port is the star of the fortified wine world. The British are credited for evolving the concept of port beginning in the 1600s, when two Englishmen first tasted a sweet, fortified wine in the Douro. It also worked out in their favor that there were embargos against the importation of French goods, and Britain's claret (red Bordeaux) supply at the time was dwindling. Much experimentation — and the realization that fortifying wine with brandy would ensure its safety for long journeys back to England — began to solidify port as a much-coveted wine. The English established their first port house, Warre, in the city of Oporto in 1670, and several others followed. Today, port is consumed on a global scale in a range of (sometimes confusing) styles. The United Kingdom consumes the most port globally, followed by France, Belgium, and Luxembourg.

Port: The glory of Portugal

Port wine takes its name from the city of Oporto, situated where the northerly Douro River empties into the Atlantic Ocean. But its vineyards are far inland, in the hot, mountainous Douro Valley. Some of the most dramatically beautiful vineyards in the world are on the slopes of the upper Douro — still very much a rugged, unspoiled area.

Port wine is fermented and fortified in the Douro Valley, and then most of it travels downriver to the coast. Large shippers finish and mature the wine in the port lodges of Vila Nova de Gaia, a suburb of Oporto, while most small producers mature their wine upriver. From Oporto, the wine is shipped all over the world — hence the name "port."

WARNING

The term "port" has been borrowed extensively around the world. Many countries outside the European Union (EU) make sweet, red wine in the port style and label it as port. Some of it can be quite good, but it's never as fine as the genuine stuff that is made only in Portugal.

TIP

The trick to identifying authentic Portuguese port is to look for the word *Porto* on the label, which lets you know that the wine was in fact made in the designated port region.

If you think sherry is complicated (see Chapter 7), port will make you think twice! Although all port is sweet because it is fortified with brandy during fermentation, it's not all made from the same grapes and isn't all one flavor profile. The styles vary according to the quality of the base wine (ranging from ordinary to exceptional), how long the wine is oak-aged before bottling (ranging from 2 to 40-plus years), whether and to what extent it is also aged in bottle, and whether the wine is from a single year or blended from wines of several years. All things are possible with port (and a lot of time).

TECHNICAL STUFF

Port estates or wineries are referred to in Portugal as *Quintas (keen-tahs)*. The authorized varieties for port wine are a tongue-twisting, Portuguese alphabet soup of native grapes. In truth, most wine lovers — even port lovers — can't name more than one or two varieties. For the record, the five most important varieties are touriga nacional, tinta roriz (tempranillo), tinta barroca, tinto cão, and touriga franca.

White port is the only style made from white grapes, and this caramel- to golden-colored wine can be off-dry to sweet. White ports can be aged in barrels (minimum of two years) or in the bottle (less than two years before going into the bottle, then upwards of 20 years in the bottle thereafter for vintage white ports). White ports can develop delicious nutty, dried fruit, and butterscotch flavors depending on their style.

Non-vintage ports

REMEMBER

Most port wine is not *vintage-dated* (meaning made from grapes that were all harvested in the same year) and is blended from wines of various years. The majority of non-vintage ports you will find are:

>> **Ruby port:** This young, non-vintage style is usually a blend of red grape varieties. It's aged in large oak vats or stainless steel tanks for about three years before release. Ruby port is fruity, vibrant in color, simple, and inexpensive ($14 to $16 for major brands), it's the best-selling type of port. If labeled *Reserve* or *Special Reserve*, the wine has usually aged about six years and costs

a few dollars more. Ruby port is a good introduction to the port world, with soft notes of red and blackberries, plums, dates, and figs, and baking spice.

» **Reserve port:** This is actually premium ruby port blended from higher-quality wines of several vintages and matured in oak for anywhere from four to six years on average. This wine is full-bodied, rich, and ready to drink when released. This wine is also a good value at about $18 to $23. Labels may or may not carry the phrase "reserve" on them. Examples include Sandeman's Founder's Reserve, Fonseca's Bin 27, Graham's Six Grapes, Taylor-Fladgate's First Estate and Warre's Warrior. Typical tasting notes include prunes, apricots, figs, and vanilla.

» **Tawny port:** Tawny is the most versatile port style. It can be made from white or red grapes. The key difference between ruby port and tawny port is the size of the aging vessel: tawny ports are aged in smaller oak barrels which gives them a browner (hence the term "tawny") hue and more caramel and nut flavors. Tawnies can range in color from amber to garnet or shades of brown, thanks to the more stringent, seven-year minimum oak-aging requirement (which is also a key difference between tawny and ruby ports). Labels carry an indication of the average age of the wines from which they were blended. Ten-year-old tawnies start at $30, 20-year-olds sell for $50 and up, 30-year-olds $135 and up, and over-40 $200 or more. We consider 10- and 20-year-old tawnies the best buys. Tawny ports have more finesse than other styles and are appropriate as apéritifs, with dessert, and dinner. Kick off your evening with a "Tawny and Tonic" and you won't regret it!

Vintage-dated ports

Although the port wines described in the preceding section can be excellent, the ports made from grapes grown in a single year are generally of a higher caliber and are more expensive. These vintage–dated ports include the following styles (only one of which is actually called "vintage port"):

» **Colheita:** Often confused with vintage port because it is vintage-dated, *colheita* is actually a tawny port from a single vintage. In other words, it has aged (and softened and tawnied) in oak for many years (technically just seven is the minimum, but ambitious quintas have set the standard in the 50ish year range). Unlike a typical aged tawny, it's the wine of a single year. Niepoort is one of the few *quintas* that specializes in colheita.

» **Late bottled vintage (LBV) port:** This type is from a specific vintage, but usually not from a very top year. The wine ages four to six years before bottling and is then ready to drink, unlike vintage port, which requires additional aging in the bottle.

- **>> Vintage port:** The pinnacle of port production, vintage port is the wine of a single year blended from several of a house's best vineyards. It's bottled at about two years of age, before the wine has much chance to shed its tough tannins. It requires, therefore, a lot of bottle aging to achieve the development that didn't occur in oak. Vintage port is usually not mature (ready to drink) until at least 20 years after the vintage.

- **>> Single *quinta* vintage port:** These are vintage ports from a single *quinta* that is usually a producer's best property (such as Taylor's Vargellas or Graham's Malvedos). They're made in years that are good but not in the best vintages, because in the best years their grapes are needed for the vintage port blend. They have the advantage of being readier to drink than vintage ports — at less than half their price — and are usually released when they're mature. You should decant and aerate them before serving, however.

WARNING

Because it's very rich and very tannic, vintage port throws heavy sediment and *must* be decanted, preferably several hours before drinking (it needs the aeration). Vintage port can live 70 or more years.

Most good vintage ports sell for $100 and up when they're first released (years away from drinkability). Mature vintage ports can cost well over $100. For a complete list of Vintage Port vintages, see Appendix C.

REAL DEAL

Higher-end port producers include Cockburn, Dow, Fonseca, Graham, Quinta do Noval, and Taylor-Fladgate. Widely available producers also include Churchill, Delaforce, Niepoort, Quinta do Infantado, Ramos Pinto, Warre, and Sandeman.

Dão: Fine wines of the rivers

Defined by the Dão and Rio Mondego rivers, the Dão DOC is one of Portugal's oldest wine regions. Immediately southeast of the Douro, Dão is a mountainous region with warm, dry summers, and wet, cool winters. Granite, sand, and schist soils, coupled with higher-elevation vineyards give the Dão's wines a racy acidity while still maintaining a certain richness and texture. Both white and red wines are here, and most wines are blends of various native varieties. Key white grapes include bical, cercial, encruzado, malvasia fina, and rabo de ovelha. Alfocheiro, jaen (*ha-en*, known as mencia in Spain), touriga nacional, and tinta roriz dominate for red wines. High-quality producers include Quinta da Pellada, Quinta do Vale, and Quinta dos Roques.

Bairrada: Bubbles and baga

Bairrada DOC is a flatter coastal region with the Atlantic Ocean moderating its temperatures and rainfall. Clay, limestone, and sand are common soil types, of which limestone has played an important role in encouraging sparkling wine production.

REMEMBER

Sparkling or *espumante* wines from Bairrada are typically blends all made in the traditional method (see Chapter 3) or *método tradicional*, with secondary fermentation occurring in the bottle. The sparklers from this region are so unique simply because you won't be able to taste these grapes in this format anywhere else in the world!

Still whites, rosés, and reds are also made here. The main white grape in Bairrada is fernão pires (*fer-now pee-res*, known as maria gomes in the region), in addition to arinto, cical, cercial and rabo de ovelha. The reds are dominated by baga followed by alfrocheiro, tinta pinheira, and touriga nacional. Some of our favorite producers from the region include Colinas de São, Encontro, Luis (and his daughter, Filipa) Pato, Nieeport, and Quinta das Bágeiras.

CHEAP DOESN'T MEAN BAD IN LISBOA

Many people get confused by the cost of wine in Lisboa specifically (since this is a typical tourist stop) and Portugal more generally. Does a $4 glass mean the wine will be flat and flabby? Not necessarily. Wine is inexpensive in Portugal for a variety of reasons: first, up until the 20th century, Portuguese wine marketing wasn't nearly as strong as it is today. While loads of wine were produced, much less was exported and appreciated than today. Second, there is wine everywhere in Portugal. Similar to some parts of France, wine is a part of everyday culture and is as common to have on the table as a jug of water. Third, indigenous grapes dominate, making higher levels of production for wines that have thrived in the country for centuries easier.

With that said, there are certainly age-worthy wines from top Portuguese producers that will not cost $16 a bottle. Still not anywhere as high in price as Casa Ferreirinha's Barca Velha (around $700 a bottle from the Douro) or Jupiter Code 01 from Herdade do Rocim (around $1,000 a bottle from Alentejo), Casa Santos Lima's Confidencial Reserva from Lisboa may cost just around $30 a bottle. You decide what's best!

Beira Interior: Old vines

The Beira Interior DOC, located in Portugal's central inland, is known as one of the oldest winemaking regions in the country. Evidence of winemaking stretches back at least 2,000 years. Old vines are so pervasive that there are actually names assigned to vines of different age ranges (young, adult, mature, and old, with the oldest being at least 25 years old and in some cases, 50 and over)!

The region is divided into three sub-regions: Castelo Rodrigo, Cova da Beira, and Pinhel. The sub-regions are separated by the Estrela, Gardunha, Malcata and Marofa mountains. Vineyards can reach up to 2,460 feet (750 meters) above sea level here, making them the highest-elevated winegrowing areas in Portugal. All this height makes for more extreme continental influence: short, hot summers, and long, cold winters. Granite and schist soils are the most common, producing wines with balanced acidity, freshness, and mineral-driven characteristics. The main white grape varieties are arinto, fonte cal, malvasia fina, rabo de ovelha and síria for whites, and bastardo (that's one you won't forget!), marufo, rufete, tinta roriz and touriga nacional. From these varieties, still white, rosé, and reds are made, as well as sparkling *método tradicional* wines.

Lisboa: Wine by the boatload

Colorful architecture, *bacalhau* (salted cod), and old cobblestone streets usually come to mind when people think about Lisbon, or Lisboa in Portuguese. Hidden away from the city but very much a part of its culture are Lisboa's vineyards, producing wines of excellent value.

Lisboa is a geographical region on Portugal's western Atlantic coast that encompasses nine DOCs: the northern is Encostas d'Aire, the central are Alenquer, Arruda, Lourinhã, Óbidos, and Torres Vedras, and the southern are Bucelas, Colares and Carcavelos. The climate in each of these sub-regions varies, with proximity to the Atlantic Ocean resulting in maritime influences, and inland vineyards enjoying more Mediterranean patterns. Calcereous and sandy clay dominate in Lisboa, with clay producing grapes that can make more robust, fuller-bodied wines and sand resulting in grapes that encourage both bright acidity and earthy or floral characteristics. Both native and international varieties are cultivated in Lisboa, including arinto, fernão pires, malvasia, seara-nova and vital for whites, and alicante bouschet, aragonez, castelão, tinta miúda, touriga franca, touriga nacional and trincadeira for reds. It is not uncommon to find chardonnay, cabernet sauvignon, or syrah as well. Indigenous varieties are often blended to make still wines in Lisboa (and throughout the country).

TIP

Wine geeks love Lisboa because it's a place where you can get great wine for as low as $4 a glass or $16 a bottle while enjoying fresh seafood or tinned fish with ocean views! Some of the most popular Lisboa producers are Casa Santos Lima, Companhia Agrícola do Sanguinhal, DFJ, Quinta de Sant'Ana, and Vale de Mata.

Tejo: Horses and wine, why not!

This is the central core of Portugal, an hour's drive north from Lisbon. Tejo is a historian's fantasy: Roman ruins, ancient treasures, castles, enchanting cork forests, olive groves, and pure-blood Lusitano horses. This is also a place to visit if you're into the foot-treading tradition of pressing grapes, which goes back centuries! Known as Ribatejo until 2009, Tejo gets its name from the river that defines the boundaries of all six of its sub-regions (now all assigned to the Tejo DOC): Almeirim, Cartaxo, Chamusca, Coruche, Santarém, and Tomar. As in other parts of the country, wine is part of life, and lots of it is made here.

Most Tejo wines tend to be lighter than the big bodies of Douro and Dão. The predominant white grapes are alvarinho, arinto, chardonny, fernao pires, and sauvignon blanc. Red wines are typically made from aragonez, castalão, cabernet sauvignon, syrah, touriga nacional, and trincadeira. Sparkling wines in Tejo are mostly made from blends of arinto and chardonnay, using both tank and *método tradicional* styles. Top-quality producers include Adega de Almeirim, Adega de Cartaxo, Quinta do Monte d'Oiro, and Quinta de Pancas.

Alentejo: Serious wines

The Alentejo region has quickly become a major forerunner to the Douro in terms of both production and quality. Sharing its eastern border with Spain, the Alentejo stretches across Portugal's southeast coast with one of the country's most diverse arrays of soil, including schist, clay, marble, granite and limestone. Climate is Mediterranean, with southern sub-regions getting the brunt of sunny, hot, and dry growing seasons. The Alentejo is known for its tropical, aromatic whites and well-structured, tannic reds. Juicy but mineral-driven rosés are also on the rise. The Alentejo DOC includes Borba, Évora, Portalegre, Granja-Amareleja, Moura, Redondo, Reguengos, and Vidigueira. Wines from these sub-regions must include 75 percent of specific native varieties, with the remaining 25 percent permitted with international grapes. The most popular red grape varieties are aragonêz, trincadeira, castelão, alfrocheiro, and alicante bouschet. Whites include arinto, antão vaz, fernão pires, and roupeiro.

TIP

This is a region where you're more likely to find collector and age-worthy wines. Top producers include Cartuxa, Herdade do Mouchao, Herdade do Rocim, Fitapreta Chao, Herdade do Mouchão, and Tapada do Chaves. This region is a must-know for anyone interested in uncovering Portugal's true potential!

Setúbal: Breathtaking sweetness

Portugal's southernmost regions are stunning, ocean-kissed areas that will make you think more about your next beach vacation than wine. Connected to Lisbon via the Peninsula de Setúbal and the River Tagus estuary, there is water everywhere. The Costa da Caparica, which runs along the western edge of the Peninsula de Setúbal, is a stretch of breaktaking limestone cliffs, and cerulean blue waters that give wines from this region a special flare. Peninsula de Setúbal's flatter sub-regions are juxtaposed with the more mountainous areas of the Serra da Arrábida.

Both the Peninsula de Setúbal and the Algarve (which also makes wine although production is much less than the other regions described in this chapter) make up the south of Portugal, and have their own distinct wines and styles.

REMEMBER

The Península de Setúbal has two DOCs (Palmela and Setúbal), and is best known for its lucious, golden, fortified dessert wine, Moscatel de Setúbal, made mostly from Muscat of Alexandria (minimum 85 percent to be labeled as such) grapes. Moscatel de Setúbal is made by adding brandy to the grape must once it achieves the desired level of sweetness. The wine is then left (still with the skins) for at least three months before being transferred to large oak casks to age for at least another 18 months. Moscatel de Setúbal wines can be made from a single vintage or blended from different vintages. Fresh and fruity moscatels are usually ready to drink around five or six years of age. Aromas may include apricots, orange peels, honey, and caramel. With age, darker brown and mahogany colors evolve, and more nutty, white raisin and tea notes become apparent.

TIP

The Moscatel de Setúbal producers to know are Bacalhôa, Horácio Simões, José Maria da Fonseca, and Venâncio da Costa Lima. Still white and red wines are also made in Peninsula de Setúbal. Most red wines come from castelão grapes, and most whites from arinto and fernão pires.

Madeira: The colonial legend

In addition to Portugal's most famous fortified wines from Porto and Peninsula de Setúbal, there is also madeira (from the island of the same name). Madeira is actually one of several islands in the Atlantic Ocean archipelago off the north-west tip of Africa, and is home to precarious hillside vineyards with volcanic soils rising straight up from the ocean.

TECHNICAL STUFF

The island is a province of Portugal, but the British have dominated its wine trade since it was colonized in the 1600s. Madeira also happens to be the wine that most American colonists drank and wrote letters about (Thomas Jefferson and John Adams to name a few).

Although Madeira's fortified wines were quite the rage 250 years ago, the island's vineyards were devastated at the end of the 19th century, first by mildew and then by phylloxera (see Chapter 2). Most vineyards were replanted with lesser grapes. Madeira has spent a long time recovering from these setbacks. In the 19th century, more than 70 companies were shipping madeira all over the world. Now, there are only eight producers: Barbeito, Blandy's, Borges, Henriques Henriques, J. Faria & Filhos, Justino's, Madeira Vintners, and Pereira D'Oliveiras.

Madeira can lay claim to being the world's longest-lived wine. A few years ago, we were fortunate enough to try a 1799 vintage madeira that was still perfectly fine. Only Hungary's Tokaji Aszú (see Chapter 10) can rival vintage madeira in longevity, and that's true only of Tokaji Aszú's rarest examples.

Madeira styles and grape varieties

The best madeira comes in four styles, two fairly dry and two sweet. The sweeter madeiras generally have their fermentation halted somewhat early by the addition of brandy. Drier madeiras have alcohol added after fermentation.

The grapes include five main or *noble* varieties (labeled as such historically for their high quality and traditional use in madeira). Each variety corresponds to a specific style of wine. We list them here from driest to sweetest:

- » **Sercial:** The white sercial grape grows at the highest altitudes. Thus, the grapes are the least ripe and make the driest madeira. The wine is high in acidity and very tangy.

- » **Verdelho:** The white verdelho grape makes a medium-dry style, with nutty, peachy flavors and a tang of acidity.

- » **Bual (or Boal):** Darker amber in color, bual is a white grape that makes a rich, medium-sweet madeira with spicy flavors of almonds and raisins and a long, tangy finish.

- » **Malmsey:** Made from the white malvasia grape, Malmsey is dark amber, sweet, and intensely concentrated with a very long finish. Drink it after dinner.

- » **Terrantez:** Another white grape that makes medium-sweet madeira with lots of acidity that falls between verdelho and bual in style.

The less-noble red tinta negra mole is the dominant grape for today's madeira production (used for more than 90 percent of madeira wines), because it grows more prolifically than the five varieties listed above. Also, it is less site-specific: it can grow anywhere on the island, unlike the noble grapes, which grow in vineyards close to the sea where the urban sprawl of Funchal, Madeira's capital city, impinges on them. Previously, the less-regarded tinta negra mole wasn't identified as a variety on madeira bottles, but increasingly it is.

Madeira-making in action

A special element of madeira production is a baking process called the *estufagem* (*es-too-fah-jem*), which follows fermentation. Madeira's potential to improve with heat was discovered back in the 17th century. When trading ships crossed the equator with casks of madeira in their holds, the wine actually improved!

TECHNICAL STUFF

Today's practice of baking the wine at home on the island is a bit more practical than sending it around the world in a slow boat. In the *estufagem* process, madeira spends a minimum of three months, often longer, in heated tanks, in *estufas* (heating rooms). Any sugars in the wine become caramelized, and the wine becomes thoroughly *maderized* (oxidized through heating) without developing any unpleasant aroma or taste. A more laborious and considerably more expensive way of heating madeira is the *canteiro* method, in which barrels are left in warm lofts or exposed to the sun (the weather in Madeira stays warm year-round) for as long as three years. The same magical metamorphosis takes place in the wines. The *canteiro* method is best for madeira because the wines retain their high acidity, color, and extract much better in the slow, natural three-year process. The finer madeiras use this method of aging.

TIP

You never have to worry about madeira getting too old — it's indestructible. The enemies of wine — heat and oxygen — have already had their way with madeira during the winemaking and maturing process. Nothing you do after it's opened can make it blink.

The wine that never ends

Technically, almost all the best madeira starts as white wine, but the heating process and years of maturation give it an amber color. It has a tangy aroma and flavor that's unique, and as long a finish on the palate as you'll find on the planet.

REMEMBER

When madeira is made from any of the island's five noble grapes, the grape name indicates the style. When madeira doesn't carry a grape name — and most younger madeiras don't — the words dry, medium-dry, medium-sweet, and sweet indicate the style. Vintage madeira must spend at least 20 years in a cask. Historically, the aging was even longer.

If a madeira is dated with the word *solera* — for example, Solera 1890 — it is not a vintage madeira but a blend of many younger vintages whose original barrel, or solera, dates back to the date indicated (although the term *solera* here is not to be confused with the *solera* system used in Spain for producing sherry, the reference does suggest the wood that's used to make aging vessels in both contexts). Solera-dated madeiras can be very fine and are generally not as expensive as vintage madeiras — nor as great. But solera madeiras are becoming more obsolete. In their place is a newer style called *colheita* or harvest madeira. This style is modeled after colheita port in that colheita madeira is a single vintage-dated madeira wine. Colheita madeira has spent a minimum of five years aging in cask — or seven for the driest, Sercial. Colheita madeira is much less expensive than vintage madeira. Most of the major madeira shippers now sell colheita. Vintage, colheita, and solera-dated madeiras are made from a single-grape variety that is typically included on the label.

WORTH THE SEARCH

If you can afford to buy an old bottle of vintage-dated madeira, you'll understand our enthusiasm. In the meantime, for a less expensive madeira experience, look for wines labeled *15 years old, 10 years old*, or *5 years old*. Don't bother with any other type, because it will be unremarkable, and then we'll look crazy.

Chapter **10**

Central, Eastern, and Southeastern Europe: Old to Wine, New(er) to You

Although France, Italy, and Spain are considered the top wine producers internationally, wine was made much earlier in other parts of the world. This is especially true in the countries of central, eastern, and southeastern Europe. This chapter uncovers the wine regions of what may feel like new, unexplored territory for some wine drinkers. Although most of these countries share membership in the European Union (EU), some shared history and characteristics of *terroir* (find out more about *terroir* in Chapter 2) in common, each country and its wines is totally different. Read on to find out more!

The Laws and the Labels

With the exception of Turkey that is not (at the time of this writing) an official member of the EU, most other wine-producing countries of central, eastern, and southeastern Europe follow the EU Protected Designation of Origin (PDO) and Protected Geographical Indication (IGP) frameworks. These guidelines designate specific regions for winemaking of different styles and quality levels. In PDO regions, wine is produced entirely within the designated area and must have characteristics directly tied to that region. Wine with the broader IGP designation is primarily produced in the demarcated region, but may include grapes from outside the region as well. The most prestigious and noteworthy regions tend to carry the PDO designation.

In addition to PDOs and IGPs, some countries such as Austria, Romania, and Switzerland use their own designations, as discussed later in this chapter.

Regions, Varieties, and Styles

Figure 10-1 shows each of the major wine-producing countries of central, eastern, and southeastern Europe. Each country and its respective regions, varieties and styles are explored in this chapter.

Central Europe

Although the countries described in this section are geographical neighbors, each has their own specialty in grapes and styles. This section introduces you to the wines of Central Europe.

Austria: Crisp, clean, and a little luscious

Winemaking in Austria dates back to at least the fourth century BCE, but Austria's wines as we know them today are the result of tremendous 20th-century investments. Recovering from the dissolution of the Austro-Hungarian empire after World War I and mass production that focused more on quantity than quality, Austria is now poised as a country with an unwavering commitment to both quality and individuality in its wines.

Austria makes less than 1 percent of all the wine in the world — about 24 million cases a year. Nearly 75 percent of the wine produced never leaves the country, and is consumed within Austria, leaving only a few drops for the rest of the world. This, coupled with the fact that the Austrians have embraced a high-quality image, explains why even the more budget-friendly, great Austrian wines start at around $15 a bottle.

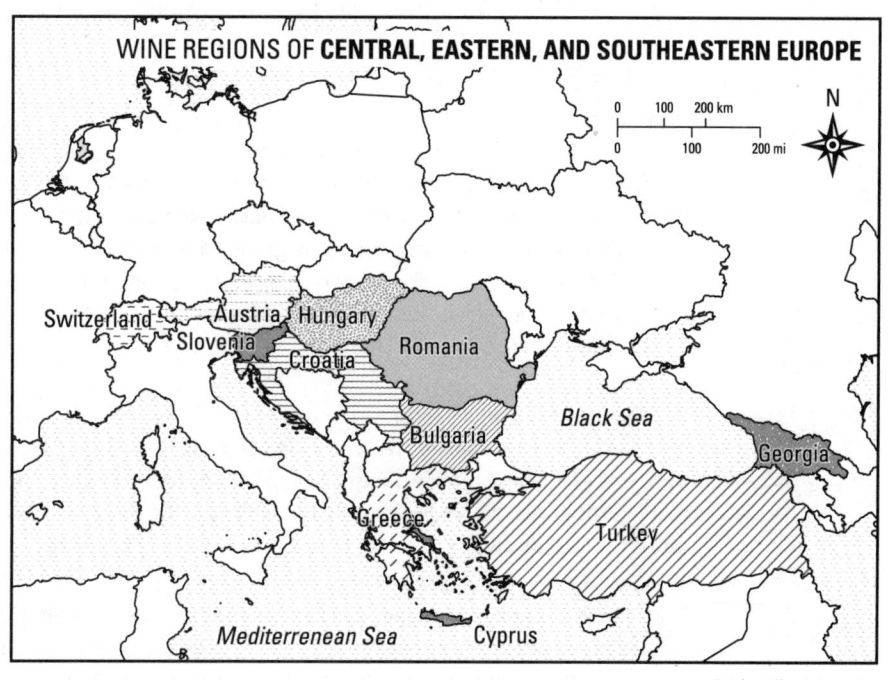

FIGURE 10-1:
The wine regions of central, eastern, and southeastern Europe.

Austria is landlocked on all sides by the Czech Republic, Slovakia, Hungary, Slovenia, Italy, Switzerland, and Germany. Its wine comes from mostly small wineries in the east, where the Alps recede into hills and the Danube River flows into the Hungarian and Slovakian borders. The climate consists of cold winters, hot summers, and mild autumns. Alluvial soils, clay, gravel, limestone, loess (coming from windblown sediment, which is an important factor for grüner veltliner), slate, and volcanic soils can all be found in Austria and make for a diversity of wines.

REMEMBER

Austria's sweet whites have long had a reputation for excellence (in particular, *ausbruch*, pronounced *ows-bro*), but dry whites and reds have gained recognition in the last 35 years. The most common wines are:

>> **White wines:** Apart from the luscious, late-harvest dessert wines made from either botrytized (see Chapter 6), extremely ripe, or dried grapes, Austria produces dry wines ranging from light- to full-bodied, generally unoaked. The infamous grüner veltliner along with riesling are the primary white wines you

will find. Grüner veltliners can be zipping with acidity, pronounced vegetal, herbal, and white pepper notes, and gentle, lemon and lime citrus characteristics. They can range from lighter to fuller in body depending on the region and producer. The rieslings are fresh, clean, stone-fruit driven, and mineral-forward. Although Austria is known for its grüner veltliner, it is often more loved for its rieslings!

» **Red wines:** These are still in the minority but growing faster than expected. Red wines hail mainly from the area of Burgenland (bordering Hungary), one of the warmest parts of the country. They're medium- to full-bodied, often provocatively spicy, with vivid, fruity flavors and sometimes an oaky character. Many of them are based on native grape varieties such as the spicy blaufränkisch (*blao-fran-kish,* also known as lemberger), the gentler St. Laurent, or zweigelt. Zweigelt is the most-planted red grape in Austria. It is a crossing of blaufränkisch and St. Laurent.

Austria has 16 *Districus Austriae Controllatus* (DAC) zones. The DAC operates like the AOCs of France or DOCs of Italy, created to protect and market the unique characteristics of specific *terroirs* (see Chapter 2) inherent in wines from those areas and made only from grapes grown within each specific zone. Three DACs are the most important to know:

» Lower Austria (also known as Niederösterreich, *need-er-os-trysh*) is situated in the northeast and known for the country's best grüner veltliners and rieslings. Lower ustria is the country's most celebrated region, home to the Carnuntum, Kamptal, Kremstal, Traisental, the Wachau (Austria's most prestigious wine region), and Wagram. The Wachau is the only region to have an additional tier of quality distinction that requires hand-harvesting and prohibits *chaptalization* (adding sugar to grape must or juice before fermentation to increase the alcohol content) and oak aging (the former which is legally banned in Austria anyway). Wines increase in ripeness of fruit and alcohol from the first to third tiers of Steinfeder, Federspiel, and Smaragd.

» Burgenland is the second largest region with vines basking in heat from the Pannonian Plain, known for its reds made from blaüfrankisch, st. laurent, and zweigelt, as well as dessert wines made mostly from botrytized, dried, and/or frozen welschriesling, muskat ottonel, and gelber muskateller.

» Steiermark, also known as Styria, is known for its Chablis-like chardonnays and clean sauvignon blancs.

Some of our favorite Austrian producers include FX Pichler, Heidi Schröck, Krutzler, Laurenz V, Prager, Schloss Gobelsburg, Weingut Knoll, and Uwe Shiefer.

WORTH THE SEARCH

Riesling and reds from Austria are hard to find unless you visit a wine shop with a broad selection, a wine bar, or an Austrian restaurant. These wines are worth the search and incredibly food-friendly!

Switzerland: Slopes of wine

The oldest evidence of winemaking in Switzerland dates back to a bottle found in a Celtic tomb from the 2nd century BCE — which means people knew how to stay warm in this cold country! Today, Switzerland is arguably better known for skiing, luxury watches, and milk chocolate than wine. Nonetheless, this is a country whose wines you should try if you can find them. This small (about the size of New Hampshire and Vermont combined), highly elevated (thanks to the Alps) country is mighty in its winemaking, producing wines in every one of its 26 states (called *cantons*). The main wine-producing regions to know are Deutschschweiz (German-speaking), Geneva, Three Lakes, Ticino (Italian-speaking),Valais (French-speaking, where most wine is made), and Vaud.

TECHNICAL STUFF

Very cold winters and very hot summers make Switzerland a unique (and difficult) place to make wine. Many vineyards are planted on steep slopes (over 1,000 meters in some areas of the Valais), making for challenging harvests that require true persistence!

Switzerland produces mostly dry style whites and reds with bright acidity and tart to ripe fruit flavors. Primary white varieties include the indigenous amigne, arvine, and chasselas. International varieties such as chardonnay, savagnin, and pinot gris are also planted. Dessert wines called *flétri* are made from botrytized white grapes.

WORTH THE SEARCH

Switzerland exports about two percent of its wine, and the United States is a small importer, which means you are lucky if you can find these wines anywhere! Michelle buys wine for her bar near Washington, D.C., and always has to search for months to find just one Swiss wine that is available, delicious, and budget-friendly.

Hungary: The dynasty and modern-day renaissance

Hungary's location makes it the entryway into Eastern Europe. Celts first planted vines here about 2,000 years ago. Hungary has developed its own traditional grape varieties over centuries and was considered an elite global producer in the 17th and 18th centuries.

Hungary turned to the popular French varieties in the 20th century, after the phylloxera epidemic hit its vineyards hard in 1882 (for more on this nasty little bug, see Chapter 2). Hungary began growing chardonnay, cabernet sauvignon, merlot, cabernet franc, and pinot noir. Wines are still being made from these varieties in Hungary, but the native varieties from the region make the most interesting and exported wines today.

Hungary has 22 wine-producing regions and over 200 different varieties planted. Its wine production is about 60 percent white and 40 percent red. Its most renowned wine, by far, is its dessert wine, Tokaji Aszú (*toq-ay a-su*), based on the native white furmint grape (with other grapes also permitted such as hárslevelű, sárgamuskotály [known as muscat à petits grains in France] zéta, kövérszőlő, and kabar). We discuss Tokaji Aszú in the nearby sidebar. Hungary's dry white wines are medium to full-bodied and unique. Furmint is also Hungary's most prominent white varietal wine: it is dry, distinctive, and reasonably priced at $20 and up. Furmint also makes a late-harvest wine, retailing for $20 or more. Hungary produces other white wines from native varieties, but furmint is the one you are most likely to see.

Two of Hungary's leading red varieties are kékfrankos (Austria's blaufränkisch) and blauer portugieser. Both are made as varietal wines and also used in blends. The wines are medium-bodied, spicy, and food-friendly. Another red wine, egri bikavér, produced around the town of Eger, and often labeled by its nickname, "Bull's Blood," is an inexpensive ($12) wine to enjoy with a casual dinner. Top-quality Hungarian dry wine producers include Demeter Zoltán, Egerszalók, and Heimann & Fiai.

MAKING TOKAJI ASZÚ AND TOKAJI ESZENCIA

Hungary's most renowned wines are its sweet wines from the Tokaj region. Tokaji Aszú's reputation as a regal wine traces back to King Louis XIV's of France's first taste (a gift from Transylvania), followed by Queen Victoria of England's lavish birthday gift of 972 bottles. Assuming this to be true, Tokaji Aszú has been served side by side with champagne as the beverage choices for Europe's elites for centuries.

The Tokaj region sits in the foothills of the Carpathian Mountains in northeastern Hungary, close to the Slovakian border. Both dry and sweet wines are made here, mainly from the furmint grape variety.

Tokaji Aszú is a sweet, intense dessert wine with high acidity and intense aromas of orange peel, apricots, and honey. This luxuriously delicious treasure is packaged only in 500 milliliter bottles. You can find bottles of Tokaji Aszú labeled "3 Puttonyos" to

"6 Puttonyos" (outlined in the next paragraph). Excellent and widely available Tokaji producers include Disznókő, Patricius Borház, and the Royal Tokaji Company.

The process for making Tokaj Aszú is laborious and time consuming: a thick, pulpy mixture is made from delicately crushed Aszú grapes (Aszú refers to botrytis-infected berries). This mixture is added in varying quantities (final proportions of which determine the sugar levels in the finished wine, measured in *puttonyos*, a term derived from the 25-liter basket that was once used to collect the Aszú berries) to base wines made from grapes that have been harvested separately from the Aszú grapes. The Aszú mixture can be added to the base wine before, during, or after fermentation to bring sweetness to the wine while maintaining a bracing acidity. The more Aszú mixture added to the base wine, the more concentrated and sweet the wine is. The higher the number of *puttonyos* (traditionally, from three to six), the sweeter the wine.

A rare and coveted variation among collectors is Tokaji Eszencia, made only from the free-run (rather syrupy) juice of the aszú berries, without blending into dry wine. Because of its scarcity, Eszencia is quite expensive (from $600 to $1,200, depending on the vintage). Due to its high residual sugar, Eszencia can take years to ferment, but the finished wine remains very low in alcohol — typically less than 5%. Eszencia is enormously concentrated, with very high acidity — so much so that it is often served by the spoonful rather than by the glass!

Slovenia: A wine and cask hub

Slovenia is north of Croatia and east of northern Italy. Evidence of Slovenia's winemaking goes back to the fifth century BCE. This fairly small European country drinks most of its own wine (unfortunately for us). The United States and Slovenia's neighbors receive the small remainders. Despite such small export and global consumption, there are more than 30,000 grape growers in Slovenia making wine from 60 differerent varieties (and counting).

REMEMBER

The three main wine regions to know are Podravje, Posavje, and Primorska, with Primorska known for most of the high-quality wine that makes it to the United States. The climate is Mediterranean, which allows a range of varieties and styles. Primorska's four main winemaking districts are:

>> Goriška Brda (*gor-eesh-ka bur-dah*), which sits on the Italian border, is known for white and orange (white grapes fermented in contact with their skins for anywhere from a few days to several months) wines made from rebula (called ribolla gialla in Italy). These wines are aged underground in large clay amphora (referred to in Slovenia as *kvevri*, pronounced *keh-vev-ree)*. Red wines are made mostly from cabernet sauvignon and merlot blends. Sparkling wines

are made in the Charmat, traditional, and ancestral or *pétillant naturel* styles (see Chapter 3). Sparkling wines are typically made from blends of chardonnay, malvasia, pinot noir, and rebula.

>> Koper is Slovenia's warmest district, on the edge of the Adriatic sea, making full and rich whites from malvazija istarska and full-bodied, herbaceous reds from refošk.

>> Kras is to the north of Koper, and is home to lighter, acidic red wines made from the teran variety.

>> The Vipava Valley's specialties are light- to medium-bodied white wines from pinela and zelen. Pinela wines are crisp, refreshing with tree and tropical fruit flavors. Zelen wines are typically more aromatic, showing riper stone fruit, nutmeg, and allspice characteristics.

Located in Slovenia's northwest, Podravje produces whites from chardonnay, furmint, laški rizling (also known as welschriesling),and sauvignon blanc. Posavje is southeast of Podravje and is Slovenia's smallest wine region, producing almost all red wines from the native variety cviček and blaüfrankisch. Slovenia grows all of the renowned international varieties as well.

WORTH THE SEARCH

From the Slovenian part of the Istria peninsula, adjoining Friuli-Venezia-Giulia in Italy, look for the red and white wines of Santomas. For pinot noir, which does well in Slovenia, look for Movia's Modri Pinot from the Brda region, well-priced for a pinot of this quality (about $35), and Tilia's Modri pinot (about $30). Both producers are among the best in Slovenia and their wines are more easily accessible in the United States.

Croatia: Stunning coasts and wine hills

Situated directly opposite Italy across the Adriatic Sea, Croatia has been producing wines since at least 2500 BCE, when Greeks settled in the region. Croatia today has one of the fastest growing wine industries in Europe, and boasts one of the world's highest per capita consumption levels, higher even than that of France!

Croatia's modern wine renaissance began in the early 1990s, when the country separated from communist Yugoslavia. Croatia quickly transitioned from large wine cooperatives producing ordinary wines to private ownership of vineyards and more distinctive quality. Despite its rather small size, Croatia has over 300 separate wine zones growing 130 native grape varieties, all subdivided into *vinogorje* (wine hills). The four main regions are Istria and Kvarner (northern peninsula areas), Dalmatia (southern coast), the Croatian Uplands (an inland region), and Slavonia and the Danube (an inland region). Coastal Croatia and its islands make the country's most renowned wines.

Winters are mild and summers are warm and sunny (hence the annual flock of tourists to Croatia's glistening coastline). Croatian wines are dominated by whites, followed by reds, rosés, and sparkling wines made in Charmat, traditional, and ancestral methods. Distinctive white wines made from malvasia are perhaps better here than anywhere else in the world. Croatia's most renowned red varietal wine, plavac mali, is a close relative of zinfandel and primitivo that grows along the coast.

Like the wines of Switzerland and Slovenia, Croatian wines aren't always easy to find. Some of our favorite producers include Cattunar, Grgić Vina, Kozlović, Kutjevo, Movia, Pomalo Wine Co., Tercolo, and Vina Laguna.

Eastern and Southeastern Europe

Moving east and southeast within Europe, a strong emphasis on indigenous varieties takes hold. This region contains some of the oldest evidence of winemaking as we know it.

Georgia: The cradle of wine

Georgia's wine scene has experienced a serious boom in the United States and abroad over the last two decades. This country makes up the *Fertile Crescent* (covering the modern-day countries of Egypt, Iraq, Lebanon, Israel, Palestine, Turkey and Syria) where evidence of winemaking as we know it began nearly 8,000 years ago. Today's winemakers, marketing organic and biodynamic approaches, and unique styles and flavors are making Georgian wine more relevant (and cool) now than ever before. The sheer number of registered wineries in Georgia rose from 80 in 2006 to over 2,000 at the time of writing.

Georgia is located in the Caucusus region that straddles eastern Europe and western Asia. It has survived countless wars, benefited from the dedication of monks who planted and studied vines, and flourished after decades of Soviet rule that effectively decimated the wine industry until the 1990s. Georgia has over 540 grape varieties, with close to 40 being used for commercial production. Climate varies by region, with sub-tropical patterns closer to the Black Sea coast, and more continental towards the eastern plains. The Greater Caucasus mountain range insulates the country from extreme cold air flows from the north and moderates heat from the south. White, orange, rosés, reds, dessert wines, and sparklers are all made in Georgia.

Georgia is best known for its winemaking in *qvevri* — a large, mineral-rich clay vessel ranging in size from 20 to over 10,000 liters (called *kvevri* in Slovenia). Some *qvevri* are so large that a person can climb in to clean them! The traditional method of Georgian winemaking involves setting *qvevri* either under or above ground in the cellar to maintain stable temperatures and achieve the winemaker's desired profile.

The main exported Georgian wines come from kisi, tsolikouri, mtsvane, and rkatsiteli for white grapes and aleksandrouli, ojaleshi, saperavi, and tavkeveri. Some of our favorite producers are Baia Abuladze (and her sister, Gvantsa), Lago, Mildiani Family Winery, Telavi, Teleda, Teliani, and Tamarisi.

Romania: Wine and Count Dracula

Pushing towards the farthest eastern point of Europe, Romania is situated directly west of Georgia, with its eastern coast hugging the Black Sea. Known for the Carpathian Mountains (Europe's second largest range) and the idyllic castlescapes of Transylvania (the setting for Count Dracula's legend), wine may feel like an afterthought for visitors. It's anything but!

Like many other countries in this region, winemaking is rooted in Romania's rich history, with Greeks bringing vines to the area between 600 and 500 BCE. Also similar to other countries of the region, war and communist rule created a yo-yo of quality and export to the rest of the world. Both EU funding and foreign investment have revamped the Romanian wine industry in the last thirty years. Although Romania ranks fifth in Europe for vines planted, only about half is used for commercial purposes, which means you're unlikely to find many shelves of Romanian wine in your local wine store.

Romania generally has a continental climate with cold winters and hot summers, which gives its wines the potential for bright acidity and freshness. The three main winemaking regions are the intra-Carpathian plateau, the Carpathian foothills, and the Pontic-Danubian area. Romania makes white, red, rosé, dessert, and sparking wines from both native and international varieties. Whites are made from mainly fetească regală, fetească albă, and welschriesling. Reds are a broader mix of merlot, cabernet sauvingon, and fetească neagră. Sparklers are blends of mostly chardonnay, pinot noir, fetească albă, and fetească regală. Although these wines can be hard to find, they are bright, interesting, and continuing to evolve. Some producers to note include Avincis, Aurelia, Darabont, Davino, Jidvei, Liliac, Lorena Deaconu, Ville Budureasca, and Villa Vinea.

Bulgaria: The Thracian wine dynasty

If you're tired of imagining the destructive impacts of war and state-led regimes on winemaking in this region of Europe, unfortunately the story continues here. Sandwiched between Romania to the north and Turkey to the southeast lies Bulgaria. Grapes were likely grown here among the Thracians as far back as 6,000 BCE. Indeed, both Homer's *The Iliad* and *The Odyssey* reference Thracian wine.

After many wars, the collapse of the Soviet Union, and the dismantling of the Bulgarian communist regime, winemakers mustered up blood, sweat, and tears to revamp the industry. This period of change, improvements in quality, and significant investment didn't really take off until the 2000s. It's safe to say that Bulgaria is still rebuilding its reputation in the wine world.

The remnants of the past are still somewhat evident, with most of Bulgaria's production (about 70 percent) being red wine from international varieties that were mandated during the communist era (although whites and sparklers from Charmat, traditional, and *pétillant naturel* styles are also made). Bulgaria's two wine regions include the the Continental Danube Plain in the north (very cold winters, hot summers) and the sunnier, warmer Thracian Valley in the south. The Danubian Plain is known for its black earth, chalky limestone, and loess soils that inspire mineral-driven wines. The Thracian Valley's calcareous, reddish, and sandy clay soils make for dense, rich, and age-worthy wines. Dominant red grapes include cabernet sauvignon, cabernet franc, kadarka, mavrud, melnik ("55"), and rubin. Whites include chardonnay, dimyt, muscat blanc (known here as tamianka), red misket, and rkatsiteli. Bulgarian wines are increasingly easier to find in wine shops. Some producers to seek out are Borovitza, Bratanov, Château Burgozone, Eolis, Ivo Varbanov, Orbelus, and Rossidi.

Greece: The goddess's wine gift

REMEMBER

We are perturbed by the fact that a country credited with making some of the world's first wines as early as the 7th century BCE could be considered an "emerging" wine region. We think this has a lot more to do with our lack of education (and laziness, quite frankly) about Greek wine than its availability or any other factor. Greece is not only considered the birthplace of western art, philosophy, politics, and science, but the place where wine's spiritual ability was cemented through its gift to man from the god Dionysus. Talk about divine intervention!

Greece never stopped making and trading in wine for all these centuries, but its wine industry suffered through Turkish rule, political turmoil, and a period of generally low-quality exports that lasted well into the 1990s. Greece's entry to the EU helped to improve quality dramatically by increasing investment to the wine industry, driving modernization, and establishing standards through classification. The industry has since been on the rise in quality for both indigenous and international varieties.

TECHNICAL STUFF

Greece's appellation system for wine, which had previously involved separate tiers for dry versus sweet wines, has been simplified by the country's complete adaptation of the new EU PDO/IGP system. Twenty-nine wine zones fall into the PDO category, and most will carry the phrase Protected Designation of Origin in English. IGP wines mainly carry the phrase Protected Geographic Indication in

English. Other terms that have formal definitions under Greek wine regulations include *reserve* (PDO wines with a minimum two or three years aging, for whites and reds respectively), *grande reserve* (three years of aging for whites and four years for reds), and *cava* (non–PDO wines with one year of aging for whites and three years for reds; no relation to the sparkling wine from Spain detailed in Chapter 7). These terms all require that a specified portion of the wines' aging takes place in barrel.

Although Greece is a southern country and famous for its sunshine and sparkling, sapphire waters, its grape–growing climate is actually quite varied from the standard Mediterranean feel because many vineyards are situated at high altitudes where the weather is cooler. Most of Greece is in fact, mountainous. Nearly 60 percent of Greece's wine is white, although there are rosés, reds, sparkling, and dessert wines made as well. There are more than 300 different grapes in Greece that make wines here particularly exciting for curious wine lovers to explore, but their unfamiliar names may make the wines challenging to sell. Greece also produces wines from international varieties, such as chardonnay, merlot, syrah, and cabernet sauvignon, but producers seem more committed than ever to their native varieties (and blending them with international ones) rather than international varieties alone. The most important grapes to know from Greece include:

>> **Assyrtiko (ah-*seer*-tee-koe):** A white variety that makes delicate, bone-dry, crisp, very long-lived wines with citrus and mineral aromas. Although assyrtiko grows in various parts of Greece, the best assyrtiko wines come from the volcanic island of Santorini. Any wine named Santorini is made from at least 90 percent assyrtiko. Two outstanding Santorini producers are Domaine Sigalas and Gai'a (*yah-yah*).

>> **Moschofilero (*mos-cho-feel-eh-roe*):** A very aromatic, pink-skinned variety that makes both dry white and pale-colored rosés. Top-quality wines come from areas around Mantinia (*man-the-nee-ah*), in the central, mountainous Peloponnese region. If a wine is named Mantinia, it must be at least 85 percent moschofilero. Wines made from moschofilero are medium- to full-bodied, with stone fruit, honeydew, and mineral notes.

>> **Agiorgitiko (*eye-your-yee-tee-koe*):** The name of this grape translates in English as "St. George," and a few winemakers call it that on the labels of wines destined for English-speaking countries. Greece's most planted and probably most important native red variety, it grows throughout the mainland. Its home turf, where it really excels, is in the Nemea district of the Peloponnese region. Any wine with the place-name Nemea is 100 percent agiorgitiko. Wines from this variety are medium to deep in color, have complex aromas and flavors of plums and/or black currants, and often

have a resemblance to cabernet franc or spicy Merlot wines. Agiorgitiko also blends well with other indigenous or international varieties.

>> **Xinomavro (*ksee-no-mav-roe*):** This is the most important red variety in the Macedonia region of northern Greece. Xinomavro produces highly tannic wines with considerable acidity that have been compared to nebbiolo wines of Piedmont, Italy. Wines made from xinomavro have complex, spicy aromas, often suggesting dried tomatoes, olives, and/or berries. Xinomavro wines are dark in color but they lighten with age and have great longevity. Their home base is the Naoussa district of Macedonia. Any wine named Naoussa is entirely xinomavro.

Other important indigenous varieties in Greece include roditis (actually a pink-skinned grape), which makes Patras white, and savatiano, the most widely planted white grape. Retsina, a traditional Greek wine made by adding pine resin to fermenting grape juice (resulting in a flavor not unlike some oaky chardonnays), is made mainly from savatiano. Mavrodaphne is an indigenous Greek red variety that's becoming increasingly important, both for dry and sweet red wines.

REMEMBER

There are about 6,000 islands in Greece (about 200 which are inhabited). Greece's main wine regions include both islands and mainland areas:

>> **Macedonia:** The northernmost part of Greece, with mountainous terrain and cool climates. Naoussa wine (from the xinomavro grape) comes from here.

>> **The Peloponnese:** A large, mainly mountainous, peninsula in southwestern Greece with varied climate and soil. Noteworthy wines include the dry, medium- to full-bodied reds from agiorgitiko, the dry whites from Patras and Mantinia, and the aromatic moschofilero.

>> **Crete:** The largest Greek island, which makes both white and red wines, many of which are varietally named along with the place-name of Crete.

>> **Other Greek islands:** Besides Crete, the four most important islands that make wine are Santorini, Rhodes, Samos, and Cephalonia.

WORTH THE SEARCH

Many Greek wines in the United States are top quality, especially the wines of small, independent wineries. The following are some of our favorite Greek wine producers:

>> **From Macedonia:** Alpha Estate, Domaine Gerovassiliou, Kir Yianni Estate, and Tsantali-Mount Athos Vineyards

>> **From the Peloponnese:** Antonopoulos Vineyards, Gai'a Estate, Katogi & Strofilia (with operations also in Macedonia), Mercouri Estate, Papantonis Winery, Domaine Skouras, Domaine Spiropoulos, and Domaine Tselepos

>> **From the islands:** Boutari Estates (six estates throughout Greece, including Crete and Santorini), Gentilini (on Cephalonia), and Domaine Sigalas (Santorini)

Cyprus: In Commandaria

Nearer to the Middle East than to its European neighbors, Cyprus is part of the region known as the Levant. The center of ancient civilations (including the legends of Aphrodite and her attempts to make wine inspired by her love affair with Dionysus and trade with pharaonic Egypt), Cyprus's wine world eroded with Ottomon rule (more than 600 years leading up to its dissolution in 1922) and the more dominant international wine trade in central and eastern Europe. Like its neighbors in the region, Cyprus continues to thrive on ancient native varieties grown in high altitudes influenced by the Mediterranean. Despite the high altitudes, this is primarily a hot, dry winemaking country that is adapting in the face of climate change. White, rosé, red, and sparkling are made in Cyprus from indigenous varieties using French and American oak barrels as well as ancient-style clay amphora. Wine grapes include xynisteri, promara, vasilissa, and spourtiko. Red grapes are lefkada, mavro, maratheftiko, ofthalmo, and yiannoudi.

REMEMBER

Cyprus is most known for its lucious dessert wine called Commandaria—an amber-color dessert wine made from sun-dried mavro and xynisteri and grapes. Some say that Commandaria is the oldest named wine produced in the world!

Turkey: Old, but new

If you haven't noticed the trend, the countries of central, eastern, and southeastern Europe have been making wine for ages — literally. Turkey is no exception. Although 420,000 hectares of vines are planted here, only about 15 percent is dedicated to wine grapes. Three major periods had lasting impacts on Turkish wine: Ottoman rule from 1299-1922 (during which non-Muslim populations were the only ones permitted to make wine); population exchanges between Turkey and Greece in the 1920s; and the influence of the Tekel monopoly from 1925 until 2003. In many ways, Turkey's industry is still quite new. With the advent of privatization, many family-owned and boutique wineries have emerged in Turkey with a renewed sense of vigor and passion for Turkish wines.

Similar to its neighbors, Turkey is a mountainous country with many different climactic influences. Mediterranean conditions dominate west and southern regions, while the northern Black Sea has more of a moderate maritime climate. Central and eastern regions range from warm to hot continental. Combined with volcanic, limestone, pebbly clay, and gravelly loam, Turkey's wines can be light and friendly to full, rich, and powerful depending on producer and region.

Turkey doesn't have an official geographic designation system for wine regions. But the majority of high-quality wines are from three main areas: the Aegean Coast, Marmara, and Anatolia. White, rosé, red, dessert, and sparkling wines are all made here. The main white grapes are the native varieties of emir and narince, producing dry, refreshing wines with citrus and stone-fruit notes. The primary reds grapes are boğazkere, Öküzgözü, and kalecik karasi, from which light- to full-bodied wines full of spice, incense, and baked berry flavors are made.

Turkish wines can be found in larger wine shops, wine bars, and Turkish or Mediterranean restaurants. They are often a great buy at $20-40 a bottle, and a suitable alternative to international vareities if you're feeling adventurous. High-quality Turkish producers include Doluca, Kavlakidere, Kayra, and Paşaeli.

3

The World of Wine: The Americas

IN THIS CHAPTER

» Understanding the laws and labels
of North America

» Exploring wines and wine regions
in the United States, Mexico, and
Canada

Chapter 11

North America: Modern Winelands

N orth America's wine story began as early as the 16th century with European settlers, but wine as we know it from the continent really took off in the 20th century. Discover more about the wines of North America, Mexico, and Canada in this chapter.

The Laws and the Labels

Even though the United States produced wine commercially in the late 18th to early 19th centuries, the legal framework for today's industry really took hold between the 1960s and 1970s. In 1978, the first American Viticultural Areas (AVAs) were named by the then Bureau of Alcohol, Tobacco, and Firearms. Like the classic French model (see Chapter 6) it identifies numerous vineyard regions. But the United States system of American Viticultural Areas (AVAs) establishes only the geographical boundaries of wine zones; it doesn't stipulate which grape varieties can be planted, the maximum yield of grapes per acre, or anything else that would link the geography to a particular style of wine. Thus, AVA names — the names of the regions of production — have secondary importance on wine labels after the grape name.

Wines labeled with the name of a grape variety in the United States must contain at least 75 percent of that grape variety, according to federal law. Wines with an AVA indication must be made at least 85 percent from grapes of that viticultural area. Wines with vintage years must derive at least 85 percent from the named vintage. The words *reserve, special selection, private reserve, barrel select, vintners reserve, classic,* and so on, have no legal definition in the United States. Although many premium wineries use these terms to indicate their special or better wines, most of the larger wineries use the same terms on their inexpensive bottlings as marketing tools.

Mexico does not have a denomination or appellation system similar to the AOCs of France (Chapter 6) or AVAs of the United States. Nor does it have any aging or blending requirements for wines from different places, making the country an attractive place for winemakers looking to experiment or get creative. The only and most important requirement is that wine labeled as Mexican is made in Mexico.

In Canada, winemaking laws are governed primarily at the provincial level (the equivalent of a United States state). Each province has its own licensing, production, and quality standards, with some provinces such as Ontario and British Columbia having their own regulatory agencies (Ontario Wine Appellation Authority and British Columbia Wine Authority, respectively).

BROADER OR MORE SPECIFIC AVAS?

United States winemakers often choose to use a broader AVA designation rather than a smaller, more specific one, in order to widen their options in buying grapes and wine. For example, a winery in Alexander Valley, within Sonoma County, could use the broader *Sonoma County* AVA rather than *Alexander Valley* if it sources grapes from other areas of the county. It could use the larger *North Coast* AVA if it blends in grapes or wine from neighboring counties, like Napa. And if low price is a goal, the winery could even use the broadest AVA, *California,* in order to buy less expensive grapes from the industrially farmed vineyards of the Central Valley or other parts of the state where grapes and wine are less expensive than in Sonoma County.

Sometimes, wineries use the *California* appellation even for their better wines, for name recognition and to give themselves complete freedom in sourcing their grapes. While specificity of place is admired, on the one hand, making a good wine at a good price through geographical blending is also admired. The relative merits depend on who's doing the admiring.

Traditional or not, America's way of making and naming wine sits just right with its local wine drinkers: American wines now account for roughly 65 percent of all wine sales in the United States.

Regions, Varieties, and Styles

The following sections dive deeper into the major wine regions (and in this case, states) of the United States, including California, Washington, Oregon, and New York as the country's heavy hitters.

The United States' main regions

Today, wineries exist in all 50 states, making the United States the world's fourth largest wine producer behind Italy, France, and Spain.

Although simple wines from muscadine (*Vitis rondofilia* species) and other grapes were produced in the colonies now comprising the United States during the 16th and early 17th centuries, early records show that *Vitis vinifera* vines were brought to the east coast from Europe by Lord Delaware in 1619 (see Chapter 2 for more on *Vitis vinifera*'s journey). For the next 100 years, wealthy landowners and elites (including President Thomas Jefferson in Virginia, for whom wine was among his many indulgences) would collaborate with European immigrants and viticulturalists to experiment with native varieties, *Vitis vinfera*, crosses, and also hybrids of the two. Thus were the true humble beginnings of wine in the United States.

Another batch of juices began fermenting on the west coast in the 17th and 18th centuries. When the Spanish *conquistadores* came to what they called the "New World" (which we know is a misnomer: although this part of the globe was new to explorers, people had lived there for centuries), missionaries accompanied them, planting the first *Vitis vinifera* vines (specifically listán prieto or misión which had arrived in Mexico at least a century before) to make wines in celebration of Catholic mass. The land that occupied these vineyards is now in parts of New Mexico, Texas, and Baja (lower) California, with ownership changing from indigenous to Spanish, Mexican, and finally American hands. These *mission grapes,* as they were called, still exist, but today's broader, international range of varieties now dominates the American wine industry. California still remains the star of America's wine story.

REMEMBER

The biggest wine-producing states in the United States account for nearly 1 million acres of vineyards, concentrated across the country. The lion's share of them are in California, Washington State, Oregon, and New York which we discuss in detail in the following sections. The *terroir* (see Chapter 2) of each varies, in many instances down to varieties, soil types, and mesoclimates of particular sites within an AVA.

CELEBRITY GRAPES

The wines of the United States — especially California — embody what we like to call "new age" wine-think. Producers may plant whatever grape variety they wish, wherever they wish, without restrictions imposed by tradition or regulations. This doesn't mean that the choice of grape variety is haphazard: with increased awareness of the importance of *terroir*, United States producers today are mindful about where to plant vineyards, which varieties to grow, and why.

United States wines have elevated grape varieties to celebrity status in ways the French probably never intended (who ever really knew what was in Bordeaux until sommeliers — also now with celebrity status — started rattling them them off eloquently to sell high-end bottles in restaurants?) For more on the role of a sommelier, check out Chapter 20. Until California began naming wines after grapes, chardonnay, cabernet sauvignon, merlot, and pinot noir were just behind-the-scenes ingredients of wine — but now wine drinkers all over the world recognize these grape names as actual wine names, and the United States (if not just California) certainly deserves some credit for it.

California: Sunshine and wine

REMEMBER

California is the heartbeat of American wine. In 1960, only 256 operating wineries existed in all of California, less than 25 percent of the pre–Prohibition number. Today, there are nearly 5,000! Almost 90 percent of all American wine is made in California, but growth of California's wine business has stimulated interest in this juice all across the country.

Considered one of the sunniest places in the entire country, California doesn't lack warm climate for growing grapes. For *fine wine* (top-quality wine characterized by reflection of *terroir*, complexity, and aging potential) production, the challenge is to find areas cool enough, with poor enough soil, so that grapes don't ripen too quickly, without full flavor development (see Chapter 3 for more details on winemaking). Distance from the pacific coast and relatively high altitudes are more important determinants of cooler climates than latitude is in California. High-quality wines, therefore, come from vineyards up and down almost the whole length of the state.

Besides proximity to the coast and colder currents coming from the Pacific Ocean, two other crucial ingredients shape California's viticultural landscape:

>> **The coastal ranges:** These are a 400-mile stretch of mountains between Humbodlt and Santa Barbara counties that provide shade, funneling cool air from the Pacific Ocean, and generating fog to help balance temperatures.

High-quality wines in or near the ranges typically have slower ripening times which leads to higher acidity and more complexity in finished wines. Key mountains in the range include the Mayacamas on the west side of Napa Valley, the Vacas Mountains on the east, the Mendocino Range covering the northern Mendocino County region of the north coast, and the Santa Cruz Mountains, covering San Mateo, Santa Clara, and Santa Cruz counties.

>> **Diurnal shifts:** If you've ever been to California, you can *feel* what we mean here. A *diurnal shift* is the difference between the lowest and highest temperature within a 24-hour period. The cycle of cold pacific currents, fog, and daily sunshine means that the majority of California's wine regions are places where before noon, you may need a jacket. By noon, you'll take it off and want to sunbathe. Then again, when the sun sets, you will reach for your jacket once more (and maybe even a hat). While this yo-yo of activity can be frustrating for us humans, it's just what the grapes in California would order: juicy ripening in the sunshine by day, and cool, retained acidity by night.

TECHNICAL
STUFF

Weather variations from year to year do exist in California but they tend to be far less dramatic than in most European wine regions. One major reason is that rain doesn't fall during the growing season (early August through late October or early November) in much of California. Contrastingly, rain at the wrong time is usually the cause of Europe's poorer vintages. California's most serious vineyard threats at the time of writing are climate change and temperature increases, droughts that can limit the amount of water available for irrigation, and wildfires that can destroy entire vineyards in a matter of hours. Unfortunately all of these are becoming more common, with devastating examples recording billions of dollars in wine industry losses in 2017 (Tubbs Fire), 2018 (Camp Fire), 2020 (LNU Complex and Glass Fire), and 2025 (Palisades and Eaton Fires).

That said, the effects of global climate change have pushed even more advancement in California in recent years, including the development of sustainable practices and certifications (Napa Green Vineyard and Napa Green Winery are the most popular) designed to address common threats and unite the state's winemakers in the quest for sustainability.

TECHNICAL
STUFF

There are more than 100 different soil variations in Napa Valley alone, representing nearly 50 percent of the entire world's soil orders. The most common types of soil found in high-quality wine production areas include loam, clay, gravel, granite, limestone, alluvial, and volcanic soils.

If your head isn't spinning yet about all that California has to offer, then just remember that although there are around 75 different types of grapes grown in California, only seven of them are the most important today. In order of production volume, they are cabernet sauvignon, chardonnay, pinot noir, zinfandel, merlot, syrah, and sauvignon blanc. Dry styles are by far the most popular, followed by sparkling wines made in traditional and Charmat methods (see Chapter 3). Very small quantities of botrytized and port-style fortified wines are also made (see Chapters 6 and 9 for more on these styles of wine), although these are more expensive and difficult to find.

TIP

You can find chardonnays, cabernet sauvignons, pinot noirs, and merlots from California at prices less than $10 a bottle. Better wines can be quite expensive, however. Most mid-range varietal wines are in the $25 to $60 range. Special bottlings and limited-production wines such as reserve bottlings and single-vineyard wines generally can cost $60 to $200 and up. Sauvignon blanc wines — growing in popularity with some of the most prestigious examples dubbed the *Super Sauvignons* by famed wine journalist Karen Macneil — are the best values among California's premium wines. You can find some sauvignon blancs for less than $15, with many good ones from $18 to $20, although a few are priced as high as $70 (hello, Illumination and Merry Edwards). Red zinfandels are also on the rise in price, with entry-level examples selling for around $20 a bottle, to higher-end versions well over $40 a bottle. If you like white zinfandels, actually pink in color, which can be distinctly sweeter than the reds, you can save yourself a bundle — they're in the $7 to $10 range.

California's important fine wine regions and districts include the following (also shown in this book's color section):

>> **North Coast:** Napa Valley, Sonoma County, Mendocino County, and Lake County

>> **North-Central Coast:** San Francisco Bay area (Livermore and Santa Clara Valleys), Santa Cruz Mountains, Monterey County

>> **Sierra Foothills:** Amador County and El Dorado County

>> **South-Central Coast:** San Luis Obispo County, Santa Barbara County

THE CALIFORNIA WINE DREAM

You would probably think we were lying if we told you that many of the largest wine companies in California were started by people who learned how to grow grapes and make wine from watching their parents, taking *ad hoc* courses, and simply renting out library books. Even though they were educated in their own right (Robert Mondavi at Stanford University (Michelle's alma mater), the Gallo brothers at Modesto Junior College), it would take years of trial and error, millions of dollars, and a lot of patience to form the American wine empires that we so know and love today. This is the story for some of the best-known California wine names, many with founders who were first- or second-generation immigrants from Italy, Germany, France, and Switzerland.

California's Gallo Winery (formerly known as E. and J. Gallo) is the largest winery in the state. In fact, until recently, it was the largest wine company in the world, producing one out of every four bottles of wine sold in the United States. Within the last decade, a large New York–based corporation, Constellation Brands, became the world's largest wine company through a series of acquisitions.

It was another California company, the Robert Mondavi Winery, however, that stimulated fine-wine production in the United States. In 1966, Mondavi left his family's winery (Charles Krug) to start his own operation, a winery dedicated to making premium wines. These finer wines — his own and those of the many producers who would follow in his steps — would be varietally named cabernet sauvignon, chardonnay, and so on. Identifying the wines by their grape varieties was a reaction against the low-priced "jug wines" that were then popular. Today, even Gallo is very much in the varietal wine business. Robert Mondavi Winery is now also part of the huge Constellation Brands corporation.

NAPA VALLEY

Napa Valley is about a 90-minute drive northeast of the beautiful bay city of San Francisco. Many of California's most prestigious wineries — and certainly its most expensive vineyard land — are in the small Napa Valley, where about 475 wineries have managed to find space. Hundreds more brands of Napa Valley wine exist, including producers who make wine in shared facilities. Nearly 95 percent of Napa Valley wineries are family-owned. Despite these numbers, the region's wine production is actually much tinier than its reputation: Napa Valley produces 4 percent of California's wine — and much of that is fine wine.

The Napa Valley floor is only 30 miles long and 5 miles wide at its widest point. The southern part of the valley, especially the Carneros district, is the coolest area, thanks to ocean breezes and mists from the San Pablo Bay. Carneros — which extends westward into Sonoma County — is the vineyard area of choice for grape varieties that enjoy a cooler climate, including chardonnay, pinot noir, and riesling among others. North toward Calistoga — away from the bay influence — the climate can get quite hot (but always with cool nights).

REMEMBER

Cabernet sauvignon is Napa Valley's most important wine in terms of production, followed by chardonnay, merlot, sauvignon blanc (sometimes labeled fumé blanc), pinot noir (mainly from cool Carneros), and zinfandel. *Blended wines*, which do not carry the name of a single-grape variety, are also important. If red, these blends are usually made from red Bordeaux varieties (cabernet sauvignon, cabernet franc, merlot, and sometimes even malbec and petit Verdot). If white, they're usually made from the white Bordeaux grapes (sauvignon blanc and sémillon). Some of these blends are referred to as *Meritage* wines — not just in Napa but across the United States — although few carry the word *Meritage* on their labels. (The term *Meritage*, promoted by the Meritage Alliance, can be used only for red or white wines that utilize grape varieties traditional for making red or white Bordeaux wine; see Chapter 6 for info on Bordeaux.)

TIP

If just about every winery in Napa makes a chardonnay and a cabernet sauvignon, how can you distinguish the wineries from one another? Good question — with no easy answer. The following alphabetical list indicates some of the most popular, high-quality producers in Napa Valley, as well as a some of their best wines and price points ($: $20-$40, $$: $41-99, $$$: $100 and up) to help steer you in the right directon. We do the same for Sonoma County (see the next section) as Napa and Sonoma are the most reputable for fine wine, and often the most difficult to navigate for an everyday wine consumer. This list could go on for several pages but we've limited it to those wines that are more accessible around the country.

>> **Brown Estate ($$ and up):** Cabernet sauvignon, chardonnay, merlot, red blends, zinfandel

>> **Charles Krug ($ and up):** Cabernet sauvignon, chardonnay

>> **Chappellet ($$ and up):** Cabernet sauvignon, chardonnay, chenin blanc, merlot

>> **Clos du Val ($$ and up):** Cabernet sauvignon, chardonnay, merlot

>> **Far Niente ($$ and up):** Cabernet sauvignon, chardonnay

>> **Heitz ($$ and up):** Cabernet sauvignon, chardonnay

>> **Inglenook ($$$ and up):** Cabernet franc, cabernet sauvignon, sauvignon blanc, syrah

>> **Kongsgaard ($$$ and up):** Cabernet sauvignon, chardonnay, syrah

>> **Opus One ($$$ and up):** Red Bordeaux-style blends

>> **Quintessa ($$$ and up):** Cabernet sauvignon, red Bordeaux-style blends, sauvignon blanc ("Illuminaton")

>> **Robert Mondavi ($ and up):** Cabernet sauvignon, chardonnay, merlot, pinot noir, rosé, sauvignon blanc

>> **Shafer ($$ and up):** Cabernet sauvignon, chardonnay, merlot

Wineries and vineyards occupy almost every agricultural part of Napa Valley. Many vineyards are on the valley floor, some are in the hills and mountains to the west (the Mayacamas Mountains), and some are in the Vaca Mountains to the east (especially Howell Mountain). Napa includes 16 sub-AVAs besides the broad Napa Valley AVA itself (which always appears on the label alongside a sub-AVA, if any). The most important to know are currently:

>> Spring Mountain, Diamond Mountain, and Mt. Veeder (all in the Mayacamas Mountains)

>> Howell Mountain, Stags Leap District, and Atlas Peak (all hilly or mountainous areas in eastern Napa Valley)

>> Calistoga, St. Helena, Rutherford, Oakville, Yountville, and Oak Knoll District (from north to south along the valley floor)

>> Los Carneros (part in Napa Valley, part in Sonoma)

SONOMA COUNTY

If you drive from San Francisco over the beautiful Golden Gate Bridge, you'll be in Sonoma in an hour. The differences between Napa (detailed in the previous section) and Sonoma are remarkable. Many of Napa's wineries are ornate (downright luxurious if you ask us) with many visits by appointment only, whereas most of Sonoma's are rustic, countrylike, and laid back (with some exceptions, of course).

As examples of the exceptions, the famously successful Gallo company, based in the Central Valley, also owns vineyards and wineries in Sonoma. Also here are Sebastiani, Glen Ellen, Korbel (technically California's first producer of traditional method sparkling wine), Kendall-Jackson, Simi, Ravenswood, Francis Ford Coppola, and Jordan wineries — not exactly small-time operations! We have the sneaking suspicion that at some point in the future, Sonoma will bear a striking resemblance to Napa. We hope not — we like it just the way it is.

Just south of Napa, Sonoma is more than twice as large, more spread out, and with almost as many wineries — more than 425. Its climate is similar to Napa's, except that some areas near the coast are distinctly cooler. Although there's plenty of chardonnay, cabernet sauvignon, and merlot in Sonoma, the region's varied microclimates and terrain have allowed three other varieties — pinot noir, zinfandel, and sauvignon blanc — to excel. In fact, Sonoma produces more pinot noir than any other county in the state!

The following are a few of the most important AVAs of Sonoma County to know, listed roughly from north to south:

>> Sonoma Coast: includes West Sonoma Coast AVA and Fort Ross-Seaview AVA (within West Sonoma Coast)

>> Dry Creek Valley

>> Alexander Valley

>> Knights Valley

>> Russian River Valley: includes Chalk Hill and Green Valley AVAs

>> Sonoma Valley: includes Bennett Valley, Moon Mountain District, and Sonoma Mountain AVAs

The largest three Sonoma AVAs in terms of vineyard acreage and number of wineries are Alexander Valley, Russian River Valley, and Sonoma Valley.

WORTH THE SEARCH

Pinot noir lovers should look for wines from Russian River Valley producers, such as Williams Selyem, Rochioli, and Dehlinger. Another new area for pinot noir — referred to informally as the Extreme Sonoma Coast or the True Coast — is ideal for growing pinot noir. See the nearby sidebar "The True Coast" for details.

TIP

The following list includes some of Sonoma's high-quality producers, shown alphabetically, along with their best wines and price guide ($: $20–$40, $$: $41-99, $$$: $100 and up).

>> **Ferrari-Carano ($ and up):** Cabernet sauvignon, chardonnay

>> **Flowers Vineyards & Winery ($$ and up):** Chardonnay, pinot noir

>> **Gloria Ferrer ($$ and up):** Chardonnay, malvasia, pinot blanc, pinot noir, traditional method sparkling, rosé

>> **Gundlach Bundschu ($$ and up):** Bordeaux blends, chardonnay, gewürztztraminer, pinot noir, rosé, tempranillo

>> **J Vineyards ($ and up):** Chardonnay, pinot noir, traditional method sparkling

>> **Jordan Winery ($$ and up):** Cabernet sauvignon, chardonnay

>> **Littorai ($$$ and up):** Chardonnay, pinot noir

>> **Merry Edwards ($$ and up):** Chardonnay, pinot noir, sauvignon blanc, traditional method sparkling (rare)

>> **Peter Michael ($$$ and up):** Cabernet sauvignon, chardonnay, pinot noir

>> **Rochioli ($$ and up):** Chardonnay, pinot noir, sauvignon blanc

>> **Three Sticks ($$ and up):** Chardonnay, pinot noir

>> **Willian Selyem ($$$ and up):** Cabernet sauvignon, chardonnay, gewürztraminer, pinot noir, zinfandel

MENDOCINO AND LAKE COUNTIES

Mendocino County is directly north of Sonoma County. Lake County (dominated by Clear Lake), a region with few wineries, is Napa's neighbor to the north. If you have the chance, it's worth your while to drive up the beautiful California coastline from San Francisco on Route 1 to the quaint, old town of Mendocino — perhaps with a quick stop to view the magnificent, redwood forests. Tourists are scarcer up here than in Napa or Sonoma, and that makes it all the nicer: you'll be genuinely welcomed at the wineries!

THE TRUE COAST

Called by its fans simply, "The True," the True Sonoma Coast, also known as the Extreme Sonoma Coast, refers to a section of the huge Sonoma Coast AVA along the Pacific Ocean, from the town of Fort Ross north to Annapolis. It includes the towns of Occidental and Freestone, and the Sebastopol hills. The name evolved because wine producers and growers in that area felt the need to distinguish their area from the rest of the Sonoma Coast AVA: Their coastal *terroir* is unique, and so are its wines. The first step toward formally redefining the overly broad Sonoma Coast AVA took place in January 2012, when the Fort Ross-Seaview AVA was created, covering an important vineyard area on the Extreme Sonoma Coast, close to the Pacific Ocean.

One of the main climatic influences in the True Coast area is the Petaluma Gap, a 15-mile virtual wind tunnel of ocean breezes that sweep through an opening in the mountain ranges at Bodega Bay (a village hugging the Pacific Ocean). This cool, windy effect, along with plenty of sun, makes an ideal growing climate for pinot noir and chardonnay. Pinot noir grapes ripen later on the True Coast, and the wines are typically lower in alcohol than pinot noirs from other, warmer parts of Sonoma. True Coast pinot noirs tend to be somewhat lighter in color and weight than most other California pinot noirs. They possess elegance and balance, plus a delicacy and finesse not usually found in United States pinots.

Quite a few top wineries specializing in pinot noir — such as Williams Selyem, Littorai, Hartford Court, Failla, DuNah Vineyard, and Willowbrook Cellars — purchase grapes from True Coast growers and make their own single-vineyard Sonoma Coast pinot noirs. The wineries actually situated in the True Coast area are miniscule, producing only a few thousand cases of wine annually (mainly pinot noir).

The elegant, cooler Anderson Valley in Mendocino County is ideal for growing chardonnay, pinot noir, gewürztraminer, and riesling, and for the production of sparkling wine. The French Louis Roederer Champagne house bypassed Napa and Sonoma to start its sparkling wine operation, Roederer Estate, here. Scharffenberger Cellars (now owned by Louis Roederer) and Handley Cellars, are two other successful producers of sparkling wine in Anderson Valley. Lake County is a well-established hotspot for sourcing grapes to larger producers across California, including Beringer, Sutter Home, and Kendall-Jackson.

TIP

The following list includes recommended Mendocino and Lake County producers and their best wines. We list the producers alphabetically in each county.

» **Mendocino County**

- **Edmeades:** Zinfandel

- **Fetzer Vineyards:** Cabernet sauvignon, gewürztraminer, pinot oir

- **Goldeneye Winery (Duckhorn):** Cabernet sauvignon, pinot noir, sauvignon blanc

- **Husch:** Pinot noir, sauvignon blanc, gewürztraminer

- **Navarro Vineyards:** Gewürztraminer, chardonnay, riesling

- **Theopolis Vineyards:** Petite sirah, pinot noir, white and red blends

» **Lake County**

- **Guenoc Winery:** Cabernet sauvignon and cabernet sauvignon blends, chardonnay, petite sirah

- **Langtry Estate & Vineyards:** Petite sirah, sauvignon blanc

- **Steele Wines:** Chardonnay, zinfandel, pinot noir, pinot blanc

THE SAN FRANCISCO BAY AREA

The San Francisco Bay area includes Marin County to the north, Alameda County and Livermore Valley to the east, and San Mateo County to the south.

The urban spread east and south of San Francisco, from the cities of Palo Alto to San Jose (Silicon Valley) and eastward, has taken its toll on vineyards in the Livermore and Santa Clara Valleys (all just about gone from Santa Clara Valley). Livermore Valley, cooled by breezes from the San Francisco Bay, is now relatively small. In Livermore, directly east of San Francisco, you can find all the usual suspects like chardonnay and sauvignon blanc, plus everything else from Spanish varieties like albariño and verdelho to Bordeaux blends and elegant petite sirahs.

TIP

We list our recommended producers and their main wines alphabetically, by locality.

>> **Marin County**

- **Sean H. Thackrey:** Petite sirah and syrah blends

>> **Alameda County/Livermore Valley**

- **A Donkey and Goat Winery:** Chardonnay, mourvèdre
- **Concannon Vineyard:** Chardonnay, petite sirah
- **Dashe Cellars:** Zinfandel, grenache, riesling
- **Longevity Wines:** Cabernet sauvignon, chardonnay, rosé, traditional method sparkling
- **Murrieta's Well:** Zinfandel, meritage
- **Wente Family Estates:** Chardonnay, sauvignon blanc

>> **San Mateo County**

- **Cronin Vineyards:** Chardonnay, cabernet sauvignon
- **Thomas Fogarty Winery:** Gewürztraminer, chardonnay, pinot noir

>> **Santa Clara County**

- **Ridge Vineyards (also in the Anderson Valley and Paso Robles):** White and red blends, zinfandel, rosé

THE SANTA CRUZ MOUNTAINS

Standing atop one of the isolated Santa Cruz Mountains, you can quickly forget that you're only an hour's drive south of San Francisco. The rugged, wild beauty of this area has attracted quite a few winemakers, including some of the best in the state (Paul Draper of Ridge Vineyards and Randall Grahm of Bonny Doon are just two). The climate is cool on the ocean side, where pinot noir thrives. On the San Francisco Bay side, cabernet sauvignon is the important red variety. Chardonnay is a leading variety on both sides.

TIP

We list our recommended Santa Cruz Mountains wine producers alphabetically, along with their best wines:

>> **Bargetto:** Chardonnay, pinot noir, cabernet sauvignon, merlot

>> **Bonny Doon Vineyard:** Rhône blends (grenache, syrah, mourvèdre)

>> **David Bruce Winery:** Pinot noir

- **Kathryn Kennedy Winery:** Cabernet sauvignon, syrah

- **Mount Eden Vineyards:** Chardonnay Estate, Pinot Noir Estate

- **Ridge Vineyards:** Cabernet Sauvignon Monte Bello, Geyserville

- **Santa Cruz Mountain Vineyard:** Pinot noir, cabernet sauvignon

MONTEREY COUNTY

Monterey County has a little bit of everything — a beautiful coastline, the chic town of Carmel, some very cool (as in temperature) vineyard districts in the north, some very hot areas in the south, mountain wineries, Salinas Valley wineries, a few gigantic wine firms and lots of small ones. Chardonnay is the leading varietal wine in Monterey County — as it is in most of the state. But the cooler parts of Monterey are also principal sources of riesling and gewürztraminer. Cabernet sauvignon and pinot noir are the leading red varieties in the mountain areas.

Like most California wine regions, Monterey has been changing rapidly during the past three decades, and now ten official sub-AVAs exist here, with the larger Monterey AVA covering close to 349 wineries at the time of writing (but that number is changing rapidly). In addition to producing wines in their respective AVAs, many Monterey wineries (especially in Santa Lucia Highlands) supply fruit to larger producers throughout California, including Belle Glos, Kosta Browne, Chamisal, and Wrath among others. The smaller AVAs within Monterey include:

- Arroyo Seco
- Carmel Valley
- Chalone
- Gabilan Mountains
- Hames Valley

- Monterey
- San Antonio Valley
- San Bernabe
- San Lucas
- Santa Lucia Highlands

TECHNICAL STUFF

Santa Lucia Highlands is also home to the fabled "Samsonite Cuttings" brought to the region by one of the highland's first avid promotors, Gary Pisoni (founder of Pisoni Vineyards). These are pinot noir vines, allegedly from a famous Vosne-Romanée vineyard in Burgundy, France. This and several other tales of suitcase smuggling are common in Calfornia's wine history, highlighting not only California's fine wine potential, but also its nod to France as the global trendsetter for quality and prestige. More than any other world wine region, California is known for its use of *clones* (genetically identitical copies of "mother vines" created through cuttings or vine grafting) identified through research and development of varietites such as cabernet sauvignon, chardonnay, and pinot noir.

The following list includes our recommended producers in Monterey County, listed alphabetically, along with one producer from neighboring San Benito County:

- **Albatross Ridge:** Cabernet sauvignon, chardonnay, pinot noir

- **Bernardus Winery:** Cabernet sauvignon, chardonnay, pinot noir, sauvignon blanc

- **Calera (San Benito County):** Aligoté, chardonnay, pinot noir, viognier

- **Chalone Vineyard:** Chardonnay, chenin blanc, pinot blanc, pinot noir

- **Château Julien:** Chardonnay, merlot, cabernet sauvignon

- **J. Lohr:** Bordeaux blends, cabernet sauvignon, chardonnay, merlot, pinot noir

- **Hahn Estates/Smith & Hook Winery:** Chardonnay, pinot noir, Smith & Hook Cabernet Sauvignon

- **Morgan Winery:** Chardonnay, pinot noir, syrah

- **Wrath:** Chardonnay, pinot noir, sauvignon blanc, syrah

- **Scheid Vineyards:** Albariño, chardonnay, gewürztraminer, grüner veltliner, Rhône blends, petite manseng, pinot blanc, riesling, roussanne, sangiovese, sauvignon blanc, petite sirah, pinot noir

- **Talbott Vineyards:** Chardonnay, pinot noir, traditional method sparkling

SIERRA FOOTHILLS

No wine region in America has a more romantic past than the Sierra Foothills. The Gold Rush of 1849 carved a place in history for the foothills of the Sierra Nevada Mountains. It also brought vineyards to the area to provide wine for thirsty miners. One of the vines planted at that time was certainly zinfandel — still the region's most famous wine. Many of the oldest grapevines in the United States, some more than 100 years old and mainly zinfandel, are here in the Sierra Foothills. In fact, very little has changed in the Sierra Foothills over the years. This is the one of the most rustic, charming wine regions on the west coast.

The Sierra Foothills is a sprawling wine region east of Sacramento, centered in Amador and El Dorado Counties, but spreading north and south of both. Two of its best known viticultural areas are Shenandoah Valley and Fiddletown. Summers can be hot, but many vineyards are situated as high as 1,500 feet (457 meters) and evenings are very cool. Volcanic soils can be found throughout the region.

TIP

The following are our recommended producers in the Sierra Foothills (listed alphabetically), along with some of their best wines:

>> **Amador Foothill Winery:** Zinfandel

>> **Donkey & Goat Winery:** Cabernet sauvignon, chardonnay, Nero d'Avola

>> **Lava Cap Winery:** Barbera, cabernet sauvignon, petite sirah

>> **Montevina Winery:** Zinfandel, barbera, syrah

>> **Shenandoah Vineyards:** Zinfandel, sauvignon blanc

>> **Sierra Vista Winery:** Zinfandel, syrah

>> **Sobon Estate:** Zinfandel, viognier

SAN LUIS OBISPO COUNTY

San Luis Obispo County — in the heart of California's South-Central Coast, about equidistant from San Francisco and Los Angeles — encompasses vastly diverse viticultural areas. These include, for example, the hotter, hilly Paso Robles region (north of the town of San Luis Obispo) where reds dominate, with cabernet sauvignon, zinfandel, and Rhône varieties like grenache, syrah, and mourvèdre, and the cool, coastal Edna Valley and Arroyo Grande (south of the town), home of some very high-quality pinot noirs and chardonnays.

Paso Robles is one of California's fastest-growing wine regions, with 200-plus wineries — more than twice as many as it had just eight years ago. Its wines are very different from those of the North and North-Central coasts (explained earlier in this chapter).

TIP

We recommend the following producers in San Luis Obispo (listed alphabetically, along with their best wines):

>> **Paso Robles**

• **Adelaida Cellars:** Pinot noir, zinfandel, cabernet sauvignon

• **Daou Vineyards:** Cabernet auvignon Reserve, pinot noir

• **Eberle Winery:** Zinfandel, cabernet sauvignon, syrah, viognier

• **Justin Vineyards:** Isosceles (cabernet sauvignon blend)

• **J. Lohr Winery:** Chardonnay, cabernet sauvignon, syrah

• **Saxum:** Grenache, syrah, and mourvèdre blends

• **Tablas Creek Vineyard:** Mourvèdre, grenache, syrah, roussanne

>> **Edna Valley and Arroyo Grande**

- **Alban Vineyards:** Viognier (Estate), roussanne, syrah, grenache

- **Chamisal:** Chardonnay, pinot noir, traditional method sparkling

- **Edna Valley Vineyard:** Chardonnay, pinot noir

- **Laetitia Vineyard:** Chardonnay, pinot noir

- **Talley Vineyards:** Chardonnay, pinot noir

WORTH THE SEARCH

Adelaida Cellars and Daou Vineyards are making high-quality wines at a range of price points, some of the most popular in California from their hillside vineyards. Look especially for their cabernet sauvignons and pinot noirs.

SANTA BARBARA COUNTY

Some of the most exciting viticultural areas in California — if not in the entire country — are in Santa Barbara County. Even though Spanish missionaries planted vineyards there, it wasn't until 1975 that the first major winery (Firestone Vineyards) opened. In light of what we now know — that is, how well suited Santa Barbara County is to grape growing — this was a late start.

The main growing areas of the county are the Santa Maria, Santa Ynez, and Los Alamos Valleys, which lie north of the city of Santa Barbara. Unusually in California, these cool valleys run east to west, opening toward the Pacific Ocean and channeling in the ocean air. The cool climate is ideal for pinot noir and chardonnay. In the Santa Maria Valley, for example, the average temperature during the growing season is a mere 74°F (23°C).

The southernmost of the three valleys is the Santa Ynez Valley. It boasts a cool climate on its western end, while the eastern end of the valley is warm enough to grow red grapes, such as grenache and syrah. The Sta. Rita Hills AVA in the cool, western end is particularly known for pinot noir and chardonnay, and is one of the three important Santa Barbara AVAs. The other two are the Santa Maria Valley AVA and the Santa Ynez Valley AVA.

REMEMBER

Pinot noir has earned Santa Barbara County much of its acclaim as a wine region. Santa Barbara is generally recognized as one of the six great American wine regions for pinot noir — the other five being Carneros, the Russian River Valley, the Sonoma Coast, Mendocino County's Anderson Valley, and Oregon's Willamette Valley (which we discuss later in this chapter). In Santa Barbara, pinot noir wines seem to burst with luscious strawberry fruit, laced with herbal tones. These wines tend to be precocious: they're delicious in their first four or five years compared to the longer-lived, sturdier, wilder-tasting Russian River or the softer

"True Sonoma Coast" pinot noirs seem to be. But why keep them when they taste so good?

TIP

The following are some recommended producers in Santa Barbara (listed alphabetically), and their best wines:

- >> **Alma Rosa:** Chardonnay, pinot gris, pinot noir
- >> **Au Bon Climat:** Chardonnay, pinot noir
- >> **Babcock Vineyards:** Chardonnay, pinot noir, sauvignon blanc
- >> **Byron Vineyard:** Chardonnay, pinot noir
- >> **Cambria Winery:** Chardonnay, pinot noir, syrah
- >> **Daniel Gehrs:** Chenin blanc, riesling, gewürztraminer, syrah
- >> **Diatom:** Chardonnay, pinot noir, syrah
- >> **Longoria Wines:** Pinot noir, syrah
- >> **The Ojai Vineyard:** Chardonnay, pinot noir, syrah
- >> **Presqu'ile Winery:** Chardonnay, pinot noir
- >> **Sandhi:** Chardonnay, pinot noir, syrah, traditional method sparkling
- >> **Sanford:** Chardonnay, pinot noir, rosé
- >> **Santa Barbara Winery:** Pinot noir, chardonnay, syrah
- >> **Zaca Mesa Winery:** Syrah, roussanne, chardonnay, viognier

Washington State: Fire and ice

Compared to California and Oregon, Washington arrived on the serious wine scene much later. With the exception of Château Ste. Michelle (now called Ste. Michelle Wine Estates with no actual French connection — it was named this because it sounded French enough at the time for marketing purposes!) and Columbia Winery, both founded in the 1960s, only 19 of the current 1,070-plus wineries existed before 1980. Washington is now second in the country in wine production.

TECHNICAL
STUFF

Long before Microsoft and Starbucks (as in, at least 6 million years ago), a foundation for sustainable viticulture was forming in Washington State. A basalt bedrock formed by some of the largest volcanic lava flows ever documented would result in soils rich in nutrients with the (almost as if determined by fate) ability to retain moisture and produce complex, mineral-driven wines. Fast-forward to at least 15,000 years ago at the end of the last ice age, and the burst of the ice dam

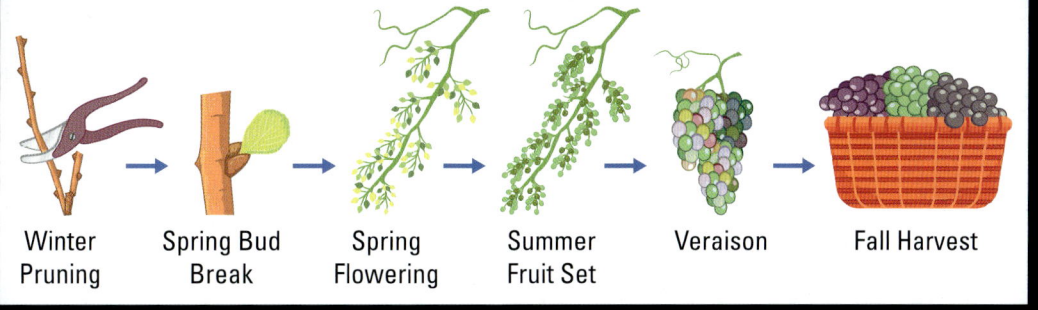

| Winter Pruning | Spring Bud Break | Spring Flowering | Summer Fruit Set | Veraison | Fall Harvest |

The life cycle of a vine (Chapter 1).

Pale straw ⟶ Deep gold

White

Pale pink ⟶ Raspberry red

Rosé

Cherry red ⟶ Opaque purple

Red

The many colors of wine (Chapter 3).

WINE REGIONS OF **ITALY**

The wine regions of Italy (Chapter 5).

WINE REGIONS OF FRANCE

English Channel

Belgium

Lille

CHAMPAGNE

Luxembourg

Germany

Reims

Lorraine

Paris

Strasbourg

Seine

Vosges
Mountains

Marne

ALSACE

Rhine

Yonne

LOIRE VALLEY

Loire

BURGUNDY

Dijon

Loire

Saône

Nantes

Jura Mountains

Jura

Switzerland

BEAUJOLAIS

Alps

ATLANTIC OCEAN

Lyon

Savoie

BORDEAUX

Dordogne

RHÔNE VALLEY

Rhône

Bugey

Bordeaux

Italy

Landes
Forest

Garonne

Montpellier

Aix-en-provence

SOUTH
WEST

Toulouse

Nice

Marseille

Spain

LANGUEDOC-
ROUSSILLON

PROVENCE

CORSICA

MEDITERRANEAN SEA

Sardegna
(Italy)

N

0   50   100   200 mi

0   50   100   150   200 km

The wine regions of France (Chapter 6).

The wine regions of Spain (Chapter 7).

The wine regions of Germany (Chapter 8).

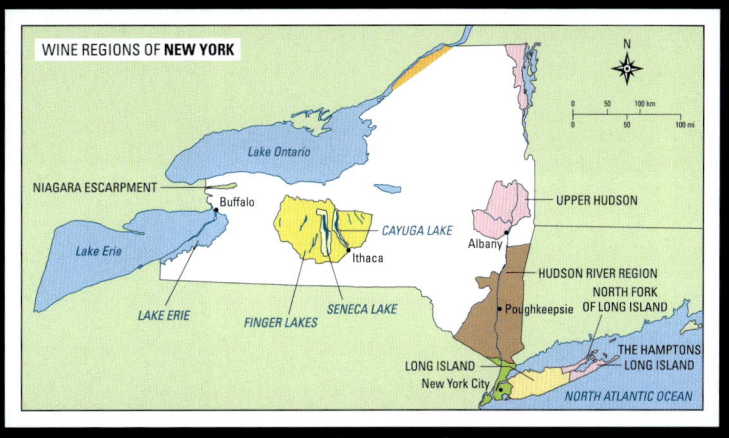

The wine regions of New York (Chapter 11).

The wine regions of California
(Chapter 11).

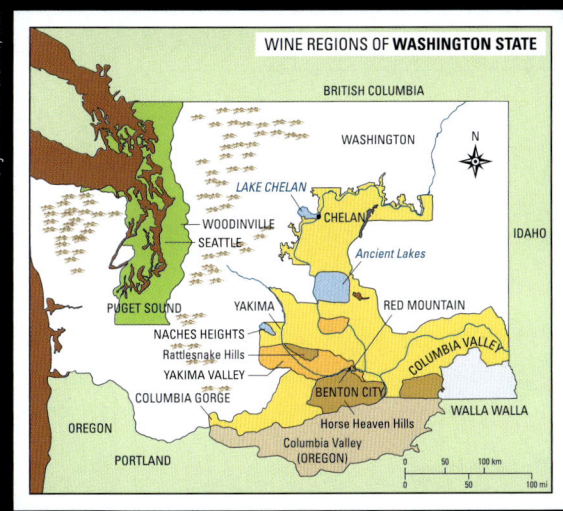

The wine regions of Washington State
(Chapter 11).

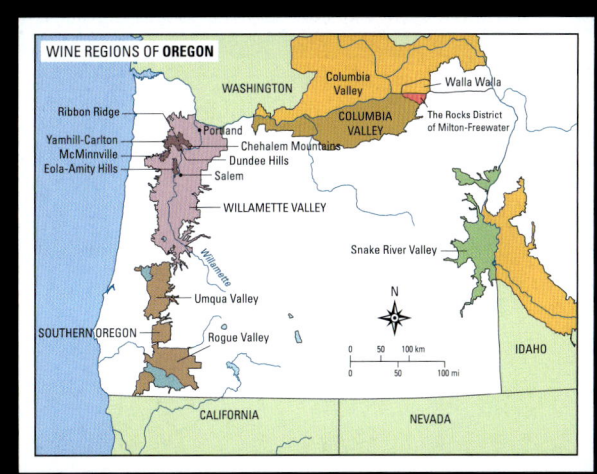

The wine regions of Oregon (Chapter 11).

The wine regions of Chile (Chapter 12).

The wine regions of Argentina (Chapter 12).

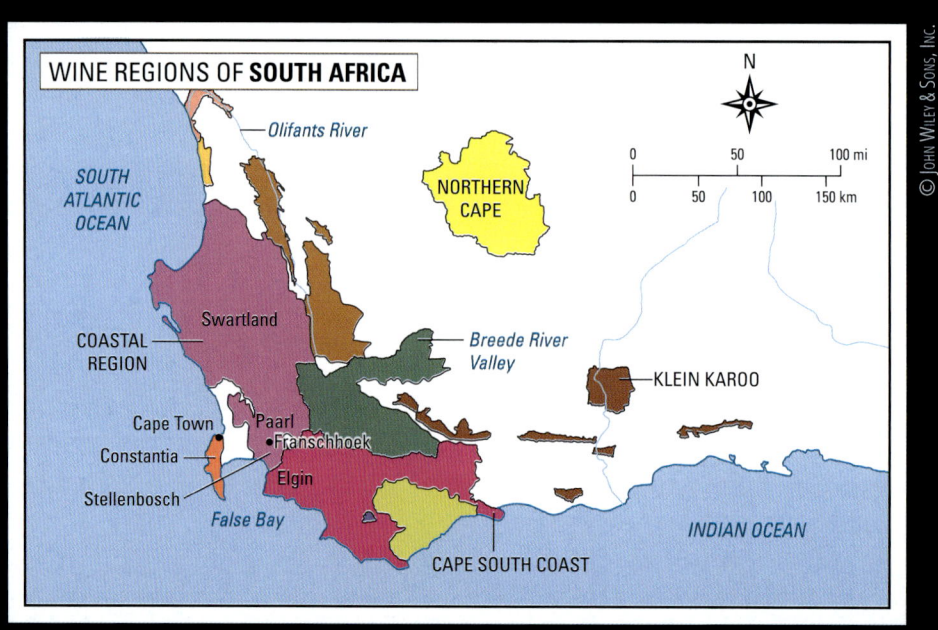

The wine regions of South Africa (Chapter 15).

Wine from sobretabla or other *solera* system

Wine with the youngest average age

3rd *criadera*

2nd *criadera*

1st *criadera*

CRIADERA (up to 14 possible)

Wine with the oldest average age

SOLERA

Sherry for sale, blending, or to another *solera* system

The *solera* system (Chapter 7).

© John Wiley & Sons, Inc.

Fino

Manzanilla

Amontillado

Palo Cortado

Oloroso

Pale cream

Medium

Cream

Pedro Ximénez

Moscatel

Different styles of sherry (Chapter 7).

© John Wiley & Sons, Inc.

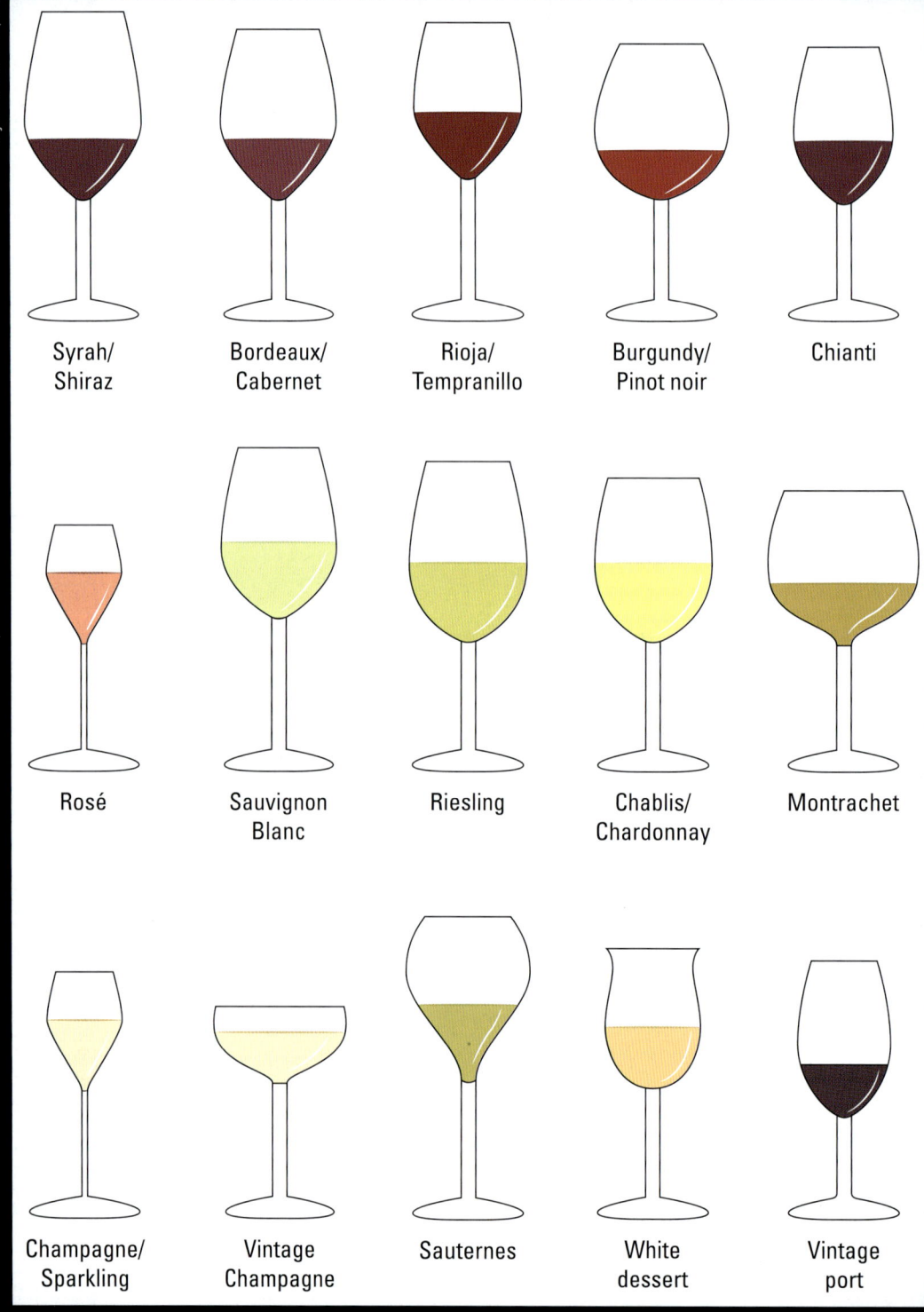

© John Wiley & Sons, Inc.

Syrah/
Shiraz

Bordeaux/
Cabernet

Rioja/
Tempranillo

Burgundy/
Pinot noir

Chianti

Rosé

Sauvignon
Blanc

Riesling

Chablis/
Chardonnay

Montrachet

Champagne/
Sparkling

Vintage
Champagne

Sauternes

White
dessert

Vintage
port

Wine glass shapes (Chapter 20).

that created the icy Lake Missoula released flood waters across Washington and Oregon before emptying into the Pacific Ocean. A gargantuan flood carved out the Columbia Valley, vigorously depositing trees, boulders and — most importantly — forms of silt that would later come to be known as Warden Silt Loam. These lower-nutrient, well-drained deposits just happen to make an ideal viticultural environment in which vines have to dig deep to extract nutrients, resulting in higher acidity and more concentrated fruit flavors in finished wines.

Although Washington and Oregon are neighboring states, their wine regions have vastly different climates due to their vineyard locations relative to the Cascade Mountains, which cut through both states from north to south. On Washington's western, coastal side, the climate is maritime — cool, plenty of rain that we've come to know as distinctly Washingtonian, and a lot of vegetation. East of the mountains, the climate is continental, with hot, very dry summers and cold winters. Most of Washington's vineyards are situated in this eastern area, in the vast, sprawling Columbia Valley, which encompasses the important Yakima Valley. Because it's so far north, Washington also has the advantage of long hours of sunlight, averaging an unusually high 17.4 hours of sunshine during the growing season (about two more than Napa or Sonoma Valley per day, for perspective). See the color section of this book for more details on the wine regions of Washington State.

More than 80 grape varieties grow in Washington, with the big five being cabernet sauvignon, riesling, chardonnay, merlot, and syrah. Washington first became well-known for the quality of its merlots. Ste. Michelle Wine Estate and Columbia Crest dominate United States sales of merlot in the over $10 per bottle price category. But Washington's rieslings and syrahs are among the country's sales and quality leaders for these varietal wines. Ste. Michelle Wine Estates also leads United States sales in American-made riesling.

REMEMBER The types of wine produced in Washington have dramatically changed during the past two decades. In 1993, about two-thirds of Washington's wines were white, one-third red. Reflecting Americans' changing tastes, Washington's wines are now about 60 percent red, 40 percent white.

Ste. Michelle Wine Estates, along with Columbia Crest and 14 Hands (all under the same corporate ownership) account for more than 60 percent of all Washington's wine sales at present. There are a number of excellent smaller wineries high-quality wines throughout Washington's key regions as well.

Washington has 21 AVAs. One of them is the gigantic Columbia Valley AVA which encompasses ten other AVAs within its macro-appellation (an *appellation* is a legally defined geographical area characterized by a specific *terroir* or certain grapes that are representative of the area). These ten (listed in order of importance) are:

>> **Yakima Valley:** This region is the second largest in acreage, behind the huge Columbia Valley itself. It is Washington's oldest viticultural region, accounting for nearly 40 percent of the state's annual wine production.

>> **Walla Walla Valley:** This fast-growing region is in the southeast corner of Washington, extending into northeast Oregon. It is home to some of the state's top wineries, such as Leonetti Cellar, Woodward Canyon, Waterbrook Winery, Canoe Ridge Vineyard, and L'Ecole No 41 — as well as some of the state's best red wines.

>> **Red Mountain:** The tiny, prestigious Red Mountain area is actually within the Yakima Valley AVA, but its red clay soil and high altitude earned it a separate appellation in 2001. A handful of wineries, including Hedges and Kiona Vineyards, concentrate on red varieties such as cabernet sauvignon, merlot, cabernet franc, and syrah.

>> **Horse Heaven Hills:** This area in the southernmost part of the Columbia Valley, just north of the Columbia River, has long been known as an ideal location for cabernet sauvignon. Many of Washington's leading wineries, including Ste. Michelle Wine Estates, use grapes from vineyards here.

>> **Wahluke Slope:** One of the state's warmer appellations, known for its merlot and cabernet sauvignon, and home to Charles Smith's K. Vintners, and LUKE Wines.

>> **Rattlesnake Hills:** A tiny appellation, Rattlesnake Hills is actually a sub-appellation of Yakima Valley that boasts Yakima's highest elevation (more than 3,000 feet, or 914 meters). The wineries are small and focused. Temperatures are moderate in this beautiful region, thanks to the altitude.

>> **Snipes Mountain:** This AVA is another sub-appellation of Yakima Valley. Snipes Mountain was the first region in the state of Washington to grow wine grapes.

>> **Lake Chelan:** Located in northern Columbia Valley, Lake Chelan became the state's tenth AVA in 2009. It boasts high elevation and temperate climate.

>> **Naches Heights:** The smallest appellation (with 37 acres and seven vineyards), Naches Heights is a high plateau, ranging up to 2,100 feet (640 meters), with volcanic soil. It is within the Columbia Valley, west of the city of Yakima.

>> **Ancient Lakes of Columbia Valley:** Ancient Lakes is also known as Quincy Basin. It's in the northwest part of Columbia Valley. Chardonnay and riesling grow especially well here.

Columbia Gorge, a beautiful area in southwest Washington crossing into Oregon, is another important Washington AVA. It actually has an equal number of wineries within Washington State and Oregon boundaries. The Greater Puget Sound/Seattle Area AVA encompasses the Puget Sound Islands and has more than 300 wineries in Puget Sound alone. In this cool, moist climate, pinot gris and pinot noir are leading varieties, as well as riesling and gewürztraminer.

Finally, 16 wineries, including Arbor Crest, are located in Lewis Clark Valley (shared with Idaho). At the time of writing, Washington State's newest AVA is Beverly, located in central Washington. The number of newly named AVAs continues to soar.

TIP

The following are some of our recommended wine producers in Washington, listed alphabetically, along with some of their best wines:

>> **Cayuse Vineyards:** Grenache, syrah, tempranillo, viognier

>> **Château Ste. Michelle:** Merlot, cabernet sauvignon, chardonnay (especially Cold Creek Vineyard), Eroica Riesling (with Dr. Loosen)

>> **Chinook Winery:** Sauvignon blanc, sémillon, chardonnay

>> **Col Solare Winery:** Meritage (mainly cabernet sauvignon, a Château Ste. Michelle/Piero Antinori collaboration)

>> **Columbia Crest Winery:** Red blends, sémillon, syrah, merlot, cabernet sauvignon, sémillon, Chardonnay

>> **Columbia Winery:** Cabernet sauvignon, cabernet franc, syrah, merlot

>> **Cote Bonneville:** Riesling, cabernet franc, cabernet sauvignon, chardonnay, red blends

>> **DeLille Cellars:** Cabernet sauvignon, red and white blends, syrah

>> **Gramercy Cellars:** Syrah, cabernet sauvignon

>> **The Hogue Cellars:** Merlot, cabernet sauvignon, chenin blanc, lemberger, white blends

>> **Kiona Vineyards:** Lemberger, cabernet sauvignon, merlot

>> **Klipsun:** Cabernet sauvignon and red blends

>> **L'Ecole No 41:** Merlot, sabernet sauvignon, sémillon

>> **Leonetti Cellar:** Cabernet sauvignon, merlot, sangiovese

>> **Quilceda Creek Vintners:** Cabernet sauvignon, merlot

- **» Savage Grace:** Cabernet franc

- **» Seven Hills Winery:** Merlot, cabernet sauvignon

- **» Snoqualmie Vineyards:** Cabernet sauvignon, merlot, syrah

Oregon: Wine trails

Because Oregon is north of California, most people assume that Oregon's wine regions are cool. And they are. But the main reason for Oregon's relatively cool climate is that its vineyards aren't separated from the Pacific Ocean by any high mountain ranges. The ocean influence brings low temperatures and rain. Oregon is generally wetter and cooler for longer periods of time than both Washington State and California.

Oregon's suitability for viticulture stems from a similar history to Washington State and California (detailed earlier in this chapter) — the country's other star-studded wine states. A combination of techtonic plate collisions, basaltic rock formations from erupting volcanos, and soil deposits from the Missoula floods from thousands to millions of years ago carved out what we know today as the Willamette Valley. A combination of *terroir* and tenacity among new winemakers are what built Oregon's wine industry from the ground up — literally. See the color section of this book for Oregon's main wine regions.

Winemaking has grown at warp speeds in Oregon. From five wineries in 1970, the state now has 1,116 with the majority in its humble yet powerful wine region, the Willamette Valley. Most of Oregon's wineries are small, family-owned operations, started by ex-professionals from other industries who made the trail to the state from places like California, setting up shop and building a community of other new winemakers who would place Oregon in a league of its own within the United States.

Because chardonnay is the companion grape to pinot noir in France's Burgundy region (see Chapter 6), and because chardonnay is popular in America, it's an important variety in Oregon. However, pinot gris actually out-produces chardonnay in Oregon. The late David Lett, founder and winemaker of The Eyrie Vineyards and Oregon's pinot noir pioneer, is the man acknkowledged as making Oregon's first pinot gris, around 1970, followed by Ponzi Vineyards and Adelsheim Vineyard. Today, most wineries in the Willamette Valley make pinot gris, along with pinot noir.

REMEMBER

Two styles of Oregon pinot gris exist. You will have to ask a shop attendant (if in a wine store) or a sommelier (if in a bar or restaurant) the producer, vintage, and wine name to be sure you're getting the style you want, as there are no labeling requirements for these in Oregon:

» A lighter, fruity style, from early-harvested grapes. Always made without oak, these wines can be consumed as soon as they are released.

» A medium-bodied, golden-hued wine from grapes left longer on the vine, which sometimes has a little oak aging. These wines can age for five or six years or longer.

In general, Oregon pinot gris has aromas reminiscent of ripe to baked pears, apples, and sometimes of melon, with surprising depth for generally great value wines (between $15 and $25 a bottle for some producers). It's an excellent food wine, even when it's slightly sweet. Pinot gris works especially well with seafood, spicy dishes, and fish — just the kind of food that it's paired with in Oregon.

TIP

The United States' most popular white variety, chardonnay, is now being made better than ever in Oregon. It seems inevitable that Oregon will eventually make chardonnay its most popular white variety, despite the state's excellent pinot gris wines.

WILLAMETTE VALLEY

The home of pinot noir and pinot gris in Oregon is the Willamette Valley, directly south of the city of Portland in northwestern Oregon. The Willamette Valley has established itself in the last 50-plus years as one of the most important wine regions in the United States. Two-thirds of Oregon's wineries are situated there.

TIP

Willamette Valley is a convenient wine destination to visit because the vibrant city of Portland, with all its restaurants, hotels, and shops, is just 30-plus minutes north. If you're into hazelnuts, you would also be visiting the country's largest producer and finding foods made with hazelnuts you didn't even know existed!

Willamette Valley is huge and encompasses several counties. Yamhill County, directly southwest of Portland, has the greatest concentration of wineries, all of which produce pinot noir. Its county seat, McMinnville, is a destination point for wine tourists. But quite a few wineries are located in Washington County, west of Portland, and in Polk County, south of Yamhill. In addition to the general Willamette Valley AVA, 11 nested AVAs now exist in the Willamette Valley: Chehalem Mountains, Dundee Hills, Eola-Amity Hills, Laurelwood District, Lower Long Tom, McMinnville Foothills, Mount Pisgah, Ribbon Ridge, Tualatin Hills, Yamhill-Carlton District, and Van Duzer Corridor. At Oregon's rate of success, we predict that there are many more AVAs to come.

TIP

Here are some of the best producers in the Willamette Valley, primarily for pinot noir and pinot gris (but sometimes also chardonnay or riesling):

- 00 Wines
- Adelsheim Vineyard
- Antica Terra
- The Audeant Wines
- Beaux Frères
- Benton Lane Winery
- Bergström Wines
- Bethel Heights Vineyard
- Big Table Farms
- Brittan Vineyards
- Chehalem Winery
- Cristom Vineyards

- Domaine Drouhin Oregon
- Domaine Serene
- The Eyrie Vineyards
- Gran Moraine
- Ken Wright
- Lingua Franca
- Rose & Arrow Estate
- Shea Wine Cellars
- Soter Vineyards
- Stoller Family Estate
- Tualatin Estate
- Yamhill Valley

UMPQUA AND ROGUE VALLEYS

Two other wine regions of note in Oregon are both in the southwest part of the state: the Umpqua Valley (around the town of Roseburg) and the Rogue Valley farther south, next to California's northern border.

Considerably warmer than Willamette, the Umpqua Valley is the site of Oregon's first winery, Hillcrest Vineyard, founded in 1961. The main grape varieties in Umpqua are pinot noir, chardonnay, riesling, and cabernet sauvignon. High-quality producers include Abacela, Brandborg, Cooper Ridge, and Reustle-Prayer Rock.

The Rogue Valley is warmer still. Cabernet sauvignon and merlot often perform better here than pinot noir. Chardonnay is the leading white wine, but pinot gris and viognier are on the rise. High-quality producers are Foris (specializing in cabernet sauvignon and merlot), Kriselle Cellars, Ovum, and Weisinger Family Winery.

PRECISELY PINOT NOIR

Oregon first gained respect in wine circles for its pinot noir, a grape that shows its most elegant, sultry side in cooler climates. The Eyrie Vineyards released Oregon's first pinot noir in 1970, but national recognition for the state's pinot noirs came only after the excellent 1983 and 1985 vintages. Pinot noir is still Oregon's flagship wine, and a vast majority of the state's wineries produce it. Oregon's finest pinot noirs show perfectly perfumed, floral notes, dry to just slightly ripe red and black fruit, and earthy, almost rustic characteristics that will leave you spellbound.

Red wine encompasses 60 percent of Oregon's wine production today. The remaining 40 percent are white wines made from pinot gris, chardonnay, and riesling. In recent years, Oregon's chardonnays have surged in quality, thanks to the replanting of many vineyards with French clones of the chardonnay grape, as opposed to the original plantings that some producers reported were more suited to California's warmer climate.

New York: An Empire State of mind

New York City may be the capital of the world in many ways, but its state's wines haven't always received the recognition they deserve. In many ways, as big as New York's cultural personality is, it's never really crept out of California's wine shadow. New York actually ranks as the fourth-largest wine-producing state in the United States, after California, Washington, and Oregon. Wineries have burgeoned in recent decades and now number more than 450. There are seven main wine regions (shown in this book's color section): The Finger Lakes, Long Island, Hudson River Region, Upper Hudson, Champlain Valley, Niagara Escarpment, and Lake Erie. The Finger Lakes, Long Island, and the Hudson River Region are the three most important to know.

TIP

Most wineries in New York State are small, family-run operations. The following are lists of recommended producers in New York's three major wine regions, mentioned alphabetically.

> **The Finger Lakes region**

- Anthony Road Wine Company
- Dr. Frank's Vinifera Wine Cellars
- Fox Run Vineyards
- Hermann J. Wiemer Vineyard
- Heron Hill Vineyards

- Lakewood Vineyards
- McGregor Vineyard
- Ravines Wine Cellars
- Wagner Vineyards

>> **Hudson River region**

- Benmarl Vineyards
- Brotherhood Winery
- Millbrook Vineyards and Winery

>> **Long Island region**

- Bedell Cellars
- Laurel Lake Vineyards
- Lieb Family Cellars
- Macari Vineyards
- Martha Clara Vineyards
- Paumanok Vineyards
- Pindar Vineyards
- Rose Hill
- Sparkling Pointe

THE FINGER LAKES

Common wisdom held that the relatively cold New York winters could not support *Vitis vinifera*. But a Russian immigrant, the pioneering Dr. Konstantin Frank, proved all the naysayers wrong when he succeeded in growing riesling (followed by many other *Vitis vinifera* varieties) in 1953 in Hammondsport, in the Finger Lakes region. The first wines from *Vitis vinifera* grapes were made in 1961 (and released in 1962) at his winery, Dr. Frank's Vinifera Wine Cellars. His son, Willy Frank, ran one of the most successful wineries in the state, with an entire line of still and sparkling wines. The winery carries on today under the leadership of Dr. Frank's grandson, Fred.

The northern Finger Lakes region, where four large lakes temper the otherwise cool climate, is still New York's most important wine region. This AVA produces the largest number of New York's wines and has more than 130 wineries. Riesling, the Finger Lakes region's most renowned (and best) wine, is available from most Finger Lakes' wineries, which are almost exclusively small operations.

LONG ISLAND AND THE HUDSON RIVER REGIONS

Long Island has three AVAs: the North Fork of Long Island (the most important), the Hamptons (on the island's South Fork), and Long Island itself, applicable to wines made with grapes from all over Long Island. There are 57 wineries (at the time of writing) on Long Island, mainly in the North Fork AVA.

Long Island's wine roots date back to 1973, when Alec and Louisa Hargrave got the idea that Long Island's North Fork — about a two-hour drive east of New York City — had the ideal climate and soil for *Vitis vinifera* grapes. They founded Long Island's first winery, Hargrave Vineyards. Some believe that Long Island is particularly suited to merlot, but chardonnay, riesling, cabernet sauvignon, cabernet franc, and sauvignon blanc are also grown, plus some gewürztraminer, pinot noir, and numerous other varieties.

The Hudson Valley AVA is situated along the Hudson River north of New York City. In the earlier days (prior to 1960), most wines in the Hudson Valley were made from indigenous American varieties, such as concord, as well as French-American hybrid grapes, such as seyval blanc. Wines from native American species and from hybrid varieties are still produced in the Hudson Valley, but their popularity is waning. Now most Hudson Valley producers make wines from the classic European grapes, especially chardonnay.

Other regions in the United States

As we mentioned at the beginning of this chapter, wine is made in all 50 United States. Although California, Washington, Oregon, and New York are the largest producers, you can find high-quality wine in all forms and fashions around the country. The wineries range from small, boutique ones that only sell wines out of their tasting rooms to multi-million dollar joint ventures with high-end consultants funded by executives, politicians, and other members of the American elite.

Here is a quick snapshot, including some of our favorite wineries from around the country and their main varieties:

>> **Michigan:** Home to mostly cool climate varieties such as chardonnay, riesling, pinot gris, and gewürztraminer. Recommended producers include Black Star Farms, Bonobo Winery, Chateau Grand Traverse, Left Foot Charley, Mari Vineyards, Modales Wines, and Wyncroft Wines.

>> **New Mexico:** Winemaking started here with misión (listán prieto) grapes planted by missionaries in the 17th century. Today, New Mexico is best known for cabernet sauvignon, chardonnay, and pinot noir, although scores of other European varieties are also popular. Producers to know include Casa Rodeña, Gruet,Luna Rossa, and Vivac.

- » **Texas:** Another start to winemaking with listán prieto and missionaries in the 17th century, Texas produces wine out of eight AVAs, with nearly 80 percent of wine coming from the Texas High Plains AVA. Cabernet sauvignon, merlot, and tempranillo are the main varieties, although others are planted in smaller quantities. Some of our recommended producers include Fall Creek Winery, Duchman Family Winery, Kuhlman Cellars, and McPherson Cellars Winery.

- » **Virginia and Maryland:** In 2023, *Wine Enthusiast* magazine named Charlottesville, Virginia and the Monticello AVA "Wine Region of the Year" for good reason. A lot of trial, error, and persistence since the first wines were made in 1607 transformed Virginia into one of the most exciting places to taste American wines today. There are now eight AVAs, producing a range of sparkling, white, rosé, and red wines, including albariño, cabernet franc, cabernet sauvignon, merlot, petite manseng, petit verdot, viognier, and nebbiolo. Top-quality producers include Barboursville Winery, Crimson Lane Vineyards, Early Mountain Vineyards, King Family Vineyards, Paradise Springs Winery, RdV, Veritas Vineyard and Winery, and Walsh Family Wine. In less than two hours' drive, you can also taste amazing Maryland wines from excellent-quality, family-owned producers such as Big Cork, Loew Vineyards, and Old Westminster Winery. We've also got our eye on *cooperatives* (a group of winegrowers who may collectively own and/or operate a winery, including those that use shared facilities for production) in Maryland. Some of our favorites include Port of Leonardtown Winery and Philosophy Winery.

Mexico

Not to be confused with the state of New Mexico, the country of Mexico is also on the rise in international wine fame. Figure 11-1 shows the country's main wine regions. Winemaking here set the foundation for the world to come in Calfornia and Texas, with Spanish missionaries planting misión (listán prieto) as early as the 1500s. Today, three main regions produce most of the high-quality wine, including the northwest states (Baja California is the state to know), north central states, and central states. Many top vineyard sites in these regions enjoy more Mediterranean climates, thanks to the Sierras de Baja ranges, without which tequila would likely overshadow wine. A smattering of grapes are grown in Mexico, but some of the most well-regarded wines are made from cabernet sauvignon, chardonnay, chenin blanc, malbec, merlot, syrah, tempranillo, and red blends. Top producers include Adobe Guadalupe, Finca La Carrodilla, Finca Sala Vive, Los Cedros, Monte Xanic, and Vinícola Parvada.

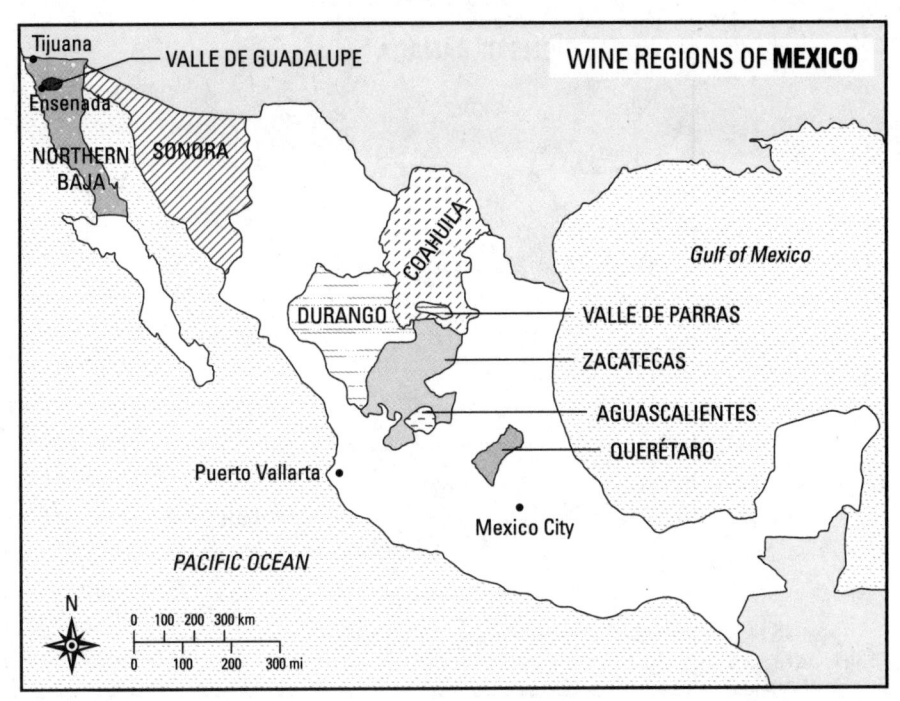

© John Wiley & Sons, Inc.

FIGURE 11-1:
The wine regions
of Mexico.

Canada

We would be remiss not to include a brief overview of Canada, whose modern-day wine industry really took off in the 1980s and 1990s. Canada is by far the coldest winegrowing region in North America, with the majority of its wines made in two provinces on opposite sides of the country: in the east, Ontario, and in the west, British Columbia. See Figure 11-2 for Canada's main wine regions.

Ontario's main wine districts include Lake Erie North Shore, Niagara Peninsula, and Prince Edward County. White and red cool climate varieties are planted here, the most popular being cabernet franc, chardonnay, gewürztraminer, pinot noir, riesling, icewine, and traditional method (explained in Chapter 3) sparkling wines. A few top Ontario producers include Cave Spring Cellars, Checkmate Artisanal Winery, Inniskillin, Jackson-Triggs, and Peller Estates.

REMEMBER

Canada is the world's largest producer of icewine. The country's icewines are known as some of the best quality and value, and have gained a reputation as Canada's top wine delicacy. *Icewines* are made by allowing grapes to freeze on the vine, then harvesting them one by one when the outside temperature is no higher than 17.6°F (-8°C), a temperature mandated by Canadian law.

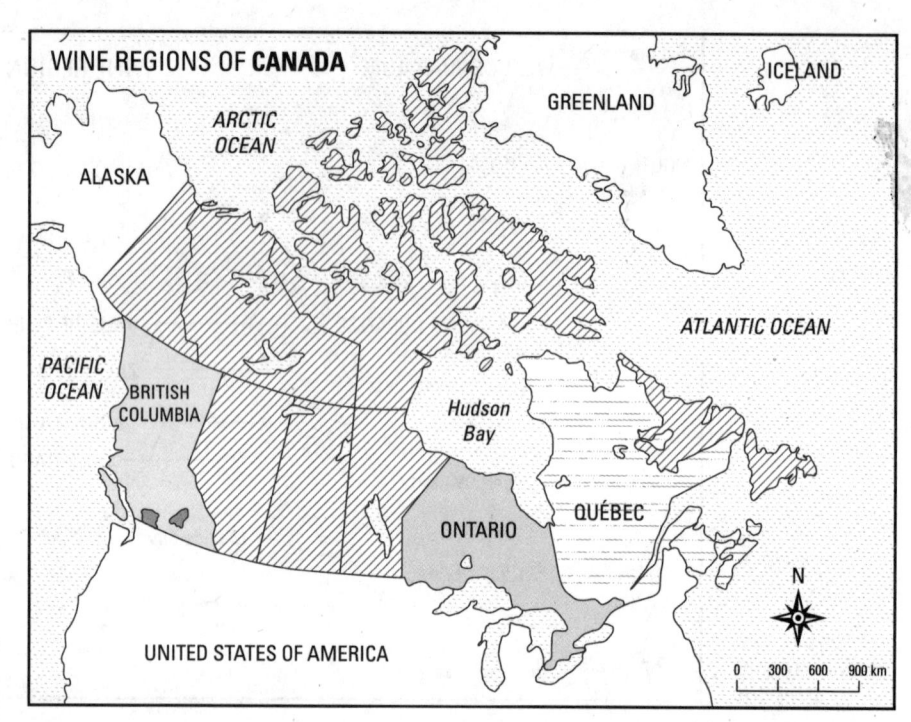

FIGURE 11-2:
The wine regions
of Canada.

REAL DEAL

The average price of a good-quality icewine from Ontario or Canada's other wine regions ranges from $18 to more than $100 a bottle, which is still a steal when compared to alternatives from regions such as France, Germany, Austria, or Switzerland.

British Columbia is Canada's western wine province, growing increasingly popular with international wine enthusiasts and tourists. The province includes five main wine districts: Okanagan Valley, Similkameen Valley, Fraser Valley, Gulf Islands, and Vancouver Island. Excellent wines are made here from cabernet franc, cabernet sauvignon, pinot gris, pinot noir, and riesling. Top producers to seek are Burrowing Owl, Clos du Soleil, Mission Hill, Osoyoos Larose, Quail's Gate, and Tantalus.

Chapter **12**

South America: Bold and Beautiful

Two generations ago, the northern hemisphere was the top dog of the wine world. The most well-known and sought after wines came from either Europe or North America. Wines from larger southern hemisphere countries were popular mostly in their home markets.

But times must and do change. The rise of the southern hemisphere has altered the wine world profoundly, changing the palates and drinking habits of wine novices and connosieurs alike. South America in particular has stunned the world over the last 50 years, shifting from producing basic, inexpensive wines in the 1980s and 1990s to competing on the world stage with more crafted and sophisticated fine wines.

Although wine is produced in much smaller quantities in countries such as Bolivia, Colombia, and Peru, the larger South American countries dominate the region. In this chapter, we explore the wines of South America's wine giants: Chile and Argentina. We also put Brazil and Uruguay on the radar as important wine regions to know with international acclaim.

The Laws and the Labels

Wine laws in Chile are the result of multiple amendments to the first laws from Decree 464 of 1994. The first wave introduced *Denominaciónes de Origen* (DOs), or legally protected geographic regions, sub-regions, and zones for specific grapes. It also included guidelines for wine labels, specifically that a varietal wine must constitute 75 percent of the named grapes and that vintage-dated wines should have at least 75 percent of grapes harvested in the named year. Each region is either named for (or contains several) valley, sub-region, or zonal names that appear on wine labels. At the highest level, Chile's main DOs to know include Atacama, Coquimbo, Aconcagua, Central Valley (which includes the Maule Valley), and Sur (or southern) regions, which includes Itata Valley, Bío Bío Valley, and Malleco Valley.

REMEMBER

Chile's wine laws were revised in 2012, 2018, and 2024 to name new appellations and varieties — it's an ongoing process. One of the more important recent changes includes three zonal designations relative to the Pacific coast that give consumers a better sense of what to expect from wines in different areas: *Costa* areas (coastal), *Entre Cordilleras* areas (between the coastal mountains and the Andes), and *Andes* areas (interior, in the hills of the Andes). *Costa* and *Andes* areas are those that benefit the coolest climate influences. To include a DO on its label, 85 percent of a wine's grapes must come from the defined origin.

Similar to Chile's legal wine history, that of Argentina has evolved to quickly adjust to the country's international rise to fame. In 1959, the National Viticultural Institute (INV) was created which would establish wine as a food product by law (wish we could have been there!) and continues to play a role in providing a legal framework for the country's wine production. It wasn't until the 1990s — a period marked by political and economic shifts in trade liberalization and tax reform — that considerable amounts of Argentinean wine were actually exported to other countries. Between 1993 and 2021, the number of exporting wineries mushroomed from just 10 to over 520.

REMEMBER

In 1999, Argentina's Geographical Indications (GIs) and Denominations of Controlled Origin (DOCs) were created that would further boost the export market for quality wines. The main difference between Argentina's GIs and DOs has to do with place versus style: a GI describes wines recognized for quality attributed to their *terroir* (the characteristics associated with a particular place for a certain grape variety: Mendoza's Malbec, for example). These wines generally follow Argentinean political boundaries and can have the GI listed on their label. There are 106 Argentinean GIs at the time of writing. There are only two DOCs in Argentina, and both of them are in Mendoza: Luján de Cuyo and San Rafael. What differentiates them is a requirement of cellar aging for least one year in oak barrels and one year of bottle aging before release.

Argentinean law follows the European Union (EU) standard that varietal-specific wines such as malbec or cabernet sauvignon must be made from at least 85 percent of that grape. Red wines labeled as *Reserva* must be aged for at least 12 months, while white and rosé wines require at least 6 months — both in the cellar.

Wine production was banned in Brazil under Portuguese rule until 1822. Although general designations for wine were codified in Brazilian law as early as 1988, Geographical Indications (GIs) were not formally delineated until 1996. In 2002, the first GI was actually recognized for still and sparkling wines from Vale dos Vinhedos in Rio Grande do Sol. GIs designate origins of wine in Brazil only, but do not attest to their quality. Rules mandate that grapes used in production of GI wines come from a designated region, although specific requirements may vary depending on the GI in question. This includes variables such as permitted varieties and production methods specific to the GI, among other factors. Denominations of Origin (DOs) associate a wine with a specific *terroir* characteristic of that place. Today, Vale dos Vinhedos is Brazil's one DO; several GIs exist including Pinto Bandeira (dedicated exclusively to traditional method sparkling wines), Monte Belo, Farroupilha, Altos Montes, Vales de Uva Goethe, and Vale do São Francisco.

Wine is made in 16 of Uruguay's 19 departments (similar to states in the United States) around the country. While there isn't an official appellation system (see Chapter 11), there are some laws that govern winemaking. Wines for commercial trade must be produced from *Vitis vinifera* vines (see Chapter 2). There are two general quality classifications: *Vino Comun* (common or table wine, VC), made primarily for domestic consumption, and *Vino de Calidad Preferente* (wine of preferred quality, VCP), a quality wine made from *Vitis vinifera* grapes, sold in bottles sized 75cl (750 milliliters) or less, and fermented to between 8.6% and 15% alcohol by volume (ABV).

Regions, Varieties, and Styles

Although they share the same continent, the wines of South America could not be more varied in *terroir*, grapes, or styles. This section discusses the major wine regions of South America, including Chile, Argentina, Brazil, and Uruguay.

Chile: A rapid rise to fame

Spanish colonialists (known as *conquistadores*) and Catholic missionaries brought *Vitis vinifera* vines (specifically the red, listán prieto locally referred to as "criolla") to Chile from Spain and established vineyards in the mid-16th century. Over the next two generations, Chile would look more to France for its grape inspiration, with wealthier Chilean landowners importing French varieties like cabernet sauvignon, carménère (a cross of cabernet franc and gros cabernet usually written without the accents in Spanish), and merlot, and building Bordeaux-inspired *chateaux*.

TECHNICAL STUFF

While Chilean wines have thrived at home for centuries, their modern, global footprint is really only about 50 years old. Chile's transition to democracy following the Augusto Pinochet Ugarte regime in the late 1980s and early 1990s resulted in deregulation and more open market policies — key ingredients for foreign investments in a growing international wine industry.

Today, Chile is South America's largest wine producer and exporter. With the Pacific Ocean to the west and the Andes Mountains to the east — not to mention the Atacama Desert to the north and the ice glaciers of Patagonia to the south — Chile is an isolated and climactically diverse country (see the color section of this book). This isolation has its advantages in terms of grape growing: The phylloxera louse hasn't yet taken a strong hold in Chile — as it has done in almost every other winemaking country — and *vinifera* vines can, therefore, grow on their own roots (although some producers plant vines grafted onto American rootstocks just in case). For an explanation of phylloxera, see Chapter 2.

Chile's other viticultural blessings include:

>> The Pacific Ocean and the Humboldt Current's cold influence from Antarctica on the relatively hot and dry climate of the Aconcagua, Casablanca, and Limari Valleys.

>> The Coastal Range mountains spanning from north to south along the Pacific Ocean that shield vineyards in and around the Aconcagua, Colchagua, and Casablanca Valleys from extreme maritime impacts.

>> Cool night air and moisture from Andes Mountains that moderate temperatures in the Atacama, Coquimbo, Aconcagua, and Central Valley regions.

>> Granite-concentrated soils in some of the country's most prestigious sites that result in well-drained, mineral-rich conditions and wines with bright acidity and distinctive minerality. Additional soil types include schist, limestone, alluvial blends of sand and clay, and slate.

The main grapes of Chile include cabernet sauvignon, sauvignon blanc, merlot, chardonnay, carménère, and syrah. Red grape varieties represent the lion's share of Chile's production, with cabernet sauvignon accounting for more than 30 percent of all grapes. Chilean carménère accounts for nearly 96 percent of the world's production. It is often blended with other grapes like cabernet sauvignon, petit verdot, and/or syrah. Single varietal syrah and pinot noir are also important.

Among white varieties, distinctive sauvignon blancs and chardonnays dominate the scene. Sparkling wines are also made in Chile with increasing popularity, including mostly Charmat and some traditional method wines from pinot noir, chardonnay, muscat, and pais (a Spanish red grape with a long Chilean history dating back to the 16th century).

REAL DEAL

Chile's wines are usually named for their grape varieties. Many wineries produce multiple tiers that rise in price (and ideally, in quality) from a basic line to a higher-level line and ultimately what the wineries call their *premium*, *icon*, or *prestige* wine. Ironically, many of the basic-level reds are labeled as *Reserve* wines (a regulated term but with a rather broad application). The reasonable prices of the entry-level wines — mainly from $10 to $15 — make Chile an excellent value for money option. The premium bottlings tend to be in the $100 and up price range. Examples include Concha y Toro's Don Melchor, Errazuriz' Don Maximo, Montes' Alpha M, Santa Rita' Real, Casa Lapostolle's Clos Apalta and Seña. These elite, age-worthy Chilean wines are often blends rather than varietal wines, and many are styled along international lines — made from very ripe grapes that give rich, fruity flavors, high (14% or higher) alcohol levels, and the baking spice notes of French oak.

From north to south, here's a summary of Chile's wine regions and sub-regions today:

>> **Atacama region (Entre Cordilleras):** Likely known more for its pisco production (a Chilean brandy distilled from moscat, torontel, and/or pedro ximenéz) than wine, the Atacama region is charactertized by the desert of the same name — one of the driest deserts on the planet. Its saving grace for viticulture is its definition as a "mild" desert compared to hotter deserts like the Sahara of Africa, for example. Daily highs around 80°F (27°C) and lows around 60°F (16°C) pace the ripening process and make the Atacama an interesting place to grow grapes and produce distinctive, complex wines. Whites are made mostly from chardonnay, sauvignon blanc, and Muscat of Alexandria. Reds are generally dry styles from cabernet sauvignon, merlot, syrah, malbec, and petit verdot. Well-known producers include Ventisquero and Ayllu.

>> **Coquimbo region (Entre Cordilleras):** There are two areas to explore in this region:

- **Elqui Valley:** Close to the Atacama Desert, which covers much of northern Chile, this coastal valley runs east to west. The climate of this smaller sub-region is cool and damp near the ocean and much warmer inland, where skies are so clear that major astronomical research facilities like the Inter-American Observatory are situated here. For nearly 30 years, the Viña Falernia winery has been making reds from syrah, cabernet blends, and carménère here. Additional high-quality producers include Vinedos de Alcohuaz and Viña Mayo.

- **Limarí Valley:** A small, semi-arid territory about 250 miles northwest of Santiago. Proximity to the Pacific Ocean brings cool morning fog and ocean breezes that blow through the valley during the day. Parts of this sub-region are classified as *Entre Cordilleras* but it is mainly coastal. Chile's three largest wineries, Concha y Toro, San Pedro, and Santa Rita all own land in Limarí. Sauvignon blanc, chardonnay, and syrah are the main wines. Producers to seek include Tabali, Reta, and Miguel Torres (for its Cordillera de los Andes brands, the most popular being a toasted, tropical fruit-flavored chardonnay).

» **Aconcagua region (Costa, Andes, and Entre Cordilleras):** This region has three areas of note:

- **Aconcagua Valley:** North of Santiago, the dramatic Aconcagua Valley is named for the continent's highest mountain, Mount Aconcagua, and is one of the warmest areas for fine wine grapes. But Aconcagua also includes many cooler, high-altitude sections, and in fact has vineyards in all three east–west zones. Cabernet sauvignon grows especially well here, and more recently, syrah. A new development is fine white wine from vineyards planted in Aconcagua Costa. Viña Errázuriz, Viña Seña, Clos des Fous, and Viña von Siebenthal and are a few top-quality producers.

- **Casablanca Valley:** This sub-region was the first of Chile's newer coastal wine regions. Some of Chile's most remarkable chardonnays and sauvignon blancs are made in Casablanca, while quality merlots and pinot noirs come from higher-altitude areas. Many wineries throughout Chile also source fruit from Casablanca Valley. High-quality producers include Casas del Bosque, Cono Sur, and Casa Lapostolle. Veramonte and Loma Larga are two other wineries known for inexpensive, everyday drinking wines.

- **San Antonio Valley and Leyda Valley:** These two coastal areas (technically Leyda is part of San Antonio, but you can find it mentioned in its own right on wine labels) are south of Casablanca Valley and are exciting, newer wine zones. The maritime influence produces impressive sauvignon blancs and chardonnays in Leyda, while pinot noir and syrah are growing especially well on cool, steep slopes. Viña Matetic is the most iconic winery of San Antonio Valley, best known for its syrah and pinot noir. Casa Marin is also a producer to seek out. Leyda Valley's star producers include Viña Garces Silva, and Montes.

» **Central Valley region (Entre Cordilleras):** This is Chile's most famous wine region, surrounding Santiago to the southwest. The Central Valley is sandwiched between the Andes and Coastal Mountain ranges, and is home to some of Chile's most prestigious wineries:

- **Maipo Valley:** Just north of Rapel Valley and south of Santiago, the Maipo Valley is one of the oldest in Chile, with vines planted here as early as the 1540s. Concha y Toro, Viña Don Melchor, Santa Rita, Carmen, Cousiño Macul, Almaviva, and Viñedos Chadwick are a few of Maipo's premium producers. Cabernet sauvignon and red Bordeaux blends are king in this region, and syrah also does very well. Chardonnay and syrah from Baron Phillippe de Rothschild's Escudo Rojo are excellent. Some vineyards in Maipo Valley are classified as *Andes*, but are mainly *Entre Cordilleras* areas.

- **Rapel Valley:** The large Rapel Valley, south of Maipo Valley, has two wine zones, Cachapoal Valley and Colchagua Valley. Cachapoal Valley, nearest to the Andes, is a mostly red wine area whose soil and climate varies depending on distance to the mountains. Cabernet sauvignon, Bordeaux blends, and carménère are important here. High-quality producers include Altair, Aristos, Chateau los Boldos, Santa Ema, VIK, and Viña San Pedro.

  Colchagua Valley's diverse *terroir* includes vineyards situated on the slopes of the Andes in the east, to sites with more maritime microclimates in the west, bordering the Pacific Ocean. This is home to many of Chile's most well-known and prestigious wineries, and is a hotspot for cabernet sauvignon, Bordeaux blends, carménère, and syrah. Renowned wineries specialize in full-bodied, juicy, and powerful wines ready to drink now, as well as more age-worthy wines whose tannin and juicy fruit flavors become more subtle with time. These include Casa Silva, Casa Lapostolle, Clos Apalta, Emiliana, François Lurton (from the Bordeaux-based Lurton family), Montes, and Neyen.

- **Curicó Valley:** One of Chile's oldest and largest wine areas, the Curicó Valley is directly south of Rapel Valley. Because of its diverse microclimates, both red and white varieties grow well here. The acclaimed San Pedro Winery and Viña Miguel Torres are based in Curicó, although their wines are also made from grapes grown in other regions outside of Curicó as well.

» **Maule Valley region:** Chile's largest wine sub-region by area, the Maule Valley is also the southernmost of the major zones. It is the second largest wine-producing region in the country, following the Central Valley region. Because it is so huge, it has many diverse microclimates, and both red and white varieties grow well, especially sauvignon blanc, cabernet sauvignon, and merlot. Top-quality producers include De Martino, Garage Wine Co, J. Bouchon, Miguel Torres, and O. Fournier.

Argentina: *Llevo unos tintos*

We can guess two things about you if you're a regular wine drinker: (1) That you've said "Llevo unos tintos" as they say in Argentina ("I'm bringing a few red wines") and (2) that at least one of those red wines has at some point been a malbec from Argentina!

Argentina boasts the second largest wine production in South America and ranks fifth in the world among wine-producing countries. Argentina is also a major wine-consuming country: only in the last 30 to 40 years have producers looked beyond their own borders to develop a strong export trade. Now, Argentinean wines have become so popular in North America and Europe that we would have to describe Argentina's ascendancy as meteoric. Not only is Argentina now a major player in the world wine market, but it's also one of the world's most exciting countries for wine production.

Wine grapes have grown in Argentina since the mid-16th century, after the Spanish *conquistadores* arrived in 1516. Many vines came to Argentina with waves of Italian, French, and Spanish (in particular Basque) immigrants between 1850 and 1880. The creation of the first school of agriculture (*Quinta Normal de Agricultura*) in 1853, coupled with government incentives for immigrant wine enthusiasts and new railways connecting winegrowing regions to city centers ignited the national viticultural industry. The history of immigration in Argentina explains the differences in dominant grape varieties when compared to Chile (detailed in the previous section), particularly malbec and bonarda.

Argentina's traditional wine regions (see the color section of this book) are situated in the north and northwestern part of the country, at the foot of the icy cold, breathtaking Andes Mountains dividing the country from Chile. But eastern regions are emerging, including some coastal zones. In the west, extremely high altitude tempers the climate. When we say high, we mean high: some of the northern regions have elevations almost 11,000 feet (3,353 meters) above sea level, requiring four-wheel drive trucks that can only ascend the hills during harvest season.

Despite the costs of manual labor, high-altitude viticulture in Argentina has a few benefits, including prolonged sun exposure leading to intense flavor concentration, cooler temperatures resulting in ideal levels of ripeness, and natural irrigation created by snowmelt from the Andes' tips. Nevertheless, most of the vineyards are still very warm by day, cool by night, and desert-dry. Sandy loam, alluvial, and franco soils are most common in Argentina's top vineyard sites.

Argentina's red wines are by far more popular and plentiful than its whites. Reds include malbec, cabernet sauvignon, bonarda (which actually exceeds cabernet sauvignon in plantings but is less evident among exports), and several Italian varieties such as Barbera, dolcetto, and sangiovese, which also are uncommon in exported wines. Given its red-centered viticulture, Argentina also produces amazing rosés from its red varieties that are widely available in the United States.

REMEMBER

Malbec, indigenous to the Cahors region of southern France (known there as Côt) — is Argentina's flagship red variety. It's become so popular that most people probably think it's the only place in the world that actually makes malbec! This variety has adapted extremely well to the mendoza region, and winemakers are discovering the nuances its wines develop when grown in different microclimates. Argentinean cabernet sauvignon and malbec/bonarda blends have also developed cult followings, but the fact remains that malbec is Argentina's signature wine.

Apart from torrontés, most of the white wines are chardonnay and sauvignon blanc. Sparkling wine made in both Charmat and traditional methods from chardonnay, pinot noir, and torrontés is gaining popularity. Dessert wines made from late harvest torrontés and malbec are also made in much smaller quantities and are more difficult to find in the U.S. market. Argentina has several wine provinces that can be grouped into three main regions: the North, Cuyo, and Patagonia and the Atlantic.

MALBEC'S MIGRATION

At one point in the 19th century, the malbec grape variety was a major player in France's southwest, Bordeaux region (see Chapter 6). Then natural disasters all but wiped out malbec there. When replanting the vineyards, many producers planted less malbec because Bordeaux's cool, maritime climate doesn't always provide the amount of sun and warmth that it needs to ripen fully. Malbec is also prone to vine diseases and is vulnerable to frost — all dangers in the region. A second natural disaster, the catastropic 1956 frost in Bordeaux, wiped out 75 percent of the malbec crop. Very few Bordeaux producers bothered to replant malbec after that. Ironically, a similar fate happened to Bordeaux's carménère variety, which ripens too late for Bordeaux's climate. Carménère found a new home in Argentina's next-door neighbor, Chile.

Meanwhile, malbec has been flourishing in Argentina's Mendoza region, where French agronomist Michel Pouget introduced it in the mid-19th century. Today, more malbec grows in Mendoza than any other wine region in the world. Mendoza's warm, dry climate is perfect for malbec, and the grape does particularly well in districts such as Luján de Cuyo and the Uco Valley in the foothills of the Andes, where vineyards are situated as high as 5,000 feet (1,524 meters) in altitude.

(continued)

(continued)

In France, malbec is still an important grape variety in the Cahors region in southwestern France, where it makes dark-colored, medium-bodied, tannic wines. Malbec makes dark, juicy wines in Argentina that tend to be more powerful, inky, and higher in alcohol than their Cahors counterparts.

The north

This region includes Jujuy, Salta, Tucumán, and Catamarca, and encompasses the highest geographical points of Argentinean viticulture. Main varieties include cabernet sauvignon, malbec, torrontés (generally the star of the show here), cereza (red Spanish variety meaning "cherry"), and syrah. Sand and sandy loam soils dominate. Top-quality northern producers include Bemberg Estate, Bodega Colomé Bodegas El Esteco, and Bodegas El Porvenir.

**WORTH THE
SEARCH**

Salta is particularly famous for Torrontés, a variety known as Argentina's signature white grape. Actually, as many as three different types of torrontés grow in Argentina in various regions, but the best and most popular is torrontés Riojano, with some wine labels specifying this name.

Cuyo

Cuyo is the heart of Argentina's wine industry, situated west of Buenos Aires. The region enjoys the sunny, inland microclimate that is generally warmer than the north. It is the arid, fertile home to the provinces of La Rioja, San Juan, and the infamous Mendoza. Similar to the North, Cuyo is mostly irrigated from the snowmelt of the Andes, and has warm days and cool nights ideal for grape growing. Malbec (85 percent of the country's supply comes from here), bonarda, cabernet sauvignon, syrah, and torrontés all thrive in Cuyo, where Argentina's most well-regarded wines are made. Luján de Cuyo DOC and Uco Valley are Cuyo's most important sub-regions, both located in Mendoza.

The vast majority of Argentina's vineyards are in the western province of Mendoza, which lies at roughly the same latitude as Santiago, Chile and produces at least 70 percent of the country's wine. Within the Mendoza region are various wine districts (the names of which sometimes appear on wine labels) such as Luján de Cuyo, Maipú, Tupungato, Uco Valley, and San Raphael. Most of Argentina's oldest wineries and their vineyards are clustered close to Mendoza city but Uco Valley, in the southern part of the province and close to the Andes, has attracted many newcomers as well as several established wineries that have relocated there.

The province of San Juan, just north of Mendoza and considerably hotter, is Argentina's second-largest wine province. La Rioja province, Argentina's oldest wine-producing region, is east of San Juan. Some (of many) producers to know from Cuyo include Alto Las Hormigas, Bodega Norton, Bodegas y Cavas Weinert, Catena Zapata, Cheval des Andes, Familia Zuccardi, Luigi Bosca, Rutini, Susana Balbo, and Viña Cobos.

Patagonia and the Atlantic

Representing less than 2 percent of Argentina's production, this region covers lower altitude and highly forested areas, and includes the provinces of La Pampa, Neuquén, Río Negro, Chubut, and Buenos Aires. A cooler climate creates the ideal conditions for cold-hardy varieties such as chardonnay and pinot noir. Malbec, cabernet sauvignon, merlot, and sauvignon blanc are also planted here. Patagonia — with its cooler climate and chalky soils — is the bedrock of Argentina's sparkling wines made in both traditional and Charmat methods (see Chapter 3 to learn more about sparkling wine methods). Top-quality producers from Patagonia and the Atlantic Region include Bodega Noemia, Familia Schroeder, Matias Riccitelli, and Otronia.

REAL DEAL

Torrontés is generally an inexpensive ($12 to $16 retail), aromatic white variety with tropical fruit flavors and (when well-made), sunbursting acidity. It is one of the few white wines in the world that can do well with some oak aging (sauvignon blanc blends, chenin blanc, viognier, and chardonnay are other examples; see Chapter 3) and is delicious with light appetizers, seafood, and spicy dishes. Distinguished torrontés wines are on the rise in Argentina. Salta's sub-region, Cafayate, which has many vineyards growing at altitudes over 5,000 feet (1,524 meters), has emerged as a prime area for this grape. The torrontés wines from these vineyards have bracing acidity and are gaining a reputation as Argentina's best. Torrontés is by far the most popular white wine in Argentina.

THE EURO CONNECTION

Thanks in part to its high altitudes and sunny days, Argentina's natural resources for grape growing are among the strongest in the world. Foreign investment continues to bring the capital and the winemaking know-how to make the most of these assets. Below are some of the most important investments and joint ventures.

- Bodega Norton, a winery that was purchased by Austrian crystal producer Gernot Langes-Swarovski in 1989, makes distinctive wines in Mendoza.

(continued)

(continued)

- Terrazas de los Andes was founded in 1996 in Luján de Cuyo by Hervé Birnie-Scott, a French immigrant.

- Bordeaux's elite Cheval Blanc winery partnered with Terrazas de Los Andes in 1999 to create Argentina's iconic Cheval des Andes, a blend of malbec, cabernet sauvignon, and petit verdot.

- Dutch entrepreneur Mijndert Pon owns the state-of-the-art Bodegas Salentein winery and its sister winery, Finca El Portillo, both in Mendoza.

- Bordeaux's Lurton family owns Bodega J. & F. Lurton in Uco Valley.

- In 2002, Bordeaux *enologist* (a winemaker or specialist in the study of winemaking) Michel Rolland created Clos de los Siete, an enclave of wineries in the Uco Valley, most of which are owned by Bordeaux families, including Rolland himself. He also makes a collective red wine from the group of wineries called Clos de Los Siete, an excellent, affordable wine that retails around $20 a bottle.

Brazil: *Ordem e Progresso*

To be the biggest country in South America, it may seem odd that Brazil trails behind Chile and Argentina in wine production. Like its neighbors, Brazil has been producing wine for hundreds of years, but its modern, international wine image is still evolving. Brazil's national motto of *Ordem e Progresso* translates to "Order and Progress," and is the paraphrase of the French philosopher Auguste Comte, who wrote, "Love as a principle and order as the basis . . . Progress as the goal." Brazil's wine industry could be summed up with this quote alone (which is also on the Brazilian flag). But you're reading this book, so we will give you a little more information!

Like Argentina, *Vitis vinifera* came to Brazil with immigrants, most notably the Portuguese colonists (called *colonizadores* in Portuguese) from 1532 to 1822, and Italian settlers from the 1870s onwards. The Italians brought American, Italian, and French varieties with them to places like the Serra Gaúcha region of Rio Grande de Sol that are considered the heart of Brazil winemaking to this day.

Although the first Brazilian sparkling wine production (a 100 percent chardonnay) was documented in 1899 by Manuel Peterlongo (the founder of Peterlongo winery) it would be more than 100 years until Brazil would rise to global interest for not only its sparkling wines, but also for dry styles from international varieties. As early as the 1970s, global companies like Moët Hennessy saw the potential of Brazil and launched a sparkling wine hub (Chandon Brasil) there that remains dedicated to traditional method wines in Garibaldi and Rio Grande de Sol.

REMEMBER

Brazil is South America's third-largest wine producer and 14th largest producer in the world. We suspect that this may change in the generations to come. See Figure 12-1 for an overview of Brazil's wine landscape.

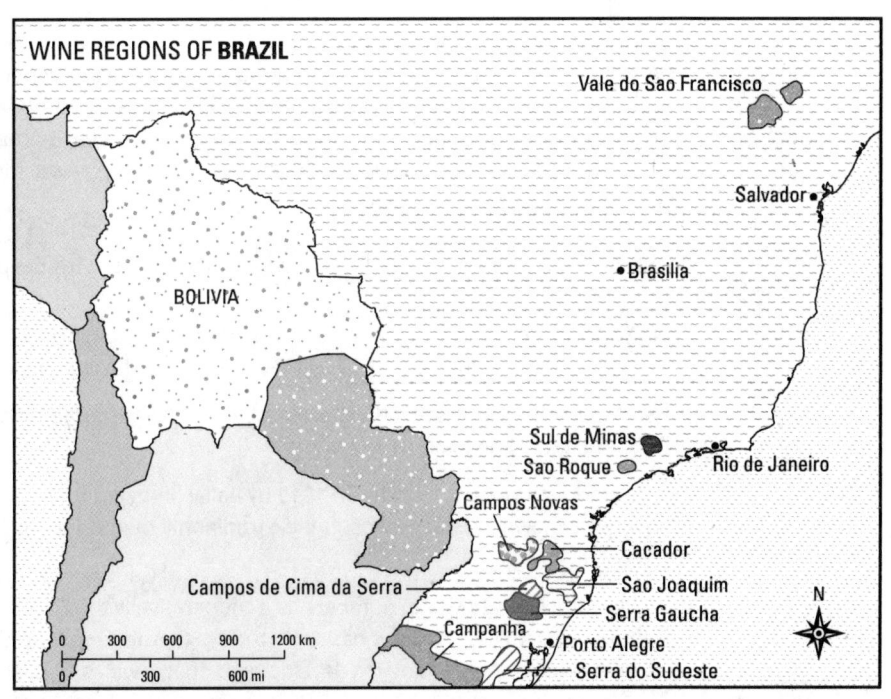

WINE REGIONS OF BRAZIL

Vale do Sao Francisco
Salvador
Brasilia
BOLIVIA
Sul de Minas
Sao Roque
Rio de Janeiro
Campos Novas
Cacador
Campos de Cima da Serra
Sao Joaquim
Serra Gaucha
Campanha
Porto Alegre
Serra do Sudeste
N

0 300 600 900 1200 km
0 300 600 mi

FIGURE 12-1:
The wine regions
of Brazil.

© *John Wiley & Sons, Inc.*

Brazil's massive landmass (it is the fifth largest country in the world, after all) means that grapes are growing in varied climates. Most wine production takes place in Brazil's cool, dry, southernmost areas, although experimental techniques and new investment are popping up farther north towards Rio de Janeiro as well. Basaltic rock, iron-rich clay, and volcanic soils contribute to complex, mineral-driven wines. The most important wine area of the south is the state of Rio Grande do Sol, and within it, Serra Gaúcha as the hilly, star region. Estrelas do Brasil, Don Giovanni, and Salton are the most important producers to know, making white wines from chardonnay, glera, and moscato, and red wines from alicante bouschet, cabernet sauvignon, and merlot. Sparkling wines from chardonnay, glera, malvasia, and pinot noir made in both Charmat and traditional methods (described in Chapter 3) are some of the south's most prestigious wines.

The remainder of Brazil's wine regions are scattered in the central and northern parts of the country. Central Brazil's production remains mostly dedicated to table wines intended for domestic consumption made from non-*Vitis vinifera* varieties.

Northern Brazil's best-quality producers are clustered in Vale do São Francisco, which is typically drier than the south and requires innovative techniques to cultivate vines in the more tropical climate. Brazil's north is likely one of the few places in the entire world where harvests can (and typically do) take place more than once a year!

The grapes that dominate Brazilian domestic table wine consumption — some hybrid and some American — include isabella, niagara, and bordô. The majority of export wines are made from cabernet sauvignon, chardonnay, pinot noir, as well as the Italian-originated trebbiano and tannat (grown mostly in Serra do Sudeste and Campanha Gaúcha).

Most of Brazil's top wine producers are also its oldest, with deep Italian roots:

>> Familia Salton was first started in 1878 by Antonio Dominco Salton and carried into the future in 1910 by seven brothers who were Italian immigrants.

>> Miolo, Brazil's largest wine exporter by volume, was started by Italian immigrant, Giuseppe Miolo in 1897.

>> Peterlongo Winery, founded in 1915 by Italian immigrant Manoel Peterlongo, is well-known as Brazil's most prolific traditional method sparkling winery.

>> Vinícola Garibaldi, founded in 1931 in the city of Garibaldi (of Rio Grande do Sul), shows power in numbers as a cooperative with 70 founders from different families. Today, it has more than 450 producing families who pool resources and technology to develop high-quality wines. Similarly, Vinícola Aurora was founded in 1931 by 16 grape-producing families who still follow a cooperative model to this day.

They produce a range of wines and styles, with some of them available at larger retailers or South American leaning wine shops and bars.

Additional high-quality Brazilian producers include Carraro, Geisse, Lidio, Pizzato, Valmarino, and Vinhas e Vinhos. Moët and Chandon Brasil (now global conglomerate Louis Vuitton Moët Hennesy, or LVMH) also launched a sparkling house in the Serra Gaúcha region of Rio Grande do Sol. It remains an important force for sparkling wine in the country since 1973.

Brazilian wines can also be hard to find in U.S. markets. Larger retails, global wine bars, and South American-focused wine shops may offer both entry level options around $14-$16 a bottle and higher-end bottlings upwards of $50 per bottle.

Uruguay: Hidden gems

The entire country of Uruguay is just slightly larger than the state of New York. Like its other South American neighbors, *Vitis vinifera* arrived with Spanish and Italian immigrants in the late 19th century. The most important of these was the originally French tannat (known in Uruguay as Harraigue, after the first documented plantings by Pascual Harraigue in 1871) which came with Basque settlers — a thick-skinned red grape that makes full bodied, tannic, powerful wines and is Uruguay's national grape today.

Uruguay is a generally flat country, with an astonishing 99 documented soil types. It borders Argentina to the west and Brazil to the north, with stretches of Atlantic coastlines to the east and south (see Figure 12-2). Uruguay's more extensive international wine industry took shape beginning in the 1980s and 1990s, and continues to evolve through many boutique, family-owned wineries and some foreign investment. Production remains small with around 200 wineries making the same volume as countries such as Japan or Switzerland.

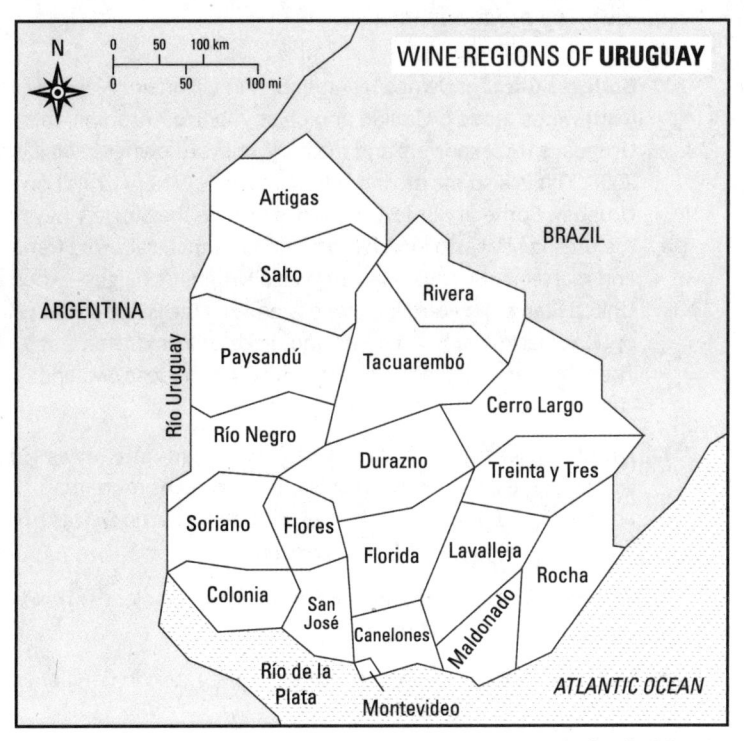

FIGURE 12-2: The wine regions of Uruguay.

© John Wiley & Sons, Inc.

Alluvial clay, silt, sand, gravel, and limestone are common soils at the best viticultural sites. Antarctic currents from the Atlantic create maritime climates in southern and coastal regions — a vast difference from the hot, arid climates of Argentina and Chile.

The most important winegrowing region is Canelones, just outside of Uruguay's capital city of Montevideo, where nearly 90 percent of all commercial wine production takes place. The most common grapes are albariño, chardonnay, and sauvignon blanc for whites and tannat, cabernet sauvignon, and merlot for reds. In addition to these main varieties, you can find everything from pinot noir to nebbiolo and Nero d'Avola in Uruguay, reflecting the rich Italian and French wine histories of the families who own most of the wineries. Other coastal regions to know include the area of Maldonado (home to the massive, award-winning winery of Bodegas Garzón, where excellent albariño, cabernet franc, and tannat is made), Colonia on the southwest banks of the Rio de Plata, Sierra de Mahoma, and Rocha. More inland regions to note are the northern Rivera and central Durazno areas.

Uruguay's wine industry remains dominated by families who have made wine for centuries. Top producers include:

>> **Bodegas Garzón:** Owned by Argentinean billionaire Alejandro Bulgheroni (with wines made by Italian enologist, Alberto Antonini), this is one of Uruguay's top exporters and majority vineyard owner in Maldonado since 2008. This is also the most modern, majestic winery to visit on a wine trip to Uruguay. Some of our favorite wines include the Single Vineyard Albariño and the prestige Ballasto, which is a blend of tannat, cabernet franc, petit verdot, and marselan. Bodegas Garzón is also Uruguay's biggest exporter to the United States. You can find these wines in larger wine shops with entry level options starting at $14 a bottle and more collector's items at $100 and up. There are several mid-tier selections between these two ends of the spectrum as well.

>> **Familia Deicas:** The family purchased vineyards as early as 1979, but launched their own brand in 2000 and now owns more than 12 vineyards around the country. Wines to seek include Massimo Deicas from Juanicó and Extreme Vineyards from Lavalleja.

>> **Pisano:** A fourth generation family winery in Canelones. The Axis Mundi is its prestige tannat from Progreso.

>> **Marichal:** Another fourth generation winery, also in Canelones, most known for its tannat, pinot noir, and chardonnay.

4

The World of Wine: Australia and New Zealand

Discover Australia's powerful wines from South Australia to Tasmania.

Learn how New Zealand became famous for sauvignon blanc. Go deeper with sparkling wines and best-kept pinot noir secrets from Central Otago.

Chapter **13**

Australia: A True Wine Power

D espite its ranking as the sixth largest country in the world, Australia only dedicates about 1 percent of its land to viticulture. This may be hard to believe given the oceans of Australian wine you've probably seen in your local grocery store or on shelves of large wine shops.

For the last 25 years, Australia's mass produced, forgettable wine flooded the world in what felt like infinite proportions (hello, Yellow Tail and Little Penguin). Not to be dismissed entirely, these wines met an important demand for inexpensive, sweeter, easy-drinking juice that could be gulped down on its own, thrown into a holiday sangria, or gifted at a college dorm gathering. Thankfully, times have changed. It turns out that the wines previously dominating the global marketplace are actually just a smidgeon of what real Australian winemakers have to offer. Today's Australian wines range from budget-friendly, small producer gems to high-end collectibles that could easily substitute a small home mortgage.

Discover the wines of Australia in this chapter.

The Laws and the Labels

Managed by Wine Australia (a government authority formed under the Wine Australia Act of 2013), The Australian Geographical Indication (AGI) system designates states (also referred to as zones), regions, and sub-regions for wine. Similar to the French *Appellation d'Origine Contrôlée* (AOC; see Chapter 6), a *Geographical Indication* (GI) is an officially recognized zone, region, sub-region, or "super zone" tied to the geographic origin of specific grapes and wine styles. All wines made by GIs must have 85 percent of the grapes sourced in the GI, with the GI printed on the label. The GI distinction on an Australian wine label is the only other important information included besides a producer's name and address, alcohol content, variety, style, and vintage (if appropriate).

There are more than 100 GIs across 65 wine regions in Australia, many whose names are becoming more visible on labels of exported wine. Some of the official geographic areas are large zones, but most are specific regions or sub-regions. We discuss the five most important ones in this chapter.

Regions, Varieties, and Styles

Australia's land is old — ancient in fact, with some of the world's oldest rock and mineral findings dating back billions of years. The vast landmass and positioning of the continent means that climate varies from desert to tropical. Most of the wine is only made in the south, southwest, and on the island of Tasmania where sunny, maritime climates are the norm. Australia's most pressing climate concerns are usually related to extreme heat, drought, and wildfires — three catastrophes that can decimate entire crops. At its best, warm, dry days and cool to cold nights are great for Australian vines in their top winemaking states and regions.

Two important waves of *Vitus vinifera* migration (find out more in Chapter 2) built the foundation for Australia's modern wine industry. Both took place during the period of British colonization of what were then *Aborigine* (indigenous Australian) lands. The first wave of vine migration resulted in failed plantings of South African vines (likely of muscat blanc à petits grains that were planted in the Cape of Good Hope to make the sweet wines of Constantia; find out more in Chapter 15). The vines were brought to New South Wales in 1787 by Admiral Arthur Phillip and the First Fleet (11 ships holding somewhere around 1,500 people). Most passengers were brought to Australia to create penal colonies — resettlement camps characterized by forced isolation and labor. Most passengers were British and Irish children and young adults who were convicted of one or more crimes from Britain's infamous list of "19 Crimes." You can thank Australian history and Treasury Wine

Estates (the global wine conglomerate that also owns brands such as Beringer and Chateau St. Jean) for the 19 Crimes wine brand, a series of $8 to $20 a bottle blends (of shiraz plus any other number of available grapes).

The second wave of vine migration was more critical to the development of Australia's wine industry, and included the transport of more than 300 vine cuttings from France, South Africa, and Spain. These vine voyages were led by enthusiasts like James Busby, Gregory Blaxland, and John MacArthur. What really drove the rapid growth of viticulture in Australia was the large-scale migration of Europeans who already had winemaking skills, knowledge and experience, and saw the potential of Australia's *terroir* (discover more about *terroir* in Chapter 2). This included Swiss, Irish, and Prussian immigrants in particular, some of whom founded fine wine companies that still exist to this day.

REMEMBER

Today, Australia ranks fifth in the world for wine production, and sixth for export, sending most of its wines to the United Kingdom and United States Despite what your grocery store shelves may present, there are many small, family-owned wineries in addition to the giant wine corporations of Australia, some which we will highlight later in this chapter.

Beyond its vast wine production, Australia is a world leader in enological and viticultural studies. The Australian Wine Research Institute, based in Adelaide, is a powerhouse for research and development in grape genetics, technology, and sustainability.

Australia's top grape for fine wine is syrah, locally called *shiraz,* followed by cabernet sauvignon, merlot, chardonnay, pinot noir, riesling, sauvignon blanc, and semillon (pronounced *sem-eh-lon* in Australia, as opposed to the French *seh-mee-yohn* used elsewhere in the world). The order and volume of planting depends on the region.

TIP

Shiraz wines are particularly interesting because they come in different styles, from inexpensive, juicy wines brimming with ripe plum and blackberry fruit to serious wines that express specific regional characteristics, such as spice and pepper from cool-climate areas (Yarra Valley and the Adelaide Hills for example) or sweet-fruit ripeness from warmer areas (including regions such as McLaren Vale, Barossa Valley, and Clare Valley). Australia may be the only country in the world that also produces sparkling shiraz!

The wines of Australia have two distinct faces:

> **»** **Inexpensive varietal wines that sell for under $15 a bottle and have historically fed the boom of Australian wines on international markets.**
> These wines are generally labeled as coming from *South Eastern Australia,*

meaning that the grapes can come from any of three states (a huge territory). Often sporting whimsical, animal-centered labels, they are user-friendly wines that preserve the intense flavors of their grapes and are usually juicy and easy to drink young.

>> **Higher-priced wines that carry more focused regional designations, such as single states (South Australia or Victoria, for example) or even tighter region-specific designations (such as Barossa Valley, Coonawarra, or Yarra Valley).** Although these wines are also enjoyable when released, many of them are more serious, age-worthy wines that offer a more complex, precision-focused, and nuanced style.

TECHNICAL STUFF

Although winemakers all over the world make blended wines — wines that feature more than one grape variety — generally the grape combinations follow the classic French models: cabernet sauvignon with merlot and cabernet franc, for example, or semillon with sauvignon blanc. Australia, however, has invented two completely original formulas: blending shiraz with cabernet sauvignon and semillion with chardonnay are the two dominant inventions. The grape in the majority is listed first on the label for wines sold in the United States, and the percentages of each grape are indicated. These blends give many Australian wines a distinctive flavor that not only reflects different *terroirs* but also the magic that can happen with experimentation in the winery!

The following sections describe the main regions, varieties, and producers in each of the five major wine-producing states of South Australia, New South Wales, Victoria, Western Australia, and Tasmania. Refer to Figure 13-1 for details of Australian wine regions.

South Australia

South Australia is the country's most important and driest wine-producing state. About 50 percent of the entire country's wine and 80 percent of its fine wine is made here. Many of the Australian "forefathers" of wine founded their estates here. South Australia has a total of 18 GIs, and includes the prestigious regions of Adelaide Hills, Barossa Valley, Clare Valley, Eden Valley, McLaren Vale, and Limestone Coast.

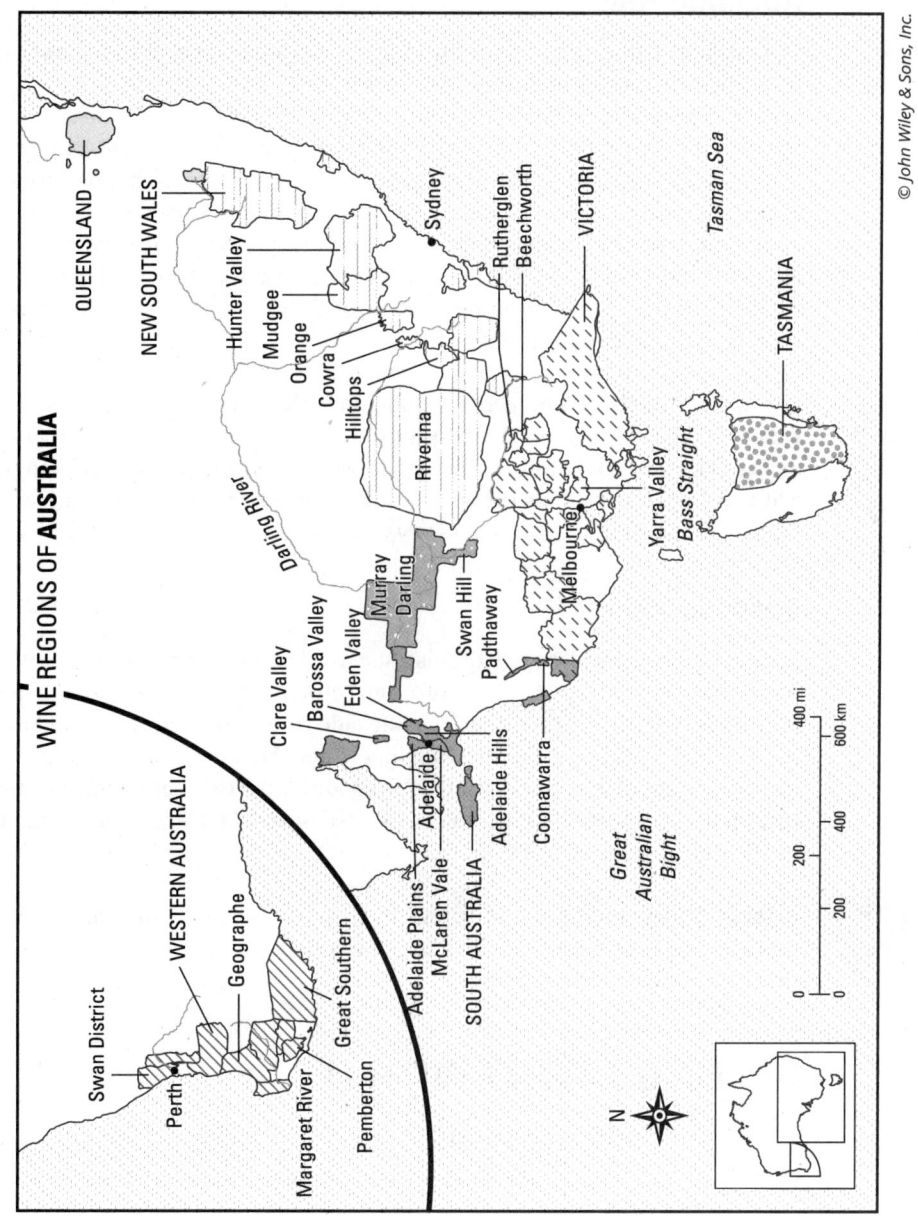

FIGURE 13-1: The wine regions of Australia.

Adelaide Hills

The Adelaide Hills is one one of the highest-elevated and coolest regions of South Australia, with cooler nights as low as 40°F (10°C) and hotter days as high as 80°F (27°C). A generally cooler climate means slower ripening for grapes, which can translate to concentrated, richly flavored wines. White, rosé, red, and sparkling wines are all made here. The main grape varieties are those that perform best in cooler climates to make elegant, well-balanced wines. They include chardonnay, pinot noir, sauvignon blanc, and shiraz. Besides the ideal grape-growing climate, Adelaide Hills soils are a combination of clay, limestone, sand, and stones — all of which made the region attractive to some of the region's heavy hitters that set up shop here in the late 19th century.

TIP

Top-quality Adelaide producers include both (relatively) smaller, family-owned wineries like Deviation Road, Grosset (with some wineries here and others spread across Clare Valley), Murdoch Hill, Ochota Barrels, Shaw + Smith, and Yangarra, in addition to giants such as Hardy's, Penfolds (whose first Magill estate was here, but is now based in the Barossa Valley), Wolf Blass, and Yalumba.

Barossa Valley

North of Adelaide, this is one of Australia's oldest areas for fine wine with a history of both English and Central European settlement and winemaking in the area. Barossa is typically warmer than the Adelaide Hills and famous first and foremost for its robust shiraz. Cabernet sauvignon and blends of syrah, grenache, and mourvèdre are also popular for reds, in addition to rich semillons and rieslings (grown in the cooler hills) for whites. Most of Australia's largest wineries, including Penfolds, are based here.

TIP

Barossa Valley producers to know include Henschke, John Duval, Penfolds, Seppeltsfield (specifically for its Para Tawny liqueur), Torbreck, and Two Hands.

GETTING TAWNY WITH IT

In Barossa, McLaren Vale, and Rutherglen (in Victoria), *tawnies* (borrowing the name from the ports of Portugal but made with different grapes) are made by adding neutral grape spirit to shiraz, grenache, and/or mourvèdre blends. These wines are aged for an average of 5 to 30 years, and carry with them the prestige and price tag of fine port or madeira with an Australian twist. They are thick and rich, with chocolate, coffee, caramel, dried citrus, and spice flavors. Penfolds and Seppeltsfield make some of the most prized examples.

Do you remember when we said that Australian wines can range from cheap to super expensive? The most expensive Australian wine ever sold was a bottle of 1951 Penfolds Grange Hermitage "Bin 1" Shiraz. One bottle sold for $157,624 at a Langton auction in December 2021.

Clare Valley

North of Barossa in the Mounty Loft Ranges, this climatically and soil-diverse plateau makes signature rieslings in a dry, weighty yet crisp style, in addition to shiraz and cabernet sauvignon. Excellent Clare Valley riesling producers include Jim Barry, Loosen Barry (a collaboration of Ernst Loosen of Dr. Loosen from Germany and Jim Barry from Australia), and Grosset.

Eden Valley

Northeast of Clare Valley and technically considered part of the Barossa zone in the Mounty Loft Ranges, Eden Valley is a plateau that sits above the Barossa Valley. It is home to some of the oldest riesling vines in the world (the oldest dating back to 1847)! The region is known for its elegant, austere, and more delicate rieslings when compared to the same wines from Clare Valley. In addition to riesling, softer, elegant versions of shiraz and viognier are made in Eden Valley. High-quality producers include Henschke, Langmeil, Peter Lehmann, Pewsey Vale, and Yalumba.

McLaren Vale

South of Adelaide and situated on the coast, with a relatively mild climate influenced by the Gulf of St. Vincent and the Southern Ocean, this region is particularly admired for its powerful, peppery shiraz, its rising star grenache, and cabernet sauvignon. Iron, clay, and stone soils contribute to these wines' structure, body, and high value in the Australian fine wine market. Recommended McLaren Vale producers are Clarendon Hills, Hardy's, Hickinbotham, Mollydooker, Mitolo, Two Hands, and Yangarra.

Limestone Coast

Thanks to limestone soil (hence the name) and a cool, maritime climate, this large zone along the southern coast of South Australia is an important area for both great value and higher-end white and red wines.

Two of the six regions within the Limestone Coast zone are famous in their own right — the warm Coonawarra region for some of Australia's best cabernet sauvignons, and Padthaway for its cabernet sauvignon, chardonnay, and merlot. Producers to know from the Limestone Coast include Bowen, Casella Wines, George Wyndham, Greg Norman, Katnook, and McGuigan.

New South Wales

To the east of South Australia and about 75 miles north of Sydney lies New South Wales, which is Australia's second largest wine-producing region, with a total of eight GIs. Although it may be better known today for whisky production (along with that of its southerly neighbor, Tasmania) New South Wales was the first thriving wine region of Australia, with some vines more than 100 years old to prove it.

High-volume production of everyday wines comes from the state's largest region called the Riverina (we're still trying to pronounce its alternate name, Murrumbidgee). Fine wine, for now, comes from three other areas:

» **Hunter Valley:** A historic grape-growing area that begins 80 miles north of Sydney. Climate here ranges from warm and humid to too hot and too dry to grow grapes. Thanks to large-scale irrigation efforts beginning in the 19th century, today's well-known wines from Hunter Valley include chardonnay, semillon, and shiraz. Dessert and fortified wines are also made from botrytized semillion grapes (made possible by the humidity produced from the Murray and Murrumbidgee Rivers that also serve as the key irrigation points for otherwise water-starved areas of the region), as well as blends of grenache, Muscat of Hamberg, and red frontignac grapes. Important producers to know include Brokenwood, Clonakilla, De Bortoli, De Beaurepaire, Mount Pleasant, and Tyrrell's.

» **Mudgee:** An interior area near the mountains. Mudgee specializes in reds such as merlot and cabernet sauvignon but also makes chardonnay.

» **Orange:** A cool, high-altitude area making distinctive wines from chardonnay, sauvignon blanc, cabernet sauvingon, and shiraz.

Victoria

This southeastern region is now Australia's third-largest wine-producing area after South Australia and New South Wales. Although South Australia is home to most of Australia's largest wineries, Victoria has more wineries than any other Aussie region, most of them small. Wine is made in 15 key regions within Victoria. Those located closer to the Bass Straight and Tasman Sea enjoy more of a maritime climate with winds coming off the waters to cool down the vines of well-adapted grapes like chardonnay and pinot noir. More inland regions have drier, warmer climates resulting in more full, richer style chardonnays, cabernet sauvignons, and shiraz. Sparkling wines are made here in different styles from pinot noir, chardonnay, and shiraz.

The luxury beverage and goods giant Louis Vuitton Moët Hennessy (LVMH) has a Chandon hub in Victoria. A number of other important family-owned wineries like Dal Zotto, Castagna, and Seppelt, one of Australia's oldest sparkling wine producers are also based here.

Principal wine regions include the following:

» **Murray Darling:** Formerly known as Murray River, this area stretches into New South Wales. This region is an important source for Australia's good-value for money wines, but drought continues to threaten its viability.

» **Rutherglen:** In the northeast, this long-established, warm climate zone is a historic winemaking outpost, and home of the distinctive Australian fortified wines called muscats and tokays (the latter now renamed in Australia as topaque) that are world-renowned. Referred to by Australians as *stickies*, the muscats are made from muscat à petits grains, and the topaques are made from muscadelle. To make the wines, the grapes are *late harvested* (meaning left on the vine to shrink and shrivel), which makes the resulting juice incredibly concentrated and rich (or sticky). After being gently pressed, neutral grape spirits are added to the wine which haults fermentation and leaves a lot of leftover, or residual, sugar. The fun really begins while the wines age for 10 or more years in oak barrels. These wines can sell from $18 a bottle to over $400 a bottle depending on the producer.

» **Goulburn Valley:** In the center of the state, Goulburn Valley makes a specialty of white varieties that are best known in France's Rhône Valley, specifically marsanne, roussanne, and viognier.

» **Heathcote:** East of Goulburn and due north of Melbourne (the capital of Victoria), this area boasts high altitudes and ancient red Cambrian soils formed from whethered greenstone that make distinctive, rich yet elegant shiraz and cabernet sauvignon.

» **Yarra Valley:** In southern Victoria, and close to Melbourne, Yarra Valley boasts a wide diversity of climates due to altitude differences of its vineyards. The Yarra is noted for its cabernet sauvignon, pinot noir, shiraz, chardonnay, and sauvignon blanc, as well as its sparkling wines. It is one of Australia's most dynamic winemaking scenes.

» **Mornington Peninsula and Geelong:** South of Melbourne and separated by Port Phillip Bay, these two cool, maritime regions specialize in fine pinot noir and chardonnay.

TIP

Producers to seek out from Victoria include Giaconda Estate, Mount Mary, and Yarra Yering for dry styles and Campbell and Chambers Rosewood for muscats and topaques.

Western Australia

Western Australia grows only two percent of the country's wine grapes, and for the most part, the quality is top notch. This is a fairly temperate region near the Indian Ocean. Western Australia — younger than other regions with some of the first vineyard plantings showing up in the 1960s — is home to five wine zones, nine regions, and six sub-regions that are all classified as GIs. The most important regions to know are Margaret River, Great Southern, Swan Valley, Blackwood Valley, and Geographe.

Margaret River

Margaret River is the most prestigious of Western Australia's wine regions, with a cool climate and gravelly soils ideal for sauvignon blanc, semillion, chardonnay, and red Bordeaux varieties like cabernet sauvignon and merlot. In fact, Margaret River is better known for its Bordeaux blends than shiraz, which is typically seen as more of a flagship grape across Australia.

Great Southern

Cooler than Margaret River, Great Southern's specialty is crisp, age-worthy riesling — one of our favorites. This huge, diverse region also produces intense, aromatic cabernet sauvignon as well as cool-climate shiraz and chardonnay on the southern coast. Pinot noir is also successful. Top-quality producers to know from Western Australia include Cape Mentelle, Clairault, Leeuwin Estate, Moss Wood, Vasse Felix, and Xanadu.

Tasmania

Centered in the cold Southern Ocean, Tasmania is Australia's smallest state with one GI covering the entire island. There are seven main winegrowing areas, but most production comes from Tamar Valley in the north and Coal River Valley in the South. Winemakers here focus on cool climate-friendly grapes for white, red, and sparkling wines. The main varieties include chardonnay, pinot noir, riesling, and sauvignon blanc.

WORTH THE SEARCH

Tasmania is best known for its hard-to-find sparkling wines made from chardonnay, pinot noir, and pinot meunier. Top producers to seek out include House of Arras, Jansz, and Pirie that all make affordable and more prestigious versions of their blends.

Chapter **14**

New Zealand: Young and Powerful

To say the New Zealand wine industry has grown in the last 30 years would be an understatement. The number of family and corporate wineries has mushroomed from less than 100 in the 1990s to more than 670 today. Yet, compared to the rest of the world, New Zealand is small in production, making about 1 percent of the world's wine. Moreover, New Zealand isn't drinking most of its juice — the rest of the world is! Nearly 90 percent of New Zealand's wine is exported!

New Zealand is a fascinating, melting pot of cultures from Māori to descendents of Asian, European, and Pacific immigrants. This diversity translates to a community of winemakers with French, German, Spanish, and other winemaking histories that have influenced styles and commitment to quality throughout the country. In this chapter, we dive into New Zealand's wine world, focusing on the top regions, styles, and producers.

The Laws and the Labels

New Zealand's youth in the wine industry is related first to its international history, and second to its national laws during the 20th century. British colonization of New Zealand began in 1840 and lasted until 1907. But British fascination with and journeys to the region started much earlier. The first *Vitis vinifera* (see Chapter 2) vines were planted by English missionaries in 1819. Throughout the 19th century, scores of Europeans would migrate to New Zealand, where over 100 indigenous groups (referred to collectively today as Māori, or *maw-ree*) had lived since 1200 CE.

The 20th century witnessed multiple bans on alcohol production and sales across several years between 1911 and 1987. A commerce-friendly environment for wine in New Zealand really began with the passing of the Sale of Liqour Act, which didn't happen until 1989.

REMEMBER

The Geographic Indications (GI) Act of 2006 is New Zealand's legal framework created to designate specific regions for wine and spirit producers throughout the country. Not as strict as the appellation systems of France, Italy, or Spain (which require specific grapes, aging requirements, and so forth for each region), the GI approach still puts important New Zealand wine regions on the map and helps to promote quality and visibility in the global market. Today, 21 New Zealand wine regions have GI status, and registered GI names must be used on labels. Other requirements for front labels include the variety, vintage (if applicable), and alcohol by volume.

New Zealand instituted additional wine-focused laws in 2016 (the GI Registration Amendments Bill) and 2021 (Wine Regulations) to increase protections and maintain quality standards for GIs, in addition to providing more specific guidelines on winemaking standards and practices.

Regions, Varieties, and Styles

New Zealand is one of several islands in Oceania (sometimes referred to as Australasia) — the area which includes Australia, Papua New Guinea, Fiji, and a number of other islands in the South Pacific Ocean. New Zealand's location gives it a maritime climate, which can (when in balance with dry, sunny days) create ideal conditions for grape growing. This is particularly true for thinner skinned grapes like sauvignon blanc and pinot noir, which dominate New Zealand's wine economy. There are close to 25 other grape varieties also grown in the country, although sauvignon blanc and pinot noir continue to take the lion's share.

REMEMBER

There are only a few countries in the world where going south translates to getting cooler (thanks to the earth's tilt as it rotates around the sun), and New Zealand is one of them (Argentina and Chile are a couple other examples — see Chapter 12 for more on winemaking in South America). Just remember that it's summer in New Zealand when it's winter in New York, and vice versa when you plan your next harvest visit to the country!

New Zealand is divided into two overarching regions: the North Island and the South Island (see Figure 14-1). North Island is the warmer of the two. We explore these two regions in the sections below.

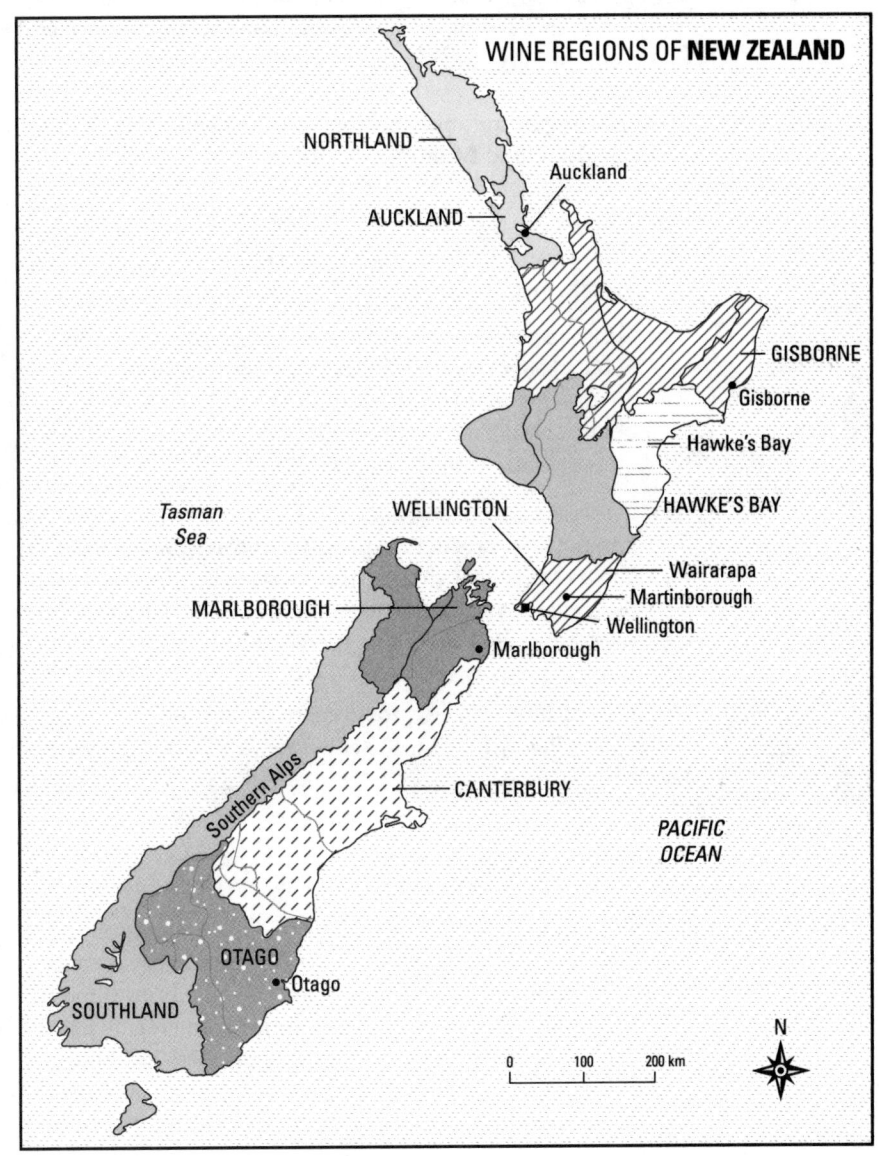

WINE REGIONS OF NEW ZEALAND

NORTHLAND

Auckland

AUCKLAND

GISBORNE

Gisborne

Hawke's Bay

Tasman Sea

WELLINGTON

HAWKE'S BAY

Wairarapa

Martinborough

MARLBOROUGH

Wellington

Marlborough

Southern Alps

CANTERBURY

PACIFIC OCEAN

OTAGO

Otago

SOUTHLAND

0   100   200 km

N

© John Wiley & Sons, Inc.

FIGURE 14-1:
The wine regions of New Zealand.

North Island

Generally warmer than its South Island neighbor, the North Island sits close to the equator. Alluvial soils pad sandy and volcanic subsoils throughout the region, with gravelly soils (ideal for merlot and syrah) found towards the southern tip of the island. In addition to sauvignon blanc, wines from chardonnay, pinot gris, and pinot noir are made here.

The most important, overarching wine regions of the North Island are Hawke's Bay, Auckland, and Wairarapa:

>> Hawke's Bay is situated in the central eastern area of the North Island. It is relatively warm, dry, and sunny, and known as one of the few ideal locations for cabernet sauvignon, merlot and syrah.

>> Auckland (also the name of the city center towards the north) is a commercial hub for larger wineries, but smaller in terms of actual vineyards. Still warm but often wetter than Hawke's Bay, smaller producers are prevalent here. Many boutique firms are making excellent chardonnay, syrah, and merlot and cabernet sauvignon blends in Auckland.

>> Wairarapa sits on the southern tip of the North Island, and is best known for its pinot noirs produced in the small, cooler sub-region of Martinborough (*Martin-bro*). Although some pinot noirs here are compared to those of Burgundy, we would say that there is a distinct difference between the two. Wairarapa's pinot noirs are generally darker, more tannic, and savory.

North Island high-quality producers to try include Ata Rangi, Church Road, Craggy Range, Dry River, Kumeū, Kusuda, Osawa Wines, Paddy Borthwick, and Palliser Estate.

TIP

South Island

The South Island's best wine regions have a moderate climate that includes maritime influences in addition to warm, dry summers. A range of soils make for a variety of wines, including acidic, podzol soils, brown and palli soils, and semi-arid stony soils (unique to the drier Central Otago region). Marlborough (*Marl-bro*) in particular is known for its Greywacke (*grey-wacky*, because of their grey color) riverstone soils, formed from sandstone remnants. Greywacke not only provides drainage to the vines, but also helps to absorb heat during the day that is released at night as the temperatures fall. The stones also contain clay-based soils that help to retain water and nutrients. Although wine is made in several areas of the South Island, Marlborough and Central Otago are the most important ones to know.

Marlborough: The heart of New Zealand sauvignon blanc

On the South Island, Marlborough — the country's largest and commercially most important wine region — is New Zealand's largest production. Sunny, and dry, this area accounts for roughly 70 percent of all wine produced in New Zealand. Almost 90 percent of New Zealand's sauvignon blanc comes from here as well. Many wine producers in Marlborough make both sauvignon blanc and pinot noir.

TIP

High-quality Marlborough producers include Allan Scott, Astrolabe, Babich, Brancott Estate, Cloudy Bay, Greywacke (named for the soil), Lake Chalice (known for amazing, traditional method sparkling in addition to still wines), and Wairau River.

A QUICK SIP: WHY SAUVIGNON BLANC IS SO GREEN

At their best, wines made from ripe sauvignon blanc grapes in New Zealand are mouth-wateringly delicious symphonies. Fresh citrus (especially grapefruit and lemon), tropical fruits, and green fruits and vegetables (green mango, fresh-cut green grass, crisp, and green asparagus) are common flavors. The green grass and other green vegetal aromas that distinguish sauvignon blanc (in New Zealand especially and other world regions generally) comes from chemical compounds found in the grapes called *pyrazines* (short for the longer, more difficult to pronounce term of methoxypyrazines). When sauvignon blanc is grown in cooler climates, these compounds become even more pronounced, and the wines create a lip-smacking, zingy, eye-widening effect that makes you wonder whether you're drinking wine or actually eating a green grass salad with a fresh squeezed lemon on top!

There can of course, be a downside to pyrazines. Climate, vintage differences, or vine-yard practices (harvesting the wine with stems, harvesting too early, or over-watering, among others) can all result in less-than-desirable pyrazine levels in a finished wine. Aromas may include overcooked, boiled, or rotten asparagus, decaying cabbage, and so forth. At their worst, pyrazines are no longer considered a pleasant byproduct of winemaking — instead, they're an actual chemical fault in the wine. Learn more about wine faults in Chapter 4.

Much of sauvignon blanc's green flavor profiles also come from their fermentation in stainless steel tanks. Using stainless steel allows winemakers to preserve the inherent flavors of the grapes at harvest, and results in wines that are clean and unadulterated

(continued)

(continued)
(continued)

versions of *terroir* (see Chapter 2). With that said, many New Zealand winemakers are experimenting with partial and full oak fermentations that, similar to the white sauvignon and sémillon blends of Bordeaux, can create a richer texture, add complexity, and result in more long-lived wines.

Beware of mass-produced sauvignon blanc from New Zealand. While inexpensive and quaffable, it can be one-dimensional flabby, and disappointing. These wines are made from grapes sourced throughout the country (mostly picked and/or sold to large corporations in Marlborough) that are quickly pressed, and processed (often with selected yeast strains used to enhance the favorable "green" characteristics we know and love). Top-quality producers focus on smaller yields, owning or managing the vineyards directly, selectively harvesting, and using techniques that result in more nuanced and expressive wines.

Central Otago and the pinot noir push

Although sauvignon blanc from Marlborough is the biggest breadwinner of the South Island, Central Otago is the region (and the country's) important for pinot noir. Nestled inland on the foothills of the Southern Alps (resulting in more sunshine and less frost-risk for vines), Central Otago is the southernmost of the South Island's (and the world's) wine regions. The Alps form a broad rain shelter over the Central Otago, making the perfect combination of warmth and dryness for grapes like pinot noir. Mica, schist, and loam are the dominant soil types, with most vineyards situated along several lakes scattered throughout the region.

WORTH THE SEARCH

The low-yielding vines of Central Otago produce highly concentrated pinot noirs. The number of high-quality producers has grown substantially in the last 10 years. Some of our recommendations for top Central Otago pinot noir producers include Akarua, Burn Cottage, Mt. Difficulty, Felton Road, Peregrine, Prophet's Rock, and Two Paddocks.

New Zealand pinot noirs vary in taste from region to region. The wines of Martinborough and Marlborough, for example, can show more red fruit (cherry, raspberry, and strawberry among others) characteristics and have brighter acidity. Central Otago is known for richer, spicier, more full-bodied pinot noirs with darker fruit flavors (plums, blackberries, and cassis for example) and more pronounced tannins.

256   PART 4 The World of Wine: Australia and New Zealand

BEYOND SAUVIGNON BLANC: NEW ZEALAND'S FUTURE

New Zealand sauvignon blancs and pinot noirs are still coming on strong to the wine world. But New Zealand is more than just a two-grape country. In the white wine category, we're impressed with the chardonnays, rieslings, and pinot fris from many of the top-quality producers named in this chapter. Among red wines, New Zealand's cabernet sauvignons, merlots, and Bordeaux blends deserve a following — particularly those from warmer-climate North Island regions such as Hawke's Bay. Finally, don't forget about rosés of pinot noir and sparkling wines made from sauvignon blanc, chardonnay, and pinot noir. They are crisp, refreshing, and fruity. They may also make a more cost-effective alternative to champagne or other traditional method sparklers. Wine bars are great places to try some of these more difficult finds.

5

The World of Wine: Africa, the Middle East, and Asia

Chapter **15**

Africa: Roaring Wines of the Continent

This chapter includes a deep dive on South Africa — the continent's premier country for wines made and exported from *Vitis vinifera* worldwide. Brief overviews are provided for three additional African countries (Algeria, Morocco, and Tunisia), all of which have rapidly expanding wine industries making their mark on the world scene.

The Laws and the Labels

From producing oceans of average quality wine for most of the 20th century to focusing on more sophisticated, *terroir*-driven (see Chapter 2) wines today, South Africa now ranks eighth in world wine production. Formed in 1973, The Wine of Origin (WO) system sets standards for variety, vintage, single-vineyard definitions, and geographic designations for wines made in any of its 60 *appellations* (defined territories where grapes are grown for making wine). From smallest to largest, categories of classification include wards, districts, regions, and geographical units. All WO wines are required to contain 100 percent of grapes only harvested in the specific geography of origin.

REMEMBER

Varietal wines in South Africa must contain at least 75 percent of the named grape variety. Exported wines — complying with stricter European Union (EU) regulations — must contain 85 percent of the named variety. About 35 percent of South Africa's wines qualify as Wine of Origin (WO). WO wines must be produced entirely from grapes of the designated area on the label.

In addition to alcohol level, variety, classification, and vintage if applicable, South African wines are prohibited from using terms such as "natural wine" or "gluten free" because of these terms' potentially misleading effects on consumers. WO laws are increasingly concerned with accuracy and direct, literal interpretations on South African wine labels, particularly in the global marketplace. The point of the South African wine label is simply for you to know what's in the bottle and where it's from without guessing or having to do much work (which we like)!

REMEMBER

In sharp contrast to the South African WO system, the countries of Algeria, Morocco, and Tunisia share a French colonial history that resulted in a loose adoption of the French *Appellation d'Origine Contrôlée* (AOC, see Chapter 6) system by designating, protecting, and promoting specific wine regions for their *terroir*, grapes, and styles. Brief highlights of each country's system are as follows:

>> **Algeria:** The Office National de Commercialisation des Produits Viti-vinicoles (ONCV) is an agency within the Ministry of Agriculture (formed in 1968) responsible for regulating and marketing Algerian wine. It is now known as the Société de Transformation Viticole (Sotravit). The agency established seven wine quality zones that may appear on wine labels.

>> **Morocco:** In Morocco, the wine industry also falls under the Ministry of Agriculture, with seven wine regions. Other than producer and varietal information, "origin label guaranteed" or "guaranteed vintage wine" on a label refers to one of 14 designated appellations of origin within the five main regions.

>> **Tunisia:** This country's system most closely mirrors the French AOC system, with designations such as *Premier Cru* or *Grand Cru* (see Chapter 6's section on Burgundy) on wine labels from any of the country's seven main wine regions, or AOCs. Similar to Burgundy, these designations should indicate quality and are likely to ascend in price from *Premier Cru* to *Grand Cru*.

Regions, Varieties, and Styles

Evidence of winemaking on the African continent dates back to 3500 BCE in Egypt, with remnants of sealed containers and grape residue, as well as tomb paintings and texts describing viticulture and winemaking skills (see Chapter 2 for more on the journey of *Vitis vinifera*). Today, while wine is still made in Egypt, much of what the world knows and can access about Africa's modern wine industry lies farther (technically furthest) south, in South Africa.

South Africa

The first major waves of *Vitis vinifera* arrived in South Africa as early as the 1650s. Dutch colonialists and settlers stopped in Table Bay (named then as the Cape Colony and now as Cape Town) setting up fleet provision stations and eventually colonizing the land. The Dutch East India Company — the world's first massive international trading firm whose first charter involved deals between Europe and what is now south and southeast Asia — was at the forefront of migration to Africa from other parts of the world.

TECHNICAL STUFF

Between 1652 and at least 1834, waves of both vines and people were imported to the region — the vines from Europe and the people enslaved from within the African continent, as well as various countries of southeast Asia. Together with throngs of Dutch, English, and French (Huguenots in particular) who would come to the colony at the promise of fertile land and opportunity, South Africa's commercial wine industry was born. Although the Dutch ceded the Cape Colony to the British who abolished slavery in 1814, the next 150 years of South Africa's wine history unfortunately doesn't tell a better story. The formation of South Africa's largest wine cooperative, the KWV (*Köoperatieve Wijnbouwers vereniging van Zuid Afrika* or the Cooperative Winegrowers' Association of South Africa) marked many more years of discrimination and manipulation of viticulture in South Africa. This resulted at first in a focus on quantity at the expense of quality, and much later in the monopolization of the wine industry entirely. The apartheid regime, which lasted from 1948 to 1994, was a system of racial segregation and discrimination enforced by the white minority government that resulted in legal separation and social, economic, and political oppression of the black majority. Apartheid had crippling effects on South African wine exports specifically, and international trade more generally as the world refused to do business with the country, imposing sanctions and divesting from South African industries.

While apartheid officially ended in early 1990s, the wine industry would still have an uphill battle to climb. Fast-forward to the last ten years, which has included everything from government bans on alcohol during the COVID-19 pandemic to documented abuses of vineyard (referred to in South Africa as "wine farms") laborers, and it's safe to say that South Africa's wine industry is all but perfect. Nonetheless, winemakers continue to strive.

There are six major wine areas in South Africa called *geographical units*. Contrary to popular belief, South Africa's leading varieties are white! The most-planted grape in South Africa is chenin blanc, sometimes referred to locally as *steen.* South

Africa produces more chenin blanc than any other country in the world. It is also home to the oldest known chenin blanc vines on the planet, with some dating back at least 120 years. South African chenin blanc is also known for its versatility: it can range from light and citrus-forward with bright acidity to full, rich, and supple with dried, baked, and/or candied fruit flavors depending on the region and producer. Finally, this star grape is also used to make sparkling (called *méthode cap classique*, or MCC if made in the traditional method in South Africa), late-harvest, and wines made with grapes that have been intentionally infected with *Botrytis cinerea* (see Chapter 6).

Sauvignon blancs from earthy and vegetal to fruity and tropical styles, in addition to chardonnay in both Burgundian (see Chapter 6) and Sonoma Coast (see Chapter 11) styles are all made in South Africa. Serious rosés and reds from cabernet sauvignon, merlot, shiraz, and pinot noir continue to gain international acclaim.

REAL DEAL

And then you have pinotage. Uniquely (and proudly) South African, pinotage is a cross of pinot noir and cinsault developed in 1925. However, pinotage didn't appear as a wine until 1959. Pinotage wine combines the cherry fruit of pinot noir with the earthiness of a Rhône (French) wine. Pinotage can vary from a light to medium-bodied, easy-drinking wine, to a high-powered, big-bodied wine only fit for a steak dinner. We are increasingly seeing less entry-level pinotage in the market, with a shift to higher-end, age-worthy producers that retail for $25 and up per bottle. Kaapzicht, Kanonkop, and Simonsig are excellent examples.

REMEMBER

The most prestigious area to know for high-quality wines is the Western Cape, situated on and around South Africa's southeastern coast. The Western Cape has five major regions in ascending order of popularity and prestige for fine wine: Olifants River, Klein Karoo, Breede River Valley, Cape South Coast, and the Coastal Region (which encompasses Cape Town and surrounding areas). Almost all the country's vineyards are within 90 miles of Cape Town, South Africa's most fascinating and picturesque city — see the color section of this book.

Despite its many political wine obstacles, South African *terroir*, and especially that of the Western Cape doesn't disappoint. This is one of the few places on continental Africa where climate is mostly Mediterranean, with warm, dry days, cold nights, and mild winters. Hotter days are tempered by the (sometimes very intense) winds blowing off the Atlantic and Indian Oceans. It is almost impossible to stand outside in the Western Cape and not see a mountain of some sort. The word "mountain" doesn't really do the wonders of Table Mountain, Simonsberg, or Stellenbosch Mountain justice: these are ancient (formed from geologic activity from at least 250 million years ago), dramatic cropped sandstone mounds that seem like they touch the sky. You can imagine what all of this elevation does for viticulture in the Western Cape: in some of the higher elevated, cooler climate regions of Cape South Coast, chardonnay and pinot noir can thrive. In the warmer, flatter areas of Stellenbosch and Franschhoek Valley, thicker skinned grapes like cabernet sauvignon and syrah (sometimes referred to in South Africa and Australia as shiraz) flourish.

Here are the four major districts and their high-quality producers in the Coastal Region:

>> **Stellenbosch:** East of Cape Town, the most important wine district in quantity and quality, especially for fine wines. Producers to seek include Aslina (especially for its skin contact chenin blanc and Bordeaux-inspired blend, Umsasane), Capensis, De Toren, De Trafford, Kaapzicht, Ken Forrester, Kumusha Wines (for its Hurudza Bordeaux blend in particular), Neil Ellis, Raats Family Wines, Rust en Vrede, Simonsig (South Africa's first Cap Classique estate), Stark-Condé, and Tokara.

>> **Paarl:** North of Stellenbosch, with warmer days and cool nights, home of the famous Nederburg Estate. Additional producers to note include Alheit, Vilafonté and Vondeling.

>> **Franschhoek Valley:** Southeast of Paarl, this district is surrounded on three sides by mountains. Many innovative winemakers and culinary attractions are here. Top producers include Alheit, Anthonij, Colmant and Haute Cabrière (for Cap Classique in particular), Holden Manz, Leeu Passant, and Normandie Est. 1693.

>> **Swartland:** North of Cape Town, this district has evolved in recent years from an area known for inexpensive wines to an exciting center of high-quality winemaking by smaller producers. Syrah and old-vine chenin blanc are particularly important. High-quality producers include David and Nadia, Mullineux, and Sadie Family.

Not a district but a free-standing ward, Constantia is the oldest wine-producing area in the country, located south of Cape Town and cooled by Atlantic and Indian ocean breezes. The highly coveted dessert wine, Vin de Constance, made from late harvest muscat frontignan (also known as Muscat à Petits Grains) by Klein Constantia dates back to 1653. Aromas of baked apricots, honeysuckle, and crème brulée will quickly reveal why this wine was a favorite of nobility and royalty in the 18th and 19th centuries, in addition to one of the most mentioned wines from legendary authors such as Alexander Dumas, Charles Dickens, and Jane Austen.

The small, cool Walker Bay district is part of the Cape South Coast region. Bordering the Indian Ocean, it is a key area for pinot noir and chardonnay production, led by the iconic Hamilton Russell Winery. Another district to note, Elgin, is on the coast between Stellenbosch and Walker Bay. A cool plateau area,

Elgin is known for its intensely flavored sauvignon blancs and pinot noirs. Top producers include Boschendal (for Cap Classique especially), Downes Family, Paul Cluver, and Richard Kershaw.

Other African wine regions

South Africa remains the continent's biggest wine producer and exporter. This is in part due to its history, but also to its unique *terroir* and maritime to Mediterranean climate. Mild seasons with warm days and cool nights, coupled with cooler, rainy winters provide the ideal conditions for *Vitis vinifera* in particular. Moving further north on the continent towards the Equator, temperatures are simply too hot for grapes to thrive.

As mentioned at the start of this chapter, other important African wine regions are in Algeria, Morocco, and Tunisia (in ascending order of production). All three countries were colonized by the French and, as a result, cultivate many French varieties and have appellation systems mirroring the French *Appellation d'Origine Contrôlée* (AOC, see Chapter 6) regime:

>> **Algeria:** Although tiny in terms of world production, Algeria is Africa's second largest wine producer. Algeria's seven main wine regions (also known as *quality zones*) are located in the northwest, and include Coteaux de Tlemcen, Monts du Tessalah, Coteaux de Mascara, Dahra hills, Coteaux du Zaccar, Médéa, and Aïn Bessem Bouira.

  Mostly full-bodied, deep-colored red wines are made from alicante bouschet, carignan, cinsault, and grenache. Popular producers include Sotrait and SGCO.

>> **Morocco:** This country follows Algeria in total production, with most of its winemaking in the north. Five main wine regions are subdivided into 14 areas with *Appellation d'Origine Garantie* (AOG) and *Appellation d'Origine Contrôlée* (AOC) designations as follows:

  • **The East:** Berkane AOG, Angad AOG, and Beni Sadden AOG

  • **Fès-Meknès:** Guerrouane AOG, Beni M'tir AOG, Saiss AOG, Zerhoune AOG, Coteaux de l'Atlas Premier Cru AOC, Crémant de l'Atlas AOC, Côtes de Rommani AOC

  • **The Northern Plain:** Gharb AOG

  • **Rabat/Casablanca:** Chellah AOG, Zemmour AOG, Zaër AOG, Sahel AOG, and Zenatta AOG

  • **El-Jadida:** Doukkala AOG

TECHNICAL STUFF

While AOG is a geographic designation, the term *Premier Cru* on a label may be assigned by a producer to their highest-quality wine, as in the French Burgundy system (see Chapter 6). AOC generally represent tighter quality control and prestige than AOG wines, similar to the difference between DOC and DOCG wines in Italy (see Chapter 5).

Like Algeria, Morocco is also red-wine dominant, focusing mostly on medium- to full-bodied, perfumed versions of alicante bouschet, carignan, cabernet sauvignon, cinsault, and syrah. Medium-bodied to rich white wines are made from chenin blanc, faranah (palomino), and the aromatic muscat. Morocco also has a number of popular indigenous varieties such as maticha for whites and abbou and doukkal for reds. High-quality Moroccan producers include Alain Graillot (whose Syrocco is one of Michelle's favorites), Domaine Ouled Thaleb, Celliers de Meknès, and Château Roslane.

» **Tunisia:** The main wine regions in Tunisia are located mostly in the north of the country, including the Cap Bon peninsula and surrounding areas of Aryanah, Béja, Jendouba, Ben Arus, Bizerte, Nabeul, and Zagwhouan. Chardonnay, clairette, Muscat of Alexandria, and ugni blanc are the main white varieties, while richer, sometimes spicy wines from alicante bouschet, cabernet sauvignon, carignan, merlot, mourvèdre, and syrah dominate reds. Well-known producers include Ceptunes, Domaine Neferis, and Jean Boujnah.

TIP

Algerian, Moroccan, and Tunisian wine can be difficult to find. Our recommendation is to visit wine bars or restaurants that feature products from these countries to get a taste of what these wines have to offer. In our experience, this is the most efficient approach to then finding higher-quality retail options to enjoy at home!

Chapter **16**

The Middle East: Ancient Vines and Modern Appeal

lthough not as long as its northern neighbors of Turkey, Georgia, or Greece (see Chapter 10), the Middle East's history of winemaking is both majestically ancient and provocatively modern. People have been making and enjoying wine here for centuries. This chapter explores the major wine-producing countries of the Middle East, focusing on the contributions of Lebanon, Israel, and Palestine.

TECHNICAL STUFF

We cover Turkey — sometimes considered part of the Middle East — in Chapter 10. Despite the fact that only about 5 percent of Turkey's landmass sits in Europe (with the rest technically on the Asian continent), the country is aligned to the European Union (EU) in terms of both winemaking industry standards and larger economic development goals through the EU–Turkey Customs Union. This union allows free movement of goods between Turkey and member countries without customs regulations. Turkey's legal frameworks for wine, coupled with its proximity to the EU, made it a better fit for Chapter 10's focus on European wine.

The Laws and the Labels

Each of the countries explored in this chapter has their own wine laws, some more strict and tied to place or production than others. Similar to the EU's Protected Designation of Origin (DOP) and Protected Geographical Indication (IGP) — more on these in Chapter 10 — the International Organisation of Vine and Wine (OIV) was developed in 2001.

Although the OIV is based in Dijon, France, it has a much broader reach than France or even Europe. The OIV is an inter-governmental organization made up of 50 member states across Asia, Africa, Europe, Oceana, and South America. It provides regulatory frameworks, common definitions, enological research and best practices, guidelines for international wine trade, and standardized methods for analyzing wine quality. Of the countries we explore in this chapter, only Lebanon and Israel are members.

Lebanon, Israel, and Palestine do not have extensive labeling laws for wine, other than requirements for ingredients, production dates, contact information, and country of origin in specific languages. Although not required, Israeli winemakers are encouraged to obtain kosher certifications that are printed on bottles, making their wines more marketable locally.

If you are lucky enough to find Lebanese, Israeli, or Palestinean wine in a shop, chances are, it's worth trying!

Regions, Varieties, and Styles

Lebanon, Israel, and Palestine have a lot in common besides the extent of their winemaking history. Their shared eastern coastline with the Mediterranean Sea (see Figure 16-1) results in moderate to warm temperatures with less seasonal change when compared to the major wine-producing countries of Europe. Average annual temperatures in Lebanon, Israel, and Palestine present the perfect recipe for grapes (and a nice summer vacation!). The elevation of some of these countries' vineyards is also ideal for grape growing, generating the diurnal shifts and acidity needed for well-balanced wines. (For more on the importance of acidity, check out Chapter 3).

All three territories make white, rosé, red, sparkling, and dessert-style wines. Israel leads the region in production, with 2023 data showing around 40 million bottles from 300 wineries, followed by Lebanon with 60 wineries and 11 million bottles in the same year. Given the humanitarian and political crises unfolding in Palestine at the time of writing, accurate estimates of existing wineries and production from the same time period are unknown. The most recent, reliable information we found was the monetary value of wine exports coming from Palestine in 2022, which amounted to just $284,000.

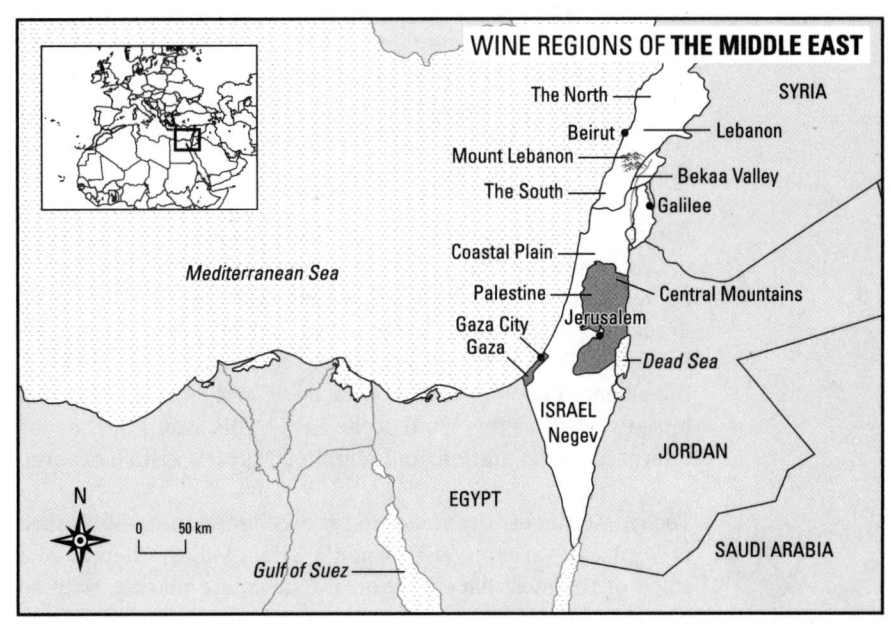

FIGURE 16-1:
The wine regions of the Middle East.

Lebanon

Evidence of the Phoenicians (semitic peoples living in the eastern Mediterranean coast between 1200 and 332 BCE) planting vines and drinking wine takes us as far back as the 7th century BCE, making Lebanon anything but new to the beverage. Lebanon's winemaking story has had some interesting twists since then, including a post-World War I League of Nations mandate requiring that France serve as a political administrator to both Lebanon and Syria. Wine-wise, both French citizenship and French grape-planting expanded (which explains why more French varieties are widely available in Lebanon than native ones to this day). Today, there are somewhere between 70 and 90 wineries in Lebanon, and most of this growth has happened only in the last 20 years.

REMEMBER

Lebanon technically has a Mediterranean climate, although many of its top-quality vineyards are located in higher elevated, mountainous areas (as high as 9,843 feet, or 3,000 meters, above sea level). The Mediterranean coastline and northern Batroun Mountains, coupled with the cool nights and warm summers of the eastern Bekaa Valley are an ideal couple for winemaking here. Clay, limestone, and sand soils result in varied wine styles with a range of dried to baked and ripe fruit flavors, bright to smack-you-in-the-face acidity, and low to high alcohol.

Lebanon's wine production is still predominantly steeped in the French grape-growing tradition, although experimentation with native varieties is growing, especially among younger generations of winemakers. The main white varieties are chardonnay, sauvignon blanc, merwah (*mer-waa*), and obaideh (*uh-by-duh*). The latter two are also used in blends to make Lebanon's famous distilled spirit, *arak*. Red varieties include cabernet sauvignon, grenache, cinsault, carignan, syrah, malbec, and petite verdot.

For years, one winery in particular has dominated the U.S. market and recognition of Lebanese wine: Chateau Musar. Founded by Gaston Hochar in 1930 (he was only 20 years old at the time), the winery was inspired by one of Hochar's trips to Bordeaux. Several years of technical and cultural exchange between the Hochar family and French winemakers would ensue. At the 1979 Bristol Wine Fair, Michael Broadbent, a popular British wine critic and journalist, named the 1967 Chateau Musar vintage as the "Find of the Fair." This award further solidified the brand's international reputation, and reignited Musar's British exports and global appeal.

WORTH THE SEARCH

Today, Musar sets the standard for excellent wine quality, specifically for the use of Bordeaux varieties in Lebanon's Bekaa Valley. Chateau Musar wines are also some of the most expensive on the Lebanese market, with some vintage wines well over $100 a bottle. Younger generations of winemakers continue to work with international varieties while exploring new avenues for indigenous Lebanese grapes to chart their own path. Some high-quality and available producers (in addition to Musar) include Chateau Belle-Vue, Château Kefraya, Chateau Ksara, Domaine des Tourelles, Massaya, and Mersel.

TIP

More affordable, great-quality examples from these producers can be found in the $30 to $50 range in specialty and/or larger wine shops. If you are looking to try Lebanese wines for the first time, Lebanese restaurants are an excellent way to try many different producers and varieties at once.

Israel

Bordered by Lebanon to the north and Egypt to the south, Israel is another country with an ancient history of winemaking, evidenced by archaeological finds dating back at least 3,000 years. Biblical references to wine used for religious ceremonies, feasts, as a form of payment, almsgiving to the poor and — last but certainly not least — the feats of Jesus of Nazareth, have all shaped the modern world's perception of wine as more than just fermented grape juice. Indeed, the formation of the state of Israel (which didn't actually happen until 1948) didn't come pre-packaged with a wine industry. For centuries before the formation of Israel, this stretch of land has been contested for political and economic control. Over the course of centuries, the land was appropriated first by the Arab conquest of 637 CE and much later by the Ottoman Empire between 1517 and 1917. Both regimes marked stagnant to non-existent wine industries in which Muslims were forbidden from making wine or consuming alcohol.

Not until the 1880s was the wine industry reinvigorated with new investments from France and a renewed sense of optimism among the Israeli Jewish population for the region's winemaking potential. In addition to increased research and development within Israel, Jewish migration to the region from Europe further boosted the wine industry and its expertise. Over time, both small and larger wine producers put Israel back on the map.

REMEMBER

Relatively speaking, both Israel and its wine industry are small. The state of Israel is no bigger than one fifth of the entire state of California. Today, there are several hundred wineries, but only about 70 engaged in commercial production and export. There are six main regions with varied climates depending on their proximity to the Mediterranean Sea in the west, and their elevation in Israel's several mountain ranges. The most important ones to know are the Coastal Plain, Galilee, Golan Heights, Judea, and the Negev. Soils vary, from limestone and terra rossa in the Judean Hills to volcanic, gravelly soils in Galilee and Golan Heights. Both native and international varieties are planted to make dry, sparkling, and late harvest dessert wines, although the majority of more popular wines are made from French varieties. Chardonnay and sauvignon blanc, gewürztraminer, jandali, marawi, Muscat of Alexandria, and riesling dominate white wines, while argaman carignan, cabernet sauvignon, grenache, and marselan (a genetic cross of grenache and cabernet sauvignon) make up most of the red wines.

TIP

Some top Israeli wine producers include Barkan, Carmel, Dalton, Margalit, Recanati, Teperberg, Yarden, and Yatir.

EVERYTHING'S KOSHER

Many people (at least those in the United States aged over 21) have probably already tried an Israeli wine and don't even know it! The country may be more famous for its *chaptalized* (sugar added — not necessarily a great thing in the wine world because of its attempts to focus on quantity versus naturally-occuring quality, or allowing grapes to express themselves naturally) red called Manischewitz *(ma-nuh-sheh-vuhts)*. Nonetheless, this grape juice-like stuff (made from concord grapes, after all) gives us a reason to talk

(continued)

(continued)

about kosher wine. To be a kosher wine has nothing to do with how the grapes are grown or even how the wine itself is made. What makes a kosher wine kosher is the person handling it. To be called *kosher,* a wine has to be touched only by a Jewish person that observes the sabbath, from the moment the grapes are picked and crushed, to the moment that the wine is bottled. Additionally, any additives to the wine (yeast, filtering or fining agents, and so on) must also be kosher. Thankfully, we are seeing more and more kosher brands on shelves that strive for go beyond Manischewitz, with winemakers aspiring to be taken seriously for more *terroir*-driven styles.

Palestine

Technically speaking, today's Palestine is the area of the eastern Mediterranean region that contains parts of modern Israel, as well as the Gaza Strip and West Bank. As in Lebanon and Israel, winemaking in Palestine is an ancient tradition. The Natufians (Palestinian ancestors) were making wine for consumption in at least 1300 BCE. Evidence of exports to regions of Cyprus, Egypt, and Georgia in clay amphora solidifies the role that wine played in economic, social, and cultural life over the centuries.

The climate in Palestine is generally Mediterranean but changes depending on the region. Summers are hot and dry, and winters are wet and mild. Major soil types for viticulture include red sandy soils, volcanic terra rossa, chalk, and marl. The Al-Khader region of Bethlehem on the south/central West Bank and the Gush Etzion area (called Al-Shefa locally) of the Judean Mountains south of Bethlehem and Jerusalem are the two main wine-producing sub-regions of Palestine. Similar to Israel, both native and international varieties are planted, producing white, red, sparkling, and dessert-style wines. White wines are made from the native dabouki, hamdani, jandali, and zeini grapes, in addition to sauvignon blanc. Reds are made from the native baladi and bittuni, in addition to cabernet sauvignon, merlot, and syrah.

TIP

Some of the top Palestinian producers include Ashkar, Cremisan, Domaine Kassis, Philokalia, and Taybeh. Michelle served Cremisan's 2019 Baladi to bar guests in celebration of Passover and Easter. The wine was the perfect companion to the stewed and roasted meats of the season, complete with mesmerizing baked berry, forest floor, and sandalwood notes!

The ultimate fate of Palestine's wine industry hinges on the extent to which wars, extreme famine, and a crumbling infrastructure continue to dominate. At the time of writing, most of the wine industry — particularly its export sector — is halted. We are hopeful that domestic wine production will rise again in the future.

Chapter **17**

Asia: Wine's Next Wave

Thirty years ago, this chapter wouldn't have existed! Today, there is simply no wine book in the universe that should omit Asia when it comes to the most rapid and significant changes in the global market. China, Japan, and India are the three largest wine-producing regions of Asia, although there are several others on the continent that also make wine.

We discuss each of these key countries in this chapter, focusing on the main regions, top producers, and trends to follow as each country stakes its claim in the wine world. With the exception of a few Chinese wines, many of the top producers described in this chapter are not widely imported or distributed to the United States yet. We are hoping you will use this chapter as your introduction to the countries and perhaps your travel map for tasting on your next visit to each one!

The Laws and the Labels

Although China, Japan, and India are ancient civilizations, their wine industries and wine laws are moving with the times and evolving. At the time of writing only Japan has regions with Geographical Indication (GI) status, which are designated regions with wines made from grapes grown in specific areas in accordance with required specifications. However, winemaking hotspots and top-quality producers have quickly surfaced and are here to stay.

TIP

China, Japan, and India require producer name, variety, net volume, alcohol, and any special ingredients to be printed on labels. If you're lucky enough to see a bottle from these countries on a wine shelf, it may be worth a try! But other than the name of the grape and vintage, you won't learn much else from the label alone.

Regions, Varieties, and Styles

China, Japan, and India are three very different countries with their own histories and folklore around wine. Read on for the most important regions and wines to know.

China: The modern wine revolution

Evidence of winemaking in China dates to at least 9,000 years ago (which would technically predate what we know about Georgia as the "cradle of wine" starting 8,000 years ago; for more on this, see Chapter 10). Archaeological findings suggest that winemaking during this time wasn't just *Vitis vinifera* (see Chapter 2) as we know it, but rather a fermented beverage made from other berries and rice as well. Nonetheless, it's safe to say that for centuries, China's agricultural society has been an integral part of its people and national identity.

Wine may not be the first thing that comes to mind when we think of China due to its towering production of beer and the sorghum-based spirit, *baijiu* (and less but still significant, its "yellow wine" called *huanjiu*, made from millet, rice, and/or wheat). The wine industry as we know it began first in 1978 with the formation of the People's Republic of China, and has grown through rapid economic development, international trade, and the development of Chinese industries. These highly productive and efficient years solidified the rise of China's wealthy elites. Today, China is only second behind the United States in the total number of millionaires, at 6 million people and counting.

Interest among China's wealthy and elite population in wine is inextricably linked to its own wine industry's development. With the resources, land, and people to build it, the country has evolved from simply consuming some of the world's best wines (specifically from Bordeaux and Burgundy — see Chapter 6 — where Chinese buyers spend hundreds of millions of dollars per year) to actually producing some amazing wines with the help of French winemakers and luxury goods conglomerates.

It seems everything is big in China: the history, the population, the sheer number of people and most importantly, the amount of land for wine. In terms of land-mass, China is the fourth largest country on the planet. With an almost infinite Pacific coastline and shared borders with a whopping 14 countries, the variation in climate depending on where you're standing in China almost begs for vine growing. Today, there are vineyards in almost two million acres across China. Most of the top wine regions are aligned to the administrative provinces (not necessarily by design) and are spread across the north and northeast, central, south, and western parts of the country. Although white grapes are planted, red wine dominates in China (the color being loved for more reasons than wine)!

REMEMBER

Today, there are more than 450 wineries in China, with many making mass-produced, quaffable wine at affordable prices. Then there are a handful of wineries investing the time and resources at promising sites to make top-quality wines for more discerning Chinese and international consumers. Any visitor to China will observe the deference for French wine culture through its construction of several *châteaux* (see Chapter 6) in these areas — all with designs inspired by the great *châteaux* of Bordeaux. Figure 17-1 shows China's wine regions.

FIGURE 17-1:
The wine regions of China.

© John Wiley & Sons, Inc.

WARNING

BUYER BEWARE!

Black market traders looking to turn a profit from high-end French wines in China have been caught replacing empty Bordeaux or Burgundy bottles with fake wines, creating fake labels to sell wines under well-known names for thousands of dollars per bottle. This problem was at one point so rampant in China that the value of fake wines sold was estimated in the hundreds of millions of dollars.

This scam worked for a few years (the worst throughout the early 2000s) and probably made a few criminals temporarily cash-rich. But long gone are the days of large-scale, counterfeit wine schemes: high-end producers are using a number of cunning counter-techniques: printing traceable serial numbers on bottles, using holograms, printing with invisible inks, creating producer-specific and bottle-specific markings that can only be seen with special types of lighting, implementing blockchain technology, and more. As producers get smarter, the black market is prevented from tarnishing producer and broker reputations.

If you or someone you know suspects a fraudulent bottle, this doesn't mean that the suspect is Chinese. Fraud happens everywhere in the world, and winemakers are getting smarter about how to combat the worst of it in their own countries.

North and northeast

This region includes Shandong, Hebei, Beijing, Tianjin, Liaoning, Jilin, and Shanxi. Climate ranges from moderate maritime to continental monsoon in further inland areas, all thanks to the Bohai and Yellow seas. Winemakers here are constantly wary of excessive humidity and resulting mold for grapes. Soil ranges from gravelly loam to sand, clay, and limestone.

REMEMBER

Shandong is considered the first and most important region for the modern wine revolution in China, particularly because its climate is shielded from the harsh, cold, and hot extremes in the center of the country. It has the ideal diurnal temperature shifts (the difference between the highest daytime and the lowest nighttime temperature within a 24-hour timeframe to grow grapes with well-balanced sugar and acidity levels. A range of international varieties are grown here for white, red, and sparkling wines, including chardonnay and riesling for whites, in addition to cabernet sauvignon, cabernet gernischt (carmeneree), merlot, syrah, petite verdot, and cabernet franc. Beichun is a main native red variety.

Shandong is home to Domaine de Long Dai (founded by Barons de Rothschild of Château Lafite Rothschild) as well as China's oldest (founded in 1892) and largest winery, Changyu Pioneer Wine Company. Additional high-quality producers from the north and northeast include Château Martin, Château Reifeng-Auzias, Château Rongzi, Château State Guest, and Grace Vineyard. Changyu and Liaoning San are well-known for their icewines made from vidal blanc in Liaoning as well.

Central

This area covers the wine regions of Inner Mongolia and the prestigious Ningxia. These are highly elevated areas with many vineyards planted on the foothills of mountains that stretch to more than 13,124 feet (4,000 meters) above sea level. The Helan Mountain Range protects vineyards of Inner Mongolia and Ningxia from frost, improves sunshine exposure, and preserves acidity with diurnal shifts. Winemakers in Inner Mongolia have also adapted to extreme temperatures by identifying more cold-resistant varieties and vineyard management techniques. Red wines dominate in Inner Mongolia, with Château Hansen as the top producer for cabernet franc and cabernet sauvignon.

REAL DEAL

Ningxia is often referred to as China's Napa Valley, complete with the prestige and price tag to match. Ningxia is home to Chandon China (partnership with Louis Vuitton Moët Hennessy, or LVMH, which makes traditional method sparkling wines from chardonnay, pinot noir, and marselan), Silver Heights, Helan Mountain, and a number of other high-end wineries including Jade Vineyard, Kanaan Winery, and Helan Qingxue.

South

Historically known more for their global culinary contributions than their wine, Yunnan and Sichuan Provinces line the autonomous region of Tibet and the stunning Himalayas. As you can guess, this means elevated vineyards and cooler, sunnier days. Although not as large or established as the regions of Shandong or Ningxia, both Sichuan and Yunnan are hotspots to keep on your radar. Well-known producers include Ao Yun (a full-bodied, age-worthy cabernet sauvignon from another generously funded LVMH venture selling for $250 a bottle), The Spirit of the Highland, and HongXing.

West

The Xinjiang Autonomous Region was an important crossroad for *Vitis vinifera* to China from Europe in 300 BCE. Today, it is remote and isolated from many other winegrowing regions, but still has the largest grape production in the country.

The specialty of this region is a cooked wine called *Musailaisi*, consumed among the Muslim Uyghur population. This warm drink is first cooked mostly with native grapes called hashihaer and munage, in addition to other berries, saffron, and cloves. It is then strained and jarred, leaving it to ferment for several weeks. Other grapes cultivated in Xinjiang include chardonnay, cabernet sauvignon, marselan, syrah, merlot, and interestingly, rkatsiteli and saperavi — eastern European varieties grown in the Manas and Yanqi basin areas. Good-quality producers include Citic Guoan, Puchang Winery, and Tiansai.

Japan: Koshu and more

Japan is well-known as Asia's center of fashion, gastronomy, sake, spirits, and more. If you ask an American chef where they wish their next restaurant could be, we can guarantee you that a city in Japan such as Tokyo, Osaka, or Kyoto is somewhere on that list.

Japan's wine journey is a little different from its neighbors in the region. The country may be more known for its vast wine scholarship than for making wine from *Vitis vinifera* grapes as we know them. In 2023 there were 40,000 sommeliers in Japan accredited by the Japan Sommelier Association. ProWine Tokyo — Japan's only tradeshow for wine and beverage professionals — welcomes close to 60,000 people per year. The wine scene is serious, and the resulting standards for making top-quality wines (even if not mandated by law) is palpable.

Unlike China with its massive landmasses suitable for various types of viticulture, the Japanese archipelago is essentially a collection of over 14,000 islands (and 111 volcanoes) to the east of China, Russia, North, and South Korea. Japan is surrounded by water, including the Sea of Japan, the Sea of Okhotsk, the East China Sea, and the Pacific Ocean. The resulting influence ranges from extreme cold to stickily hot and humid — all factors that can completely destroy a crop. Even so, the Japanese drive for precision winemaking persists. Figure 17-2 shows Japan's wine regions.

Documents suggest that Japan was first exposed to *Vitis vinifera* of winemaking in the 16th century during a visit from Portuguese missionaries to the southern-most region of Kyushu. But the fun really began in the late 19th century, when the Meiji Restoration encouraged re-integration of social, political, and economic life with the rest of the world. Travel, exploration, and experimentation were encouraged. Many Japanese visited and studied wine in France, returning with new knowledge and excitement to plant vines, all of which was encouraged by a newly open government and society.

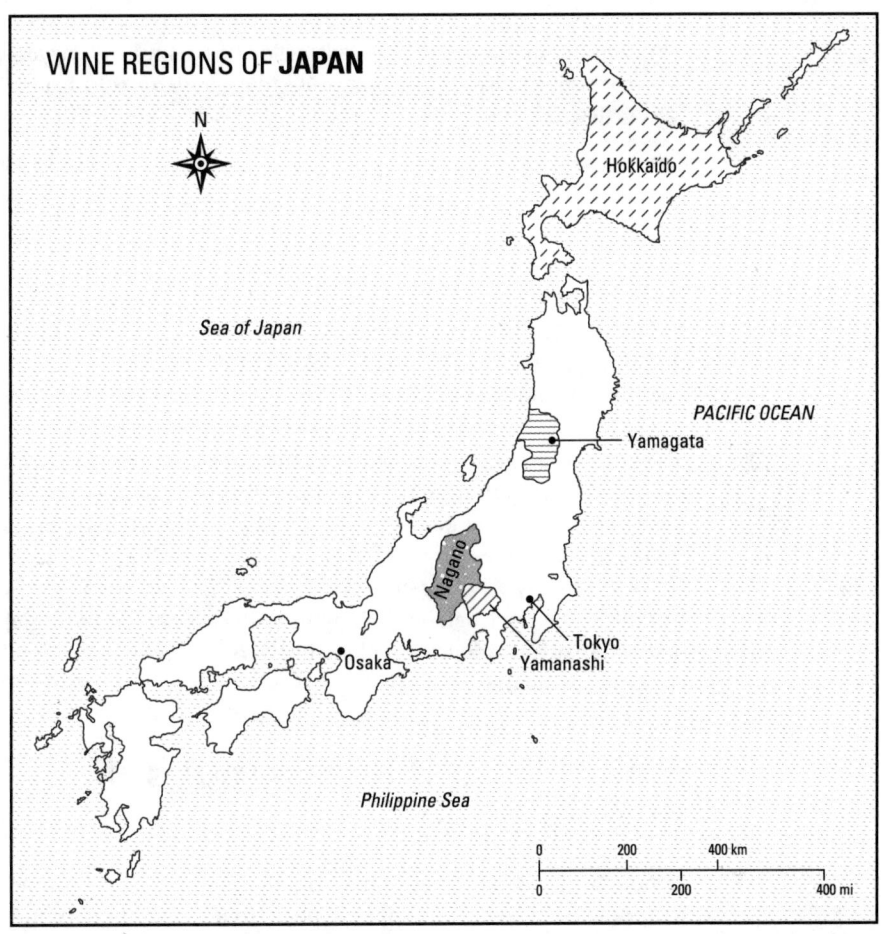

FIGURE 17-2: The wine regions of Japan.

WINE REGIONS OF **JAPAN**

N

Hokkaido

Sea of Japan

PACIFIC OCEAN

Yamagata

Nagano

Tokyo

Osaka
Yamanashi

Philippine Sea

| 0 | 200 | 400 km |
| 0 | 200 | 400 mi |

© John Wiley & Sons, Inc.

There are five main wine regions —or GIs — to know in Japan, all corresponding to their respective prefecture or administrative region:

» **Hokkaido:** Podzolic, acidic brown forest, and peat soils here tend to create well-structured, elegant wines.

» **Nagano:** Well-drained gravel, sand, and volcanic ash soils are known for making crisp, dry, acid-driven wines.

» **Osaka:** Named in 2021, Osaka's soils are mostly sand and clay, contributing to balanced and light- to full-bodied wines.

>> **Yamagata:** Named in 2016, this region has many low-lying areas with soils consisting mostly of clay and gravel that can make bold, full-bodied, and well-structured wines.

>> **Yamanashi:** Considered the cradle of Japanese wine. Known for its granite and volcanic soils, contributing minerality and freshness to its wines.

Koshu, Japan's most planted and successful grape, is a white grape cross of a *Vitis vinifera* variety and a native Japanese variety. It's known for its big, pinkish, juicy berries and bright citrus aromas. Koshu wines can range from light and whimsical to full, rich, and creamy. Additional varieties planted include chardonnay, sauvignon blanc, and Muscat Bailey A (a cross of bailey and muscat hambourg).

TIP

Similar to China, Japan is charting the course for its own transformation. With new investments in research and development, winemakers are working meticulously to expand the quantity and quality of *Vitis vinifera* wines in Japan. Larger beverage companies own wineries and are expanding their landholdings. Smaller firms started by newer generations of Japanese winemakers are leading the way to find the perfect balance of Japanese individualism with global appeal. High-quality Japanese producers include Lumiere, Grace Winery, Hombo Shuzo, Katsuki Wines, and Takahata Winery.

India: Hot and humid (but still making wine)

Although not as advanced in its winemaking journey as China or Japan, India's history with *Vitis vinifera* grapes appears to have begun with the Persian invasions beginning in 5000 BCE. Winemaking was encouraged (if not mandated in some areas) centuries later during the British colonization of India between 1858 and 1947. While most of the wine made during this time may have been served to members of the British colonial regime and Indian elites, the period marked an important starting point for what would grow into a mainly domestic market for today's wines. Figure 17-3 shows India's wine regions.

India has a tropical monsoon climate in most regions of the country, which can be as perilous for winemaking as it sounds. Seriously — it's the hottest and most humid country featured as a winemaking region in this entire book! There are just under 3,000 hectares of vines planted in the country, and most of these are located in the two states of Maharashtra in the western peninsula region and Karnataka in the southwestern region. The majority of grapes grown in these regions aren't even for wine — they're for raisins and table grapes that are staples in everyday and fine dining cuisine.

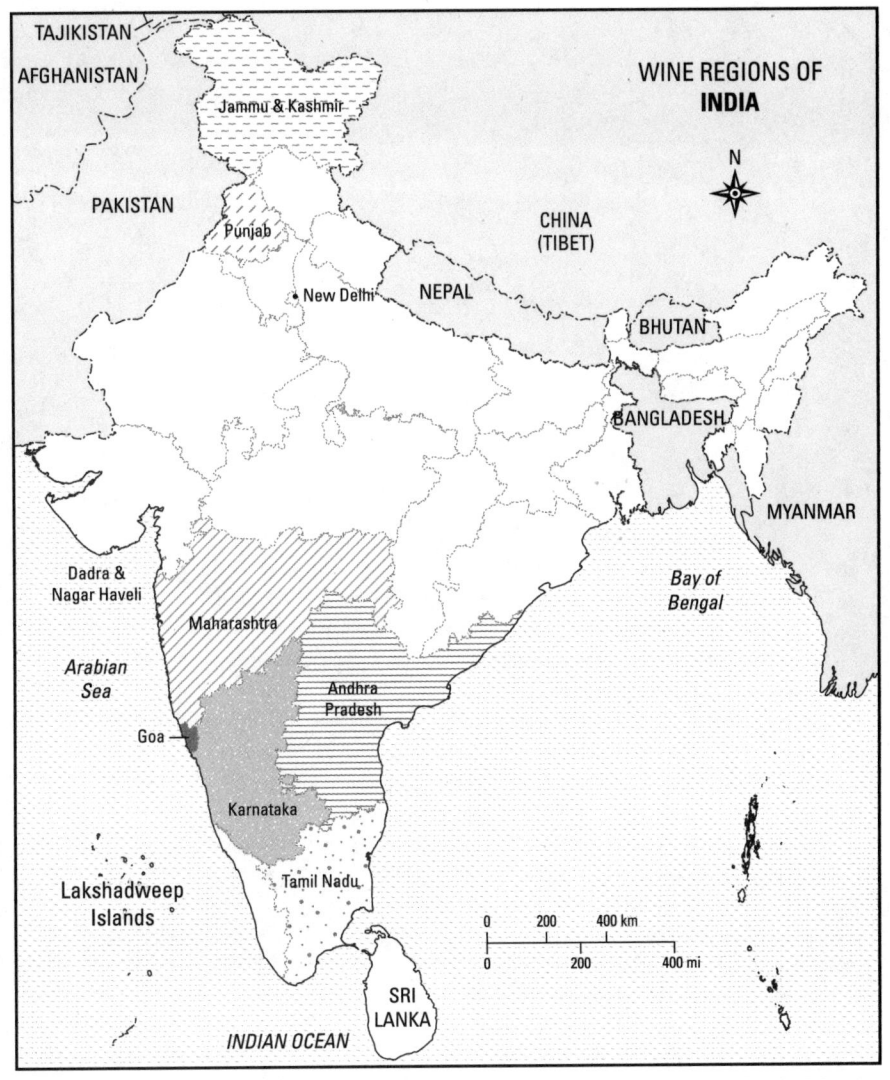

WINE REGIONS OF **INDIA**

TAJIKISTAN

AFGHANISTAN

Jammu & Kashmir

PAKISTAN

Punjab

CHINA (TIBET)

New Delhi

NEPAL

BHUTAN

BANGLADESH

MYANMAR

Dadra & Nagar Haveli

Bay of Bengal

Maharashtra

Arabian Sea

Andhra Pradesh

Goa

Karnataka

Tamil Nadu

Lakshadweep Islands

0   200   400 km

0   200   400 mi

SRI LANKA

INDIAN OCEAN

FIGURE 17-3:
The wine regions of India.

© John Wiley & Sons, Inc.

Nonetheless, Indian winemakers plant ambitiously, with mainly sauvingon blanc and chenin blanc for white grapes and cabernet sauvignon and dyrah for red. Most of the top-quality producers are located in the Nashik region of Maharashtra where some vineyards have the benefit of elevation and the diurnal shift is a bit more forgiving (relative to the rest of the country, between 45°F and 79°F (7°C and 26°C). Most of the high-quality producers are based in or around Nashik including Fratelli, Grover Zampa, and Sula Vineyards. Chandon India (the Indian division of LVMH) produces sparkling wines from chenin blanc, chardonnay, pinot noir, and shiraz in the Dindori region, and also in Nashik.

6 Building Your Wine Muscles

Understand the concept of taste and how wine interacts with food. Discover delicious pairings for any occasion and budget.

Build your confidence in buying wine to enjoy at home. Learn how to leverage experts to get the best bang for your buck.

Serve wine like a sommelier. Practice at home using a simple process to keep yourself feeling safe and looking cool.

Shake your wine list jitters with some practical advice for buying wine in restaurants and bars. Learn about the hidden gems of wine bars.

Get more recommendations for continuing your wine journey, including blogs, podcasts, magazines, and memberships.

Chapter **18**

Pairing Food and Wine

Michelle gets countless calls, text messages, and emails asking her for the "best" wine to go with a meal — a friend trying to impress a date, a non-profit leader looking to wow potential donors with five-course pairings, the list goes on. Unfortunately, her answers are rarely straightforward. They typically involve lots of clarifying questions and "if–then" statements.

There are no rules when it comes to food and wine pairing. There are, however, some guiding principles that can help you build a vocabulary for food and wine pairing and help to make the universe of food and wine a little less daunting. Your goal should be to find pairings that work for you and the occasion, while keeping in mind that wine was created to enjoy. Don't take it too seriously. In the end, the best pairing for a great bottle of wine is good company!

REMEMBER

While it's not an exact science, we know some things about how different tastes in food interact with the chemical makeup and flavor profiles of different wines. You are the expert of your own palate, armed with a lifetime of sensory memories unique to you, your culture, and your preferences.

Understanding Taste

Taste is a perfectly arranged symphony of many different sensations. It can be impacted by temperature, smell, or consistency. It's also sensitive: if one instrument of the symphony is off (you have a stuffy nose, for example), your sense of taste can be compromised. Taste starts in your mouth, primarily on your tongue but also in other areas with taste buds. Your soft palate or the back of your throat are two examples. As a substance — ideally food or a beverage — touches your tongue, messages are passed from your taste buds to your brain telling you how that substance tastes. Discover more about taste in Chapter 4.

TECHNICAL STUFF

When combined with aromas or how substances smell, our brain builds the story of flavor. Humans can detect at least 1 trillion aromas, making us one of the most complex (and culinary) species on the planet. Flavors in both food and wine are the foundation for perfect pairings, whatever you decide they should be.

REMEMBER

We can all agree on five well-known tastes. How we detect those tastes changes with wine type and flavor profile.

>> **Sweet:** Usually comes from sugar, fructose, amino acids, or alcohol. Sweetness tickles the tip of your tongue, hits your mid-palate, or registers when you swallow. Think bananas, dates, honey, or sweetcorn. Sweet foods need wines with just as much if not more sugar for you to taste the flavors in both the food and the wine simultaneously. For example, dry Oregon pinot noir can have tasting notes of red berries, florals, baking spice, and potting soil. Drinking a dry Oregon pinot noir with a peach cobbler will make this wine taste drier, sour, bitter, more vegetal, or fruitless. Drinking a Hungarian Tokaji (which is known for its dried apricot and honey aromas) with the same peach cobbler will accentuate the fruit of the dessert while highlighting the acidity and fruit flavors in the wine.

>> **Sour:** Typically comes from organic acids (citric and carbonic are common examples) or acidic solutions. Sourness is often detected on the sides of our tongue. Sour tastes activate our salivary glands (hence mouth-watering and puckering) to counteract the acid and prevent enamel erosion on our teeth. Some sour substances include lemon juice, vinegar, grapefruit, tamarind, kimchi, and sauerkraut. Sour or high-acid foods need wines with just as much if not more acid. A wine's acidity can balance acidity in sour foods, creating a pleasant, mouth-watering effect between each bite versus a clash of weight or flavors. New Zealand sauvignon blanc is famous for its tart citrus (ripe lemon or white grapefruit, for example) and grassy notes. A chilled New Zealand sauvignon blanc will do wonders for ceviche or green salad with citrus vinaigrette by creating harmony. The same foods' flavors will be completely decimated with a Napa Valley cabernet sauvignon or Venetian Amarone.

These wines are known for their rich, dry and/or ripe red fruit flavors. They are also typically higher in alcohol and lower in acidity, making a balance with light Iceberg or Butterhead lettuce nearly impossible.

>> **Salty:** Generated from sodium and chloride ions. Mineral salts can produce the same effects. We have sodium sensors on our taste buds that send signals to our brain about too little, just enough, or too much salt. Many foods are naturally salty, including briny oysters, bacon, soy, and olives. Salt makes the world go round! It adds flavor and softens wines by making them taste juicier and less astringent or bitter. The wine matchmakers here are either intensity (meaning degree of power in the flavors) or acidity. There is nothing like a glass of dry, bubbly champagne with salty french fries or an Argentinean malbec (known for bold red and black fruit flavors coupled with baking spices and/or tobacco) with a seasoned New York strip steak.

>> **Bitter:** 35 proteins in our sensory system respond to bitterness, including polyphenols, catechins, flavanoids, and caffeine. Arugula, dark chocolate, Brussels sprouts, coffee, eggplant, and ginger fit the description here. Pairing bitter or tannic wine with bitter foods constitutes a no-go zone. Acidic and less tannic wines rule here by complementing bitter flavors without intensifying them beyond enjoyment. Give your next endive salad or roasted eggplant a try with Austrian grüner veltliner, Loire Valley sauvignon blanc, or Venetian Soave. The drier styles of these wines are all lighter in body with some fruit flavors, but a great balance of acidity that works for even the most challenging ingredients.

>> **Umami:** First identified by Japanese scientist, Dr. Kikunae Ikeda, this taste is derived from glutamate — a protein building-block and one of the most common amino acids found in both food and the human body. Umami can be detected in a range of foods, including seaweed, mushrooms, tomatoes, beef, and fermented or cured items. Foods rich in umami can often make wines seem richer or more bitter. Lower tannins and more moderate acidity can help to create balance. Truffles and dolcetto (a medium-bodied Italian red wine with both fruit and earth characteristics), or a cheese and charcuterie board with red Burgundy (dried red and black fruits, mushrooms, earthy aromas), won't disappoint.

Spice is worth mentioning here because of its impact on food and wine pairing. Spice is a sensation — not a taste — that sends signals to your brain about temperature. Our mouth identifies capsaicin, a chili pepper extract typically found in spicy foods, making our bodies feel hot. Brain command receives the signals, your blood vessels dilate, your body temperature rises, and you can feel a burning sensation on your tongue and lips. Just like pulling over your car when the engine is overheated, your body takes the necessary steps to cool itself down, generating sweat or a runny nose to dissipate the heat. Spicy food can overpower a wine with its heat by making it flavorless, bitter, or at its worst, just as hot as the food if it's high in alcohol. Lower-alcohol and higher-acidity wines allow you to taste both the food and the juice. These characteristics also generate the salivating sensation that keep you wanting more of both! Off-dry German riesling, South African chenin blanc, and Alsatian pinot gris are excellent partners for curries, tandoori, Sichuan, wasabi, and Mexican chili-driven dishes.

Similarly, fat is not a taste. But its presence in the foods we eat and its impact on wine is remarkable. Different neurons in our brain respond to different representations of fat in our mouths (think steak fat versus vegetable or cod oil). Our brain recognizes that we're eating something fatty through any combination of taste, texture, or even temperature. Fatty foods can diminish a lot of wine elements, including acidity and tannins. Powerful wines (higher in alcohol and tannins) and acidity play a role here as they combat and "cut" the fat in certain foods. Generally, the fattier the food, the more powerful wine you need. Fried chicken and Crémant de Loire, grilled ribeye and Australian shiraz, and macaroni and cheese with Napa Valley chardonnay are tried and true pairings.

Discovering How Wine and Food Interact

Sure, a big bowl of Bolognese pasta and a goblet of Chianti might sound good, but what does it mean? The building blocks of a wine's *character* —such as acid, alcohol, sugar, or tannin — are just as important as the components of taste in food.

Acid, alcohol, sugar, and tannin

Sommeliers (a wine professional responsible for all aspects of wine service, typically in a restaurant or bar) love to talk about tart red cherries, limestone, or leather in wines (Michelle is guilty as charged). While this exercise is fun, fruit, soil, or aging characteristics may not be the first thing your mouth detects when you sip a wine. Acid, alcohol, sugar, and tannin may be more apparent at first.

REMEMBER

You can start with the food or start with the wine when assembling a pairing. Consider a food's sweetness, sourness, saltiness, bitterness, or umami characteristics. Think about spice and fat with the goals of creating harmony and balance from sip to bite and vice versa. A wine's acid, alcohol, sugar, and tannin will change the presence and intensity of different foods.

Acid

Acid makes your mouth water — literally. Saliva is your body's way of diluting the acid to restore balance. You will detect acid in a wine when the sides of your mouth and back of your throat tingle, or when you swallow. If you can remember the last time that you drank a cold glass of lemonade or bit into a tomato, then you know acid.

The highest-acid wines tend to come from cooler climates where grapes are less exposed to sunlight or grow under other cooling influences such as higher altitudes, oceans, or fog. Higher-acid wines often make food-friendly companions because of their versatility. They can complement spice, make rich foods less intense, and serve as palate cleansers for everything from deep-fried foods to nuts and creamy desserts.

Alcohol

Alcohol is a byproduct of the fermentation process. Wine is made when yeasts transform the sugar in grapes to carbon dioxide (CO_2) and alcohol. We can detect a wine's alcohol levels in the amount of heat we feel at the back of our throat or when we swallow (can you remember what happened the last time you took a shot of tequila or Irish whiskey)? We can also take a hint from the thickness or viscosity of the wine. The thicker the wine on the palate (imagine the range of texture from water to honey going down your throat), generally the higher the alcohol in the wine.

REMEMBER

Wines can range in alcohol from 5.5% to 23% depending on the style (dry, off-dry, fortified, and so on). These percentages are calculated using 17 grams per liter of sugar to generate one percentage point of alcohol. Chemically, the higher the alcohol, the lower the acidity and vice versa in wine as a finished product.

TIP

You can consider the alcohol in a wine as it pertains to its weight (also known as its *body*) — heavier wines generally pair well with heavier foods. A Lodi zinfandel at around 15% alcohol will drown out the flavors of a delicate Irish Point oyster. The same wine will make a spicy lamb vindaloo burn because of its low acidity. The wine will clash with the complexity of the dish's spice blend, making it taste like rubbing alcohol instead of a dry, fruit-forward wine.

In some instances, a high-alcohol or full-bodied wine can complement or contrast foods in a delicious way. A Napa cabernet sauvignon stands up to the fatty richness of a grilled ribeye steak. A tawny port's sweetness counterbalances Stilton or Roquefort cheese's strong, salty flavors.

Sugar

Sugar and alcohol go hand in hand because alcohol is after all, converted sugar! To be considered sweet, a wine must have some sugar left in it by the time it's bottled (meaning not all the sugar was converted to alcohol during the fermentation process). Sweet wines can highlight flavors in salty foods. They can also neutralize spice and bring out sweetness. Gewürztraminer with Singapore noodles (sweet wine, spicy food) or Spätlese riesling with sweet and sour chicken (sweet wine, sweet food) are solid examples here.

Tannin

Have you ever had a cup of black tea thinking that it would help with a cold, but it really just ended up drying your throat out even more? That's tannin. *Tannins* are chemical compounds found in a range of food and beverages, including tea, coffee, chocolate, and of course, wine. Tannins in your wine can come from grape skins, seeds, and stems. They can be introduced via aging vessels such as oak barrels. Winemakers can also alter tannin levels through macerations, added oak, or tannin-based products.

TECHNICAL STUFF

Tannins interact with proteins in our saliva, which causes a drying, gritty, or puckering sensation that can sometimes feel uncomfortable. Protein-rich foods can bond with tannins to "cut it" or remove it from your palate, increasing both comfort and pleasure. The result is the best of the flavors in your food: the rich red cherry of your red Bordeaux with the salty, savory flavors of your New Zealand lamb rack.

Awesome sauce and seasonings

Some of the largest restaurant kitchens in the world have a person whose entire job is dedicated to making sauce: the *saucier.* Classic French cuisine thrives on sauces with simply prepared proteins or starch (think béchamel for au gratin potatoes, hollandaise for eggs benedict, or meunière for Dover sole). The importance of sauce (and the esteem that comes with being the person who made it) cannot be understated in Italian culture. In the American south, is a pork chop really a pork chop if it is not smothered in sauce? No matter the country or culture, sauce can make or break a dish.

When it comes to wine, sauce is no different. The same Chianti Classico that will do wonders for fettucine Bolognese will wreak havoc on fettucine alfredo. Because the sauce's flavors are driving your taste of the dish, the wine should focus more on the sauce than it does on the starch, protein, or vegetables it's covering. The same can be said for seasonings. Grilled chicken tastes totally different with a záatar versus a mesquite barbeque rub. The former emphasizes toasted and savory herbs such as oregano, thyme, and marjoram while the latter may have a foundation of apple cider vinegar, Worcestershire sauce, paprika, and honey.

TIP

Look to the key ingredients of sauces and seasonings to create the best pairings using the same principles of sweet, sour, salty, bitter, umami, spice, and fat described earlier in this chapter.

Sauces and seasonings also create wonderful opportunities to dig a little deeper with fruit, mineral, and earth characteristics in wine. For example, Thanksgiving turkey dressed in cranberry sauce can be enjoyed with fruity pinot noirs or rosés thanks to the sauce itself (and lighter weight of the wine with the leaner meat of turkey). The honeydew and saline mineral flavors of Muscadet can highlight the slight saltiness and melon notes in pacific oysters with green apple mignonette. If you're in the "faster" lane, try an off-dry chenin blanc with a spicy chicken sandwich. This can be drizzled (or drenched, your pick) in spicy barbecue sauce. The chenin blanc's slight sweetness and acidity will harmonize the sweet spiciness of the sandwich and sauce.

Pairing Principles for Food and Wine

Armed with your taste buds and wine-tasting skills, you are ready to make heaven-sent pairings.

REMEMBER

There are different ways to pair wine with food that should all be based on your personal preferences, the occasion, and budget:

>> **Congruent pairings:** Create harmony between the food and wine by highlighting their shared flavors.

>> **Contrasting pairings:** Accentuate different flavors between the food and wine that still results in a well-balanced combination.

TIP

If you're in a pairing bind and unsure which wine to choose or how to match food tastes with wine characteristics, start with the weight of the wine (see earlier in this chapter). Matching the weight of a wine to the weight of a dish is something you likely already do but don't even notice. Choose a light-bodied wine for a lighter meal, and a medium- to fuller-bodied wine for a heavier one.

Wine shops or grocery stores may also provide clues with country or region signage that will help you make a great choice. For example, if you are in the Austrian section, you can deduce that wines coming from this country generally enjoy a cooler climate and more acidity than those from Napa Valley in California or Central Valley in Chile. You may want to stay in the latter for those short ribs because heavier wines will stand up to the fat in meat cuts like these.

REMEMBER

If all else fails, remember that what grows together goes together. Wine grapes and other agricultural products are all a reflection of *terroir* (a combination of soil, climate, and topography — find out more in Chapter 2). Every wine region has its own culinary history of growing, preserving, and preparing foods. These histories have influenced factors such as seasonality and adaptability of different food (and wine grapes) to the regions that they come from. We learn what to eat and drink from the people who have grown grapes and harvested their own food with regional recipes for centuries. While everything that grows in the same region may not make a perfect pairing, understanding these nuances (and a little history) can certainly help.

TIP

Mastering the art of food and wine pairing requires that you know or can recall how different food and wine tastes. If you are new to tasting and describing wine (which most people are), rely on wine merchants, bartenders, or service staff in restaurants to learn more. Don't be shy to ask what their favorite pairings are, and why. They have the interest and the time to learn about why some pairings work while others don't. They're also excited to share what they know and see how it works for you. Find out more about tasting in Chapter 4.

Fancy food and wine pairings

Let's get serious. You're probably not shucking oysters, making foie gras, or shaving truffles for dinner every night. There are what we like to call "fancy" pairings because of the cost, time, and occasions that are typically involved in eating these foods. Nonetheless, some classic, fancy pairings have been around for ages and are worth knowing. Some are congruent pairings, and others are contrasting pairings (outlined earlier in this chapter). The list in Table 18-1 might help you order your next wine in a restaurant or grab a nicer bottle on your next shopping trip.

TABLE 18-1 **Fancy Pairings**

Pairing	Type
Oysters and unoaked Chablis	Congruent
Caviar and champagne	Contrasting
Nigiri sushi and brut champagne	Contrasting
Poached lobster with drawn butter and blanc de blancs	Congruent
Foie gras and Sauternes or gewürztraminer	Contrasting
Seafood bisque and dry sherry	Contrasting
Chilean seabass and Pouilly-Fuissé	Congruent

Pairing	Type
Duck a l'orange and Alsatian pinot gris	Congruent
White truffle risotto and vermentino	Congruent
Beouf Bourgignon with red Burgundy	Congruent
Ribeye steak and Napa Valley cabernet sauvignon	Congruent
Stilton or Roquefort cheese with port	Contrasting

Everyday food and wine pairings

Most of us mortals just want a nice, inexpensive bottle of wine to enjoy with a meal or a few friends. Enjoying wine with great food shouldn't (and doesn't) require that you break the bank. In fact, wine can be enjoyed with fast foods, raw foods, packaged and processed foods, desserts — you name it. If you don't happen to have any fancy food or wine lying around (like us), check out Table 18-2 for everyday pairings in the real world.

TABLE 18-2

Everyday Pairings

Pairing	Type
Pasta with tomato sauce and Sangiovese	Congruent
Lean, smashburgers and Beaujolais	Congruent
Thick, hearty burgers and Crianza Tempranillo	Congruent
Macaroni and cheese and Sonoma Coast chardonnay	Contrasting
Fried chicken and brut Crémant de Loire	Contrasting
Shrimp and grits and Sonoma chardonnay	Congruent
Indian, Thai, or Caribbean curry and Kabinett riesling	Contrasting
Green salads and sauvignon blanc	Congruent
Potato chips and blancs de blancs	Contrasting
Tuscan salmon and pinot noir	Congruent
Barbeque ribs and shiraz	Congruent

TIP

When visiting some of the world's major wine countries, here are a few of our favorite regional pairings you can try to test the theory that what grows together goes together:

>> Apfelstrudel and beerenauslese or eiswein (Bavaria)

>> Arachon oysters with Entre-Deux-Mers (Bordeaux)

>> Gambas al ajillo and fino sherry or albariño (central and southern Spain)

>> Goat cheese and Sancerre (Loire Valley)

>> Ligurian pesto and vermentino or pigato (northwest Italy)

Cooking with Wine

Humans have been drinking wine and cooking with it for centuries. Some wines are marketed specifically for cooking (usually with lower to no alcohol content), while others are marketed to drink but can be used in cooking (typically sold in bottles of 187.5ml, 375ml, 750ml, or more).

TIP

Adding wine to food can enhance the food's structure, complexity, richness, and flavor. Contrary to popular belief, the wine's condition and quality can have a profound impact on a dish. When cooking with wine, you're using it as an ingredient. Unless you're making a fancy dinner for a special occasion, treat your wallet as you would with any other ingredient when it comes to purchasing wine for cooking.

When to cook with champagne or sparkling wine

Champagne or sparkling wine can add acidity and freshness to a dish by enhancing citrus flavors, cream, toast, or nuttiness. Add champagne or sparkling wines to vinaigrettes, butter-based sauces, or marinades for chicken, pork, or seafood. Champagne also adds dimension to desserts. Champagne vanilla cupcakes, sparkling wine panna cotta, or champagne pound cake are just a few.

TIP

Keep the sugar levels of the champagne or sparkling wine in mind, as very sweet sparklers will sweeten your dish. Brut or off-dry styles usually make the best companions. If a dish becomes too sweet, adding more fatty products like butter or duck fat can counteract the overdone sugar effect if caught early.

REMEMBER

Don't break the bank to cook with bubbles. Budget-friendly proseccos, cavas, or sparkling wines that aren't made in the traditional champagne method will work just fine. Purchasing a sparkling wine that you would like to drink is key — chances are you'll have some left over after cooking!

When to cook with white wine

The land of white wine cooking is vast. White wines can add complexity, balance sharp or creamy accents, tenderize, sharpen, lighten heavier foods, and enrich flavor. Not only can white wine be an ingredient or additive to food — it can serve as the liquid that a food is cooked in all alone. Michelle once used an entire bottle of Piedmont arneis to make a big pan of wild mushroom risotto.

You can use a Sardinian vermentino to steam seafood or shellfish, or a Loire Valley sauvignon blanc to sauté fresh vegetables. White wines can also be used to braise, marinate, or poach foods. We would be remiss here not to mention Coq au Vin, the classic French dish that can use either red or white wine for the "Blanc" version. Unoaked Chablis can do wonders for poached lobster tails or French onion soup.

On the less French side, white wines can even enhance the taste of processed foods. Try adding some pinot grigio to your next jar of alfredo sauce or instant mashed potatoes. Add some dry sherry to a Moroccan lentil soup or Cantonese steamed fish. You can also use white wine to simply *deglaze* a pan (remove or dissolve food residue to flavor a gravy, sauce, or soup).

When to cook with rosé wine

As far as we're concerned, the phrase "rosé all day" applies to both drinking and cooking! Rosé provides red and pink fruitiness along with the acidity of some white and sparkling wines which makes it a great cooking companion. You can use it to sear, sauté, baste, poach, or marinate. Marinate leaner cuts of meat (lamb leg or pork tenderloin, for example) with herbs, spices, and rosé. Add a bit of nebbiolo rosé to your next shrimp scampi or oyster mignonette. You can also keep rosé on hand for basting roasted chicken or turkey. Drier style rosés tend to complement more savory dishes, while fruitier and sweeter rosés can accentuate fruit flavors in sweeter foods. Fresh plums or apricots are delicious when poached with a rosé of grenache or syrah.

When to cook with red wine

Red wine is by far the most well-known wine for cooking. You can probably recall the number of movies you've watched with someone pouring red wine into a pasta sauce then serving up a quick sample on a wooden spoon (of course it's always delicious). Red wine adds depth, flavor, and richness to a range of foods, but usually rises to fame with heftier proteins. It can be used as a sauce base, for braising, or for roasting. It can add complexity to sweeter sauces such as barbeque or molé. Chianti for tomato sauces, red Burgundy for Bœf Bourguignon, or shiraz for barbeque marinades are tried and true companions.

REMEMBER

Like champagne or sparkling wine, mind your wallet when purchasing red wine for cooking. Buy bottles that you can enjoy drinking after all the work is done.

When to cook with dessert or fortified wine

REAL DEAL

The dessert and fortified wine aisles are the most underrated places in a wine shop. They're quickly overlooked for the $8 Chilean sauvignon blanc or the $10 magnum of Barefoot shiraz. What most people don't know is that these wines have a wide range of uses, and awesome preservation potential, which makes them a great value. Dessert and fortified wines can infuse flavor, depth, and richness to anything from salty snacks to decadent desserts.

Here are the most common dessert and fortified wines for cooking; check out Chapters 5, 7, and 9 to learn more about these wines and how they're made:

>> **Port:** Made in the Douro Valley of Portugal, port wine is made in ruby (young, fruity) and tawny (wood-aged, browner in color, imparting more cocoa, caramel, and/or toffee characteristics) styles. Port can be added to sauces for stewed or braised meats and mushrooms. It can be infused into fruit or chocolate desserts or used in reductions or glazes. Ruby or tawny ports should be used in cooking rather than vintage or "Late Bottle Vintage" (LBV) ports. These are intended to be enjoyed on their own, and usually command a higher price tag.

>> **Madeira:** Also made in Portugal, but comes from an island with the same name off the coast of Morocco. Madeira's flavor profiles can include nuts, caramelized sugar, baked or stewed fruit, and coffee. Tried and true madeira dishes include the infamous Chicken Madeira (made with madeira, beef broth, and cream sauce), stroganoff, and veal saltimbocca. Madeira can also add richness and dried fruit character to sweeter cheese tarts, butter-based cakes, and more.

>> **Sherry:** This comes from southwest Spain. It can be made in a range of styles from bone dry (manzanilla, fino) to sweet and syrupy sweet (oloroso and cream). Depending on the style, sherry will add nuttiness, dry herbs, mushrooms, fresh dough, coffee, or toffee notes to a dish. Given its range of flavors, sherry can complement salty or savory dishes like marinated

artichokes, olive-oil pan-cooked potatoes, pork shu mai, or crab bisque. In its sweetest (and highest alcohol) forms, it can elevate desserts (plum cakes, pumpkin pie, or berry trifles, for example). Hungry yet?

>> **Marsala:** Marsala comes from the town with the same name on the western coast of Sicily. It's made by first making a white wine with Sicilian grapes, then adding locally made brandy and aging in oak barrels for anywhere from one to ten years. Marsala is made in dry (*secco*) and sweet (*dolce*) styles, and can impart flavors of dried or baked apricots, honey, nuts, tamarind, tobacco, or vanilla. Leather and mushroom notes can be detected in more aged marsala wines. These wines can add richness and complexity to turkey, chicken, or pork dishes. They can add a dried fruit or nutty dimension to beans or lentils. They can even pump up the sugar or caramel on desserts made with mascarpone cheese, cream, or egg yolks.

Dessert wines that are not fortified can also be used in cooking. Some examples you may find include late harvest reds or whites, or icewine made in colder climates (think Austria, Canada, Germany, or Switzerland), *noble rot* wines such as Sauternes or Tokaji, *passito* styles (Italian wines made from dried grapes), and more.

REMEMBER

Many dessert wines are made in small quantities (and sold in smaller bottles) because of the painstaking process involved in growing and harvesting grapes with the right amount of sugar to make the cut. With many dessert wines, we recommend simply drinking and enjoying them on their own. Understanding the grapes that make the wine and how their flavor profiles change in their sweetest forms will guide you to your next perfect pairing.

Chapter **19**

Buying Wine to Enjoy at Home

U nless you're best friends with a passionate wine expert, you must make your own wine-buying choices. If you're lucky, you will meet someone who works at the grocery store or wine shop whose life purpose is to teach people about wine. But the chances are that most of the time you'll feel as if you're lost in a fog, surrounded by lots of bottles and price tags.

When Ed and Mary wrote earlier editions of *Wine For Dummies,* they bought almost all their wine in wine shops that they visited in person. Online shopping has changed a lot for both consumers and winemakers, and now the next transaction is just a click away. As convenient as online shopping is, there's still much to be said for browsing in person, especially if you're just beginning to learn about wine. Finding a knowledgeable wine merchant can make wine shopping a lot easier.

In this chapter, we discuss various types of wine retailers and how to choose those best for you. Arming yourself with this information may help you to overcome any fears you feel about buying wine.

Getting Started as a Buyer

Common sense suggests that buying a few bottles of wine should be less stressful than, say, applying for a mortgage or interviewing for a job. What's the big deal? It's only grape juice.

But memories tell us otherwise. One time, Ed and Mary pretended they knew what they were doing and bought a full case — 12 bottles — of a French wine based on the brand's general reputation, not realizing that the particular vintage they purchased was a miserable aberration of the wine's usual quality. Why didn't they just ask someone in the store, or do a little research in advance? Sigh.

We can all recall the many times we spent staring at shelves lined with bottles whose labels might as well have been written in an alien language. Fortunately, our enthusiasm for wine motivated us to persevere. We eventually discovered that wine shopping can be fun!

TIP

Our experience has taught us that the single, most effective way to ensure that you have more good wine-buying experiences than bad ones is to come to terms with your knowledge — or lack thereof — of the subject.

REMEMBER

Too much information about wine — new vintages each year, hundreds of new wineries, new brands, and so on — is changing too quickly for *anyone* to presume that they know it all, or for anyone to feel insecure about what they don't know.

Checking Out Your Retail Options

Buying wine in a store to enjoy at home is great for several reasons, not the least of which is that stores usually have a much bigger selection of wines than restaurants do, and they charge you less for them because you're not paying for the experience of drinking the wine there. You can examine the bottles carefully and compare the labels. You can drink the wine at home from the glass — and at the temperature — of your choosing. But of course, a big selection of wines from a store can be downright daunting.

Depending on where you live, you can buy wine at all sorts of stores: grocery stores, wine superstores, discount warehouses, general wine and liquor stores, and small specialty wine shops. Each type of store has its own advantages and disadvantages in terms of selection, price, or service.

Wine, being an alcoholic beverage, is regulated in many countries. Governments dictate where and how wine may be sold. Some states within the United States and some provinces in Canada have raised government control of alcoholic beverage sales to a fine art, deciding not only *where* you can buy wine, but also *which wines* are available for you to buy. If you love wine and live in one of those areas (you know who you are), take comfort in the fact that (a) you have a vote; (b) freedom of choice lies just across the border; and (c) if cars can drive themselves, there's hope for freedom in wine buying.

We'll assume a healthy, open-minded, free-market economy for wine in the following discussions on wine retail. We hope that scenario applies where you live, because your enjoyment of wine will blossom all the more easily if it does.

Grocery and wholesale stores

In truly *open* wine markets, you can buy wine in grocery stores, like any other food product. Grocery stores and their large-scale brethren, discount warehouses and wholesale stores, make wine accessible to everyone.

In grocery and wholesale stores, the mystique surrounding wine sometimes dissipates: who can waste time feeling insecure about a wine purchase when many more critical issues are at hand, such as the amount of time left before the kids turn into monsters, or where to find the shortest checkout line, not to mention the 50 other items you're supposed to be buying besides wine? You will likely stroll by dozens of wines for under $20 a bottle. You'll pick up the first California cabernet sauvignon (see Chapter 11) you see with a cool label and call it a day.

WARNING

The downside of buying wine in these stores is that your selection is often limited to wines produced by large wineries that generate enough volume to supply larger retailers. You'll seldom get any advice on which wines to buy unless a store employee or brand representative happens to be there pushing their products. Basically, you're on your own.

TIP

Some discount and wholesale stores are good places to find *private label* wines — wines that are created especially for the discount chain and that carry a brand name that's owned by the store. These wines are usually quaffable, and if you like them, they can be excellent values. Some of the "club" chains may also offer — in smaller quantities — higher-end wines that are not the usual supermarket fare.

The bottom line is that grocery and warehouse stores can be great places to buy everyday wine for casual enjoyment or home-based entertaining. There is usually no limit to the amount you can buy, which has its advantages if you want to get a whole case of wine for some special occasion, or if you want to get a bunch of boxed wine (which isn't all bad). But if what you really want is to become knowledgeable about wine as you buy it, or if you want an unusually interesting variety of wines to satisfy your rapacious curiosity, you'll probably find yourself shopping elsewhere most of the time.

Specialty wine shops

Wine specialty shops come in all shapes and sizes: some are small, carrying a couple hundred labels, and others are megastores that have thousands of wines and wine accessories. These shops sometimes sell beer, liquor, and specialty foods as well.

If you decide to pursue wine as a serious hobby, you'll probably end up buying your wine at specialty wine shops because they offer many advantages. For instance, these shops almost always have wine-knowledgeable staff on the premises. You can usually find an interesting, varied selection of wines at all price levels. Sometimes, the shop will offer in-store tastings of featured wines, allowing you to get a (very small) taste and potentially pick up a bottle you weren't expecting on that day.

Wine shops may organize their wines by country of origin, region, variety, color, or even weight of the wine. Some stores organize their wine sections by style, such as Aromatic Whites, Powerful Reds, and so forth. You can usually find a special section for champagnes and other sparkling wines and another for dessert and fortified options.

THE PROS AND CONS OF COMMERCIAL WINE CLUBS

When you're on the wine circuit, you'll get many offers to join wine clubs. These clubs are wine-buying programs, sometimes sponsored by respected print publications or the grocery or wholesale store itself, that send members a few preselected wines every month or so. They sound like a good deal: the club selects wines for you, offers them at attractive prices, and delivers them to your door. You'll probably like some of the wines. The catch is that the wines are unknown entities, and they're not necessarily bargains. The brands are usually private labels that are exclusive to the club (no comparative shopping is possible) and were purchased at really low prices. Plus, you have no say in the wine selection. Yes, wine clubs are convenient. But when you know about wine, you'll want to make your own selections based on your palate and preference, preferably with the aid of a knowledgeable wine merchant whom you trust.

Some wine shops have a special area (or even a super-special, temperature-controlled room) for the finer, more expensive wines. In many stores, this area is a locked, vaultlike room. In others, it's the whole back area of the store.

Near the front or around the store, you might also see boxes or bins of special sale wines. Sometimes, sale wines are those the merchant is trying to unload because they got a special deal on them or are looking to shed inventory to make space for newcomers. When in doubt, try one bottle first before committing to a larger quantity. We provide more wine shopping strategies later in this chapter.

Online retailers

The online wine-buying experience today mainly involves purchasing wines from the websites of established wineries with online sales, brick-and-mortar wine shops, or flash sites that offer an ever-changing but limited selection (read more on flash sites later in this section). A few companies do sell wine *only* online — such as Wine.com, ShopWineDirect.com, Vinfolio.com, and Vivino.com.

Most websites of established wine shops offer an extensive selection of all types of wines. However, restrictions prevent some retail stores (and their websites) from shipping to consumers who live in other states, which significantly narrows your options in terms of where you shop. At last count, only 13 states and the District of Columbia allow out-of-state retailers to ship wine to their residents. That means that 37 states prohibit alcohol shipments from out-of-state retail stores into their states. Wineries have much more latitude regarding shipments to consumers. Loss of sales taxes and powerful local wine retailer and wholesaler lobbies are the culprits.

Some mega-chains have licensed stores in most states, so that you can receive the wine legally from their local, in-state store. A few stores (and their websites) will agree to ship wine to you even if they shouldn't. The wine you buy from retailers in these 37 states can actually be legally destroyed by shipping companies because the store has no right to ship to out-of-state consumers. Or if the regulatory heat is off, you could receive your order with no problem. The situation is frustrating for both retailers and consumers.

Look for terms and conditions indicating your agreement that you are buying the wine in their retailer's respective state, and that you are shipping it out of state to yourself. Language like this probably lessens the store's risk, but maybe not yours. Wine store websites include: flatiron-wines.com, astorwines.com, chambersstwines.com (all in NYC); blmwine.com (Allston, MA); hdhwine.com (Chicago); kermitlynch.com (Berkeley, CA); rarewineco.com (Sonoma, CA); wallywine.com (Los Angeles); and winelibrary.com (Springfield, NJ).

WINE SEARCH ENGINES

When you purchase wine online rather than at a store, the issue of storage is nearly impossible to evaluate. Selection, availability, and price are the criteria that determine which online store deserves your loyalty.

When we're shopping for a specific wine online, our first stop is either Vivino (www.vivino.com) or Wine Searcher (www.wine-searcher.com). These search engines enable you to look for specific wines, even specific vintages, and discover which of the site's member retailers (including most major wine shops across the United States and online retailers) are selling that wine, and at what price. You can even find ratings and wine descriptions on these sites from other users around the world. You can then contact retailers online or by phone to purchase the wine. We don't always select the shop with the lowest price, however. Sometimes shipping charges from a distant store negate the lower price.

You won't find offerings from flash sites on Wine Searcher because the wines offered by such sites change too quickly, sometimes several times a day. Some additional flash sites to check out include Invino.com, GreatWine2U.com, and Last Bottle Wines (lastbottlewines.com). All these sites generally list wines at affordable prices (some highly discounted) and sometimes with conditional free shipping.

Unlike the websites of established wine stores, flash sites offer a limited selection of wines at any given moment, usually at very affordable prices. *Flash sites* are the wine equivalent of shopping for sale items at the mall: If you find something you want, buy it before someone else does! Most flash sites enable you to sign up for email alerts so that you can stay abreast of their offerings. You can get real bargains at these flash sites (one is called Wines Til Sold Out [www.wtso.com]), but you must act quickly because the wines do sell out rapidly.

Choosing the right retailer

Buying wine online is terrific *if you know something about wine*. If you're a novice, you're much better off relying on a knowledgeable wine retailer to help you select your wines.

Sizing up a wine merchant is as simple as sizing up any other specialty retailer, whether online or in person. The following sections outline the main criteria to look for.

Finding a trusted advisor

TIP

When you're a novice wine buyer, your best strategy is to shop around with an eye to service and reliable advice more than to price. As a starting point, ask a wine-knowledgeable friend what store(s) they recommend near you. After you've found a merchant who has suggested several wines you've liked, stick with them, even if they don't have the best prices in town. Paying a dollar or so more for wines recommended by a reliable merchant (wines that you'll probably like) makes more sense than buying wines in a discount store and saving a buck, especially if that store has no special wine advisor or if the advice you receive is suspect.

REMEMBER

Remember that as much as you love wine, it's not a necessity for survival (this sounds like the right thing to say, even if we don't agree)! Even if you're just spending a few bucks, you're consuming a luxury product that's worth the time and investment to ensure you actually enjoy it. When you have more knowledge of wine, you'll have enough confidence to shop at stores with the best prices.

Evaluating selection, expertise, and service

You won't necessarily know on your first visit whether a particular store's selection is adequate for you. If you notice a lot of wines from many different countries at various prices, give the store's selection the benefit of the doubt. If you outgrow the selection as you discover more about wine, you can seek out a new retailer at that point.

WARNING

Don't be too ready to give a merchant the benefit of the doubt when it comes to expertise. Although some retailers are extremely knowledgeable about the wines they sell and about wine in general, others know less than their customers. Just as you expect a butcher to know their cuts of meat, you should expect a wine merchant to know wine. Be free with your questions (such as, "Can you give me some specific information about this wine?" or "How are these two wines different?"), and judge how willing and able the merchant is to answer them.

Expect wine merchants to have *personal* knowledge and experience of the wines they sell. Often, larger retailers use the point-score ratings of a few critics (usually a number like 90 or higher on a scale of 100) as a sales crutch. Selling by the numbers is a quick way of communicating what one critic thought about the wine — but that doesn't mean *you'll* like the wine! Retailers' knowledge and experience of the wines simply must go beyond the critics' scores, particularly for wines that are considerable investments.

Most knowledgeable wine retailers take pride in their ability to guide you through the maze of wines and help you find one you will like. Trust a merchant's advice at least once or twice and see whether their choices are good ones for you. If they're not flexible enough — or knowledgeable enough — to suggest wine that suits your needs, it is okay to seek out another team member within the shop before moving on to another retailer.

Any reputable wine merchant will accept a bottle back from you if the wine seems damaged after you open it (*damaged,* meaning showing some form of chemical fault as described in Chapter 4; don't take something back just because you don't like it). After all, they want to keep you as a customer. But with privilege comes responsibility: be reasonable. Ask ahead of time about the store's defective and/or unopened wine policy. You should return an *open* bottle only if you think the wine is defective — in which case the bottle should be mostly full! Hold on to your receipt. In the case of unopened bottles, don't wait several months before returning a wine. By that time, the store may have a hard time reselling the bottle.

Assessing storage conditions

Here's a fact about wine that's worth understanding early on: wine is a perishable product. Even so, it doesn't go moldy like cheese, and it can't host E. coli bacteria as meat can. It normally poses no health hazard beyond those associated with alcohol and certain individuals' sensitivities, even when a wine is past its prime. But if wine isn't stored properly, its taste can suffer. For advice on storing wine in your own home, see Chapter 20.

Particularly if you plan to buy a lot of wine or expensive wine, check out a store's wine storage conditions. What you don't want to see is wine stored in a warm area, such as near the heaters where it cooks all winter or on the top floor of the building where the sun can smile on it all summer.

Although fancier shops have climate-controlled storerooms for wine, these shops are in the minority. Most stores are required to keep the ambient temperature at a level that preserves the freshness of all the wine inside. If a shop does have an additional storage facility, an attendant will be happy to show it off to you because they'll be rightfully proud of all the expense and effort they put into it.

In better wine shops, you'll see most of the bottles (except the inexpensive, large, jug-like bottles) lying in a horizontal position so that their corks remain moist, ensuring a firm closure. A dry cork can crack or shrink and let air into the bottle, which will spoil the wine. A short time upright doesn't affect wine much, so stores with a high turnover can get away with storing their fast-selling wines that way, but slower-selling, expensive bottles, especially those intended for long maturation in your own cellar or storage cabinet, will fare better in the long run when they are lying down from the start.

Many wines these days, even very good wines, have screw caps on their bottles instead of cork. These bottles can be displayed upright without risk. But normally you will see them lying sideways along with the corked bottles because that's the most practical arrangement for the store.

Unfortunately, the problem of wine spoilage doesn't begin at the retail outlet. Quite frequently, the *wholesaler* or *distributor* — the company from which the retailer purchases wine — doesn't have proper storage conditions. And in some instances, wine has been damaged by extreme weather even before it got to the distributor, while sitting on the docks in the dead of winter (or in the heart of summer). A good retailer will check out the quality of the wine before they buy it, or they'll send it back if they discover the problem after they've already bought the wine.

Strategies for Wine Shopping

When you begin to get comfortable buying wine, you can really have fun in wine shops, especially when you use the strategies in the following sections.

Above all, the most important strategy to remember is to be open to new wines. Like most people, when we first started buying wine, we'd buy the same brands again and again. We knew what to expect from them, and we liked them well enough (both good reasons to buy a particular wine). But in retrospect, we let ourselves get stuck in a rut. If wine was really going to be fun, we realized we had to be a little more adventurous.

Helping the merchant to help you

While most wine merchants love wine, they're not mind readers. Communication is key in the wine-buying experience. The most knowledgeable wine expert in the world can't recommend a wine that you'll like unless you can give them some clues about your tastes.

The following is a familiar scene in nearly every wine shop:

> **Customer:** Do you have that wine with a yellow label? I had it in this little restaurant last week.
>
> **Wine Merchant:** Do you know what country it's from?
>
> **Customer:** I think it's Italian, but I'm not sure.
>
> **Wine Merchant:** Do you recall the grape variety?
>
> **Customer:** No, but I think it has a deer or a moose on the label. Maybe if I walk around, I can spot it.

Needless to say, most of the time that customer never finds the wine they're looking for.

TIP

When you come across a wine you like in a restaurant or at a friend's house, snap a picture of the label with your cellphone or write down as much information about the wine as you can from the label. Don't trust your memory. If your wine merchant can see the name, they can help find that exact wine or something very similar to it. Tell your wine retailer anything you can about the types of wines that you've enjoyed before or that you want to try. Describe what you like in simple terms. Mention what kind of food you plan to have with the wine; the wine you drink with your halibut isn't the one you want with spicy chili! A good wine merchant is invaluable in helping you match your wine with food. Chapter 18 includes more about pairing wine with food.

Naming your price

Because the price of a bottle of wine can range from about $4 to literally hundreds, it's a good idea to decide approximately how much you want to spend and say so. Fix two (realistic, based on research in your area) price ranges in your mind: one for everyday purposes and one for special occasions or to be stored over time. These prices will probably change over time: the $10 to $12 range you start with for everyday wines often rises to $15 to $40 and above as you discover finer wines. A good retailer with an adequate selection should be able to make several wine suggestions in your preferred price category.

REMEMBER

A good wine retailer is more interested in the repeat business they'll get by making you happy than they are in selling you on a bottle of wine that's beyond your limits. If what you want to spend is $15 a bottle, just say so, and stand firm, without embarrassment. It's also totally acceptable to ask store associates what the good buys of the month or week are. Plenty of decent, enjoyable wines can be found at different price points.

Growing Your "Cellar"

Whether your wine collection is small, medium or large, your purchases can either go into that collection of bottles you're storing for the future or be consumed now. Purchasing wine to enjoy at home should factor into your immediate needs and the needs of your collection. When our budget allows, we like to purchase one bottle on our wine shop trip to be stored for later, and another to be enjoyed when we leave the shop. Different purchases should be for different purposes if your ultimate goal is to build a wine collection or cellar of your own.

WARNING

Most wine sold for under $100 bottle in a retail shop is intended to be consumed in the immediate if not near future. Wine shops with special storage rooms that offer aged wines give you an opportunity to purchase something that is not necessarily intended for immediate enjoyment. In these cases, you will need to do some research on vintages to see if the winemaker or other industry professionals (sometimes critics, journalists, or other wine experts) suggest drinking or holding the wine for some period until it reaches its peak drinking performance.

TIP

Holidays such as Easter, Memorial Day, July 4th, Thanksgiving, Christmas, and New Years' Eve are great times to visit specialty wine shops. If you are interested in collecting different types of wine and enjoy specialty boxes or labels, you can almost always find something new and interesting in specialty wine shops and wholesale stores alike.

IN THIS CHAPTER

» Knowing the tools and tricks of the trade to open your bottle like a pro

» Discovering uncorking methods and the best corkscrews

» Pouring your wine

» Drinking from tulips, flutes, trumpets, and other types of wine glasses

» Being the perfect host and looking after leftover wine

Chapter **20**

Serving Wine Like a Sommelier

et's face it: everyone has an embarrassing story about trying to extract a stubborn cork from a bottle. From wooden cooking spoons to bra straps, we've heard it all. The truth is, everyone gets a case of the clumsies when trying to open wine at least once in their life. Contrary to what the *Somm* documentary movie (2012) might show, sommeliers who work the floors of restaurants sometimes have it the worst, but you would never tell!

Whether you're an aspiring sommelier (a wine professional responsible for all aspects of wine service, storage, and business aspects in a restaurant or bar) or just someone who wants to be able to open their own wine at home, this chapter is for you. We cover the basics of presenting (and the proper etiquette for both serving and receiving) wine in Chapter 21. This chapter discusses how to open and serve wine at home, including both the tools and the savvy required.

Getting to Grips with the Tools

Here are the tools we use to offer a formal wine service. You may go through this process and decide you can do without one item or another, but at least you'll have this list as a reference:

>> A working corkscrew or other device for opening wine (see more on common types in the following sections).

>> A soft cloth for wiping any spills (just in case), folded longways into a rectangle such that it can wrap around the neck of your wine bottle.

>> Two stainless steel or other wine bottle coasters (if you plan to sit the wine bottle and the cork in front of your guests in true sommelier fashion; see the section, "Serving Wine Correctly").

>> Clean, polished glassware (we're going to get you Instagram ready, thank us later).

>> Clean, moisturized (but not greasy) hands. We can't tell you the number of bartenders and sommeliers we know who have cut their skin open on foil alone because of dry hands. This is a thing.

Ready? Let's open it!

Removing the Foil

Before you can even think about removing the cork from a wine bottle, you need to deal with whatever covers the cork. Most wine bottles have a colorful covering over the top of the bottle that's called a *capsule*. Wineries place capsules on top of corks for two reasons: to keep the corks clean and to create a sexy look.

Most producers use colored foil or plastic capsules. Whether the capsule is plastic, foil, or even cellophane, you don't want it coming into contact with the cork or the wine when you pour it. Use the small knife that's part of most *corkscrews* — devices that exist solely for opening wine bottles — and cut the capsule below the lip of the bottle, about one inch from the top. You will need to cut around the entire circumference of the top lip to get the foil off. Some opening devices come with a handy foil cutter that's already part of the corkscrew device, and shaped in a perfect circle to simply be placed around the top of the bottle. Line up the bottle with the round opening, twist a bit and your cork should be exposed and ready for the next step.

TIP

Sometimes, we encounter a plastic plug atop the cork rather than a capsule, and we just flick it off with the tip of the knife. Occasionally, the cork is covered with hardened wax. Just tap the wax gently or carve it off the rounded top until it breaks using the small knife that flips out of your corkscrew.

After removing the capsule or plug, wipe clean the top of the bottle with your cloth. Sometimes, in older bottles, the visible end of the cork is dark with mold that developed under the capsule, and in that case, you will need to wipe all the more diligently. That mold can actually be a good sign: it means that the wine has been stored in humid conditions.

Getting Uncorked

It's finally time to remove the cork! We describe our most recommended corkscrew options in this section, as well as other useful uncorking information.

WARNING

We're guilty as charged for being corkscrew snobs. But the one corkscrew we absolutely avoid also happens to be one of the most common types of corkscrews around. We don't like it for one very simple reason: It mangles the cork, almost guaranteeing that brown flakes of cork will be floating in your glass of wine. This is the infamous Wing Type Corkscrew, a bright silver or silver and black colored, metal device that looks like a cross between a pair of pliers and a drill. When you insert this corkscrew into a cork, two "wings" rise up from the side of the corkscrew, which you push down to remove the cork. The major shortcoming of this device is its meager but sharp worm, or *auger* (the curly prong that bores into the cork), which is too short for many corks and overly aggressive on all of them. Many of these corkscrews are also simply too light in weight to withstand the pressure that needs to be applied to get the cork out. Instead of finding out the hard way that this corkscrew just doesn't cut it (or cuts it too much!), invest a few dollars in a decent corkscrew from the beginning. The time and hassle you save will be more than worth the investment.

You can buy some really fancy corkscrews — some which attach to a counter or a bar — that will cost you $100-plus. Yes, most of them work very well after you get the hang of them, but frankly, we don't see the need to spend that much on a corkscrew. We'd rather spend it on the wine!

The Waiter's Corkscrew

The most commonly used corkscrew in restaurants all over the world is simply called the Waiter's Corkscrew (see Figure 20-1). A straight or gently curved base holds three devices that fold into it, like a Swiss Army knife: a lever, a worm, and a small knife. The latter is especially handy for removing the capsule from the bottle. The Waiter's Corkscrew sells for a few dollars to about $18 or more for the best versions. We use these corkscrews frequently because they're the fastest to use (after you get the hang of them).

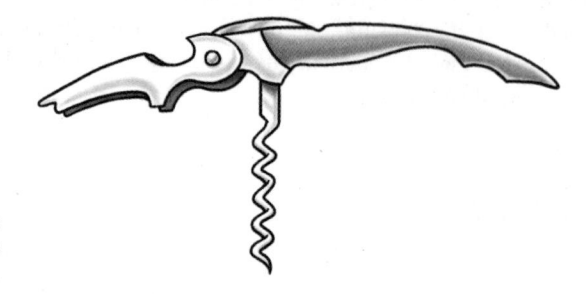

Illustration by Lisa S. Reed.

FIGURE 20-1:
The Waiter's
Corkscrew.

The Waiter's Corkscrew is the preferred corkscrew of wine professionals, but using it requires some practice. If you're used to opening wine bottles while they're sitting on a countertop, then you're in for a real transformational treat here. Remove the bottle from the counter because you're going to do all of this in mid-air.

Hold the bottle with your non-dominant hand as you stick the worm into the center of the cork. Use your dominant hand to rotate the worm deep into the bottle, turning it (not the bottle) clockwise six to nine times while holding the bottle firm with your non-dominant hand, until the worm is completely inside the cork. After the worm is fully descended into the cork, place the lever on the lip of the bottle and push against the lever while pulling the cork up. Give a firm tug at the very end or wiggle the bottom of the cork out with your hand.

TIP

Centering the worm inside the cork from the very beginning is crucial. Double check to ensure you're as centered as possible before you drive the worm further into the cork.

If your cork ever breaks and part of it gets stuck in the neck of the bottle, the Waiter's Corkscrew is indispensable for removing the remaining piece. Use the method we just described, but insert the worm at a 45-degree angle. In most cases, you will successfully remove the broken cork.

The lever-style corkscrew

Another reliable option, especially good for novices, is the lever-style corkscrew. About 6 inches long, it consists of an arched piece of plastic (which looks like a clothespin on steroids) straddling an inordinately long, 5-inch worm that's coated with Teflon (see Figure 20-2). It also comes in chrome or nickel — more expensive but worth it because it will last forever. The plastic one usually breaks after a few years. This style comes in many colors and costs about $20 to $25 in wine shops, kitchen stores, and online; the chrome or nickel version costs around $60. It's very simple to use and doesn't require a lot of muscle.

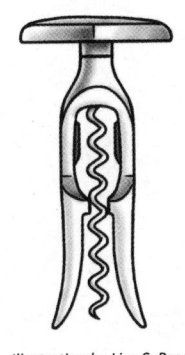

FIGURE 20-2:
The lever-style corkscrew.

Illustration by Lisa S. Reed.

To use this corkscrew, you simply place the plastic frame over the bottle top (having removed the capsule), until a lip on the plastic is resting atop the bottle. Screw the worm downward until it touches the cork. Then hold on to the plastic firmly while turning the lever atop the worm clockwise into the cork. Simply keep turning the lever in the same clockwise direction, and the cork magically emerges from the bottle. To remove the cork from the Screwpull, turn the lever counter-clockwise while holding on to the cork.

WARNING

Lever-style corkscrews can't remove some corks, including those on wider, flange-top bottles. If you go with this option, you may still need to have handy a Waiter's Corkscrew (see the previous section) or another type described in the following sections.

The Ah-So

Another recommended corkscrew is unofficially called the Ah-So because — according to legend, anyway — when people finally figure out how it works, they say, "Ah, so that's how it works!" It's also known as the *Butler's Friend*, but since this is about you opening a wine bottle we're just going to stick with the Ah-So name instead. The Ah-So sells for around $5 for the simplest version and up to $30 for the fancy ones.

This is a simple device made up of two thin, flat metal prongs, one slightly longer than the other (see Figure 20-3). To use it, you slide the prongs down into the tight space between the cork and the bottle (inserting the longer prong first), using a back-and-forth seesaw motion until the top of the Ah-So is resting atop the cork. Then you twist the cork while gently pulling it up.

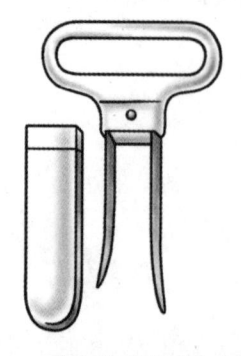

FIGURE 20-3:
The Ah-So corkscrew.

One advantage of the Ah-So is that it delivers an intact cork — without a hole in it — that can be reused to close bottles of homemade vinegar or an arts and crafts project of your choosing.

TIP

Although more difficult to operate than the Screwpull, the Ah-So really comes into its own with very tight-fitting corks that no other corkscrews, including the Screwpull, seem to be able to budge. Also, the Ah-So can be effective with old, crumbly corks that don't give other corkscrews much to grip.

WARNING

The Ah-So is useless with loose corks that move inside the bottle's neck when you try to remove them. It just pushes those corks down into the wine. At that point, you'll need another tool called a *cork retriever* (which we describe in the section "Dealing with cork in your wine" later in this chapter).

The two-part magician

A newer device is quickly gaining in popularity among serious wine types. It's a hybrid of the Ah-So and the Waiter's Corkscrew (both detailed earlier in this chapter) and is especially effective with frail or old corks. You first grip the cork with the Ah-So prongs, and then gently screw down the long worm of the corkscrew. At the moment, however, the base retail price for a good-quality device (Durand is the most popular brand) is in the $100 range.

Opening champagne and sparkling wine

Opening a bottle of sparkling wine is usually an exciting occasion. Who doesn't enjoy the ceremony of a cold glass of bubbly? But you need to use a completely different technique than you'd use to open a regular wine bottle. The cork even looks different. Sparkling wine corks have a mushroom-shaped head that protrudes from the bottle and a wire cage that holds the cork in place against the pressure that's trapped inside the bottle.

To get this right, you still need your cloth and coasters if you're trying to impress your guests (see the earlier section, "Getting to Grips with the Tools"). Hold the neck of the bottle with your non-dominant hand (and the cloth, if preferred). You can use the small knife on your Waiter's Corkscrew to remove the foil with your dominant hand. Place the foil in your pocket or disgard it immediately so that it's not in your way when you're trying to remove the cork.

WARNING

Hold the bottle at a 45-degree angle from yourself, your guests, and any fragile objects. Be careful when you remove the wire cage. From the moment you loosen the cage, keep your non-dominant hand on top of the cork as a precaution.

Removing the cork from sparkling wine with just a gentle sigh rather than a loud pop is fairly easy, and is the best way to preserve the most wine. Continue to hold the bottle at a 45-degree angle with your cloth wrapped around the top. Twist the bottle counterclockwise with your non-dominant hand, while holding on to the cork with your dominant hand (we prefer to keep the cork fully covered with our dominant hand and the cloth) so that you can control the cork as it emerges. When you feel the cork starting to come out of the bottle, push down against the cork with some pressure, as if you don't want to let it out of the bottle. In this way, the cork will emerge slowly with a hiss or sigh sound rather than a pop.

If you like to hear the cork pop, there is no law that says you can't just yank it out. When you do that, however, you'll lose some of the precious sparkler, which will froth out of the bottle. Also, the noise can interfere with your guests' conversations. At the end of the day, this approach just isn't classy unless you've just won a Formula 1 race or the Super Bowl. Those guys have bottles to spare and apparently bathing in the champagne has become an important part of the culture.

WARNING

Never, ever use a corkscrew on a bottle of sparkling wine. The pressure trapped in a bottle is about 90 pounds per square inch (psi) — roughly three times the amount of pressure found in a car tire. The pressure of the trapped carbonation, when suddenly released, can send the cork and corkscrew flying right into your own or someone else's eye, with serious consequences.

TIP

Here are some more tips for opening bottles of bubbly:

>> Never shake a bottle of sparkling wine before opening. If your bottle of bubbly has just traveled, let it rest for a day. Controlling the cork is difficult when the carbon dioxide has been stirred up.

If you're in the midst of a sparkling wine emergency and need to open a bottle that has traveled, calm down the carbonation by submerging the bottle in an ice and water bucket for about 30 minutes. Fill the bucket with one-half ice cubes and one-half ice-cold water.

>> Every once in a while, you'll come across a really tight sparkling wine cork that doesn't want to budge. Try running the bottle neck under warm water for a few moments or wrapping a towel around the cork to create friction. Either action will usually enable you to remove the cork, but keep your thumb on the cork in case it suddenly pops out.

>> Another option for a tight cork is to use a fancy gadget that you place around the part of the cork that's outside the bottle. Actually, three types of gadgets can do the trick: Champagne Pliers, a Champagne Star, and a Champagne Key. You can try using regular pliers, although lugging in the toolbox will surely change the mood.

Opening screw caps

Back in the day, only cheap, lower-quality wines had *screw cap* closures (bottles that are closed by a cap that you can twist off instead of a cork). But in the past 20 years, more and more wine producers have switched from corks to screw caps for their fine wines for a few reasons: environmental preservation (using aluminum and other recyclable materials versus natural cork, which involves harvesting it from trees), reliability, and convenience. Not only are many wineries now using screw caps for wines that are meant to be enjoyed young, but more producers, particularly in Australia and New Zealand (see Part 4), are using screw-cap closures even on wines destined for cellaring.

Screw caps are perfectly sound closures, technically speaking, and they're easier to remove than corks. They also prevent *cork taint,* a chemical flaw affecting a small percentage of corks and, consequently, the wine in those bottles (see Chapter 4 for more information on cork taint and other common wine faults). A *corked* wine — that is, one affected with cork taint — is damaged either slightly or flagrantly. In the worst-case scenarios, corked wines give off an offensive odor similar to moldy or damp cardboard.

TIP

Don't expect to see bottles of the most elite, age-worthy red wines sporting screw caps anytime soon, because many winemakers are still reluctant to use them for such wines, especially in Europe. But don't shy away from screw-capped bottles of other fine wines when you find them.

Serving Wine Correctly

Once you've finally gotten the cork out of your wine, it's time to pour!

If you want the full restaurant vibe, then pour a small (1 ounce) taste for your guest of honor or the person who chose the wine at the dinner table. Use your cloth to wipe the lip of the bottle after pouring and removing the bottle from each guest's glass. Serve each guest at the table counterclockwise from the host, pouring with your dominant hand and wiping the lip of the bottle as soon as you raise the bottle up to move on to the next person. The helps to avoid unwanted drops of wine on the sides of glasses or on the table.

TIP

Traditional Court of Master Sommeliers (www.mastersommeliers.org) etiquette dictates that ladies are served first counterclockwise from the host, followed by men, and finally the host (regardless of the host's gender identity). Two coasters are placed to the right of the host before the wine is presented and opened. Once you are finished pouring, one coaster gets the cork and the other gets the bottle itself. This may just be nice to know in the event that you ever want to simulate a restaurant in your dining room. But it's not necessary in informal settings.

Dealing with cork in your wine

Every now and then, even if you've used the right corkscrew and used it properly, you can still find pieces of cork floating in your wine. They can be tiny dry flakes that crumbled into the bottle, actual chunks of cork, or even the entire cork.

Before you start berating yourself or others, you should know that *floating cork* has happened to all of us at one time or another, no matter how experienced we are. Cork won't harm the wine. Besides, you can get a wonderful instrument called a *cork retriever* (no, it's not a small dog from the south of Ireland!) that sells for $5 to $10 online. One type of cork retriever consists of three 10-inch pieces of stiff metal wire with hooks on the ends. This device is remarkably effective for removing floating pieces of cork from the bottle. We have even removed a whole, fallen cork through the neck with a cork retriever.

Alternatively, you can just pick out the offending piece(s) of cork with a spoon after you pour the wine into your glass. This is once instance where serving your guest first is rude, because the first glass has more cork pieces in it. Or you can pour the wine through a sieve or paper coffee filter (preferably the natural brown-paper type), into a decanter or pitcher to catch the remaining pieces of cork. Michelle swears by tea strainers because they also happen to fit nicely over standard wine glasses!

Letting wine breathe

Most wine is alive in the sense that it changes chemically as it slowly grows older. When grapes turn into wine, they give off carbon dioxide, just like us (when we breathe — not when we turn into wine, although we wish we could sometimes). Wine itself absorbs oxygen, and, like our own cells, it oxidizes. So we suppose you could say that wine breathes. But of course that's not what the service team member means when they ask, "Shall I open the wine and let it breathe?"

REMEMBER

The term *breathing* refers to the process of aerating the wine, exposing it to air. Generally, the aroma and flavor of some wines improves with aeration. But just pulling the cork out of the bottle and letting the bottle sit there is a truly ineffective way to aerate the wine. The little space at the neck of the bottle is way too small to allow your wine to breathe very much.

In the following sections, we explain how to aerate your wine and list the wines that benefit from this process.

TIP

Aerating your wine

If you really want to aerate your wine, do one or both of the following:

>> Pour the wine into a *decanter* (a fancy word for a glass container that is big enough to hold the contents of an entire bottle of wine). Practically speaking, it doesn't matter what your decanter looks like or how much it costs. In fact, very inexpensive, wide-mouthed carafes are fine.

>> Pour some of the wine into large glasses at least ten minutes before you plan to drink it.

Many red wines but only a few white wines — and some dessert wines — can benefit from aeration. You can drink most white wines upon pouring, unless they're too cold, but that's a discussion for later (see the section "Getting the temperature just right." Young, tannic red wines — such as cabernet sauvignons, Bordeaux, many wines from the northern Rhône Valley, and many Italian wines — definitely taste better with aeration because their tannins soften and the wine becomes less harsh (find out more about tannins in Chapters 4 and 18).

The younger and more tannic the wine is, the longer it needs to breathe. As a general rule, most tannic, young red wines soften up with at least 45 minutes of aeration. A glaring exception to this rule would be many young Barolos or Barbarescos (red wines from Piedmont, Italy, which you can read about in Chapter 5). These wines are frequently tannic enough to make your mouth pucker, and can often benefit from one or more hours of aeration. But some Barolos and Barbarescos with softer tannins are ready to drink sooner. You can taste the wine to find out.

Some very good, dry white wines — such as full-bodied white Burgundies and white Bordeaux wines, as well as the best Alsace and German rieslings as detailed in Chapters 6 and 8 — also get better with aeration. For example, if you open a young Corton-Charlemagne (a great white Burgundy), and it doesn't seem to be showing much aroma or flavor, chances are that it needs aeration. Decant it and taste it again in half an hour. In most cases, the wine dramatically improves. Conversely, most red Burgundies usually don't need aeration or decanting. An exception to not decanting red Burgundy would be a young, dark-colored, tannic Burgundy.

One of the most famous fortified wines is vintage port (properly called "Porto"). We discuss this wine and others like it in Chapter 9. For now, we'll just say that, yes, vintage port needs breathing lessons! Young vintage ports are so brutally tannic that they demand many hours of aeration (eight would not be too many). Even older ports improve with four hours or more of aeration. Older vintage ports also require decanting for another reason: they're chock-full of sediment. Often, large flakes of sediment fill the bottom 10 percent or so of the bottle. Keep vintage ports standing for several days before you open them to allow the sediment to settle. The next section discusses how to overcome the issue of sediment.

Decanting older red wines with sediment

Many red wines develop *sediment* (tannin and other matter in the wine that solidifies over time) usually after about ten years of age. Although harmless if consumed, removing the sediment is ideal because it could taste a bit bitter or so grainy that it interferes with your perception of the wine's texture. Not to mention that the dark particles floating in your wine, or the cloudy substances accumulating at the bottom of your glass don't look very appetizing.

To remove sediment, keep the bottle of wine upright for a day or two before you plan to open it so that the sediment settles at the bottom of the bottle. Then *decant* the wine carefully: pour the wine out of the bottle slowly into a decanter at an angle while watching the wine inside the bottle as it approaches the neck. Watch the wine so that you can stop pouring when you see cloudy wine from the bottom of the bottle making its way to the neck. If you stop pouring at the right moment, all the cloudy wine remains behind in the bottle. If the wine needs aeration after decanting (that is, it still tastes a bit harsh), let it breathe in the open decanter until the wine softens to your taste. Or decant it a second time.

To actually see the wine inside the bottle as you pour, you need to have a bright light shining through the bottle's neck. Candles have traditionally been used for this purpose, and they're romantic, but a flashlight standing on end works even better because it's brighter and it doesn't flicker. Or simply hold the bottle up to a bright light and pour slowly.

The older the wine, the more delicate it can be. Don't give old, fragile-looking wines excessive aeration. Look at the color of the wine through the bottle before you decant: if it looks pale, the wine could be pretty far along in its life cycle. The flavors of really old wines will start fading rapidly after 10 or 15 minutes of air exposure.

Getting the temperature just right

Just as the right glass enhances your wine experience (see later in this chapter), serving wine at the ideal temperature range is a vital factor in your enjoyment of wine.

Most red wines are best at cool room temperature, 55°F to 65°F (13°C to 18°C). Once upon a time, in drafty old English and Scottish castles, that was simply room temperature. Actually, it was probably warm, mid-summer room temperature! Today when you hear *room temperature,* you may think of a room that's about 68°F (20°C) or higher. Red wine served at this temperature can taste flat, flabby, lifeless, and often too *hot* — you may even get a burning sensation from the alcohol. Many restaurants may unknowingly leave red wines out at their room temperature, which is is typically too warm, especially in summer.

Ten or 15 minutes in the fridge or 5 to 10 minutes in an ice bucket does wonders to revive red wines that have been suffering from heat prostration. But don't let the wine get too cold. Red wines served too cold taste overly tannic and acidic and decidedly unpleasant. Light, fruity red wines, such as the simplest Beaujolais wines and inexpensive Pinot Noirs are most delightful when served slightly chilled at about 56°F to 58°F (13° to 14°C). While many red wines are served too warm, white wines are often served too cold, again judging by our experiences in many restaurants. The higher the quality of a white wine, the less cold it should be so that you can properly appreciate its flavor. Don't use an ice bucket unless your white wine is too warm. Table 20-1 indicates our recommended serving temperatures for various types of wines.

TABLE 20-1   **Recommended Serving Temperatures for Wine**

Type of Wine	Temperature (°F)	Temperature (°C)
Most champagnes and sparkling wines	43–48°F	6–9°C
Older or expensive, complex champagnes	53–57°F	12–14°C
Rosés and blush wines	48–53°F	9–12°C
Dry sherry, such as Fino or Manzanilla	41–52°F	5–11°C
Sherry other than Dry Fino or Manzanilla	45–57°F	7–14°C
Light, dry white wines	45–55°F	7–13°C
Full-bodied white wines	50–55°F	10–13°C
Dessert wines	43–46°F	6–8°C
Most red wines	55–65°F	13–18°C
Port and Madeira	43–64°F	6–18°C

TIP

Are you wondering how to know when your bottle is 55°F to 60°F (13°C to 16°C)? You can buy a nifty digital thermometer that wraps around the outside of the bottle and gives you a color-coded reading. Or you can buy something that looks like a real thermometer that you place into the opened bottle (in the bottle's mouth, you might say). We have both of those, and we never use them. Just feel the bottle with your hand and take a guess. Practice makes perfect.

To avoid the problem of warm bubbly, keep an ice bucket handy. Or put the bottle back in the refrigerator between pourings.

Reflecting that Glassware Matters

If you're just drinking wine as refreshment with your meal, and you aren't thinking about the wine much as it goes down, the glass you use probably doesn't matter. But if you have a good wine, a special occasion, friends who want to talk about the wine with you, or someone else important at your home for dinner, *stemware* (glasses with stems) is called for. Frankly, we use fine glasses just about every night with dinner (yes, we're wine snobs but you now know this already).

Jokes aside, it's not just a question of etiquette and status. Good wine tastes better out of good glasses. Really.

Think of wine glasses as being like stereo speakers. Any old speaker brings the music to your ears, just like any old glass brings the wine to your lips. But can't you appreciate the music so much more, aesthetically and emotionally, from good speakers? The same principle holds true with wine and wine glasses. You can appreciate a wine's aroma and flavor complexities so much more out of a fine wine glass. The medium is the message.

Color, size, and shape

Good wine glasses are always clear. Those pretty pink or green glasses may look nice in your cabinet, but they interfere with your ability to distinguish the true colors of the wine.

Two other aspects of a glass are important: its size and its shape. The idea that the taste of a wine changes when you drink it from different sizes or shapes of glasses can be difficult to believe. A riot almost broke out at one wine event Ed and Mary organized because the same wine tasted so different in different glasses that the tasters thought they had served them different wines — and that Ed and Mary had just pretended it was all the same wine, to fool them!

For dry red and white wine, small glasses are all wrong — besides that, they're a pain in the neck. You just can't swirl the wine around in little glasses without spilling it, which makes appreciating the aroma of the wine almost impossible (check out Chapter 4). More importantly, who wants to bother continually refilling them? Small glasses can work adequately only for sherry or dessert wines, which have strong aromas to begin with and are generally consumed in smaller quantities than table wines.

REMEMBER

Matching glass size to wine works like this:

>> Glasses for red wines should hold a minimum of 12 ounces (355ml). Many of the best glasses have capacities ranging from 16 and up.

>> For white wines, 10 to 12 ounces should be the minimum capacity.

>> For sparkling wines, an 8- to 12-ounce capacity is fine.

Your goal should never be to fill the glass to the top. A standard glass serving of wine is five or six ounces (177ml).

The shape of the bowl matters because it affects the surface area of the wine that's exposed to air and also the manner in which the wine enters your mouth. Some wine glasses have very round bowls, while others have more elongated, somewhat narrower bowls. When we're having dinner at home, we often try our wine in glasses of different shapes, just to see which glass works best for that wine. The next section discusses the functions of various glass shapes.

Tulips, flutes, trumpets, and more

You thought that a tulip was a flower and a flute and a trumpet were musical instruments? Well, they also happen to be types of glasses designed for use with sparkling wine (see Figure 20-4):

>> The *tulip* is the ideally shaped glass for champagne and other sparkling wines. It is tall, elongated, and narrower at the rim than in the middle of the bowl. This shape helps hold the bubbles in the wine longer, not allowing them to escape freely (the way the wide-mouthed, sherbet-cuplike, so-called champagne glasses do). Riedel's Veritas and Veloce glasses are variations of the tulip that is wider yet in the middle of the glass. These are our favorite champagne glasses right now.

>> The *flute* is another type of sparkling wine glass, but it's less ideal than the tulip because it doesn't narrow at the mouth, and it does little to trap and hold the wine's aromas.

>> The *trumpet* actually widens at the mouth, making it less suitable for sparkling wine but very elegant looking. Another drawback of some trumpet glasses is that the wine can actually fill the stem itself, which causes the wine to warm up from the heat of your hand as you hold the stem.

FIGURE 20-4:
Sparkling wine glasses (from left): Tulip, flute, and trumpet.

Illustration by Lisa S. Reed.

TIP

We avoid the trumpet glass. We are not fans of flutes, either. When tulip glasses or Riedel's Veritas or Veloce glasses are not available, we use good white wine glasses for champagnes and sparkling wines.

An oval-shaped bowl that narrows at its mouth (see Figure 20-5) is ideal for many red wines, such as Bordeaux, cabernet sauvignon, merlot, Chianti, zinfandel, and most white wines. On the other hand, some red wines, such as Burgundies, pinot noirs, and Barolos — and the better chardonnays and white Burgundies — are best appreciated in wider-bowled, apple-shaped glasses (also shown in Figure 20-5). We urge you to experiment and decide for yourself which shape you prefer for any particular wine.

FIGURE 20-5:
The Bordeaux glass (left) and the Burgundy glass (right).

Illustration by Lisa S. Reed.

Buying wine glasses

Stemware made of very thin, fine crystal costs a lot more than normal glassware. That's one reason many people don't use them, and why some people do. The better reason for using stemware is that the wine tastes better out of it. Thick, heavy glass detracts from your tasting experience because it is a rude barrier between your lips and the wine. Thin crystal heightens the aesthetic experience of wine drinking.

TIP

Some of the best wine glass manufacturers include Riedel, Schott Zwiesel, Spiegelau, Zalto, and Glasvin. Riedel is an Austrian glass manufacturer that specializes in making what it considers the ideal wine glass for each kind of wine, along with high-end decanters and many other wine accessories. You can buy these glasses online or in many department stores or specialty shops.

So what's a wine lover to do: Buy a different type of glass for each kind of wine? Fortunately, some all-purpose red and white wine glasses combine the best features of most glasses in terms of size, thickness, and shape. Andrea Robinson, a Master Sommelier, has designed "The One," a glass that comes in two sizes: a larger glass for red wines, and a smaller glass for white wines. The glass shape is trapezoidal, a relatively new shape that some wine people favor for red Burgundy. In fact, we use the larger glass for both red and white wines. The Riedel 002 series is another fantastic option.

TIP

If you are interested in varietal-specific glassware, check out a few shapes that are designed specifically for different types of wine in the color section of this book.

Washing wine glasses

TIP

Strong detergents often leave a filmy residue in glasses, which can affect the aroma and flavor of your wine. We strongly advise that you clean your good crystal glasses by hand, using soft soap or even baking soda and lukewarm water. Neither product leaves any soapy, filmy residue in your glass. If you're wondering how to get the red residue out of the bottom of your glass, try a brush used for cleaning baby bottles (obviously you will need to dedicate it to this purpose only). The baby bottle brush works for any size wine glass!

Entertaining with Wine

Wine is (thankfully) a part of many occasions. When you are hosting a dinner party in particular, you probably serve more wines than you would in the course of a normal meal. Instead of just one wine, you may want to serve a different wine with every course.

REMEMBER

Because you want every wine to taste good — besides pairing perfectly with the food you're serving as described in Chapter 18 — you should give some thought to the sequence in which the wines will be served. The classic guidelines are:

>> Champagne or sparkling wine first

>> White wine before red wine (unless the white wine is clearly superior to the red wine)

>> Light wine before heavy wine

>> Dry wine before sweet wine

>> Simple wine before complex, richly flavored wine

TIP

Each of these principles operates independently. A very light red wine served before a rich, full-bodied white can work just fine. If the food you're serving calls for white wine, there's really no reason that both wines couldn't be white: a simpler, lighter white first and a richer, fuller-bodied white second. Likewise, both wines could be red, or you could serve a dry rosé followed by a red. The goal is to make sure your guests' palates are not so over-satiated by the time they get to the next wine that they can barely taste it. Excessive tannin and/or alcohol tends to have this effect.

We provide more details on how to serve wine when entertaining in the following sections.

Settling in with an apéritif

Even if you don't plan to serve *hors d'oeuvres* (small, finger foods or appetizers), you probably want to offer your guests a drink when they arrive to set the mood. This is known as an *apéritif*.

TIP

We like to serve champagne as the apéritif because opening the bottle of champagne is a ceremony that brings everyone together. Champagne honors your guests. A glass of champagne is compelling enough that to spend a thoughtful moment tasting it doesn't seem rude. Even people who think it's absurd to talk about wine understand that champagne is too special to be ignored. Also, champagne is complex enough that it stands alone just fine, without food. Nonetheless we often accompany the bubbly with crunchy fried appetizers, chilled seafood, or other light snacks.

How much is enough?

TIP

A simple rule is to figure, in total, 2 to 4 glasses per guest (total consumption). That quantity may sound high, but if your dinner is spread over several hours and you're serving a lot of food, it isn't necessarily immoderate. If you're concerned that your guests may overindulge, be sure to keep their water glasses full so that they have an alternative to automatically reaching for the wine (you can also sequence your less expensive wines upfront for the those who really don't care to know the difference between an entry-level and a collector's wine. We do this all the time when we know [insert person with reputation for drinking too much at the party's name] will be in attendance).

If your dinner party is special enough to have several food courses and several wines, we recommend giving each guest a separate glass for each wine. The glasses can be different for each wine, or they can be alike. All those glasses will look great on the table. And with a separate glass for each wine, no guest feels compelled to empty each glass before going on to the next wine. You also can tell at a glance who is drinking the wine and who isn't really interested in it, and you can adjust your pouring accordingly. If you take this approach, make sure your friends are good enough to help you clean all those glasses at the end.

Looking After Leftover Wine

A *sparkling-wine stopper,* a device that fits over an opened bottle of bubbly wine, is really effective in keeping any remaining champagne or sparkling wine fresh (often for one to two days) in the refrigerator. But what do you do when you have red or white wine left in a bottle?

You can put the cork back in the bottle if it still fits, and put the bottle into the refrigerator. Even red wines will stay fresher there. Just take the bottle out to warm up about an hour before serving it. But other methods are also reliable in keeping your remaining wine from oxidizing (read more on oxidization in Chapter 4). These techniques are all the more effective if you put the bottles in the fridge after using them, which slows down the action of oxygen on the wine:

>> **If you have about half a bottle of wine left, simply pour the wine into a clean, empty half-sized wine bottle and recork the smaller bottle.** We sometimes buy wines in half-bottles, just to make sure that we have the leftover, empty half-bottles around.

>> **Buy a can of inert gas, available in some wine stores and online.** Just squirt a few shots of the gas into the bottle and put the cork back

in the bottle. The gas displaces the oxygen in the bottle, thus protecting the wine from oxidizing. Simple and effective. This is the effect that the Coravin (a wine preservation system that relies on argon gas) has, which we highly recommend!

>> **Try using another wine preservation device called _Repour_.** This is a large plastic stopper that you insert into your opened bottle after peeling off a tiny foil cover on the bottom of the stopper. By absorbing oxygen in the airspace of the bottle, the stopper reverses the effects of oxygen interaction that the wine has experienced after being opened. We have tried it on red wines that were open for three days and witnessed the restored freshness of the wine. Repour sells for about $18 for a box of ten stoppers. Each stopper is good for one bottle of wine.

To avoid all this bother, just drink the wine! Or, if you're not too fussy, just place the leftover wine in the refrigerator and drink it in the next day or two.

Chapter **21**

Enjoying Wine in Restaurants and Bars

L et's face it: being the chosen one to select the bottle of wine for a group meal is pretty cool. You get face time (not the Apple version) with the service team member or *sommelier* (a specially trained, high-level wine specialist who is responsible for putting the wine list together and making sure that the wines offered on the list complement the cuisine of the restaurant or bar), and you instantly become the trusted advisor to your friends and family. Then you get to sit back and (hopefully) watch and listen to all the "oohs" and "aahs" at the table. Not a bad night.

But of course, this isn't always the case, even if you know a lot about wine. At the end of the day, picking a wine is a gamble if you haven't had that exact wine from that exact vintage before that exact moment. The gratification that comes from the first taste, ensuring that you've picked something quaffable is probably the biggest reward. Two decades ago, you may have relied entirely on your memory or the advice of the service staff to make these decisions. Today, thanks to the general explosion of wine consumption worldwide, in addition to resources such as technology and the internet, things are a little different.

In this chapter, we explore how wine programs work in restaurants and bars. Read on for tips on how to navigate wine lists, get the best bang for your buck, and leave the restaurant as a customer that business owners want to see again (yes, they talk about you, too).

Exploring the Art of the Wine List

REMEMBER

A *wine list* is a document printed in paper or visible on a screen or board that gives you basic information about wines available, their size offerings, and their price. To find out more about what a wine list should tell you, skip through to the cunningly named section, "What the wine list should tell you."

Restaurants and bars come in all shapes and sizes. Some are owned by a person or group of partners. Others are run by corporations and investment bankers. Why is this important? Because it often dictates the list of wines that you ultimately have to choose from. The wine business — like any other business — is full of producers and companies of different kinds. On one end of the spectrum are what we call "small producers" in the wine industry who make less than 5,000 cases of wine a year. These winemakers are more likely to sell to smaller bars and restaurants whose demand can meet their supply at a fair price. On the other hand are massive conglomerates (Louis Vuitton Moët Hennessy, or LVMH, for example) that own several large brands (not just wine), that may have multiple wines from one producer in their portfolio. Some of these mega-brands have wines produced at a rate of over 500,000 cases or more per year. Needless to say, the size of the producer is what drives the ultimate pricing and availability of a wine.

TECHNICAL STUFF

Wine is often part of a comprehensive beverage program in a restaurant or bar. The wine list(s) are some of the most important documents that a sommelier, bar manager, or proprietor will develop. These documents are usually changing on a routine basis (based on supply, seasonality, and other factors). For most bars and restaurants where wine is a focus, the wine list is a document that gets a lot of attention and requires many steps before it comes to fruition. These include:

>> Researching and tasting wines in advance with business partners, distributors, importers, and/or winemakers.

>> Determining where each wine fits within the overall program, such as happy hour, a dinner special, a general "by the glass" (BTG) or by "the bottle" offering.

>> Calculating the price per pour, glass, or bottle.

>> Educating and training staff on how to sell the wine.

When all is said and done, the wine list can be considered a work of art. Carefully planned with respect to the food menu, intentionally priced to sell, and designed to at least be consumable if not enjoyed, the wine list should be your ticket to a great time in any establishment!

TIP

The restaurant or bar has a lot on its plate (no pun intended) when it comes to wine. As a consumer, it's important for you to do a little research in advance depending on the type of wine experience you want to have. If you're indifferent to the variety or region you want to enjoy, then visiting a restaurant or bar without advance research is fine. But if you're looking to get more specific or explore a certain region, variety, or style, it may help to poke around the establishment's website or other online places to see a menu. As not all restaurants or bars publish their menus online, other clues can be the types of cuisine offered. It's unlikely that an American dive bar specializing in hot wings and 15 different beers is going to have an extensive wine selection. Chances are that if you go to a Greek restaurant, you will find Greek wine. If you go to a Spanish restaurant, you will find Spanish wine, and so forth. If you go to a wine bar with a French name, you are highly likely to find French wines. If all else fails, call the restaurant or bar before you make your reservation. A solid establishment should be able to give you a spiel on who they are and what they have to offer.

THE PRICE IS RIGHT (OR IS IT)?

Our short and best answer to this question when it comes to the price of wines in restaurants and bars is, "you will never know." Every establishment has its own operating costs based on their location, commercial property mortgage or lease, and an avalanche of other costs that consumers don't (and should never) know about. It is typical for an establishment to mark the cost of a bottle of wine up at least three times the cost that they paid for it. This cost accounts for everything you see and experience from the time you enter the building, from the lights being on, to the labor costs of the service team members on duty, to the equipment being used in the dining room and kitchen, and more. In general, most proprietors want to offer competitive pricing for their wines, even considering all the overhead costs. After all, they need customers to come and come again, and don't want to be perceived as not delivering value or the type of experience that matches their pricing. At any rate, you should expect to pay at least three times what you can purchase a bottle of wine for in a retail shop when you visit a restaurant or bar. Pricing is not something to discuss with your service team members, as they most likely didn't come up with the price themselves and can't change it (even if you don't agree with it)!

What the wine list should tell you

A decade or two ago, American wine lists were generally uninspiring. They were either one-page summaries of mostly California wines or bibles full of bottles you generally couldn't pronounce or afford. Thanks to technology and the evolution of wine culture to something much trendier, especially among younger generations, many of today's wine lists have a totally different look and feel. From tablet-displays to robot bartenders and showcase sommeliers, the totality of the wine experience has superseded the importance of a list's format or size.

You can't predict exactly what you'll find on the wine list, other than prices. Though, you might discover the wines arranged in the following categories:

>> Champagne and sparkling wines

>> Dry white and amber (or orange) wines

>> Rosé wines

>> Dry red wines

>> Dessert and/or fortified wines

Some restaurants further subdivide the wines on their list according to country, weight, or even flavor profile (the various French wine regions subdivided into light versus full-bodied, for example). U.S. reds may be divided into California, Oregon, and Washington. Some lists organize wines by grape varieties rather than by origin. Some will even have a catch-all bucket at the end for odd bottles that don't fit in any larger categories ("Other Interesting Reds" or "Michelle's Picks" for example).

REMEMBER

A bottle list may be combined with wine by the glass or divided into different size pours. In general, a restaurant or bar offers more affordable wines by the glass, with pricier wines by the bottle. In some cases, you can order a glass of something that you can also buy by the bottle if you really like it or want to share it with other guests.

TIP

As soon as your service team member comes to the table, ask to see the wine list. Besides communicating that you feel comfortable with wine (whether it's true or not), quickly asking for the list gives you more time to study it. Also, if you wait until the food is served to order a wine, you might get the wine when you're almost finished eating! This has happened to us more than once, and now we always ask for the wine list as soon as we receive our menus. This is usually a standard part of opening service, in any case.

All about the bottles

Most of the time, you'll probably end up turning to the restaurant's standard wine list to choose your wine. We use the term *standard wine list* to distinguish a restaurant's basic wine list from the special, or reserve, wine list, which certain restaurants have. Unfortunately, nothing is standard about wine lists at all. They come in all sizes, shapes, and degrees of detail, accuracy, and user-friendliness.

Some wine lists offer only wines by the bottle. Others include wines by the glass, either on a separate page or in a separate column that indicates a wine's glass price, where applicable, next to its bottle price. Later in this chapter, we explain some strategies for dealing with wine lists (see "Leveraging the List").

TIP

Some fine restaurants have a *special*, or *reserve*, wine list of rare wines to supplement their standard wine list. These special lists appeal to two types of customers: very serious wine connoisseurs and just people willing to spend more. There is no prerequisite or pressure to view any of these lists.

REMEMBER

The more serious a restaurant or bar is about its wine selection, the more information it gives you about each wine. Here's some information you're likely to find on a good menu:

>> **Item number (on a bottle list):** These numbers are sometimes called *bin numbers,* referring to the specific location of each wine in the restaurant's cellar or wine storage room. This is information that the service staff uses to find the wine once you've ordered it. The item number is typically not an indicator of price or quality.

>> **Variety and producer name:** The names of wines may be grape names or place-names, but they should also include the name of each producer (Château this or that, or such-and-such Winery), or you'll have no way of knowing exactly which wine any listing is meant to represent.

>> **Region and country:** This is critical information that tells the consumer what to expect from the wine in question. For example, A malbec from Cahors, France will taste totally different from a malbec from Mendoza, Argentina. Sometimes the region will be listed at the highest level of categorization, and others down to the exact plot where the grapes were harvested. This is common for Burgundy wines, but also important in other regions (for example, nebbiolo from the prestigious Alba commune versus other surrounding communes that also make nebbiolo). In these cases, the differentiation is critical and can tell you what you should expect to pay for the wine. For more on the different wine regions of the world, check out Parts 2 to 5 of this book.

- >> **A vintage indication:** *Vintage* is the year the grapes were harvested. If the wine is a blend of wines from different years, it may say *NV,* for *non-vintage.* Vintages are also important because they give you a sense of whether the price you're being asked to pay is on par with the market value of that wine. See the Appendix C for a list of important vintages in the world's biggest wine regions.

- >> **Description of each wine:** Sometimes, you might find a brief description of the wines. This is usually the case in wine bars or establishments with shorter wine lists, particularly for wines by the glass. However, this is unlikely if dozens of wines are on the list.

- >> **Food pairings:** Sometimes, a wine list might include suggestions for certain wines to pair with certain food items. In our experience, this information can be helpful, but you might not always like — or agree with — the wine suggestion. For more on pairing wine with food, see Chapter 18.

- >> **Prices for each wine:** Wine lists *always* include prices. If you don't see a price for a wine you're interested in, say something!

Most wines sold in restaurants and bars are intended to be consumed at the point of sale (or else they wouldn't be presented to you on a menu). Your best bet is to review the full listing, ask questions, and pick a wine that sounds interesting and falls within your budget.

WARNING

If you are in a high-end restaurant that carries several vintage-dated wines over $100 a bottle, then looking at the vintage on the wine list may help to explain its pricing. But not all vintage wines are better than non-vintage wines. If a restaurant or bar carries the same label from the same producer year after year, sometimes the vintage won't be changed on the menu, or even printed at all. This is because most restaurant and bar teams don't want to continuously print wine lists every time a vintage wine changes or becomes unavailable (this is a huge cost). It is up to the service staff to communicate those changes to you in advance of any decisions you make about purchasing a wine should the menu not be up to date.

Leveraging the List

Some people like to design their meals based on their wine selections, and others vice versa (see Chapter 18 for more on choosing complementary wine and food). We typically tend to think about what we want to eat first, then ponder over which wine (or wines as is usually our case) to get with which courses.

TIP

Here are some pointers to remember the next time you're in the hot seat for ordering from a wine list:

>> **Take your time.** It doesn't matter how many times the service team member visits or revisits your table. They are there to make sure you have an awesome experience, so don't feel pressured to rush an answer or order, especially if the wine list is extensively long.

>> **Review the entire list with your wallet in mind.** Look for price points that fit your budget and occasion. If you're in a group of picky wine drinkers who are all ordering different food items, maybe a bottle isn't a good idea, and the BTG route is better to start! Sometimes prices are listed in ascending order, and sometimes they're not. Bottle lists tend to be pricier than BTG lists, but some establishments offer steals on wines by the glass that allow you to try many different options throughout the course of your experience versus committing to one bottle if you're unsure.

>> **Don't just pick what you know.** This applies to all wines you've tried before, in addition to wines that are household names. If you can buy the wine in a grocery store, do you want to also buy it in a restaurant or bar? The choice is yours. But our recommendation is to take your time to find something different. After all, someone has taken (very likely) hours to craft the menu in front of you, with the goals of elevating your experience to beyond that of your dining table at home (as fancy as it may be)!

WARNING

Many fine dining restaurants and wine bars feature listings of elite wines by the glass with prices you could easily confuse with bottle prices. These selections are likely to be branded as *Coravin Selections*, a reference to a device that enables establishments to pour a glass of wine without removing the cork by injecting argon gas into the bottle. Using this device, restaurants and bars can offer a single glass of very old or rare wine without compromising the remainder of the bottle's contents — but the price for that single glass is commensurate with the wine's reputation, often $30 per glass or more. Sometimes these listings occupy a separate page of the wine list. These elite wines by the glass are a real boon for serious wine lovers!

REMEMBER

We can't stress enough the importance of engaging with your service team member in a restaurant or bar when it comes to the wine list and BTG versus bottle offerings. The next section offers guidance on how to have candid yet polite conversations about wine in restaurants and bars.

Having Candid Conversations

Trust us, you will not be the first person to tell a service team member that you didn't like a wine they recommended. It happens all the time. While service team members have a responsibility to try to suggest the best wine possible for your preferences and budget, they are not magicians (even if they are sometimes dressed like them). There is an implicit understanding when you walk into a restaurant or bar that you can and will pay for what you order.

TIP

To help manage your own expectations and ensure you feel that you're getting the best value for your money, we recommend:

>> **Asking about specials.** Many establishments will offer specials that might not be written clearly on wine lists or BTG menus. For example, some will offer half-off bottles depending on the day of week. Others will provide reduced-price glasses within a certain timeframe. Just because a wine is being offered at a discount, this doesn't mean that the wine is of poor quality. The point is that it's okay to ask about all these things, even down to the service team member's opinion on the wine itself.

>> **Asking for help if you're unsure.** If the restaurant is fairly formal or very wine-focused, ask whether a sommelier is on staff. More and more restaurants now employ one, or sommeliers are the actual owners, as in Michelle's case. Many restaurants and bars have sommeliers and other service staff who have already tried many of the wines and if not, they at least know what's popular or the basics of what to recommend with certain food items. There is no additional cost to you for engaging a professional, and many of them are there because this is what they like to do! If the restaurant isn't particularly fancy, ask to speak with the wine specialist or even manager. Often someone on staff, frequently the proprietor, knows the wine list well.

>> **Knowing when it's acceptable to send something back.** Some restaurants and bars offer small (typically 1 to 2 ounces) "tastes" of wine that are printed on BTG lists, giving you an opportunity to decide if you want to commit to a whole glass (by the way, this is never the case with a bottle unless said bottle is also on the BTG list in glass format).

But this isn't always the case. When you are presented with a bottle of wine and given the first taste (this dance is described in more detail in the next section), this is simply for you to agree that the wine does not have any chemical faults that would render it undrinkable. However, with wines by the glass, there are instances in which a wine may be overly oxidized or lacking freshness (because it may have been open for a few days). In those cases, it is totally acceptable to ask for a different glass and not expect to be charged twice. It is an establishment's responsibility to ensure they are serving fresh products. While it can sometimes be difficult to keep up with the quality of every wine in an establishment (even for bartenders, who spend a lot of time with the wines), a quality restaurant or bar will pour you another glass to improve your experience without question. But with this said, sending a wine that is sold by the glass back simply because you don't like it is considered poor etiquette and should be avoided. Our recommendation is to drink the wine, order something else, and move on.

>> **Knowing your opinion matters (sometimes).** Once upon a time, there was a saying called "the customer is always right." Based on our experience, fewer establishments are following this mantra in absolution. We're seeing proprietors engage in more and more meaningful discussions with consumers about how to be both good business owners and good customers. Offering your opinion about the options or quality of the wine list to service team members, especially when this opinion results in constructive criticism, should never be the focus of your visit unless you are prompted as such. Remember, every establishment has their own program for their own budget and reasons. The ethical approach is to enjoy your experience with the menus you're given, and if you have strong opinions one way or another, send them directly to the restaurant or bar (versus a public platform that proprietors are unlikely to see let alone be able to respond to). You can usually contact a restaurant or bar directly via their website or by email. Trust us, the business will appreciate that you took the time and will hopefully respond in turn.

TIP

Here are a few more specific ways you can request help when choosing a wine:

>> If you aren't sure how to pronounce the wine's name, point to it on the list.

>> Point out two or three wines on the list to the service team member and say, "I'm considering these wines. Which one do you recommend?" Doing so is also a subtle way of communicating your price range.

>> Ask to see one or two bottles but be mindful of the current flow of service. Your familiarity with the labels, seeing the name of an importer whose other wines you've enjoyed, or some other aspect of the label might help you make up your mind. With that said, if you're in a massive restaurant with a cellar that is likely on a lower level and takes at least 10 minutes for the service team member to get there, asking them to bring you bottles just to look at the labels may come off as inconsiderate, especially if things are busy.

>> Mention the food you plan to order and ask for suggestions of wines that would complement the meal.

Understanding Tasting Etiquette

When a wine bottle is ordered, the level of pomp and circumstance in presenting it to you may vary depending on your attendant and the bottle itself. Sometimes the presentation feels so much like a ceremony that you'd think you were involved in high church or temple services: the hushed tones of the sommelier, the ritualized performance, the seriousness of it all could make you want to laugh (yet this somehow seems wrong — almost like laughing during a serious church sermon).

Fortunately, service staff have become more approachable in restaurants — even higher end ones offering wines in the hundreds to thousands of dollars per bottle range. But the process and the logic behind this dance remain the same. Step by step, the ritual (and the logic) goes like this:

1. **The service team member presents the bottle to you (assuming that you are the person who ordered the wine) for inspection. They should announce the vintage, producer, and variety or blend name as they are displaying the label towards you at an angle close enough for you to read it.**

TIP

The point is to make sure that the bottle *is* the bottle you ordered. Check the label carefully. In our experience, 10 to 15 percent of the time, we receive the wrong bottle or vintage — especially when there is no sommelier on staff. Feel the bottle with your hand, if you like, to determine whether its temperature seems to be correct (see Chapter 20 for details on proper serving temperature). If you're satisfied with the bottle, speak your approval to the server. Do not just nod to them — they may consider this rude and dismissive. This isn't ancient Rome, after all.

2. **The server pulls the bottle back towards them, removes the cork, and places it in front of you (either on a coaster in a formal establishment or simply on the table if not).**

Historically, the purpose of this step was for the guest to determine, by smelling and/or visually inspecting the cork, whether it was in good condition and whether the cork seems to be the legitimate cork for that bottle of wine. Chances are that if any of these are the case, the service team member will already know this after pulling the cork out of the bottle. They will not put the cork on the table and will instead promise to return with another or offer a different selection.

WARNING

In rare instances, a wine might be so damaged (see Chapter 4 for details on wine faults) that the cork itself has an unpleasant odor. On even rarer occasions, the cork might be totally wet and shriveled or very dry and crumbly; either situation suggests that air has gotten into the wine and spoiled it.

Occasionally, you might discover an incorrect vintage year or winery name on your cork. But most of the time, the presentation of the cork is inconsequential. If the cork does raise your suspicions, you should still wait to smell or taste the wine itself before deciding whether to accept the bottle.

Once, when one of our wise-guy friends was presented the cork by the server, he proceeded to put it into his mouth and chew it, and then he pronounced to the waiter that it was just fine! We're not going out with him again.

3. **If your wine needs decanting, the service team member decants it.**

   For more information on decanting, see Chapter 20. You can (and should) also discuss whether decanting is a good or necessary option based on your selection before the bottle is presented.

4. **The service team member pours a small amount of wine into your glass and waits.**

   At this point, you're *not* supposed to say, "Is that all I get?!" You're expected to take a sniff of the wine and a little sip, and then speak your approval to service team member. Actually, this step is an important part of the ritual because if something *is* wrong with the wine, *now* is the time to return it — not after you've finished half the bottle! For a review of wine-tasting techniques, turn to Chapter 4 before you head out to a restaurant or bar.

TIP

   If you're not sure whether the condition of the wine is acceptable, ask for someone else's opinion at your table and then make a mutual decision. Take as long as you need to on this step.

   If you do decide that the bottle is not in good condition, describe to the service team member what you find wrong with the wine, using the best language you can. *Musty* or *dank* are descriptors that are easily understood. Be sympathetic to the fact that you're causing more work, but keep in mind that you're not responsible for the quality of the wine. You didn't make it after all!

   Depending on whether the sommelier or manager on duty agrees that it's a bad bottle or whether they believe that you just don't understand the wine, they might bring you another bottle of the same, or they just might bring you the wine list so you can select a different wine. Either way, the ritual begins again from the top.

5. **If you do accept the wine, the waiter pours the wine into your guests' glasses based on their training protocol, and then finally into yours.**

   Now you can relax.

REMEMBER

The sommelier or wine specialist in a restaurant is there to help you make an intelligent choice of wine(s). Don't hesitate to use their services.

Drinking Wine in a Restaurant or Bar

Drinking wine in a restaurant or wine bar requires so many decisions that you really do need a guidebook. Should you leave the wine in an ice bucket? What should you do if the wine is bad? Can you bring your own wine? Let the following list guide you:

- **Can I kick the ice bucket habit?** Many establishments use ice buckets or other chillers to keep wine cold throughout your stay. But sometimes the bottle is already so cold when it comes to you that the wine would be better off warming up a bit on the table. If your white wine goes into an ice bucket and you think it's getting *too* cold, remove it from the bucket, or ask the service team member to remove it. Just because that ice bucket is sitting there on your table (or next to your table) doesn't mean that your bottle must be in it!

  Sometimes, a red wine that's a bit too warm can benefit from five or ten minutes in an ice bucket or more efficiently, being sent back to the bar so that the bartender can *flash chill* the wine (using salt and a little ice water). Just explain that the wine is too warm — we promise that you will not be the first or last person to do this. If you want to chill your glass, you can ask for an ice cube and quickly drop it into your glass, swirling it around for about ten seconds before it melts, then removing it. Be careful not to let the ice melt into water, which will dilute the wine.

- **What's with these glasses?** When various glasses are available, you can exercise your right to choose a different glass from the one you were given. For example, if you find a restaurant's red wine glass is too small, a stemmed water glass might be more appropriate for the red wine. Ask the server what glassware options they have, and if they can accommodate you, chances are that they will. Read more on wine glass types in Chapter 20.

- **Should the wine breathe?** By *breathe,* we mean that you expose the wine to oxygen. If a red wine you ordered needs aeration to soften its firm tannins or release more aromas, merely pulling the cork will be practically useless in accomplishing that (because the airspace at the neck of the bottle is too small). Decanting the bottle or pouring the wine into glasses early is the best tactic. Don't hesitate to ask for your wine to be decanted. But be mindful that this may help more for some wines than others.

- **Where's my bottle?** Some people prefer to have their bottle of wine on or near their table, instead of out of their reach. Whatever your preferences are, just communicate them (politely).

- **» Can I "split" a glass with a friend?** This isn't really an appropriate ask in a restaurant or bar setting. We suggest asking for a taste instead before deciding about a glass. If you're unsure whether you and a friend will finish one glass of wine, then you may just have to take the risk (or drink at home)!

- **» What if the bottle is bad?** You have the right to politely refuse any bottle that tastes or smells unpleasant (unless you brought it yourself) due to chemical faults (read more about these in Chapter 4). A good establishment will always replace the wine, even if they believe there is nothing wrong with it (see the preceding section for details on returning a bad bottle during the wine presentation ritual). Just as you didn't make the wine, the restaurant or bar probably didn't either! They're not responsible for your taste preferences, but they are responsible to deliver a good-quality wine that is in drinkable condition.

- **» May I bring my own wine?** Many restaurants allow you to bring your own wine — especially if you express the desire to bring a special wine or an older wine. Restaurants will usually charge a *corkage* fee (a fee for wine service, use of the glasses, and so on) that can vary from $15 to $35 a bottle, or higher, depending on the policy of the restaurant. You should never bring a wine that's already on the restaurant's wine list — it's cheap and insulting. Call and ask the restaurant when you're not sure whether the wine is on its list. Anyway, you certainly should call ahead to determine whether bringing wine is possible — in some places, the restaurant's license prohibits it — and to ask what the corkage fee is.

- **» Can I take the remaining wine home with me?** The answer depends on where the restaurant or bar is located. Some states and municipalities prevent you from leaving an establishment with an open bottle of wine. Others permit it, often with precautions attached, such as sealing the wine in a bag with a copy of your bill for the meal showing on the outside. Ask your service team member about the local regulations.

- **» What if I'm abroad?** If you journey to wine-producing countries, try the local wines. They'll be fresher than the imports, in good condition, and the best values on the wine list.

WARNING

In many cases, you will end up paying more if you order a bottle's worth of individual glasses than you would if you had ordered a whole bottle to begin with. If two or three of you are ordering the same wine by the glass — and especially if you might want refills — ask how many ounces are poured into each glass (usually 5 to 8 ounces) and compare the price with that of a 25.4-ounce (750-ml) bottle of the same wine. You usually do have the option of buying an entire bottle. Sometimes, the cost of only three five-ounce glasses is equivalent to the price of a whole bottle.

TIP

Some restaurants offer an interesting selection of *half-bottles*. We strongly suggest you check out these bottles. Buying half-bottles (which hold two or more large glasses, depending on the pour) instead of BTG will save you money and ensure a fresh pour from an unopened bottle. This is especially important for champagne or sparkling wine.

Savoring Wine Bars

What's a wine bar, and how is it different from a restaurant? Typically, *food* is the focus in restaurants. Meaning there are more food options than there is anything else (cocktails, wines, beers, and so forth). Many restaurants are driven by a chef or a large kitchen team responsible for preparing and serving hundreds of different food items a day. The beverage programs are designed around the food. Our definition of a wine bar is a place where *wine* is the focus. This doesn't mean that delicious food can't be offered along with it or curated to pair with the wine perfectly. But a wine bar typically has a lot more wine than a restaurant, especially by the glass (many offering 25 to 100 wines by the glass alone).

Wine bars are everywhere these days. You can find them in small to large cities, major airports, hotels, and even mobile ones on wheels. New York City alone has hundreds, if not thousands. Wine bars also tend to incorporate a wider variety of options for preserving and serving wine, for example through free-standing dispensers or Coravin wine preservation systems (described earlier in this chapter).

In wine bars, you're sometimes offered a choice of two or three different size pours of wines by the glass, ranging from 2 to 9 ounces (59 to 266ml) each at different prices. People love wine bars because they can learn about and try a variety of wines in different servings, all while nibbling away at food in a leisurely fashion. It is expected by wine bar owners that their customers stay longer and get more comfortable than in standard restaurants, simply because there is so much wine to drink!

TIP

Depending on the size of the wine bar, you may also get a chance to encounter wines that you will not see in large retail shops or restaurant chains. This is because wine bars work with a network of distributors whose sole job is to bring new, interesting, and limited supply wines to wine bars and small restaurants, serving as a critical link between small producers and customers. Wine bar proprietors get excited about these wines and the stories behind each of them. Another plus of visiting a wine bar is that the entire staff will usually be more knowledgeable about wine than you would find in a restaurant. This setup makes for a non-threatening, fun environment in which to explore and enjoy. If you haven't visited a wine bar, go find one and read the next chapter of this book while tasting some new wines!

IN THIS CHAPTER

» **Picking a wine school**

» **Learning from hands-on industry experience**

» **Getting wine tasting and wine events right**

» **Visiting a winery**

» **Savoring our best recommendations for more learning**

Chapter **22**

Continuing Your Wine Journey

Learning about wine is like space travel: Once you get going, there's no end in sight. Fortunately for those who choose to be educated wine drinkers, learning about wine is a fascinating experience, full of new flavors, places, and friends.

Although we teach others about wine, we are also avid students of wine. We can't imagine we'll ever reach the point where we say, "Now we know enough about wine, we can stop here." So, off we go to another vineyard, wine bar, tasting, or deep dive into the pages of a new wine book, magazine, or website. Every step brings not only more knowledge but also more appreciation of this amazing beverage.

This chapter offers tips to maximize your benefit from a range of educational opportunities.

Going Back to School: Wine Classes

There are many ways to learn about wine depending on your goals: are you interested in working in the restaurant or bar industry? Are you considering making your own wine one day? Do you want to review and discuss wine menus in restaurants as a consumer without sounding ignorant? Ask yourself what you want to accomplish first.

TIP

If you are simply interested in learning more about wine from a consumer's perspective, you can find online or in-person wine tasting and wine-specific courses. If you live in a medium-sized or large city, you're sure to find several wine courses offered by private wine schools, universities, adult education extension programs, or through local wine shops or restaurants. If you can't access such courses, you can research the options nearest to you using social media hashtags or online search engines. You can also inquire at your nearest wine shop or restaurant about opportunities to learn more.

Most wine courses are *wine appreciation* courses — they don't teach you how to make wine, they don't provide you with professional credentials, and they're not accredited. But they do offer instruction about wine in general or specific types of wine and — just as importantly — they provide immediate, expert feedback on your tasting impressions. For information on professional wine credentials, see the sidebar "What do the initials "MS" and "MW" mean?" later in this chapter.

Introductory classes generally deal with wine varieties and how to taste wine, while more advanced classes discuss the various wine regions of the world or the wines of a particular region in depth. Instructors are usually experienced professionals who work in the wine trade or who write about wine. In the best cases, they also have some training in the principles of adult learning.

Many other wine courses are less comprehensive or less formally structured — but most wine classes have a lot in common. A typical class usually lasts about two hours. Participants listen to a lecture or engage in discussion on a specific wine theme and taste anywhere from three to eight or more wines. Maps of wine regions, videos, or slides punctuate the discussion and reiterate key facts or concepts. The instructor encourages questions and guides students through the tasting.

At most wine classes, each student sits before a place setting of wine glasses — ideally one glass per wine to be tasted. There may be printed information on the wine, regions, or producers at the place setting (or this may be displayed on a screen). Water and sometimes light snacks are available to help participants clear their palates between each taste. A large plastic cup or other vessel is provided so that participants can spit out the wines rather than swallow them, and can dump their leftover wine.

Spitting is designed to ensure you're taking in all there is to offer in each wine instead of getting drunk. We can say with confidence that it's a little more challenging to describe multiple wines in depth after you've had a few to drink. The spitting approach also helps to keep your palate fresh enough to analyze the wine's structure (find out more in Chapter 4).

If you know that you can't bring yourself to spit, be sure to have something substantial to eat before going to a wine tasting. You absorb alcohol more slowly on a full stomach — and the simple snacks at most wine tastings aren't sufficient to do the trick. Of course, don't drive afterward.

Brand promotion and education often enjoy a cozy relationship in the wine industry. Many wine instructors, such as distributor salespeople or winery representatives, have a vested interest in the brands of wine that they offer as tasting samples in class. As long as the instructor has expertise beyond their own brands, you can certainly still benefit from the instruction. But you should request disclosure of any commercial affiliations at the first class.

Getting Behind the Bar

If you want to go beyond education for consumers, our recommendation is to consider spending time (volunteering or working part-time) in a wine shop, wine bar, or wine-focused restaurant. In these settings, you will instantly gain exposure to hundreds of different types of wine, in addition to the priceless skills of learning how to talk about and even sell them.

To offer an example, Michelle is the founder and sommelier of Era Wine Bar in Mount Rainier, MD (www.erawinebar.com). Every team member Michelle hires is required to undergo one-on-one training with Michelle in the Court of Master Sommeliers (CMS) deductive tasting method. Using this method, new team members learn how to identify different types and styles of wine through the process of elimination, integrating some well-established facts about common characteristics of different varieties when cultivated in different regions of the world.

In addition to learning the ins and outs of tasting, Michelle's team members have to adapt the CMS tasting method to their personal style of selling, incorporating their own vocabulary into a customer conversation, and getting comfortable making recommendations to consumers with any level of wine knowledge. You may not want to go through all of this just to learn about wine, but we can guarantee that you will learn, and learn fast! Taking inventory and stocking wines in shops, bars, and restaurants is also an excellent approach to learning more about wine, laws, and classification systems.

WHAT DO THE INITIALS "MS" AND "MW" MEAN?

Wine professionals receive the title *Master of Wine* (often shortened to MW) by passing a grueling three-part exam. The Institute of Masters of Wine awards the credential. It offers preparatory programs and/or exams in Australia, the United States, the United Kingdom, and continental Europe. A high level of knowledge, several years of experience in the wine trade, and completion of locally available wine courses are the standard prerequisites. At the time of writing, there are 416 Masters of Wine across 30 countries.

The "MW" title is different from the "MS" title, in that "MS" stands for Master Sommelier. This is a different level of wine expert, the highest title bestowed for someone who has passed the rigoruous study and preparation for the three-part exam offered through the Court of Master Sommeliers. A *sommelier* is a wine steward whose primary focus is sales and service in restaurants, bars, and other establishments in the hospitality industry. Master sommeliers generally have deeper hands-on experience with wine in service settings than those with the MW title. They are often placed in charge of developing and managing beverage programs, partnering with importers and distributors to purchase wine, and even managing day-to-day bar operations. There are 279 master sommeliers worldwide at the time of writing.

While the MW title is accredited, meaning a certain level of educational standards are upheld, the MS title is not. In our view, the MW title is more academic-driven and theory-based, while the MS title is more practical and service-oriented. Both titles are well respected and can serve many different purposes in the wine industry. There are also other levels of knowledge and expertise within each organization that may better suit your needs. Learn more at https://www.mastersommeliers.org and https://www.mastersofwine.org.

Experiencing Tastings and Expositions

Wine tastings are events designed to give enthusiasts the opportunity to sample a range of wines. The events can be very much like classes (seated, seminar-like events), or they can be more like parties (tasters milling around informally). Compared to a wine class, the participants at a wine tasting are more likely to have mixed levels of knowledge. Tastings don't come in beginner, intermediate, and advanced levels — one size fits all.

At wine tastings, you can gain insight from your fellow tasters, and make new friends who share your interest in wine. Most importantly, you can taste wine in the company of some individuals who are more experienced than you, which is a real boon in training your palate. We have led or attended literally thousands of wine tastings in our lives — so far. And it's fair to say that we've learned something about wine at almost all of them. We're confident you will do the same!

Wine tastings are useful because they override the limitations of sampling wine alone, at home. How many wines can you taste on your own (unless you don't mind giving away three-quarters of every bottle)? How many wines are you willing to buy on your own? And how much can you really learn, tasting wine in isolation, or with a friend whose expertise is no greater than yours?

WARNING

Because smell is such an important aspect of wine tasting, courteous tasters try not to interfere with other tasters' ability to smell. This means:

>> Smoking is a complete no-no at any wine tasting.

>> Using any scent (perfume, after-shave lotion, scented hair spray, and so on) is discouraged. These extraneous odors can interfere with your fellow tasters' ability to detect the wine's aroma.

Courteous wine tasters also don't volunteer their opinions about a wine until other tasters have had a chance to taste the wine. Serious tasters like to form their opinions independently and are sure to throw dirty looks at anyone who interrupts their concentration. (Note that these wine-tasting etiquette guidelines also apply to wine classes, and remain relevant when you visit wineries around the world.)

TIP

To find out about wine tastings in your area, contact your local wine shop or bar. Your local shop might sponsor wine-tasting events occasionally (apart from informal sampling opportunities in the store itself). Staff should also be aware of wine schools or other organizations that conduct wine tastings in your area.

Wine expositions (conventions or trade shows) are another great way to meet wine professionals and taste hundreds of wines. Some of these are local events featuring just a few wineries, and others are international affairs (examples include Vinitaly, Vinexpo, ProWein, and the Bordeaux Wine Festival among others). Most of the presenters at these expositions hope not only to build their brand awareness, but to connect with importers and distributors who will help sell their wine. Be sure to read the fine print about attendance before booking to ensure the content and tastings are relevant to your needs.

TIP

We have two important pieces of advice about expositions: first, these events usually showcase hundreds of wines per day, all which are not intended to be consumed in one sitting. Second, as wine professionals, we get really irritated when consumers come to events that are intended for professionals of the trade only — meaning people who can actually buy, sell, or write about wine for a mass audience. Taking advantage of wine expositions for personal benefit (drinking loads of free wine and giving nothing in return to vendors) is unethical and tacky.

Attending Wine Dinners and "Meet the Winemaker" Events

A popular type of wine event is the wine dinner, a multi-course dinner at which a specific wine, producer, or region is highlighted. If you're lucky, an actual winemaker or winery executive is the guest of honor. Wine drinkers pay a fixed price for the meal and taste various featured wines paired with each course.

Wine dinners and related events offer the chance to taste wines under ideal circumstances, and get a glimpse into the world of winemaking from the winemaker's perspective. It's one of the few opportunities you may get to learn about how a vintage impacted the wine you're tasting, or how a new technology or viticultural technique shaped the harvest. You're getting all of this information firsthand and in the flesh from a real winemaker — it doesn't get better than this!

TIP

You may find that some of these events come with a heftier price tag, upwards of $100 per person pre-taxes or service charges. Our suggestion is to review the menu in advance (or ask for a copy of it from the restaurant or bar) to decide whether the experience will be worth the investment. After having planned and attended many wine dinners, we can say that restaurants and wine bars tend to "up their game" for these evenings in terms of food options and presentation, especially because of the work involved in designing wine pairings, which isn't easy (especially for large groups).

Visiting Wineries

One of the best — and most fun-filled — ways to find out about wine is to actually visit wineries and speak to the winemakers or other winery personnel about their wines. You get to immerse yourself in the region you visit — experiencing the climate firsthand, seeing the soil and the vineyards, touching and tasting the grapes, and so on. You can also visit nearby towns or villages, eat local food, and drink wine from the region. We can guarantee that you won't forget wines you taste (or the food you enjoy with it) when you journey to another country and enjoy its wine while taking in the region where it was made!

You will discover that there's something special about the people who devote their lives to making wine. Maybe it's their commitment to bringing pleasure to the world through their labor. Whatever the reason, they are exceptional people. We have found some of our dearest friends in wine regions throughout the world.

TIP

When you do plan to visit a winery, you usually need to call or write ahead for an appointment if the winery is small, elite, or situated off the beaten track, in an area that does not have many tourists. This advice applies to many wineries within and outside of the United States. Many wineries in the United States do have tasting rooms that are open every day during the busy tourism months and on weekends during the winter, so you don't need an appointment for the tasting room. But do check the hours in advance. You can sample wines (often for a small fee), learn about the wines from the tasting room staff, buy wine, and sometimes buy souvenirs.

Exploring from Your Armchair

Traveling around the world takes time and money. Alternatively, you can travel through the wine world from the comfort of your living room or your home office, letting the written word carry you to faraway wine regions. Apart from bookstores and online sellers, many retail wine stores sell wine books and magazines. And with every passing month, the number of websites and apps increases.

Books

The following books are some of our favorites, each serving a different purpose and having its own voice depending on the author(s)!

- **General wine knowledge**
  - Jaime Goode, *The Science of Wine: From Vine to Glass* (University of California Press, 2014)
  - Hugh Johnson and Jancis Robinson, MW, *World Atlas of Wine,* 8th Edition (Mitchell Beazley, 2019)
  - Pascaline Lepeltier, *One Thousand Vines: A New Way to Understand Wine* (Mitchell Beazley, 2024)
  - Karen MacNeil, *The Wine Bible* (Workman Publishing Company, 2022)
  - Madeline Puckett and Justin Hammack, *Wine Folly, Magnum Edition: The Master Guide* (Avery, 2018)

- **Food and wine pairing**
  - Dana Frank and Andrea Slonecker, *Wine Food: New Adventures in Drinking and Cooking* (Lorena Jones Books, 2018)
  - Vanessa Price and Adam Laukhuf, *Big Macs and Burgundy: Wine Pairings for the Real World* (Harry N. Abrams, 2020)
  - Edwin Soon, *Pairing Wine with Asian Food* (Monsoon Books Pte. Ltd, 2009)

- **Selected wine regions**
  - Jon Bonné, *The New California Wine: A Guide to the Producers and Wines Behind a Revolution in Taste* (Ten Speed Press, 2013)
  - Jon Bonné, *The New French Wine: Redefining the World's Greatest Wine Culture* (Ten Speed Press, 2023)
  - Stephen Brook, *The Complete Bordeaux: The Wines, The Chateaux, The People,* 4th Edition (Mitchell Beazley, 2022)

- Laura Catena, *Vino Argentino: An Insider's Guide to the Wines and Wine Country of Argentina* (Chronicle Books, 2014)

- Michael Cooper, *Wine Atlas of New Zealand,* 2nd Edition (Hatchette, 2010)

- Anne Krebiehl, MS, *The Wines of Germany (The Classic Wine Library)* (Académie du Vin Library, 2019)

- Benjamin Lewin, *Wines of Burgundy: Cote D'Or* (Vendange Press, 2017)

- Peter Liem, *Champagne* (Ten Speed Press, 2017)

- Shelley Lindgren and Kate Leahy, *Italian Wine: The History, Regions, and Grapes of an Iconic Wine Country* (Ten Speed Press, 2023)

- Jane Lopes, Jonathan Ross, *et. al., How to Drink Australian: An Essential Modern Wine Book* (Murdoch Books, 2023)

TIP

Ed and Mary have contributed several other wine titles in the *For Dummies* series, which we'd love you to read: *California Wine For Dummies* (Wiley, 2009) takes the varietal approach, devoting a chapter to each of California's major varieties and recommending wines in various price categories; *Italian Wine For Dummies* (Wiley, 2001) explores every Italian wine region and every major Italian wine, with special emphasis on Piedmont, Tuscany, northeastern Italy, and southern Italy; and *French Wine For Dummies* (Wiley, 2001) details every French wine region, with special emphasis on Bordeaux, Burgundy, and the Rhône Valley. Dare we say, an eminently readable list?

Magazines and newsletters

Wine magazines and newsletters can provide more topical information about wine than books can. They keep you up to date on the current happenings in the wine world, give you timely tasting notes on newly released wines, profile exciting wines and winemakers, and so on. Another insider's hint: the classified ads in the back of most wine magazines are a good way to hear about wine-related equipment for sale, wine tours, and other useful offers.

Here are some wine magazines we recommend (some require a digital subscription):

>> *Decanter* (www.decanter.com): One of the oldest and one of the best, this monthly magazine covers the world, but is especially strong on French and Italian wines. *Decanter* also frequently issues supplements on major wine regions as part of your subscription.

- » *Wine & Spirits* (`www.wineandspiritsmagazine.com`): This high-class magazine offers comprehensive, thoughtful coverage of wine and spirits. Extensive tasting notes are always included. It's published eight times a year.

- » *Wine Enthusiast* (`www.winemag.com`): A colorful, newsy monthly that includes an extensive wine-buying guide and increasingly Hollywood-style cover spreads featuring veterans and novices in wine to watch.

- » *Wine Spectator* (`www.winespectator.com`): Much of the current wine news is in the *Spectator,* but the magazine also includes rather extensive coverage of the world's major wine regions, with plenty of tasting notes. It's published 15 times a year, and includes some of the most comprehensive vintage information for the world's most age-worthy wine dating back several years.

- » *World of Fine Wine* (`www.finewinemag.com`): The wine world's equivalent of a literary magazine, this quarterly is published in the United Kingdom and covers wine-related topics at the highest levels of fine wine.

Wine newsletters have undergone a transition from printed periodicals to online platforms, and thus fall into a hybrid category that is part (online) wine magazine and part blog, with frequent video content. Most wine newsletters are intended for the intermediate to advanced wine buff, and require a subscription. Here are three newsletters we recommend:

- » *Burghound.com* (`www.burghound.com`): Allen Meadows's comprehensive, quarterly review of red and white Burgundies has become *the* most respected newsletter on Burgundy, covering what is perhaps the most challenging wines of all to evaluate. Each issue averages 150 pages. A "must read" for Burgundy lovers.

- » *Peter Liem's ChampagneGuide.net* (`www.champagneguide.net`): American journalist Peter Liem has lived in the Champagne region and is expert in its wines. His commentary on producers and champagnes are incisive and clear, making him one of the best writers on champagne today.

- » *Vinous* (`www.vinous.com`): Antonio Galloni publishes *Vinous*, the most comprehensive, up-to-date newsletter on wine today. It now incorporates Steve Tanzer's *International Wine Cellar* newsletter, long regarded highly for its comprehensive wine reviews. Galloni's *Vinous* combines thoughtful articles, extensive tasting notes, and video features and interviews with leading wine people. It makes an intelligent guide for the advanced wine buff.

Websites & podcasts

If you're thirsty for wine knowledge, you can spend hours and hours researching wine online. Most wineries and wine importers have websites, as do the promotional boards of major wine-producing countries and wine regions, and those sites can be useful. But third-party resources provide a broader selection of information. Here are some of our favorite places to discover or chat about wine online:

>> **GuildSomm Podcast:** Hosted by Geoff Kruth, MS, this is a podcast geared towards intermediate to advanced wine buffs. Topics range from technical and viticultural to economic and political. A must-follow.

>> **Jancis Robinson (www.jancisrobinson.com):** This site features articles and commentary from England's leading wine journalist and regular contributing writers, as well as lively, active chat boards with international participation. Subscribers gain access to the site's Purple Pages, where they can even search Robinson's authoritative *Oxford Wine Companion.*

>> **Métier by Julia Coney (https://juliaconey.substack.com):** A seasoned wine educator, writer, and consultant, Julia Coney has amassed a cult following for her writing on wine, winemakers, and the intersection of culture, wine, and language. Various subscription options are available.

>> **SOMM Podcast Network:** A collection of podcasts focusing on wine and food, hosted under the SOMM TV platform, which also produced the well-received "Somm" documentary series.

>> **Vine Pair (www.vinepair.com):** One of the largest digital media companies focused exclusively on "drinks culture," including articles, columns, and reviews. This site features wine in addition to beer, spirits, coffee, and cheese.

>> **Vinography (www.vinography.com):** Alder Yarrow's wine blog was one of the first to gain fame, and understandably so, because it's one of the best-written and authoritative blogs we have come across.

>> **Wine Folly (www.winefolly.com):** Founded in 2011 by Madeline Puckette and Justin Hammack, this is a go-to resource for new and young wine drinkers. Content includes an extensive library of well-designed maps, infographics, courses, videos, and articles. Several subscription options are available.

>> **Wine Review Online (www.winereviewonline.com):** Robert Whitley, a San Diego–based wine writer and radio wine show host, is publisher of this weekly newsletter, edited by Michael Franz. Contributors include a very experienced group of wine writers from all over the United States, including two authors of this book. The site's articles are free.

7
The Part of Tens

Chapter **23**

Answers to Ten Common Questions about Wine

I n our years of teaching about wine and helping customers in bars, restaurants, and shops, we've noticed that the same questions about wine pop up again and again. Here are our answers.

What's the Best Wine?

This is probably the question we get the most. It's almost impossible for us to respond without asking:

» "Do you prefer red wines or white wines?"

» "How much do you want to spend for a bottle?"

» "Are you planning to serve the wine with any particular dish?"

As all these questions suggest, the "best wine" depends on your taste and circum-stances. There's no single "best wine" for everyone.

Hundreds of very good wines can be found in most wine shops. Viticulture and the wine industry have progressed to the point that there are more high-quality options at affordable price points than not.

REMEMBER

You won't necessarily like every one of those good wines. There's simply no getting around the fact that taste is personal. If you want to drink a good wine that's right for you, you have to decide what the characteristics of that wine could be. Then get advice from a knowledgeable retailer. As we mention in Chapter 22, you can also use various applications to read unbiased reviews and ratings from consumers around the world for most wines before making a decision.

Which Vintage Should I Buy?

This question assumes that you have a choice among several vintages of the same wine. Most of the time, however, you don't. The majority of wines are available in only one vintage to consumers, which is referred to as the *current vintage*.

REMEMBER

For white wines, the current vintage represents grapes that were harvested as recently as nine months ago or as long as five years ago, depending on the type of wine. For red wines, the current vintage is a date one to four or more years ago. Non-vintage sparkling wines often have no date at all (they are usually blends of several vintages) but when they do, the date is generally three to eight years ago — or more, for the most elite champagnes.

Classified-growth red Bordeaux wines (see Chapter 6) are a notable exception: most wine shops feature several vintages of these wines. A few other fine wines — such as Burgundies, Barolos, or Rhône wines — could also be available in multiple vintages, but often they're not because the quantities produced are small and the wines sell out.

REAL DEAL

A red Rioja or a Chianti Classico could appear to be available in multiple vintages, but if you read the label carefully, you see that one vintage of the Rioja could be a *crianza* (aged two years before release), another may be a *reserva* (aged three years), and another may be a *gran reserva* (aged five years) — so they are each actually different wines, not multiple vintages of the same wine. Likewise, a Chianti or Chianti Classico could be available in an aged *riserva* version in one vintage, as well as a non-riserva style in a younger vintage.

TIP

Leveraging retailer knowledge and the internet are helpful when shopping for the best vintage to purchase and drink now versus a later date. Not all wines have aging potential. In general, more tannic (and usually more expensive) wines have the most aging potential, and are often recommended to drink several years from the vintage date.

Examples of the most outstanding vintages for some of the world's more sought after wines (usually determined by the winemakers and professional wine critics) are in Appendix C of this book (which you're welcome to take with you on your next shopping trip)!

How Should I Store My Wine?

Most wines are ready to drink when you buy them and don't require any particular aging to make them taste better. If you have a few bottles that you are waiting to drink, store them in the coolest place available to you. This might be your basement or it might be a closet in your apartment. Ideally, the temperature will be fairly constant over the seasons and the air will not be very dry (as can occur through air conditioning). Lower temperatures will slow down the chemical reactions that make wines age.

TIP

If you have a temperature-controlled refrigerator made just for wine (which we hope you do if you're purchasing more valuable, age-worthy wines), this is of course the ideal location, as wines will be ready to serve at the right temperatures whenever you're ready. But if you don't, there's no need to store them in a standard (very cold) refrigerator before opening. If you do store them in the refrigerator, you will have to wait at least an hour before serving to get them to the ideal temperature. See Chapter 20 to learn more about the best serving temperatures for different styles of wine.

How Long Will My Wine Last After Opening?

Here's another "it depends" answer. But it really does! The variety, the type (sparkling, white, rosé, red, and so on), and the storage conditions are important factors. Winemaking can also play a role: the lifespan of some wines that have gone through *secondary malolactic fermentation* (softening tannins and/or introducing buttery characteristics; see Chapter 3) tends to be shorter than those that haven't.

Generally speaking, sugar, tannin, and acid can act as preservatives. Fresh white, amber, rosé, and light red wines may still taste fresh for two to three days from opening. We've tasted some fuller-bodied red wines that still drink fresh up to four days later if the bottle has been closed properly after the first opening. Sparkling wines are at the bottom of the totem pole, unfortunately, losing their luster in as little as a day or two after opening (kind of like a soda). Coravin and other preservation systems have helped to expand the life cycles of many wines (including some sparkling wines) to at least double the shelf-life that we've described here. These systems are a worthwhile investment if you plan to open many bottles at once but don't think you will finish them, or if you simply want to preserve a bottle you really enjoyed and just drink one glass at at time.

How Do I Know whether a Wine Is Flawed?

The majority of the wines you taste will not exhibit any flaws. When a wine is flawed, your sense of smell will generally alert you. The most common flaw in a wine is *cork taint*, which is caused by a faulty cork. In serious cases of *cork taint*, the wine has an offensive, moldy odor, like damp cardboard. In fact, the corkiness gets worse when the wine is exposed to air. Cork taint is one reason why screw caps have become more popular as closures for wine.

WARNING

When a wine is just slightly corky, it doesn't have a dank odor — it just seems lifeless, as if its aromas and flavors have been neutralized. If you are not very familiar with the wine, you might not realize that this is not the normal style of that wine, but comparing the wine against another bottle of the same wine will clarify the situation. This problem occurs more frequently than the flagrantly corky wines, which are generally more obvious. If a wine smells flat or dull, and its fruit aromas seem cooked, it has probably suffered from exposure to oxygen, usually because of overly warm storage or an ill-fitting cork. If you detect a vinegary note in a wine's smell, that wine has deteriorated with age or poor storage, combined with winemaking issues. See our description of various wine flaws in Chapter 4 for more information.

If you don't like the taste of a wine — for example, it is too tannic, too acidic, too tart or too sweet, or unbalanced — the wine is not necessarily flawed. It's just not for you!

Is Wine Giving Me a Headache?

The short answer for about 99 percent of us is "no," unless you are part of the very small global population (we're talking 1 in every 100 people) that is sensitive to sulfites. Sulfur dioxide exists naturally in wine as a result of fermentation and is sometimes added in very tiny amounts by winemakers (see Chapter 3 to learn more about sulfites and all of their magical properties in more detail). Winemakers use sulfur dioxide at various stages of the winemaking process because it stabilizes the wine (preventing it from turning to vinegar or from deteriorating from oxygen exposure) and safeguards the wine's flavor. Sulfites also exist naturally in other fermented foods — such as bread, cookies, and beer — and various sulfur derivatives are regularly added as preservatives in packaged foods.

Very few winemakers refrain from using sulfur dioxide, but some do. Winemakers who produce natural wines generally do not add sulfites during winemaking, but these wines can also be more vulnerable to quicker deterioration in our experience (more on natural wines later in this chapter).

TECHNICAL STUFF

If a wine does not carry the phrase "Contains Sulfites" on its label, the sulfite content must be less than 10 parts per million according to U.S. regulations, and sulfites were probably not added during winemaking. U.S. wines that are labeled as organic wines (not to be confused with the category of wines produced from organic grapes) cannot have sulfites added. Refer to the later section for more information on organic wines.

TIP

If you wish to limit your consumption of sulfites, dry red wines should be your first choice, followed by dry white wines. Sweet wines contain the most sulfur dioxide.

What Are Organic and Biodynamic Wines?

The standards of organic agriculture established by the U.S. Department of Agriculture in 2002 contain two categories for wine:

>> **Wine made from organically grown grapes:** These are wines whose grapes come from *certified organic vineyards,* meaning vineyards that do not use synthetic pesticides, herbicides, or fertilizers.

>> **Organic wine:** These wines come from organically grown grapes and are also produced organically, that is, without the addition of chemical additives such as sulfur dioxide during winemaking. Current E.U. regulations, however, do allow organic wines to contain added sulfur.

More U.S. wines fall into the first category than the second, because most wine-makers do use sulfur dioxide in making their wines (see the previous section for the reasons.) But not all wines from organically grown grapes are labeled as such. Some winemakers whose vineyards are certified organic prefer to promote and sell their wines based on the wines' quality, not the incidental feature of their organic farming. For them, organic farming is a means to an end — better grapes, and therefore better wine — rather than a marketing tool.

Still, other winemakers who are deeply committed to organic farming have chosen not to have their vineyards certified as organic. For some of them, the certification represents unwanted bureaucracy and extra paperwork. Therefore, their vine-yards are not organic, technically speaking, even if their farming practices are.

We have the impression that organic grape growing is more prevalent than ever, whether the "O" word appears on wine labels or not. But we expect the number of wines in the more rigid "organic wine" category to remain small, because of the sulfur dioxide restriction.

Like wines made from organic grapes, *biodynamic wines* are produced without the use of pesticides or synthetic fertilizers. Rudolph Steiner, a 1920s Austrian philosopher, is credited with developing the concept of biodynamic winemaking (although several interpretations of the "how" and "when" exist). Biodynamic wine is defined by its approach to vineyard management as a holistic practice. It revolves around a biodynamic calendar made in 1962 by a woman dubbed the "high priestess" of biodynamics (Maria Thun) that coincide with the earth's elements (earth, water, wind, and fire). This calendar drives vineyard management practices such as pruning, watering, harvesting, or simply letting the vineyard be. Additional tenets of biodynamic viticulture include use of natural compost like animal manure (from horses, sheep, cattle, and so on), as well as herbs or flowers. If you're wondering whether all these special preparations make the wine taste different, our answer is "generally no," but you can be the judge!

What Are Natural Wines?

There isn't a universally accepted version of this term (also referred to as *low intervention*). Essentially, most winemakers would describe their wine as "natural" if it's made in a traditional method and nothing is added during the fermentation or aging process (especially sulfites, as described earlier in this chapter). Grapes are typically grown without any chemicals (such as herbicides and pesticides). The wines are fermented using native or ambient yeasts that are naturally occurring on the grapes or in the cellar. Natural wines are usually unfiltered and unfined, which may also give them a (harmless) cloudy appearance. See Chapter 3 for more details on different winemaking techniques.

How Do I Know When to Drink the Special Wines I've Been Keeping?

Unfortunately, no precise answer to this question exists because all wines age at a different pace. The aging curve of a wine is highly dependent on storage conditions. Even two bottles of the same wine that are stored under the same conditions can age differently.

TIP

When you have a specific wine in mind, you can get advice about its readiness to drink in several different ways:

>> Visit *Wine Spectator* magazine's vintage charts that come from years of expert panel tastings and are continuously updated (www.winespectator.com/vintage-charts).

>> Consult the comments of critics such as Jancis Robinson (www.jancisrobinson.com), Antonio Galloni (www.vinous.com), Robert Parker (www.robertparker.com), or James Suckling (www.jamessuckling.com), who almost always list a suggested drinking period for wines they review in their newsletters and books. Their educated guesses are usually quite reliable.

>> Contact the winery directly in the case of fine, older vintages. The winemaker and their staff are usually happy to give you their opinion on the best time to drink their wine — and they typically have more experience with the wine than anyone else.

>> If you have several bottles of the same wine, try one from time to time to see how the wine is developing. Your own taste is really the best guide — you may enjoy the wine younger, or older, than the experts.

Are Wine Experts Sommeliers?

The authors of this book are wine experts and sommeliers. Among us, Michelle is the *sommelier*, a French term that refers to a wine steward. This is a job title for individuals who own or manage beverage operations of a restaurant, from selecting the wines and spirits that the restaurant purchases and maintaining the inventory, to designing menus, advising diners on their beverage choices, and serving wines using a very precise methodology.

REMEMBER

From our perspective, a successful sommelier needs to have not only expert knowledge of wine but also training and experience in restaurant or bar operations and a keen understanding of food and wine pairing. A sommelier's key priorities are sales and service. The Court of Master Sommeliers (www.mastersommeliers.org) conducts a series of examinations through which individuals can prove their knowledge of wine and spirits and their service skills at different levels from beginner to certified, advanced, then master — the highest title bestowed. Other sommelier training programs also exist in the United States, Canada, and various other countries.

WARNING

Many people who have studied and successfully completed testing in wine theory or tasting identify themselves as sommeliers whether they are actively working in a restaurant or not. For that reason, the term *sommelier* has become a synonym for *wine expert* in the minds of some. But while most sommeliers are indeed wine experts, most wine experts are not necessarily sommeliers because their expertise does not center on sales or service with customers.

Chapter **24**

Ten Wine Myths Demystified

As you leaf through the pages of this chapter, you'll probably recognize several of the myths we mention. They all represent common thinking — and common misinformation — about wine. We set the record straight.

Single Varietal Wines Are Better than Blends

One advantage of *single varietal wines* — wines that are named after a grape and only made from that grape, such as chardonnay or merlot — is that you supposedly know what you're getting (actually, for most American wines, only 75 percent of the wine has to come from the named variety, and for most other wines, only 85 percent — so you don't know *exactly* what you're getting. But anyway . . .). The presence of a variety on the label, however, even a top-quality variety such as cabernet sauvignon, tells you nothing about the quality of the wine.

Similarly, the term *blend* (blending different grapes to make a wine) is thrown around all too loosely these days. Some people think they "only" like blends, and others think a blend indicates a lower-quality level. These are baseless theories, although we support the idea of just drinking whatever it is that you like. We may use this opportunity to remind you that some of the world's most celebrated wines from places like Bordeaux and champagne are blends (find out more in Chapter 6)!

Single varietal wines range in quality from ordinary to excellent, as do blends. Wines named in other ways (for their region of production or with a fantasy name) also range in quality from ordinary to excellent. Single varietal wines in general are no better and no worse than other wines.

A More Expensive Wine Is a Wiser Choice

In many ways, wine has assumed a societal position as a luxury product, especially in the fine wine and collector worlds. Is it true that more expensive wines should be of higher quality? Yes! Is this universally the case? No!

Your criteria for selecting a wine should include the following considerations:

>> **Your personal taste and preferences.** Not those of wine critics or salespeople.

>> **The occasion.** The bottle you want for a casual weeknight meetup with friends may be different from the bottle you want for Valentine's Day or New Years' Eve.

>> **Your budget.** We've seen too many people try to impress their friends or colleagues by just purchasing something expensive from a store or restaurant menu. None of this is necessary and of course, true friends are there to connect with you, not break your bank!

Level your expectations for your setting, understanding that a store-bought bottle of wine will be less expensive than that in a restaurant or wine bar. There is no shame in discussing the price point you want to stay in with either your fellow guests or even the sommelier or server at an establishment. Excellent service staff will help ease the tension by asking you what budget range you prefer.

We've enjoyed a $15 bottle of wine as much as a $50 or even $150 bottle of wine with the right people. At large family gatherings, on picnics, at the beach, and so on, an expensive, top-quality wine can be out-of-place — simply too serious and important for the occasion.

Likewise, the very finest wines are seldom the best choices in restaurants — considering typical restaurant prices. Instead, we look for the best value on the wine list (keeping in mind what we are eating, as outlined in Chapter 18) or we experiment with some moderately priced wine that we haven't tried before. There will *always* be some wines that you haven't tried!

Fortified Wines Are Actually Liquor

As sweet and high in alcohol as they may be, fortified wines such as port, sherry, and madeira are not liquor because they are not distilled from grains. Fortified wines are made by adding a distilled spirit to wine made from grapes.

WARNING

We do not recommend you go out and buy high-quality fortified wines to drink as you might some liquor (in shots or as an ingredient in an inexpensive cocktail). For the most part, the authentic versions of these wines were meant to be enjoyed on their own, and in smaller quantities per serving (typically around 3 ounces per glass versus the standard 5 ounces for a glass of dry wine). The painstaking process with which grapes are grown and harvested to extract a sufficient amount of juice for many dessert and fortified wines is in and of itself the perfect reason to explore the true essence of these wines on their own. In the case of sherry especially, you may be tasting wines that have hundreds of years of history in them — our suggestion would be to taste that history while you can, unadulterated by other liquids.

Screw Caps Are for Lower-Quality Wine

This is an outdated theory. True, screw caps are still the closure on large "jug" bottles of old-fashioned, really inexpensive wines, but that type of wine is a dying breed as people come to learn more about wine, and as the demand for higher-quality wine continues to increase. Meanwhile, screw caps have reinvented themselves as the closure of choice on many bottles of fine wine, especially white wines, from all over the world.

REMEMBER

Winemakers know that using a metal cap to close their bottles can eliminate the risk of wine spoilage from blighted corks. Research has also proven that screw cap closures don't prevent wines from aging and developing just as wines in cork-sealed bottles don't. Today's screw-cap closures are attractive, they are easy for wine drinkers to use, and they protect the wine from cork taint: all good reasons to embrace them.

Screw cap closures are not universal, and they probably won't be anytime soon (traditions die hard). You will find screw-cap closures especially on: wines from New Zealand and Australia; wines from other non-European countries; bottles of white wines (even high-quality whites) from many other countries; and on inexpensive and mid-priced bottles of red wine. You won't find screw caps on bottles of many red wines from classic European wine regions because, in some cases, the theories about proper aging and higher quality persists. We suspect that cork will continue to be the closure of choice for many of the world's most elite wines, although again, this is not a testament to the quality of these wines versus others.

When you encounter a wine with a screw cap, know that you have a wine from a conscientious producer who wants to protect their wine from off-flavors that could derive from a cork.

Red Wines Are More Sophisticated than White Wines

We know: there's something about red wine that just says "serious." Maybe this is because many people enjoy white wines when they start drinking wine, and then with experience progress to red wine (we have no idea why this is the case, perhaps because of more tart, citrus fruit flavors and less tannin or dryness). But we can assure you from our experience that, after years of drinking more red wine than white, many serious wine lovers, including us, rediscover the unique virtues of white wines, such as their compatibility with light meals and their easier drinkability. Not to mention the fact that many white wines can be serious (and pricey) indeed (hello, white Burgundy and Sauternes — check out Chapter 6).

If you have the (splendid) opportunity to drink white and red wines in one evening, our recommendation would be to start with the whites before transitioning to the reds because white wines are generally lighter and less tannic. Drinking the white wine first allows your palate the refreshment it needs to experience the full range of flavors in both the white and later the red wine, which will typically be more tannic and palate saturating.

Whether you're deciding between white and red, just know that the sophistication comes from you as you drink it — not the wine itself!

Red Wine Shouldn't Be Chilled

It is true that the suggested serving temperature for most red wines hovers between 55°F and 65°F (13°C and 18°C), and many red wines' full range of flavors are experienced at or around warmer temperatures. However, not all red wines should or have to be enjoyed in this way. Ligher style, less tannic reds are a caveat here, including some pinot noirs, gamays, mencías, dolcettos, and nebbiolos. We really enjoy some of these wines chilled, especially during the blazing months of summer. They can cool you off just as much as white wine and make excellent barbeque companions!

White Wine with Fish, Red with Meat

As guidelines go, this *generally* isn't a bad one. But we said *guideline,* not rule. Anyone who slavishly adheres to this generalization is missing out, big time.

Even if you're a perfectionist who's always looking for the ideal food and wine combination (in which case, head over to Chapter 18), you'll find yourself wandering from the guideline. The best wine for a grilled tuna steak is probably a lighter style red — like a pinot noir or a bardolino — and not white at all. Veal and pork do equally well with red or white wines, depending on how the dish is prepared. And what can be better with hot dogs on the grill than a cold glass of rosé?

TIP

Pay attention to the preparation of the protein, and not just the protein on its own. Is the fish smothered in a sauce? Is it baked, deep-fried, or grilled? Is the meat lean or fatty? These are all questions to consider because they alter the flavor and texture of the food, which has different implications for the best wine pairing.

REMEMBER

Do you want a glass of white wine with your burger? Go ahead, order it. You're the one who's doing the eating and drinking, not your friend and not the server who's taking your order. No one is going to arrest you if you have white wine with everything, or red wine with everything, or even champagne with everything! There are no rules.

Buy the Wine because Someone Gave It "90 Points"

It's natural to turn to critics for advice. We do it all the time when we're trying to decide which movie to see, when we're choosing a new restaurant to try, or when we want to know what someone else thinks of a particular book.

In most cases, we weigh the critics' opinions against our own experience and tastes. Say a steakhouse just got three stars and a fabulous review from the dining critic. Do we rush to the telephone to make a reservation? Not if we don't like red meat! When a critic gives the nod for a movie, do we automatically assume that we'll like the movie — or do we listen to their commentary and decide whether the movie may be too violent, silly, or serious for us? You know the answer to that. Yet and still, many wine drinkers hear that a wine just got more than 90 points out of 100 from a critic and go out of their way to get that wine. The curiosity to try a wine that scores well is understandable. But the rigid belief that such a wine is necessarily a great wine, and is a wine you will like, doesn't always ring true.

Critics' scores are little more than the critics' professional opinion. Opinion, like taste, is *always* personal.

Very Old Wines Are Always Good Wines

The idea of rare old bottles of wine being auctioned off for tens of thousands of dollars apiece, like fine art, is fascinating enough to capture anyone's imagination. But valuable old bottles of wine are even rarer than valuable old coins because, unlike coins, wine is perishable.

The vast majority of the world's wines don't have what it takes to age for decades. Most wines are meant to be enjoyed in the first one to five years of their lives. Even those wines that have the potential to develop slowly over many years will achieve their potential only if they are properly stored. See Chapter 19 for information on storing wines.

The purpose of wine is to be enjoyed — usually, sooner rather than later. Don't get excited because you see a wine that's 10 years old on a sale shelf. Research the vintage of that particular wine and producer to determine if you're getting a high-quality wine. You will also need to determine whether to drink or hold said wine for a longer period of time. Many of the world's best wines have a peak for drinkability. Once this threshold passes, the wine deteriorates in quality and becomes worthless (not to mention, undrinkable). Use research from various sources (including vintage charts from Wine Searcher (www.wine-searcher.com/vintage-chart), Wine Spectator (www.winespectator.com/vintage-chart), and Jancis Robinson (www.jancisrobinson.com/learn/vintages) as) that will tell you about the quality of the overall vintage from a region — these are unbiased accounts of weather patterns and other factors that could influence the quality of fruit, with differences by producer noted as feasible.

Champagne Doesn't Age Well

We don't know who started this myth, but the truth is quite the contrary: champagne *does* age well! Depending on the particular year, vintage champagne can age especially well. We have enjoyed two outstanding 1928 vintage champagnes, Krug and Moët & Chandon's Dom Pérignon, neither of which showed any sign of decline. The oldest champagne that we've ever tasted, a 1900 Pol Roger, was also in fine shape.

WARNING

Champagne demands excellent storage. If kept in a cool, dark, humid place, many champagnes can age for decades, especially in the great vintages. They lose some effervescence but take on a complexity of flavor somewhat similar to fine white Burgundy.

WORTH THE SEARCH

If you want to try some fine, reliable, older bottles of vintage champagne, look for either Krug or Salon in the 1964, 1969, 1973, or 1976 vintage. If stored well, they will be magnificent. Dom Pérignon is also reliable — the 1961 and 1969 bottlings are legendary.

The following houses produce champagnes that are known to age well:

>> **Krug:** All are remarkably long lived.

>> **Pol Roger:** Especially Cuvée Sir Winston Churchill.

>> **Moët & Chandon:** Cuvée Dom Pérignon, nearly ageless when well-stored.

>> **Louis Roederer:** Cristal, Cristal Rosé, and vintage brut all age well.

>> **Paul Bara:** Special Club and Special Club Rosé.

>> **Bollinger:** All, especially the Grande Année.

>> **Gosset:** Grand Millésime and Célébris.

>> **Salon:** Remarkable Blanc de Blancs; needs at least 15 years of aging.

>> **Veuve Clicquot:** La Grande Dame and vintage brut.

- **Taittinger:** Blanc de Blancs (Comtes de Champagne).

- **Billecart-Salmon:** Vintage Blanc de Blancs.

- **Pommery:** Cuvée Louise.

- **Laurent-Perrier:** Cuvée Grand Siècle.

- **Philipponnat:** Clos des Goisses.

Recent great, age-worthy vintages for champagne are 1996, 2002, 2008, and 2012. By the way, the champagnes listed here are prestige level.

Another related myth is that champagne is only meant for celebrating. There is no rule, rhyme, or reason to this. The legendary style icon Coco Chanel once said, "I only drink champagne on two occasions: when I am in love and when I am not." You get the point.

8 Appendixes

Master wine lingo with a pronunciation guide for the most common wine words.

Revisit key definitions with a glossary of key wine terms.

Consider whether to drink or hold some of the most prized wines from around the world, from 1996–2023 vintages.

Appendix A

Pronunciation Guide to Wine Terms

Let's face it: you probably don't speak every language from every wine region in the world. Here we offer pronunciations for some of hottest wine words you'll need to know. This list is not exhaustive, and may have variations based on sub-region or local dialects. We place accented syllables, if any, in italics.

Name or term = Pronunciation

Agiorgitiko = eye-your-*yee*-tee-koe

Aglianico del Vulture = ah-lee-*ahn*-ee-coh del *vul*-toor-ay

Albariño = ahl-bah-*ree*-nyoh

Aligoté = ah-lee-go-tay

Aloxe-Corton = ah-luss-cor-tohn

Alsace = al-zass

Alto-Adige = ahl-toh *ah*-dee-jay

Amontillado = ah-moan-tee-*yah*-doh

Anjou = ahn-jew

Arneis = ahr-*nase*

Assyrtiko = ah-*seer*-tee-koe

Name or term = Pronunciation

Auslese = *ouse*-lay-seh

Auxerrois = aus-ser-whah

Auxey-Duresses = awk-see-duh-ress

Barbaresco = bar-bah-*res*-co

Barbera = bar-*bear*-ah

Barolo = bah-*ro*-lo

Batard-Montrachet = bah-tar-mon-rah-shay

Beaujolais = boh-jo-lay

Beaulieu (Vineyards) = bo-l'youh

Bianco di Custoza = bee-*ahn*-coh dee cus-*toez*-ah

Blanchot = blahn-shoh

Botrytis = boh-*try*-tis

Name or term = Pronunciation	Name or term = Pronunciation
Bourgogne = boor-guh-nyuh	Côte Chalonnaise = coat shal-oh-naze
Bourgueil = boor-guh'y	Côte d'Or = coat dor
Brouilly = broo-yee	Côte de Nuits = coat deh nwee
Brunello di Montalcino = brew-*nel*-lo dee mon-tahl-*chee*-no	Côte de Nuits-Villages = coat deh nwee-vee-lahj
Brut = broot	Côte-Rôtie = coat-roe-tee
Cabernet Sauvignon = cab-er-nay saw-vee-nyon	Côtes du Ventoux = coat due vahn-too
Canaiolo = cahn-eye-*oh*-loh	Cuvée = coo-vay
Carmignano = car-mee-*nyah*-no	Dolcetto = dohl-*chet*-oh
Chablis = shah-blee	(Domaine) Leroy = leh-wah
Chardonnay = shar-dohn-nay	Eisele Vineyard = *eye*-seh-lee
Chassagne-Montrachet = shah-sah-nyuh-mon-rah-shay	Entre-Deux-Mers = ahn-truh-duh-mair
(Château) Grillet = gree-yay	Fleurie = flehr-ee
(Château) Haut-Brion = oh-bree-ohn	Fourchaume = for-shahm
(Château) Lafite-Rothschild = lah-feet-roth-sheeld	Friulano = free-ou-*lah*-noh
(Château) Margaux = mahr-go	Friuli-Venezia Giulia = free-*oo*-lee-veh-*netz*-ee-ah *joo*-lee-ah
(Château) Mouton-Rothschild = moo-tohn-roth-sheeld	Galicia = gah-*leeth*-ee-ah
(Château) Petrus = peh-troos	Garrafeira = gar-ah-*fay*-ah
Châteauneuf-du-Pape = shah-toe-nuf-doo-pahp	Gattinara = gah-tee-*nah*-rah
Chenin Blanc = shen-in blahnk	Gavi = *gah*-vee
Chevalier-Montrachet = sheh-vah-lyay-mon-rah-shay	Genevrières = jen-ev-ree-aire
Chianti = key-*ahn*-tee	Gewürztraminer = geh-*verz*-trah-mee-ner
(Chianti) Rufina = *roo*-fee-nah	Gigondas = jhee-gohn-dahs
Chinon = she-nohn	Givry = gee-vree
Chiroubles = sheh-roob-leh	Grands Crus Classés = grahn crew clas-say
Clos du Val = clo dew val	Graves = grahv
Colheita = col-*yay*-tah	Grenouilles = greh-n'wee
Condrieu = cohn-dree-uh	Grüner Veltliner = *grew*-ner *velt*-lee-ner
Corton-Charlemagne = cor-tawn-shahr-luh-mahn	Halb-trocken = *hahlb*-tro-ken
	Haut-Médoc = oh-may-doc
Côte de Beaune = coat deh bone	Hermitage = er-mee-tahj
	Juliénas = jhool-yay-nahs

Name or term = Pronunciation

Languedoc-Roussillon = lahn-gweh-doc-roo-see-yohn	
Les Clos = lay cloh	
Les Forêts = lay for-ay	
Les Preuses = lay preuhz	
Liebfraumilch = *leeb*-frow-milsh	
Listrac = lee-strak	
Loire = l'wahr	
Mâcon-Villages = mah-cawn-vee-lahj	
Malvasia = mal-va-*see*-ah	
Margaux = mahr-go	
Médoc = meh-doc	
Menetou-Salon = meh-neh-too-sah-lohn	
Mercurey = mer-cure-ay	
Merlot = mer-loh	
Meursault = muhr-so	
Moët = moh-ett	
Mont de Milieu = mon deh meh-lyew	
Montagny = mon-tah-nyee	
Montepulciano d'Abruzzo = mon-teh-pul-chee-ah-noh dah-*brute*-zoh	
Monthélie = mohn-teh-lee	
Montlouis = mon-loo-wee	
Montmains = mon-man	
Montrachet = mon-rah-shay	
Moschofilero = mos-kho-*feel*-eh-roe	
Mosel = *moh*-zel	
Moulin-à-Vent = moo-lahn-ah-vahn	
Moulis = moo-lees	
Müller-Thurgau = *mool*-lair-*toor*-gow	
Muscadet = moos-cah-day	
Muscat = moos-caht	

Name or term = Pronunciation

Nahe = *nah*-heh	
Nantais = nahn-tay	
Nebbiolo = neb-bee-*oh*-lo	
Niederosterreich = nee-der-*oz*-ter-ryke	
Nuits-St.-Georges = nwee-san-johrj	
Orvieto = or-vee-*eh*-toh	
Pauillac = poh-yak	
Pays d'Oc = pay-ee doc	
Penedés = pen-eh-*dez*	
Perrier-Jouët = per-ree-yay-joo-ett	
Pessac-Léognan = pay-sac-lay-oh-nyahn	
Pfalz = fallz	
Pinot Bianco = pee-noh bee-*ahn*-coh	
Pinot Blanc = pee-noh blahnk	
Pinot Grigio = pee-noh *gree*-gee-oh	
Pinot Gris = pee-noh gree	
Pinot Noir = pee-noh nwahr	
Pinotage = pee-noh *tahj*	
Pouilly-Fuissé = pwee-fwee-say	
Pouilly-Fumé = pwee-foo-may	
Premier Cru = prem-yay crew	
Priorato = pree-oh-*rah*-tow	
Puligny-Montrachet = poo-lee-nyee-mon-rah-shay	
Qualitätswein = *kal*-ee-tates-vine	
Quincy = can-see	
Quinta = *keen*-ta	
Reuilly = reuh-yee	
Rheingau = *ryne*-gow	
Rheinhessen = *ryne*-hess-ehn	
Rías Baixas = *ree*-ahse *byche*-ahse	

Name or term = Pronunciation
Ribera del Duero = ree-*bear*-ah del *dwe*-roh
Ribolla Gialla = ree-*bohl*-lah *jahl*-lah
Riesling = *reese*-ling
Rioja = ree-*oh*-hah
Rueda = roo-*eh*-dah
Rully = rouh-yee
Saint-Amour = sant-ah-more
St-Aubin = sant-oh-ban
St-Emilion = sant-eh-meal-yon
St-Estèphe = sant-eh-steff
St-Julien = san-jhoo-lee-ehn
St-Nicolas-de-Bourgueil = san-nee-co-lah-deh-boor-guh'y
St-Romain = san-roh-man
St-Véran = san-veh-rahn
Sancerre = sahn-sair
Sangiovese = san-jio-*vae*-sae
Saumur = soh-muhr
Sauvignon Blanc = saw-vee-nyon blahnk
Savennières = sah-ven-nyair
Savigny-lès-Beaune = sah-vee-nyee-lay-bone
Scheurebe = *shoy*-re-beh
Semillon = *sem*-eh-lon (Australian)
Sémillon = seh-mee-yohn (French)
Sèvre-et-Maine = sev'r-et-mehn
Soave = so-*ah*-vay
Spanna = *spah*-nah
Spätlese = *shpate*-lay-seh
Spumante = spoo-*mahn*-tay

Name or term = Pronunciation
Steiermark = *sty*-er-mark
Tempranillo = tem-prah-*nee*-yoh
Tinto = *teen*-tow
Tokaj-Hegyalja = toe-*kye*-heh-*jah*-yah
Torgiano = tor-gee-*ah*-no
Tre Venezie = trae veh-*netz*-ee
Trebbiano = treb-bee-*ah*-noh
Trocken = *troh*-ken
Vacqueyras = vah-keh-rahs
Valmur = vahl-moor
Valpolicella = val-po-lee-*chel*-lah
Vaudésir = voh-deh-zeer
Vendange Tardive = vahn-dahnj tahr-deev
Veneto = *ven*-eh-tow
Verdejo = ver-*day*-ho
Verdicchio = ver-*dee*-key-oh
Vernaccia di San Gimignano = ver-*nah*-cha dee san gee-mee-*nyah*-noh
Vinho = *veen*-ho
Vinho Verde = *veen*-ho *vaird-eh*
(Vino) Nobile di Montepulciano = *no*-be-lay dee mon-tay-pul-chee-*ah*-no
Viognier = vee-oh-nyay
Vosne-Romanée = vone-roh-mah-nay
Vouvray = voo-vray
Wachau = va-*cow*
Weissburgunder = *vice*-boor-gun-der
Willamette (Valley) = wil-*lam*-et
Xinomavro = zee-*no*-mav-roe

Appendix **B**

Glossary of Wine and Wine-Tasting Terms

Here, for handy reference, are definitions of the most common wine and wine–tasting terms !

acidity: A component of wine, generally consisting of tartaric acid (a natural acid in grapes) and comprising approximately 0.5 to 0.7 percent of the wine by volume.

aerate: To expose wine to air in preparation for drinking it, usually with the intention of softening the harshness of a younger wine or allowing the most attractive aromas to reveal themselves in an older wine.

alcohol level: The percentage of alcohol by volume that a wine has. Most white wines have an alcohol level between 9% and 14%, and most red wines have an alcohol level between 12% and 15%.

American oak: Oak wood from a U.S. forest, of the species *quercus alba,* with the barrels made from such wood. Some winemakers in certain wine regions (such as some in Spain and Australia) favor American oak for aging their wines.

aroma: The smell of a wine, which can include several characteristics: fruit, non-fruit, earthy characteristics such as mushrooms or potting soil, or manmade materials such as leather and cigar box.

aromatic: A descriptor for a wine that has a pronounced smell, used particularly in reference to fruity and floral smells. Some white grape varieties are also dubbed *aromatic* because they are strong in aroma compounds.

aromatic compounds: Those substances in wine — derived from the grapes, from winemaking, or from aging — that are responsible for a wine's aromas and flavors.

astringent: A descriptor for the mouth-puckering, pore-tightening, tactile character of some wines caused by tannin, acid, or the combination of both. Generally not a positive trait.

balance: The interrelationship of a wine's alcohol, residual sugar (if any), acid, and tannin. When no one component stands out obtrusively in your mouth, a wine is said to be well balanced. Wines can also have balance between their aromas/flavors and their structure.

barrel: A relatively small wooden container for fermenting and/or aging wine, generally 60 gallons in size and made of oak.

barrel-aged: A term that applies to wines that are fermented in containers of inert material, such as stainless steel, and subsequently placed into wooden barrels for a period of maturation. The term also applies to the maturation period of wines that also fermented in the barrel.

barrel-fermented: A term that applies to white wines that are fermented in oak barrels. The oaky character of such wines is generally more subtle than that of wines that have been merely barrel-aged.

black fruits: A general term for wine aromas and flavors that suggest blackberries, blueberries, black cherries, black currants, or other black fruits.

black grapes: Wine grapes that have a reddish or blue pigmentation in their skins. Used to make red wine.

bodega: A winery in Spain. Also the Spanish word for a building where wine is stored.

body: The impression of a wine's weight in your mouth. A wine's body is generally described as light, medium, or full.

bottle-age: Maturation of a wine after it has been bottled. Most wines undergo a short period of bottle aging at the winery before release. Fine wines can be aged additionally by consumers after purchase.

bouquet: An evolved, complex, mature aroma.

bright: Indicates a wine whose characteristics are perceived as vivid by the senses. A wine can be visually bright, or it can have bright aromas and flavors. In both cases, the opposite is dull.

cask: A relatively large wooden container for making or storing wine. Can range in capacity from 50 gallons to over 10,000 gallons.

castello: Italian for *castle*. Refers to a wine estate.

charry: Having aromas or flavors that suggest burnt wood or charred wood.

clone: A subset of a grape variety. A vine or set of genetically identical vines, that exhibits characteristics specific to it as compared to other vines of the same variety.

compact: A descriptor for wines that give the impression of being tight and concentrated, but not full.

complex: Having a multiplicity of aromas and flavors.

concentrated: A descriptor for wines with aromas and flavors that are dense rather than dilute.

concentration: A characteristic of wines whose flavors are tightly knit as opposed to being diluted or watery.

crisp: A wine that feels clean and slightly brittle in your mouth — the opposite of *soft*. Crispness is usually the result of high acidity, and crisp wines, therefore, are usually lighter in body.

depth: A characteristic of fine wines that give the impression of having many layers of taste, rather than being flat and one-dimensional. A positive trait.

dry: A wine that is fermented to some desired level of dryness. The word *dry* can also describe the texture of a wine that feels rough in your mouth, as in *dry texture* or *dry mouthfeel.* But when used alone, it refers specifically to lack of sweetness.

dull: A wine whose expression is muddled and unclear. This term can apply to a wine's appearance, to its aromas and flavors, or to its general style. It is a negative characteristic.

earthy: Having pleasant aromas and flavors that suggest earth, such as potting soil, forest floor, mineral-driven aromas, and so forth. This term is sometimes used as a euphemism for wines that are rustic and lack refinement.

elegance: A somewhat overused descriptor for wines that express themselves in a fine or delicate manner as opposed to an intense or forceful way — considered a positive trait.

extraction: The absorption of substances from the grapes, such as color and tannin, that occurs when the skins co-mingle with the juice or wine during the winemaking process.

finish: The final impressions a wine gives in the rear of your mouth after you have swallowed it or spat it out — the aftertaste.

firm: A descriptor for wines that are not soft but are not harsh and tough. Generally relates to the tannic content of a red wine or the acidity of a white wine.

flabby: A pejorative term used to describe wines that taste too bland or soft, generally due to a lack of acidity or tannin.

flavor intensity: The degree to which a wine's flavors are pronounced and easily perceived.

flavors: Aromatic constituents of a wine that are perceived in the mouth.

fleshy: A descriptor for a rich textural or tactile impression of some wines.

French oak: Oak wood from the forests of France, of the species *quercus robur*, considered the finest type of oak for aging most white wines and many red wines, with the barrels made from such wood.

fruit character: Those characteristics of a wine that derive from the grapes, such as a wine's aromas and flavors.

fruity: Having aromas and flavors suggestive of fruit. This is a broad descriptor. In some cases, the fruity aroma or flavor of a wine can be described more precisely as suggestive of fresh fruit, dried fruit, or cooked fruit, or even more precisely as a specific fresh, dried, or cooked fruit, such as fresh apples, dried figs, or strawberry jam.

full: A descriptor for wines that give the impression of being large and weighty in your mouth. A wine's fullness can derive from high alcohol or from other aspects of the wine. A wine can be pleasantly full or too full, depending on one's taste preferences.

generous: A descriptor for wines whose characteristics are expressive and easy to perceive. Usually describes fuller, rounder styles.

grape tannin: Those tannins in a red wine that come from the grapes from which the wine was made, from the grapes' skins and seeds, and sometimes from stems.

harmonious: A flattering descriptor for wines that are well balanced and also express themselves in a particularly graceful manner.

herbal: Having aromas and flavors that suggest herbs, such as fresh herbs, dried herbs, or specific herbs (rosemary, thyme, tarragon, and so forth).

intense: Usually used in reference to a wine's aromas and flavors, to describe the volume of those aromas or flavors — how pronounced the smell of lemon is in the wine, for example, or how flavorful the wine is.

lees: Grape solids and dead yeast cells that precipitate to the bottom of a wine vessel after fermentation.

length: A characteristic of fine wines that give a sustained sensory impression across the length of the tongue.

maceration: The process of soaking the skins of red grapes in their grape juice to leach the skins' color, tannin, and other substances into the juice. Can also be used to create amber or orange wines made from white grapes.

malolactic fermentation: A natural conversion of harsh malic acid into milder lactic acid, which weakens the total acidity of a wine. An optional process in white wine production.

maturation: The aging period at the winery during which a wine evolves to a state of readiness for bottling or for shipping. The process of development and evolution that fine wines undergo after they are bottled.

medium-dry: A term to indicate the perceived sweetness of wines that are somewhat sweet but close to dry.

medium-sweet: A term to indicate the perceived sweetness level of wines that are sweeter than medium-dry, but not fully sweet.

mineral-driven: Having aromas or flavors that suggest minerals (as opposed to organic substances, such as plants or animals). This is a broad descriptor. In some cases, the mineral aroma or flavor of a wine can be described more precisely as suggestive of chalk, iron, steel, and so forth.

new oak: Oak barrels that are used for the first time in making a particular wine. Sometimes called *"first use" oak.*

New World: Collective term for those winemaking countries of the world that are situated outside of Europe. This term is no longer in use in many circles of the wine industry given its negative connotation to the colonial periods of the 16th to 19th centuries.

nutty: Having aromas or flavors that suggest nuts. This is a broad descriptor. In some cases, the nutty aroma or flavor of a wine can be described more precisely as suggestive of roasted nuts, toasted nuts, nut butter, cashews, almonds, hazelnuts, and so forth.

oaky: Having characteristics that derive from oak, such as toastiness, smokiness, a charry smell or flavor, vanilla aroma, or a higher tannin level than the wine might otherwise have. Usually, these oaky characteristics occur as the wine ages in oak barrels, but in lower-quality wines, they may have been added as an actual flavoring.

off-dry: A generalized term for wines that suggest dryness but not completely dry.

old vines: An unregulated term for grapevines whose fruit quality presumably is quite good due to the fact the vines are old — generally 40 years old or older — and therefore produce a very small crop of concentrated grapes.

Old World: Collective term for the winemaking countries of Europe. This term is no longer in use in many circles of the wine industry given its negative connotation to the colonial periods of the 16th to 19th centuries.

palate: A term used by wine tasters as a synonym for "mouth," or to refer to the characteristics of a wine that manifest in the taster's mouth.

plummy: Having aromas or flavors that suggest ripe plums.

powerful: An anthropomorphic descriptor for wines that convey an impression of strength and intensity.

primary aromas: Fresh aromas in a wine that derive from the grapes used to make that wine.

residual sugar: Sugar remaining in the wine after fermentation.

rich: A descriptor of wines that offer an abundance of flavor, texture, or other sensory perceptions.

round: A descriptor for wines that are perceived in the mouth to be neither flat nor angular. Roundness relates to the wine's structure — that is, its particular makeup of acid, tannin, sweetness, and alcohol, which dictates texture and mouthfeel.

Secondary aromas: Aromas and flavors that derive from winemaking, such as oak-derived notes or a buttery note from malolactic fermentation.

sediment: The residue in a bottle of red wine that forms as the wine matures. Can include particles from grape skins, seeds, stems, tartaric acid crystals, yeast, and other bacteria from the fermentation process. Sediment is harmless and can be consumed.

serious: A metaphorical descriptor for a wine that is of high quality, as opposed to a popularly styled, mass-market wine.

silky: Having a supple, smooth texture suggestive of silk.

single-vineyard wine: A wine that is made from the grapes of a single (presumably exceptionally good) plot of land and that usually carries the name of the vineyard on its label. The term is unregulated, in that *vineyard* is not defined as to size or ownership.

smoky: Having aromas or flavors that suggest smoke or smoked wood, smoked meat, and similar.

smooth: Descriptor for a wine whose texture is not rough or harsh on the palate.

stems: The woody part of a grape bunch, which are high in tannin. Usually the stems are removed and discarded prior to fermentation.

stony: Having minerally aromas or flavors that suggest stones. In some cases, the stony aroma or flavor of a wine can be described more precisely as suggestive of wet stones.

structure: That part of a wine's taste that derives from perception of the wine's structural elements, including alcohol, acid, tannin, and sugar.

style: The set of characteristics defining the type of wine produced. For example, sparkling, dry, or dessert.

supple: A descriptor for wines that seem fluid in texture in the mouth, without roughness or sharpness. A positive trait especially for red wines.

sweetness: The impression of a sugary taste in a wine, which can be due to the presence of residual sugar or to other sweet-tasting substances in the wine, such as alcohol.

tannic: A word used to describe wines that seem to be high in tannin.

tarry: Having aromas or flavors that suggest fresh tar.

tart: A descriptor for aromas or flavors of underripe fruit. This term can also apply to a wine that is high in acid.

taste: A general term for the totality of impressions a wine gives in the mouth. More specifically, the primary tastes found in wine: sweetness, sourness, and bitterness.

tertiary aromas: Aromas and flavors that derive from aging of the wine, such as notes of mushroom, leather, dried fruit, and other aromas.

texture: A wine's consistency or feel in the mouth.

thin: A word used to describe wines that are lacking in substance or meager in texture.

tight: A descriptor for wines that seem to be inexpressive at the moment. This term can apply to a wine's aromas and flavors or to its structure, and is typically used to describe a wine that may need more time to reveal its aromas in a glass or bottle.

underbrush: Aromas or flavors that suggest wet leaves, dampness, and slight decay. A welcome note in many older reds.

variety: A distinct type of grape within a species.

vegetal: Having aromas or flavors that suggest vegetables, such as green peppers or asparagus. These can be pleasant or not, depending on the taster.

vinification: The process of making grape juice into wine.

viticulture: The practice of growing grapes.

weight: The impression of a wine's volume in the mouth.

wood tannin: Those tannins in a wine that are attributable to the barrels in which the wine aged, as opposed to the grapes.

yeasts: One-cell microorganisms responsible for transforming grape juice into wine.

Appendix C

Vintage Wine Chart: 1996–2023

Any vintage wine chart must be regarded as a rough guide — a general rating determined by a combination of factors, including growing conditions, changes in weather, and other viticultural considerations. Many wines can be exceptions to a vintage rating, and some wines can excel under certain conditions while others can't. For example, some producers manage to find a way to make a decent (even fine) wine in a so-called poor vintage. Use this guide to cross-reference with other sources about particular vintages (see Chapter 24).

Key:

100: Exceptional, classic

95: Excellent

90: Good with some variation by producer

85: Average with a lot of variation by producer

75: Poor

a: Too young to tell

b: Can drink now or keep for later

c: Ready to drink

d: Past peak

ND: Vintage not declared by producer

NR: Not yet rated by enough reliable sources or not yet released

Wine Region	1996	1997	1998	1999	2000	2001	2002	2003	2004	2005	2006	2007	2008	2009
Bordeaux														
Left Bank	95c	90c	90c	90b	90c	90b	90c	90b	90c	100a	90b	90c	85c	95b
Right Bank	90c	90c	95b	95b	95c	100a	90b	90a	95a	100a	90c	90c	95b	95b
Sauternes/Barsac	90c	95c	90c	95b	95b	95c	90c	95b	90c	95a	95b	90b	95a	95a
Rhône Valley														
North Rhône Valley	90c	90c	90c	95c	90c	85c	90c	90b	90c	95b	90b	90c	85c	100b
Southern Rhône	80d	80d	95c	90c	95c	75d	75d	90c		95b	90b	95c	95b	95c
Burgundy														
Côte de Nuits	95c	90c	90c	95b	90b	90c	95c	90c	90c	95b	90b	90c	90c	100b
Côte de Beaune	90c	85c	85c	85c	85c	90c	90c	90c	90c	95b	90b	90c	90c	95b
White Burgundy	95c	90c	90c	90c	90c	95c	95c	90c	90c	90c	90c	90c	90c	90c
Other Wine Regions														
Champagne	100b	90c	90b	90b	90b	ND	95b	90c		90c	90c	95c	100b	90b
Alsace	NR	NR	NR	90b	90b	90b	90b	90c	90b	90b	90c	95b	90b	90b
Germany: Riesling	90b	90b	90b	90b	85c	100b	90b	95b	94b	100b	95b	95b	90b	100b
Piedmont	100b	90c	90c	90b	90c	95b	75d	85c		95b	100c	95b	90c	90c
Tuscany: Bolgheri & Maremma	90c	100c	100c	100c	90c	90c	90c	90c	90c	90c	90c	90c	90c	90c
Tuscany: Brunello di Montalcino	85c	95c	90c	100c	90c	100c	75d	90c	90c	90b	95b	95c	90c	90c
Tuscany: Chianti & Chianti Classico	NR	100c	90c	90c	90c	90c	90c	90c	90c	90c	90c	90c	90c	90c
Douro Valley Reds	NR	NR	NR	NR	90c	90c	80d	90c	90c	90c	90c	95c	95b	90c
Vintage Port	ND	100b	ND	ND	100b	ND	ND	100b	ND	ND	ND	100a	ND	ND
Priorat	NR	NR	NR	NR	90c	95b	85c	90c	90c	90b	90c	90c	90c	90c
Ribera del Duero	NR	NR	NR	90c	90c	90b	85c	85c	100b	90b	90c	90c	90c	90c
Rioja	NR	NR	NR	NR	85c	90b	85d	85c	90c	90b	85c	90c	85c	90b
Napa Valley Cabernet Sauvignon	95c	95c	85d	100c	85d	95c	95c	85d	95b	90c	95c	100b	95b	95b
Western Cape	NR	NR	NR	85d	90c	85d	90c	90c	90c	90c	90c	90c	90c	90c

Wine Region	2010	2011	2012	2013	2014	2015	2016	2017	2018	2019	2020	2021	2022	2023
Bordeaux														
Left Bank	100a	90b	90b	90c	90a	95a	95a	90b	95a	90a	90a	85c	95b	90b
Right Bank	95a	90c	90c	90c	90b	95a	95b	90b	90a	90a	90a	85b	95b	90b
Sauternes/Barsac	95a	95a	90c	90a	95a	95a	90b	90b	90b	90b	90b	85c	95b	
Rhône Valley														
North Rhône Valley	100a	95b	95b	90b	90b	100a	95a	95a	90b	95a	95b	90b	90b	95b
Southern Rhône	95a	91b	95b	90c	85c	95a	100a	90b	90b	95b	90b	85b	90b	95b
Burgundy														
Côte de Nuits	100b	90c	95c	95c	95b	100b	100b	95b	90b	100b	100b	90b	90b	95b
Côte de Beaune	95b	90c	90c	90c	90b	95b	95b	95b	90b	95b	95b	90b	90b	95b
White Burgundy	90c	90c	90c	90c	100c	100c	90c	95c	90b	90b	95b	90b	100b	95b
Other Wine Regions														
Champagne	90c	80c	100b	95b	90b	100b	95b	80c	NR	NR	NR	NR	NR	NR
Alsace	90b	90b	90c	90c	90c	90b	90b	90b	90b	90b	90b	90b	NR	NR
Germany: Riesling	90b	95b	90b	90b	90b	95b	90b	90b	90b	90b	90b	90b	90b	NR
Piedmont	100b	90b	90b	100a	90b	95b	100b	90b	90b	100a	NR	NR	NR	NR
Tuscany: Bolgheri & Maremma	90b	100c	90c	90b	90b	100b	100b	90b	90b	100b	90b	100b	NR	NR
Tuscany: Brunello di Montalcino	100b	90c	95b	95b	90c	100b	100b	90b	90b	100b	NR	NR	NR	NR
Tuscany: Chianti & Chianti Classico	90c	90c	90c	90c	90c	100b	100b	90b	90b	90b	90b	100b	NR	NR
Douro Valley Reds	90c	95b	90b	90b	90b	90b	95b	95b	90b	90b	90b	100b	NR	NR
Vintage Port	ND	100a	ND	ND	90a	90a	95a	95a	95a	90a	90a	90a	90a	NR
Priorat	90c	90c	90c	90c	90b	90b	90b	90b	90b	90b	90b	90b	90b	NR
Ribera del Duero	90b	90b	90b	85c	90b	90b	90b	90b	90c	90b	90b	NR	NR	NR
Rioja	95b	90c	95b	90c	90b	90b	95b	90b	90c	90b	90b	NR	NR	NR
Napa Valley Cabernet Sauvignon	100b	90c	95b	100b	95b	95b	100b	95b	100a	100b	90c	100a	NR	NR
Western Cape	90c	90c	90b	90c	90c	90b	90b	90b	90b	90b	NR	NR	NR	NR

Index

everyday food and wine pairings, 295–296

expensive wines, myth about, 370–371

expertise, in retailer evaluation, 307–308

experts, wine, 61, 367–368

expositions, wine, 352

extra brut champagnes, 114

extraction, 385

F

fake wines, 278

fall harvest, 10

Familia Deicas, 238

families of flavors in wine, 60

fancy food and wine pairings, 294–295

fatty foods, 290

faults, wine, 53, 64–65, 308, 364

fermentation
  container types for, 46
  defined, 26, 36
  of red wines, 40
  secondary, 42–44, 76, 112–113, 363
  of white wines, 37–38

filtering wine, 46–47

fine wine, 196

Finger Lakes, New York, 217–218

fining, 46–47

finish, 63, 385

fino sherries, 141, 143

firmness, of wine, 59, 385

flabby wines, 385

flash chilling wine, 344

flash sites, 306

flavor intensity, 60, 385

flavors
  aspects of, 60
  defined, 385
  perception of, 50

fleshy wines, 385

floating cork, 321–322

flor yeast, 141–142

flutes (glassware), 327–328

food, cooking with wine, 296–299

food pairings
  acidity, 290–291
  alcohol, 291
  everyday, 295–296
  fancy, 294–295
  myth regarding, 373
  overview, 287
  principles of, 293–294
  sauces and seasonings, 292–293
  sugar, 291–292
  tannin, 292
  taste, understanding, 288–290
  wine list, using for, 338–339

fortified wines. *See also* dessert wines
  from Australia, 246, 249
  cooking with, 298–299
  madeira, 170–173
  making, 44–45
  myth about, 371
  port, 163–166
  from Rhône Valley, 119–120
  sherry, 140–144

four "s" method of tasting
  overview, 51
  seeing, 51–52
  sipping, 54–55
  smelling, 52–54
  speculating, 55–57

France. *See also* Bordeaux, France; Burgundy, France
  Alsace, 122–124
  Bugey, 123
  champagne, 111–116
  classification system for, 92–94
  Corsica, 126–127
  fame of wines from, 92

grapevine moths, 10

grapevines
life cycle of, 9–10
overview, 9
pests and diseases affecting, 10–11
soil, role in performance of, 13

Graves wine area, France, 96

Great Southern, Australia, 250

Greater Puget Sound/Seattle Area AVA,
Washington State, 213

Greece, 185–188

grenache, 23

grocery stores, buying wine at, 303–304

Grosse Lage wines, 150

grower champagne, 116

grüner veltliner, 17, 177–178

GuildSomm podcast, 357

Gutswein, 150

gyropallate, 136

H

half-bottles, 346

hardening elements, 62

Hargrave Vineyards, 219

harmonious wines, 386

Harraigue (tannat) grapes, 237

harvest, 10

Haut-Médoc, France, 97–98

Hawke's Bay, New Zealand, 254

headaches caused by wine, 365

Heathcote, Australia, 249

herbal wines, 60, 386

Hermitage, 117, 118

Hokkaido, Japan, 281

hondarribi beltza, 138

Horse Heaven Hills, Washington State, 212

Hudson River region, New York, 218, 219

Hungary, 179–181

Hunter Valley, Australia, 248

hybrid grapes, 153

I

ice buckets, 344

icewine, 45, 153, 221–222

India, 275–276, 282–283

Indication Géographique Protégée (IGP) system, EU,
93, 129–130, 176, 185–186

Indicazione Geografica Tipica (IGT), 70, 71

inert gas, preserving wine with, 331–332

Inner Mongolia, China, 279

intense wines, 386

intensity, flavor, 60, 385

International Organisation of Vine and Wine
(OIV), 270

Israel, 270, 272–273

Italy
central region, 82–88
classification system for, 70–71
northeast, 77–82
northwest, 72–77
overview, 69–70
south, 88–90
vintage wine chart, 392–393

item number, on wine lists, 337

J

Jancis Robinson website, 357,
367, 375

Japan, 275–276, 280–282

Jerez region, Spain, 140–144

joven (young) Rioja wines, 133

Jumilla, Spain, 140

Jura, France, 123–124

K

Karnataka, India, 282

Koper, Slovenia, 182

kosher wine, 273–274

koshu, 282

Kras, Slovenia, 182

Q

Qualitätswein, 148
quality, detecting, 60–65
qvevri vessels, Georgia, 182–183

R

Rapel Valley, Chile, 229
Rasteau, 119–120
rating wines, 61, 374
Rattlesnake Hills, Washington State, 212
Real Deal icon, explained, 3
Red Mountain, Washington State, 212
red wines
  aerating, 322–323
  from Argentina, 230–232
  from Austria, 178
  from Bordeaux, France, 94–96, 97, 100, 102
  broad categories of, 41
  from Burgundy, France, 102, 104–105, 106, 107–108, 110–111
  from Chile, 226
  cooking with, 297–298
  from Corsica, France, 127
  current vintage for, 362
  filling glasses with, 329
  from Germany, 152, 156–157, 158
  glass size for, 326
  grapes used in, 18–23
  from Hungary, 180
  from Italy, 72–75, 77–78, 82–85
  from Languedoc-Roussillon, France, 125–126
  from Loire Valley, France, 121
  myths about, 372–373
  from New Zealand, 256, 257
  from Oregon, 217
  from Portugal, 161, 163
  production of, 40–41
  from Rhône Valley, France, 117, 118–119
  with sediment, decanting, 323–324

serving temperatures for, 324, 325, 344, 373
  from Slovenia, 182
  from Spain, 130–131, 132–135, 138–139
  from Washington State, 211
reduction, 64
regions, on wine lists, 337
Remember icon, explained, 3
Repour device, 332
reserve port, 165
reserve wines
  from Chile, 227
  from Greece, 186
  from Spain, 130, 133, 362
  wine lists focused on, 337
residual sugar, 387
restaurants
  bringing wine to, 345
  drinking wine at, guidelines for, 344–346
  food pairings, finding, 338–339
  overview, 333–334
  price of wines at, 335
  requesting help when choosing wine, 340–341
  spending time learning at, 349–350
  tasting etiquette, 342–343
  wine lists, information on, 334–338
Rheingau, Germany, 154–155
Rheinhessen, Germany, 156
Rhône Valley, France, 116–120, 392–393
Rías Baixas, Spain, 137–138
Ribera del Duero, Spain, 133–134
rich wines, 387
riddling, 112–113, 136
riesling
  from Alsace, France, 122
  from Australia, 247
  from Austria, 177–178, 179
  general discussion, 15
  from Germany, 152, 154, 155, 158
  from Washington State, 211

W

overview, 35

red wines, 40–41

rosé wines, 39

steps in, 35–36

white wines, 37–39

winemaker tricks, 45–47

wineries

contacting about when to drink wines, 367

visiting, 353

Wing Type Corkscrew, 315

winter pruning (thinning), 9

WO (Wine of Origin) system, South Africa, 261–262

wood tannin, 389. *See also* tannin

World of Fine Wine magazine, 356

Worth the Search icon, explained, 3

Württemberg, Germany, 157

X

Xinjiang Autonomous Region, China, 279–280

xinomavro, 187

Y

Yakima Valley, Washington State, 212

Yamagata, Japan, 282

Yamanashi, Japan, 282

Yarra Valley, Australia, 249

yeasts, 36, 42, 46, 389

young (*joven*) Rioja wines, 133

Yunnan, China, 279

Z

zinfandel, 22, 198, 207

zweigelt, 178

About the Authors

Michelle Grant is a certified sommelier (currently an advanced candidate at the time of writing) based in Mount Rainier, Maryland. She is the owner and sommelier of Era Wine Bar and Kitchen, also located in Mount Rainier, Maryland. Michelle graduated from Stanford University with bachelor's degree in international relations, followed by Michigan State University with a doctorate in educational policy and international development. Michelle worked in global development and corporate social responsibility for 15 years before falling in love with and pursuing wine full-time. What started out as a simple food and wine blog in 2013 (more for personal therapy than media appeal) slowly burgeoned into a life with wine, food, and hospitality at the center of each day.

Era Wine Bar and Kitchen has been nominated as a finalist for Wine Program of the Year by the Restaurant Association of Metropolitan Washington for three consecutive years since its opening in 2021. The bistro has received numerous Diners Choice awards from OpenTable and Yelp, and been featured in *The Washington Post*, *Eater DC*, *DCist*, ABC7's *Good Morning Washington*, and *DC News Now*. When she's not researching wines or planning the next Era members' club excursion to a faraway place, Michelle is shuffling the loving and busy life of a wife and mom to two children under 5, as well as a very demanding English bulldog named Biko.

Ed McCarthy and **Mary Ewing-Mulligan** met at an Italian wine tasting in New York City's Chinatown and subsequently merged their wine cellars and libraries when they married. They coauthored more than ten wine books in the *Wine For Dummies* series (including two of their favorites, *French Wine For Dummies* and *Italian Wine For Dummies*) as well as *Wine Style: Using Your Senses to Explore and Enjoy Wine* (Wiley); taught hundreds of wine classes together; visited nearly every wine region in the world; ran five marathons; and raised 12 cats. Along the way, they amassed over half a century of professional wine experience between them.

Mary is president of International Wine Center, a New York City wine school for wine professionals and serious wine lovers. She is also a wine journalist, having been the wine columnist of the *NY Daily News* for more than a decade, and having written for numerous periodicals. Mary's most impressive credential is that she became the first female Master of Wine (MW) in the United States, and is one of currently only 50 MWs resident in the United States and 380 worldwide.

Ed, a New Yorker, graduated from City University of New York with a master's degree in psychology. He taught high school English in another life, while working part-time in wine shops to satisfy his passion for wine and subsidize his growing wine cellar. That cellar was especially heavy in his favorite wines — Bordeaux, Barolo, and Champagne. Besides coauthoring wine books with Mary, Ed went solo as author of *Champagne For Dummies*, a topic on which he was especially expert. Ed also wrote for *Beverage Media*, a trade publication.

Author's Acknowledgments

The wine world changes fast. Each year, there are not only new wines to explore, but new technologies, new climate challenges, new laws, new producer stories to share, and more. I wrote this book to continue the conversation on wine, making it not only more approachable, but also more relatable for people around the world. On that note, it was important to include more history, geography, and information on how wine can be used to complement daily life in this edition. I am beyond grateful to contribute to the growing body of knowledge and awareness around wine and its many magical powers.

This book would not have been possible without the team at Wiley. I sincerely thank Executive Editor Tracy Boggier for her engagement, thoughtfulness, and openness to my crazy ideas. I am especially grateful to Dan Mersey, my cheerful and encouraging development editor who kept me on track and offered such valuable guidance throughout the writing journey. I know that having this kind of all-star team when writing a book is rare. I hope you can feel our synergy as you turn each page!

Much gratitude to Tajira McCoy, my dearest family friend and agent, who brought me to the *For Dummies* series and is always there for me — in books and beyond. I am so thankful for Charles Mwalimu, who joined the team at a critical juncture to provide a thorough technical review of the book that was invaluable.

Last but never least to my family: Ka-ton Grant, my husband and unwavering support system without whom I could never appreciate a good Grüner Veltliner; Charles and Munira Mwalimu (Grandpa and Grandma), for countless hours of childcare that allowed me the time and space to write; children Leila and Lionel, whose virgin noses are currently training them for excellent wine tastings to come; and siblings Desiree, Rehana, and Charles for their enduring love, support, and encouragement.

— Michelle Grant

Publisher's Acknowledgments

Executive Editor: Tracy Boggier

Development Editor: Dan Mersey

Technical Editor: Charles Mwalimu

Managing Editor: Ajith Kumar

Illustrator: Lisa S. Reed

Cover Image: © diy13/stock.adobe.com